OLD MYTHS AND NEW APPROACHES

OLD MYTHS AND NEW APPROACHES

INTERPRETING ANCIENT RELIGIOUS SITES IN SOUTHEAST ASIA

Edited by Alexandra Haendel

© 2012 Copyright of the individual chapters is owned by the authors.
© 2012 Copyright of this collection is owned by Alexandra Haendel

All rights reserved. Apart from any uses permitted by Australia's Copyright Act 1968, no part of this book may be reproduced by any process without prior written permission from the copyright owners. Inquiries should be directed to the publisher.

Monash University Publishing
Building 4, Monash University
Clayton, Victoria 3800, Australia
www.publishing.monash.edu

Monash University Publishing brings to the world publications which advance the best traditions of humane and enlightened thought. Monash University Publishing titles pass through a rigorous process of independent peer review.

ISBN: 978-1-921867-28-6 (pb)
ISBN: 978-1-921867-29-3 (web)

www.publishing.monash.edu/books/omna.html

Design: Les Thomas

Front cover image: A 3D image of an Angkorian village shrine. Image © Tom Chandler and Brent McKee
Back cover image: *Apsaras of Angkor Wat*. Photograph © Martin Polkinghorne

The Monash Asia Series
Old Myths and New Approaches is published as part of the Monash Asia Series.

The Monash Asia Series comprises works that make a significant contribution to our understanding of one or more Asian nations or regions. The individual works that make up this multi-disciplinary series are selected on the basis of their contemporary relevance.

The Monash Asia Series of the Monash Asia Institute replaces Monash University's MAI Press imprint, which, from the early 1970s, has demonstrated this University's strong interest and expertise in Asian studies.

Monash Asia Series Editorial Board
Professor Marika Vicziany, Chair, Professor of Asian Political Economy, Monash Asia Institute, Faculty of Arts
Professor Greg Barton, School of Political and Social Inquiry, Faculty of Arts
Associate Professor Gloria Davies, School of Languages, Cultures and Linguistics, Faculty of Arts
Dr Julian Millie, School of Political and Social Inquiry, Faculty of Arts
Dr Jagjit Plahe, Department of Management, Faculty of Business and Economics
Dr David Templeman, School of Philosophical, Historical and International Studies, Faculty of Arts

Printed in Australia by Griffin Press, an Accredited ISO AS/NZS 14001:2004 Environmental Management System printer.

The paper this book is printed on is certified by the Programme for the Endorsement of Forest Certification scheme. Griffin Press holds PEFC chain of custody SGS - PEFC/COC-0594. PEFC promotes environmentally responsible, socially beneficial and economically viable management of the world's forests.

CONTENTS

Contributors viii

Introduction. ix
Marika Vicziany

PART ONE
NATURE AND HUMANS: ADAPTING TO THE ENVIRONMENT

Introduction to Part One. 3
Alexandra Haendel

Chapter 1
General archaeological aspects and speculations concerning the red soil region east of the Mekong River in Kampong Cham Province, Cambodia 5
Heng Sophady

Chapter 2
Beyond the temples. 12
Angkor and its territory
Christophe Pottier

Chapter 3
Mysteries of Angkor revealed. 28
Hydrology and the siting of Angkor
Bob Acker

Chapter 4
The dynamics of Angkor and its landscape 42
Issues of scale, non-correspondence and outcome
Roland Fletcher & Damian Evans

Chapter 5
Religious architecture and irrigation in the plain of Phan Rang 63
William A Southworth

Chapter 6
Connecting the dots 84
Investigating transportation between the temple complexes of
the medieval Khmer (9th–14th centuries CE)
Mitch Hendrickson

Chapter 7
Journeys and landscapes 103
Some preliminary remarks on ancient Javanese perceptions of
the environment
Peter Worsley

PART TWO
SITES AND GROUPS OF BUILDINGS

Introduction to Part Two 119
David Chandler

Chapter 8
Temples and landscape in south Central Java 121
Véronique Degroot

Chapter 9
Mountains, forests and water 134
A new approach to the study of the Javanese temple complex of Sukuh
Jo Grimmond

Chapter 10
Life among the ruins 159
Habitation sites of Trowulan
John Miksic

Chapter 11
Speculation on landscape use in and around Sambor Prei Kuk 180
Heng Piphal

PART THREE
LIVING THE SITES: THE COMMUNITIES AROUND

Introduction to Part Three. 201
Stuart Robson

Chapter 12
Incorporating the periphery 203
The classical temples of Southeast Asia and their social context
Alexandra Haendel

Chapter 13
Through the visualisation lens 218
Temple models and simulated context in a virtual Angkor
Tom Chandler

Martin Polkinghorne

Chapter 14
Graves, trees and powerful spirits as archaeological indicators
of sacred spaces 237
Angelo Andrea Di Castro

Chapter 15
Imagery of the temple in Old Javanese poetry. 252
Stuart Robson

Chapter 16
Mỹ Sơn and Pô Nagar Nha Trang sanctuaries and the cosmological
dualist cult of the Champa kingdom. 267
Trần Kỳ Phương & Rie Nakamura

Bibliography 281

Contributors

Bob Acker, University of California at Berkeley

David Chandler, Monash University

Tom Chandler, Monash University

Véronique Degroot, Ecole française d'Extrême-Orient

Angelo Andrea Di Castro, Monash University

Damian Evans, University of Sydney

Roland Fletcher, University of Sydney

Jo Grimmond, University of Queensland

Alexandra Haendel, Monash University

Mitch Hendrickson, University of Illinois at Chicago

John Miksic, National University of Singapore

Rie Nakamura, Universiti Utara Malaysia

Trần Kỳ Phương, Co-director of
'Crossing Boundaries—Learning from the Past to Build the Future'

Heng Piphal, University of Hawaii at Manoa

Martin Polkinghorne, The University of Sydney

Christophe Pottier, Ecole française d'Extrême-Orient

Stuart Robson, Monash University

Heng Sophady, Ministry of Culture and Fine Arts, Cambodia,
and Memot Centre for Archaeology

William A Southworth, Rijksmuseum

Marika Vicziany, Monash University

Peter Worsley, The University of Sydney

Introduction

Marika Vicziany

Director, Monash Asia Institute, Monash University

Based on a conference of the same name, and bringing together some of the world's leading scholars in their field, *Old Myths and New Approaches* represents a ground-breaking contribution to the study of the religions and cultures of Southeast Asia. A major objective of the volume is to locate temples within their general cultural and geographic surroundings. All too often temples are studied from the viewpoints of their artistic and architectural merits. These are certainly important, but in order to better understand even their aesthetic qualities it is important to place them into the context of how they were used.

The chapters that compose this collection cover a wide geographical area and use an extensive range of source materials and methodologies. Many of the approaches are innovative, pushing the research frontiers and methodologies to new limits and new speculation. Given this complexity, the chapters are grouped into three distinctive sections, each with its own introduction.

Part One focuses on how the people who inhabited these religious sites adapted to the local environments. In different ways, these chapters examine the interplay between culture and environment, with four of the contributions focussing on Angkor Wat. As Haendel notes in her introduction, the central characteristic revealed by all these studies is the diversity of the human interaction with nature.

Part Two focuses on the interrelationship between the temples and the environment and, as with the other chapters in this collection, introduces the reader to a range of new methodologies that have been used to better understand the nature of the sacred sites of Southeast Asia.

Part Three deals explicitly with the 'functionality of sacred sites' in Southeast Asia. The studies here go well beyond the older, traditional understandings of ancient temple complexes. They do not merely deal with priestly or religious power; they also examine the ways in which temples met the daily needs of ordinary people, kings, merchants and other members of society. Moreover, not all sacred sites were temples—they could also be sacred spaces, or groves or other locations of spiritual meaning.

This volume includes a rich array of photographs, diagrams and maps, which convey a more immediate sense of the nature of the ancient sacred sites of Southeast Asia.

Dr Alexandra Haendel and all the contributors are to be commended for their work in putting this volume together. We also record our appreciation to the numerous donors who have supported this research.

PART ONE

NATURE AND HUMANS
ADAPTING TO THE ENVIRONMENT

Introduction to Part One

Alexandra Haendel

Adjunct Research Fellow, Monash Asia Institute, Monash University

Part One of this volume is concerned with the environmental and cultural backgrounds, the settings, and the scale of Southeast Asian sites that can be called 'sacred'. A key characteristic of Southeast Asia is its immense diversity—ethnic, cultural and historical. It is one of those parts of the world which has, over millennia, been a passage for people, goods and ideas, and the resultant Southeast Asian cultures bear witness to an astounding capacity for cultural adaptation and amalgamation to this present day.

Several of the chapters in Part One focus on mainland Southeast Asia, covering various periods from the dawn of the Metal Age to the decline of the Angkorian Empire. Angkor, possibly the most famous of the ancient Southeast Asian political sites, almost by necessity is dealt with in greater detail than other locations. In recent years Cambodian archaeology has changed significantly, and with an ever increasing number of scholars and researchers from within and outside Cambodia examining the country, considerable insights have been gleaned into the *terra incognita* that is the history of central mainland Southeast Asia.

Heng Sophady's chapter examines the round moated sites in Eastern Cambodia, a region he has worked in for many years. Those sites date back to the late Neolithic period and are rich in archaeological data.[1] Finds indicate a long history of contact with other regions. Despite their partaking in the wider commodity exchange networks, the societies east of the Mekong River did not produce the numerous Buddhist and Brahmanical monuments that were produced by those to the west: what might be the reason for this? And what are the implications for other areas in Southeast Asia—and most notably the eastern part of the Indonesian Archipelago—that also demonstrate this lack of temple architecture?

The chapters by Christophe Pottier and by Roland Fletcher and Damien Evans—both of which focus on the largest of those temple-building societies, Angkor—have to be read in conjunction with one another. Pottier's chapter

---

[1] Many sites in the region still await discovery.

traces the development of settlements throughout the Angkor capital district in terms of their social organisation and layout in space. And Fletcher, applying a model of non-correspondence to the civilisation of Angkor, develops a much wider spatial–temporal understanding of the history of Angkor. Both Pottier's and Fletcher's research push the boundaries of our understanding of Angkor as a multifaceted settlement, and stress the need for a multi-disciplinary approach when researching its sites.

Bob Acker's chapter, again focusing on the civilisation of Angkor, discusses the relationship between water-tables levels and the development of large settlements in different parts of the Angkor plain.

Mitch Hendrickson's chapter assesses the connectivity of select 'isolated' Angkorian temple complexes through space and time. In particular, terrestrial and riverine transport routes are examined to determine the links between outlying sites and the capital at Angkor. This research offers much-needed insight into the highly complex communication and transportation networks between capital and regional centres.

Moving to neighbouring Champa, William Southworth discusses the location of the main temple complexes in the plain of Phan Rang in the 8th and 9th centuries CE, and their connections through natural and man-made features, such as rivers and canals. Specifically, Southworth examines the economic, social and religious significance of the location of the temples.

Finally, Peter Worsley shifts our attention to peninsular Southeast Asia and ancient Java. Worsley, who has undertaken extensive research on Javanese culture and texts, analyses several accounts of journeys and landscapes described in a number of literary works, mainly epic *kakawin*, to determine the types of landscape described and the roles that temples played within these landscapes.

This brings us back to the overarching theme: the settings of the 'sacred sites' themselves—which, above all, are characterised by diversity. While answering numerous questions, the chapters in Part One will most certainly create just as many more. These chapters push the boundaries of our knowledge about ancient Southeast Asian cultures, and will, it is hoped, ensure a continued dialogue about old and new mysteries.

Chapter 1

General archaeological aspects and speculations concerning the red soil region east of the Mekong River in Kampong Cham Province, Cambodia

Heng Sophady

Deputy Director General for Cultural Heritage, Ministry of Culture and Fine Arts, Cambodia, and Senior Researcher, Memot Centre for Archaeology

Introduction

Cambodia is one of the smaller countries in Southeast Asia, with a population of around 14 million, as opposed to its more populous neighbours Thailand and Vietnam which have populations of approximately 67 million and 88 million respectively. Cambodia's main geographical features are the central basin, formed by the Mekong and Tonle Sap Rivers, the surrounding mountain ranges (the Dong Rek mountains in the north and the Cardamom Mountains in the west) and the red soil plateau in the east and south.

Over the past century, many prehistoric, historic and proto-historic sites have been discovered throughout the country. Undeniably, there is a concentration of those sites in the areas west of the Mekong, with some of them dating back to 2000–3000 BCE. In contrast, in the red soil plateau region east of the Mekong River in Memot and Krek Districts, ancient temples, urban complexes and other historical sites are rare, despite the likelihood that some sites were well connected to larger socio-economic networks. For example, the Village 10.8 burial site clearly contains widely distributed artefacts such as Dong Son bronze fragments and various types of beads. Even the circular earthwork sites characteristic of the region contain pottery that was possibly widely distributed in a somewhat smaller nested exchange sphere that included sites such as Village 10.8.

Ecologically, the region is rich in forest and agroforestry resources. Lower areas along drainages can be used for wet-rice cultivation and hill areas for swidden and dry-rice agriculture. Material and ecofactual remains indicate that rice production and animal husbandry was part of the Neolithic to proto-historic economies. Although there was probably a significant arboricultural component, little research has been conducted concerning this aspect of the ancient economy. Also, neither the nature of inter- and intra-regional socio-economic relations nor the nature of total resource environment use (social and biological) has been researched.

It is possible that there were several levels, or spheres, of interaction, ranging from household, village, local region to inter-local regions. It is possible that many sites remained isolated self-sustaining settlements, but it is unlikely, given the archaeological data analysed thus far. How were these societies related to societies elsewhere which built large temple complexes and larger urban areas? Were there local environmental/ecological, settlement, social and economic factors which did not favour the construction of urban settlements and temples? Or, was it a temporal difference (that is, the Neolithic sites simply faded away over time for different reasons, possibly because they were out-competed)? The Village10.8 data and early dates from sites in Siem Reap and Takeo suggest there were significant temporal overlaps from the late Neolithic to Metal Age and proto-historic period—a transitional period we know almost nothing about.

General aspects

In the following, I focus on two districts, Memot and Krek. Both are covered by red soil and located east of the Mekong River. The red soil region is characterised by low hills, slopes and valleys that contain many small streams flowing north to south, as well as a few streams flowing from east to west. Elevations range from 50–200 metres above sea level. The iron-rich red soil is the result of soil transformation from old volcanic formations with resultant basaltic and laterite deposits. The plateau extends upwards to the highland regions in Cambodia (Rattakiri, Mundulkiri, Kratie, Steng Treng) and neighbouring Vietnam (for example, Song Be) and downwards to the western flood-plain regions of the eastern Mekong River, Kampong Cham Province.

The red soil is rich and fertile for plantations (rubber, coffee, cashew, pepper, fruit trees, cassava, etc.), mixed agroforestry and shifting cultivation. Since 1954 rubber has been imported and planted in Memot. It became one of the main economic resources for Cambodia at that time. Today, local economies are based on rubber, cashew and cassava as well as small trade with Vietnam. Rice is not a particularly important resource for local economic development because the amount of rice produced varies significantly from year to year and yields are not reliably high. Nevertheless, there are two forms of rice production in the area—irrigated and dry rice. Irrigated rice is grown in the valleys and dry rice is grown on the tops or slopes of hills. House gardens and field resources, including fruit trees, vegetables, etc., are common. River banks are frequently used for vegetable gardens in the dry season when water levels are low.

Some villages of Mon Khmer origin (Steang) still practise shifting cultivation. However, they are in a process of changing agricultural strategies to focus on cashew plantations and other crops, often at the times they would usually plant rice.

Archaeological remains

Historical remains

Historical remains in the red soil region in Krek and Memot are less well documented than in other regions in Cambodia. A few brick temples remain in the lowland of Krek District (adjacent to the red soil areas), including Choeung Ang, Banteay Prei Nokor, and Prei Ki. Choeung Ang is a brick tower built approximately in the second half of the tenth century CE by Jayavarman IV. The site includes inscriptions on a set of doorjambs that are useful for understanding part of its history. Banteay Prei Nokor was likely the early city of Jayavarman II, Indrapura, according to inscriptional evidence, and was probably constructed at the beginning of the ninth century CE. The city was surrounded by a 2.5 kilometre square earthen wall with an accompanying exterior moat. The city was apparently used as a political centre for only a short time. The political centre then moved west to the Siem Reap region (Phnom Kulen and Angkor). The two brick towers remaining in the middle of Banteay Prei Nokor were likely constructed in the pre-Angkor period (seventh–eighth centuries), but the city wall and moat were possibly built and used by Jayavarman II and reconstructed and used again around the 16th century by King Srei Chettha, or 'Kan', as his city and citadel. Prei Ki is a pre-Angkor temple, but little is known of the site and it will not be discussed in this chapter.

The temples were built presumably as local religious centres for local populations and appear mostly, but not entirely, Brahmanic. Thus far, no temples have been found in the east in Memot. Nevertheless, a lintel and other parts of temple decorations and architectural elements were discovered in the vicinity of Memot and Vietnam, which are currently kept in the pagoda at the border of Cambodia and Vietnam in Memot District. The motif on the lintel belongs to the Sambor Prei Kuk style and probably dates back to the seventh century CE. Thus, there is a possibility that unidentified temples do exist in the immediate area.

Many other archaeological sites can be found in the Memot rubber plantations. One site was found by chance when workers from the Memot rubber plantation cleared ground for replanting in May 2003. They discovered many fragments of glazed stoneware belonging to the Angkor period and possibly three different types of celadon. Whether they are Chinese, Thai, or Vietnamese remains unknown. Most of these potsherds probably belong to the 14th–16th centuries. Based on assessments of local collections whose provenance has not been determined and the limited archaeological data, we expect to find more artefacts dating from the Neolithic through the post-Angkor periods.

Prehistoric remains

Many prehistoric sites have been identified. The most numerous ones are circular earthwork sites. These have consistent features and a seemingly homogenous distribution from southern Vietnam to northeast Cambodia. Local people refer to the sites as Banteay Kou. Circular earthworks are normally located on the tops or upper slopes of red-soil hills proximate to creeks and streams.

The sites are structurally characterised by earthen embankments, inner ditches and inner platforms. They often contain two entrances on opposite sides. The diameters of the site embankments range from 150 to 280 metres. Many cultural remains, such as ceramic vessels, stone tools, glass and stone ornaments, have been recovered on the inner platform edges. Unfortunately, because of high soil acidity, organic remains rarely survive. Thirty circular earthwork sites have been documented in Memot and Krek and many others have been identified and researched in Vietnam. It is highly probable that many more exist and will be identified in the future.

The circular earthwork sites are dated to the late Neolithic period and possibly as far back as the Bronze or Iron Age periods, based on associated artefacts such as glass ornaments found at the sites and radiocarbon dates from various projects (Dega 2002; Albrecht et al 2001; Heng 2002).

An Iron Age cemetery was also found in Krek, in close proximity to circular earthwork sites located in a Krek rubber plantation. Many interesting artefacts were recovered from excavations: metal weapons, metal ornaments, pottery, a few stone tools, carnelian beads, garnet artefacts, glass beads, Dong Son drum fragments, human skeletal remains and textile impressions on the iron tools identified through technical cleaning procedures. The presence of spindle whorls and textile impressions yields clues to the technological nature of local fabric manufacture. Spindle whorls and fabric remains and impressions have been found in other Iron Age burial sites in mainland Southeast Asia. Carnelian, garnet and glass beads, as well as the Dong Son artefacts and later-period foreign ceramics (provenance unknown, but recovered from the local area), reveal that trade networks might have included direct or indirect connections with China, India and northern Vietnam.

Despite this area's seemingly long period of contact with the outside world, why did Buddhism, Brahmanism, temple construction and larger scale urbanisation not emerge in the eastern part of Cambodia, as it did in the western or central parts? What were the settlement patterns like and the relationship between settlement, environment, etc.? Are these important explanatory factors and, if they are, how do we test them? Four main factors are considered here.

1. Belief/Religion

It is possible that past people respected the living places or cemeteries of their ancestors. Thus they may have not wanted to disturb the areas, perhaps out of respect or because of perceived dangerous forces. It is possible that some cities or settlements were intentionally placed far away from old living places or cemeteries—the area of the ancestors.

2. Socio-economic and environmental push for settlement dispersal

It is possible that the social beliefs coupled with the economic systems favoured movement out of old settlements periodically (such as once or twice a year, or every few generations). Without consolidated labour forces and management, it would be difficult to build large urban areas. Additionally, aggregated large-scale settlements might have been environmentally degrading, subsequently reducing resources and weakening local economies. A more permanent city is not a good solution in such a setting without good infrastructure, access to distant resource zones and economical communication and transportation.

3. Political and economic factors

The red soil area is close to the southern part of Champa which was a strong Austronesian polity (or set of polities) during the eighth–13th centuries. If urban centres were built near the Cham territories or influence zones, they could either stimulate or be susceptible to conflict and attacks. Additionally, if the Khmer urban centres placed themselves in polities towards the centre, they would be better protected and centralised. This may have had more advantages than developing large urban areas and religious complexes on frontier zones. This is predicated on the assumption that there was a lot of planning, communication and interaction at the time, but is also supported by archaeological evidence.

4. Environment factors

The region is relatively isolated from large rivers, such as the Mekong, and has no apparent canals connecting to the larger riverine resource zones and communication routes. Certainly, there was communication and trade, but perhaps the area was unable to attain a significantly large-scale trade centre because of environment and geography.

It is possible that natural resource depletion in the area was advanced and that resources were becoming scarce so that it was economically unsustainable to acquire resources, process them and transport them. If the area was heavily populated and resources heavily utilised for several hundreds or thousands of years before the emergence of the lowland centralised urban centres and temple complexes, resource depletion may have favoured migration out of the region and dispersal of its population. The potential may have been simply exhausted before the emergence of larger urban areas and temple complexes elsewhere. On the other hand, archaeological evidence indicates that the area was still communicating with extra-regional sources up until post-Angkor times.

The potential for intensive agriculture to support a large complex urban polity, mainly irrigated rice production, animal husbandry and aquaculture was not adequate. Dangerous illnesses in the area, such as malaria, may have been a limiting factor. However, until assessments are conducted concerning potential diseases using evidence from burial remains in the various environmental zones throughout mainland Southeast Asia with the helpful analogy of modern disease assessments and their environmental correlations, it remains difficult to determine. The density and/or variety of natural resources for economic development, such as the development of urban centres and subsequent temple creation (if those variables are indeed positively correlated) may not have been sufficient.

Chapter 2

Beyond the temples

Angkor and its territory

Christophe Pottier

Head of Princess Maha Chakri Sirindhorn Anthropology Centre,
Ecole française d'Extrême-Orient

Angkor is one of the pivotal examples that will be discussed within the discourse of this volume, not only because it is one of the favourite sites for approaching the 'old myths' of the great religious sites in Southeast Asia, but also because it symbolises 'new approaches' that try to put the monumental sets of sanctuaries into wider spatial and historical frames. Angkor is a remarkable illustration of the agrarian city concept in Southeast Asia (Lombard 1970), centred as it is on a complex of temples surrounded by rice paddy fields. It was interpreted as the almost perfect expression of a huge *maṇḍala* (Higham 1989), as much for its socio-economical and political organisation as for its spatial organisation. To talk about the 'new approaches' to understanding Angkor leads us, nevertheless, to briefly recall the content of the 'old' approaches that formed the basis of our understanding of Angkor and, at the very least, to highlight the importance of the monumental heritage closely associated with it.

Angkor was 'discovered' in the second part of the 19th century when the Western world was exploring—and often colonising—the planet (Dagens 1989:192). The French protectorate in the kingdom of Cambodia presented Angkor as the symbol of a rich ancient civilisation, lost and buried under the tropical jungle, which the colonial 'civilising' mission would study and restore in order to return to the country its 'history', if not its 'magnificence'. After the first period of exploration and discovery of the archaeological remains, which inspired the myth of the Asian Atlantis, the French administration established in 1900 l'École française d'Extrême-Orient (EFEO), a scientific institution specifically dedicated to the study and conservation of the cultures of French Indochina. The creation of the EFEO and the establishment of a permanent office in Angkor, the Conservation d'Angkor, provided a framework for developing long-term research strategies (Pottier 2001b). Then, the first systematic inventories and the first studies of the sources of the civilisation of ancient Cambodia started. It is necessary to recall that these were restricted to the monuments and a limited number of inscriptions, and to even scarcer Chinese texts. In the field, the first interventions focused on clearing the main monuments of their vegetal gangue. This did not leave much time for any other activities or research in other fields, given the limited resources. The clearing out continued until the 1930s, but in the 1920s the strengthening of the administrative framework enabled the rapid development of new approaches which became apparent in the creation of the Angkor Park. The introduction of anastylosis in the restoration field is proof of development from simple operations, such as occasional and often not very efficient strengthening, to an intentional policy of highlighting the ruined structures by rebuilding them and thus asserting a rediscovered monumentality based on a deep and scientific knowledge of the monuments. Besides this, the stylistic studies by Philippe Stern reordered the chronology of monuments and opened up new historical and spatial issues. These triggered a complete revision of the interpretation of the epigraphic corpus and the development of new research in the field, using, simultaneously, prospection, aerial reconnaissance and archaeological excavations, which were for the first time implemented following specific paradigms. The Second World War and the insecure period that followed meant the interruption of at least part of the work undertaken on site. Work restarted as early as the beginning of the 1950s, accompanied by the introduction of new techniques. Restoration work incorporated large and complex anastylosis projects, associated with the development of the implementation of real strategies. At the same time archaeological research also recommenced, with more advanced use of remote sensing and the introduction of stratigraphic excavations giving rise to new reflections on the material culture and the spatial and economic organisation beyond the religious frame. All of this was brutally stopped with the closure of the site in 1970 and of the country in 1975. Studies continued outside Cambodia, but these focused only on the texts and epigraphic sources or on the studies and synthesis of data previously accumulated in the field.

In the 1980s and especially after the reopening of the country in 1992, when Angkor was placed on the World Heritage List, it became the focus of an international campaign for its safeguarding. Priority was given to the conservation of monuments, and the majority of international projects were developed for the main and most visited temples. In the field, work that focused mainly on architectural heritage resumed, leaving aside the development of research areas including archaeological ones. It is not surprising that tourist and other popular publications, which have mushroomed in the past twenty years, have presented Angkor simply as a cluster or a succession of huge monumental temples located in indeterminate surroundings. The stereotypical image is of a range of isolated temples, of capital cities geometrically surrounded by walls and with some independent hydraulic structures. This comes, of course, from the relative lack of available sources to comprehend the historical and spatial complexity of the Angkorian civilisation. The sources that are available reveal only a few aspects of this civilisation. For example, the epigraphic corpus has only 1,300 inscriptions, all originating from the temples, most of which only give direct information about the divinities and the functioning of religious foundations. These texts provide a lot of other data, but most of it constitutes indirect information often in an unknown context. A complementary source is iconographic study, especially art history, but again it mainly focuses on the representation of divinities. Secular scenes are scarce and sometimes anecdotal. Architectural remains are the third source, patiently registered, dated and chronologically ordered from the epigraphic studies and the evolution of the ornamental motifs. But these concern mainly sanctuaries, as only temples were erected using long-lasting materials. There is much more research in this field to be done, even after a century of work; there are still many grey areas and just as many possibilities for detailing them. Therefore the vision of Angkor has developed aound—and has limited itself to—its gods, its temples and its kings, in isolation from other social aspects which remain largely unknown.

It is necessary, therefore, to extend the scope of investigation beyond this restrictive framework in order to build a wider and more balanced understanding. Bernard-Philippe Groslier stressed this need when he was appointed as scientific director of the Conservation d'Angkor in 1959. He proposed developing Angkorian research by following two different but complementary directions—a horizontal one aimed at understanding the space and the paleo-environment, and a vertical one focused on the study of chronological superimpositions and diachronies (Groslier 1959b). This approach is schematic and not very specific to Angkor, but it nevertheless stresses the importance of developing a dual reading—spatial and chronological—which can found in some of Groslier's publications. Since my appointment in Angkor in 1992, in my studies I have followed this prematurely interrupted research method, considering that we are far from being able to fabricate a comprehensive interpretative model and that the available basic data should be reconsidered, and that missing information, especially archaeological information, should be collected in situ (Pottier 2003). Below, I provide examples of recent research that illustrates this double approach.

Starting with the horizontal approach, it was necessary to reconsider some basic information: firstly, the map of Angkor. Despite a century of archaeology on the site, an extensive review of its mapping was not redundant as the mapping was incomplete and had been influenced by external factors. Let us recall that the first maps drawn during the exploration at the end of the 19th century (Mouhot, Garnier, Aymonier, and others) covered the whole Angkor region from the Tonle Sap in the south to Phnom Kulen in the north. They did not have any preconceptions about the extent of the site, and gave an overall view of the main sites which was not very accurate but was integrated with the main elements of the surrounding topography. They were typical of a classical geographical style of mapping, and reached their peak with the 'Archaeological map of ancient Cambodia' from Lunet de Lajonquière (1911), with more than 900 monuments located on a large map covering the whole Khmer empire. Paradoxically, the same author simultaneously drew a new map of Angkor, one whose influence had the effect of confining maps produced over the next 70 years to a restricted geographical area. This new map focused especially on a group of monumental remains, referred to by the common denomination of 'Angkor Group' because of their remarkable density. Nevertheless, this map only shows a tiny part of the site, delimited by two big *baray*, in the north by Preah Khan and in the south slightly lower than Angkor Wat, north of the Siem Reap village. This bordering is not without foundation: it conveys the spirit of showcasing a group of main monuments that were confirmed as 'central' by the creation of visitor 'circuits' in 1915 which made them accessible. This group of monuments then became the main focus of the Conservation d'Angkor. The work done up until the 1970s unveiled new sites and generated a few new maps, but these continued to be more or less within the same central area boundaries of the 'Angkor Group' map of Lunet de Lajonquière (Fletcher and Pottier 2002; Pottier 2006). Maps now available in all the guides show these same borders, with the monumental temples scattered in countryside that is at best neutral, or evocative of a mythical forest that has almost disappeared.

This has been one of the contradictions in the understanding of Angkor, because the surrounds of the temples have been studied for a long time. Starting in the 1920s with the introduction of aerial reconnaissance, several studies tried to assess the sanctuaries in their urban surroundings, which were then characterised by large encompassing walls, causeways, dykes and canals. These first attempts to understand the temple as part of an evolving urban environment, as characterised by the model of the last capital Angkor Thom, motivated the first of the archaeological campaigns in the 1930s that focused on things other than the monuments. Followed up in the 1950s by Groslier, the research extended from the city to its territorial environment, including the remains of the hydraulic networks. Groslier tried to link them with a wider spatial and chronological context and then began to put together an archaeological atlas of the region and started several test pits. But this work was never completeded and little has been published about it, possibly because the author had too much work in managing the Conservation d'Angkor (Pottier 1993a; Groslier 1997; Pottier 1999). Nevertheless, he collected enough material to develop the model of the '*cité hydraulique*' (Groslier 1979). Although his functionalist approach now needs to be reconsidered, this synthesis remains, until now, the only work offering a comprehensive and diachronic vision of the territorial development of Angkor in which the monuments are closely associated and integrated. It is, therefore, a pity that what often persists from this model is a misunderstanding of the *baray* and an over-interpretation of the role of the Angkorian hydraulic system. These result in an impression of Angkor where the usual image of its isolated monumental temples has been superimposed with an image of similarly isolated hydraulic structures, all of which purportedly represent a remarkable symbolic and cosmogonic model.

As mentioned earlier, I don't think the current level of knowledge enables us to assemble and assess a comprehensive interpretative model. I will, therefore, present a few examples of a horizontal approach that facilitates the collection of information necessary to develop our knowledge of Angkor, especially its relationship with the environment and its region. This work commenced when I took part as a consultant in the multidisciplinary Zoning and Environmental Management Plan (ZEMP), which was implemented under the auspices of UNESCO for the site's listing as a World Heritage area: for this listing, a detailed map was required of the area to be protected. I was in charge of the drawing of a map of the known monuments in the Angkor region. The cartography of the central area was not a problem; however, as mentioned earlier, the only one to cover all the studied area was the 1911 map with its inaccurate cartographic background. Using new aerial pictures made by FINMAP for the Mekong River Commission, I started to identify by remote sensing all the features likely to be temples—these were often distinguished by a square moat—in order to locate on a new cartographic background the 300 temples in the region that were registered in the EFEO's inventories and archives. This method proved fast and efficient, but led me to identify more than 800 sites instead of the expected 300! It seemed, therefore, that the density of the sites and of the linear structures was far greater than predicted. Even more interestingly, the cartography of these new sites also showed a large undifferentiated and homogeneous pattern of small secondary sites throughout the zone, giving a completely different image of Angkor than the one conveyed by the classical maps and their cluster of huge monumental structures (Pottier 1993b). Consequently, the urban development of Angkor needed to be reviewed, taking into account this new systematic cartography that also revealed vestiges of old rice field parcelling.

I followed this up, developing a detailed cartography that restricted the study area to the Angkor zone up to the lake in the south. This 600 square kilometre zone was the cradle of Angkorian development and allowed a study of its relationship with the lake. It was also the only area at the time where security conditions allowed for safe working conditions in the field. I will not go into the methodology details, but this included crosschecking the archives and published information with systematic analyses by remote sensing, prospections and systematic surveys in the field with GPS localisation. The resulting data was entered into a database and linked with other available resources (inscriptions, statuaries, bibliographies, etc) and mapped at a 1:10000 scale, based on the only detailed cartographic information available at the time which had been ordered by Groslier in the 1960s, for the same purpose. This new cartography then served as the basis for the re-evaluation of the configuration and modality of the successive capitals of the region from the so-called 'pre-Angkorian' period to the beginning of the 11th century (Pottier 1999). These maps were digitised and integrated on a GIS platform, thanks to a collaboration with the University of Sydney, which allowed me to enter honourably into the 21st century. This cartography registers 527 archaeological structures, two thirds of which had not been mapped or registered before. But apart from the dots and registration numbers, the main features on the cartography are the remains of settlements and their associated structures (roads, canals, etc.), and plenty of evidence of old land use, such as the contours of the bunded fields. This data presents a scale of development that, if it does not go beyond, at least complements the details of our current understanding of Angkor. I think the data deserve to be looked at in more detail.

The first type of information emerging from this cartography concerns, of course, the temples—the markers most obvious and most often visible in the field and on the maps. If we do not dwell on their potential for cosmogonic representation, which are well known, we must stress a systematic feature we find in all Angkorian temples, from the smallest to the biggest: the same geometric pattern of the square or rectangular mound surrounded by a peripheral moat. There are, of course, some variations in size and orientation, but there is a significant amount of the archaeological remains from small temples spread equally across the Angkorian plain. In spite of the similarity of their disposition—which would homogenise them—the variety of materials used, especially in terms of their quantity, shows us that it is a very hierarchical and contrasted corpus that stresses the inequalities of the distribution of resources between the limited number of royal foundations and the multitude of often humble private structures. This is revealing in terms of the economic importance of these religious constructions, and in terms of the capacity of a centralised power to organise such a workforce.

Often located close to the temples, human settlements present a completely different picture—according to the mounds, earth platforms and ponds, whose topography, together with the concentration of ceramic fragments on the surface, lead us to think are the remains of human settlements. Study of the mounds shows that there is some concentration of human settlements, especially around pyramid temples (the supposed centre of the capitals). But almost all of them comprise a limited number of earth platforms, associated with—if not situated next to—classical settings of small temples, with moats and an axial pond (*trapeang*) to the east or north. This common setting can be found even inside complex and organised sites, such as some capitals or particular installations like those at Phnom Bok. Their distribution in the region studied is similar to the sanctuaries they are associated with and is, therefore, very homogenous. But that is not the case for the mounds that are independent of temples; if some densities close to pyramid temples suggest urban characteristics, others located on the edge of the flooding area of the lake seem to show modalities of primitive settlements, probably 'pre-Angkorian', as was recently shown in Trapeang Phong (see below).

The systematic cartography gives us rich data related to water management, through the identification of numerous hydraulic structures—*baray* of course, but also canals, *trapeang* and moats. They help us to reconsider diverse elements that were undeveloped but often tacitly mentioned by Groslier (1979), such as the relationships between the *baray*, the big linear structures and human settlements. At first the cartography confirms the classical image of Angkor with four *baray* more or less linked by big canals and road structures. But, in detail, the hundreds of *trapeang* show a different picture that emphasises a strong formal and functional distinction between the *baray* and the nebulas of small reservoirs spread homogeneously. The most common type of *trapeang* is 140 metres long and 70 metres wide, but their size varies a lot depending on the religious foundations they are related to; the bigger the foundation usually the larger the *trapeang*. These ponds—associated as they are with the temples and with the related settlements, or even those located independently—reveal, on the surface of their banks, signs of old occupation. They were permanent water stations and central features for inhabited areas. Some *trapeang* are also placed along several long linear structures—canals and dykes—forming stripes on the territory that suggest the existence of settlements along some of these structures. But most of them seem to be unrelated to 'nucleus' human settlements, with their earth platforms and their ponds being spread around each of the temples. This is especially the case in the northern part of Angkor, where linear structures show a peculiar density whilst at the same time remaining clearly dissociated from 'nucleus' settlements and their distribution (Evans 2002). It is clear that these function distinctly and have a separate organisational logic, proving different levels of territorial planning.

Remote sensing helps us to go further in detailing the land use, particularly through the identification of old agrarian parcels and of bunded rice fields. We can see that some of the temples and their associated structures have generated in their vicinity—often close by, but sometimes further away—their own geometrised systems, as evidenced by isocline groups of parcels. Analyses of their morphology and the study of their superimposition show clearly that they are fossilised parcels. Recently, preventive excavations done at the Siem Reap airport have stratigraphically confirmed the antiquity of these bunded fields (Baty et al 2005). These parcels show the scope of the land area linked with religious foundations (sometimes up to 70 hectares), and they also suggest a noticeable densification of specific patterns of organisation around the urban centres. Additionally, they illustrate the amount of work being done, which often goes beyond the mere development of temples to reach a real grid layout of the region. It testifies to the importance of a geometrical grid, both for what it reveals about the territory as having been deeply shaped by its people, as for what can be perceived of their search for mastery over the environment. The geometric shaping and the attempt at environmental mastery are perfectly illustrated by the grid representation of the only map of the period, which is located at the bottom of the inscription K.542 at the north Kleang. The agrarian parcels show the complex relationship with pre-existing topography which has been more or less modified in order to fit into a geometrical grid. Through morphochronological analyses, the agrarian parcels also help to reveal some moments of densification in territorial development; this can be seen especially in the south of the western *baray* where, within a mosaic of parcels, the orientations enable several groups of parcels from settlements that preceded the *baray* to be dissociated from those created during or after the realisation of the network of canals linking to the *baray* (Pottier 2001a). The dissociation shows that the creation of the *baray* helped to complete the development of rice fields in a large area downstream which had formerly only been partially cultivated.

Analyses of these cartographic data enable a better understanding of, and offer the potential for, the reconsideration of different aspects of the management and development of the space in Angkor. I will only stress here the land-planning aspect, but it is directly linked with our understanding of Angkorian urban planning and with an idealised representation of cities with huge geometrical surrounding walls, like Angkor Thom, the last capital funded by Jayavarman VII at the end of the 12th century. As mentioned earlier, the 'perfect' example of Angkor Thom, the basis for the first studies of Angkorian cities, served as a model from which the urban characteristics of older capitals were studied. Where the research focused initially on a few basic urban structures (temples, causeways, surrounding walls, network of canals, etc.), it has been remarkably extended by studies led in recent years by Jacques Gaucher (2004), who has unveiled a regular network of linear structures determining a system of rectangular blocks showing the remains of occupation (ponds, earth platforms, etc.) which could recall, at least morphologically, the rectangular grid of the inscription K.542 of the north Kleang.

If Angkor Thom's urban configuration really looks like an almost perfect schema, it cannot, however, be understood as the ultimate realisation of an urban model for earlier Angkorian capitals. Angkor Thom seems also to have been erected following a traumatic event—the fall of Angkor when it was taken by the Chams—which easily explains its enclosed configuration behind a defensive system. The Javayarman VII capital is rather a spectacular achievement in the urban planning history of Angkor, the preceding stages of which we still have to determine. Several square cities delimited by a surrounding wall have been proposed to fill this chronological gap. The most famous hypothesis is probably that formulated in the 1930s by Victor Goloubew concerning the first capital city named Yaśodharapura. He had identified the Phnom Bakheng as the central temple, funded by the king Yaśovarman at the end of the ninth century, and asserted the existence of a surrounding city wall, each side of which was four-kilometres long. The first part of the hypothesis is now taken for granted, but the delimitation of this huge city of 16 square kilometres, known as Goloupura, must now be put aside (Groslier 1979; Pottier 2000). The structure considered by Goloubew as the southwest angle of the enclosure—the only tangible archaeological remains—has been revealed as most likely a hydraulic structure constructed after the 12th century. Also, data from coring, topographic and morphological studies, as well as the comparison of epigraphic data with the old parcelling shapes, show that the Yaśovarman city was wide open to its territory downstream from Yaśodharatatāka, the eastern *baray* (Pottier 2000).

Groslier also came up with a similar hypothesis concerning 'Banteay Chhœu', one of the first cities of the pre-Angkorian period, which had a huge square moat each side of which was three kilometres long, which would have included several of the temples from this period that were discovered in the 1930s in the western *baray* area (Groslier 1979). Again, here no links can be traced between these old temples and this supposed 'enclosure'; the distribution of the temples actually extends beyond the perimeter of the 'enclosure' (Pottier 2001a). This hydraulic structure is only part of an orthogonal system of canals associated with the western *baray*, built in the 11th century, more than three centuries later than the supposed Banteay Chhœu. Moreover the name, Banteay Chhœu (the 'wooden citadel') refers to a nearby site where remote sensing has shown vestiges of a rectangular delimitation of 650 x 560 metres superimposing clearly with the Angkorian fields, but which is invisible on the ground. The toponymy reveals at its best a small, closed post-Angkorian structure (Pottier 1999). Therefore, the few hypotheses of closed cities prior to Angkor have to be abandoned, and we should now look for open configurations which are not formally delimited. A good example is the city established south of the eastern *baray* by Rājendravarman in the middle of the tenth century, sometimes called 'the eastern city' or 'Yaśodharapura Ibis'. It was the capital, and within the surroundings of its pyramid temple—Pre Rup—were a probable palace, ponds and several earth platforms whose organisation is shown by the cartography. But there are no elements that show a 'city' enclosure or an exact morphological delimitation. The parcelling studies show a gradual densification towards the pyramid temple and its southeast surroundings, corresponding to a cluster of rectangular mounds that are the only archaeological remains of an urban configuration (Pottier 1999). Next to these densities are classical sanctuary configurations with *trapeangs* and associated earth platforms, typical of supposed rural settlements, although some of them (Bat Chum for example) were created by high dignitaries of the kingdom. There is a remarkable continuum, which we could identify as rural/urban if this *rus/urbs* opposition could really be justified here. In this case, the city is not differentiated through a specific and delimited morphologic reality but by the existence of symbolic elements. So, territorial development, urban planning and architecture seem to be closely linked in an overall approach of the development of the space defined by royal and religious power.

I will end this horizontal approach by presenting briefly the developments we are presently working on as part of the Greater Angkor Project, a co-operative project between the University of Sydney, APSARA and the EFEO.[1] Because the contribution of my colleague Roland Fletcher to this volume is also about the work of the Project, I will only present here one aspect of the Project which is linked with the extension of the archaeological cartography. A preliminary remote-sensing study was done by Damian Evans (2002) on the north zone using new radar coverage, AIRSAR, completed in September 2000 and based on the cartography of the south zone (Pottier 1999) and the ZEMP data (Pottier 1993b). It is now being checked and refined by field prospections—even though they are not systematic they are nevertheless indispensable—and by aerial prospections by ultralight aircraft, which are perfect for following long linear structures in difficult to access and less safe environments. These works are still in progress (Evans et al 2007) but are already suggesting a density and modalities of occupation in the north area similar to those studied in the south. There is certainly a difference, nevertheless, in the significantly increased density of the linear structures that form a grid in the north zone, of which the history and purposes are still to be addressed.

---

[1] These developments were current at the time of the *Old Myths and New Approaches* conference in 2005; since then, however, work has continued, yielding further results. See Pottier et al 2006, Evans et al 2007, and Pottier and Bolle 2009.

I will then conclude, with a second example that illustrates the vertical approach, by presenting some of the work we have carried out since 2000 for the Mission Archéologique Franco-Khmère sur l'Aménagement du Territoire Angkorien (MAFKATA). The main focus of this archaeological mission is the study of the first phases of Angkor development: this key period witnessed the evolution from the first small-scale, pre-Angkorian installations to the emergence of the first organised and geometrised capitals around huge pyramidal architectural groups. Our preliminary studies suggested two areas that would enable us to follow this progression in the Angkor region: the western *baray* area and Roluos. Our first campaign started in the western *baray* area, and five sites that are potentially representative of this key time in Angkorian history were selected. The excavations focused mainly on the immediate surrounds of the sanctuaries, and on the study of the developments and eventual peripheral settlements. Showing a discrepancy between temple space and domestic space, they also stressed, especially at Prei Khmeng, a remarkable continuity of occupation between proto-historical periods and the pre-Angkorian period. The establishment of the Hindu sanctuary, dated from the sixth century (or perhaps the beginning of the seventh), was accompanied by a deep spatial reorganisation and a radical change in funeral rituals when the practice of inhumation ceased. But the profound changes that occurred in this area in the 11th century have hindered our research, especially around the pyramid temple of Ak Yum where an early 'Angkorian' type capital might have been founded as early as the end of the seventh century (Pottier 2010).

Since 2004, our work has shifted to the region of Roluos where there are pre-Angkorian architectural remains (such as Trapeang Phong) and monumental constituent elements of Indravarman I's capital, which is usually considered the first 'Angkorian city' to be centred on the pyramid temple of Bakong. Roluos presents several clues that potentially indicate a synchronous evolution. We have focused our research on two distinctive but comparable sites, Bakong and Trapeang Phong, which are complementary and characteristic of two types of installation.

The latter, located in the south of the Roluos region on the edge of land flooded by the Tonle Sap, seems to be typical of the first pre-Angkorian settlements, with a strong cluster of small, relatively rectangular mounds. Moreover, east and north of the temple, which shows several sanctuaries from different 'style' periods, are two large *trapeangs* which were interpreted by Groslier as 'superimposed *trapeangs*' typical of a configuration used as a prototype for the Angkorian city of Bakong (Groslier 1998). It was even ventured that this site could have corresponded to the centre of the first Hariharālaya of the Jayavarman II and Jayavarman III capitals. Research carried out in 2004 and 2005 has focused on the configuration, the chronology and the type of occupation over the large area, which is around 240 hectares. Guided by a detailed topographical survey, more than 60 corings were done on all of the site's mounds in order to assess the depth and general configurations of potential archaeological layers. At the same time, excavation of a first set of test pits was carried out in the immediate surrounds of the temple and on the two huge trapeangs; this work continued in the second year with a new set of excavations on several neighbouring mounds. Even at that time, with the studies not yet finished, it already appeared that the trapeangs were added during the Angkorian period, subsequent to a first configuration made only of mounds. If these are the missing link between small installations of isolated sanctuaries and large geometrised Angkorian organisations, the 'superimposed trapeangs' hypothesis must be abandoned. These ponds show a resettlement and a profound reorganisation of the site in the 11th or 12th centuries which could echo the architectural changes made in the neighbouring site of Trapeang Totung Tngay (Pottier and Bolle 2009).

Twenty-four test pits were examined in Trapeang Phong. Of these, the first core samples from 19 neighbouring mounds revealed a rich history of domestic occupation; located essentially west of the temple, the mounds continued to be used during the Angkorian period, when they were raised and new mounds and *trapeangs* were created. The importance of this temple is proven by the additions and restoration works on one of the central sanctuaries, possibly carried out in the tenth century (Pottier and Lujàn-Lunsford 2006); however, it now seems unlikely that it can be considered the prototype of the Angkorian city. On the contrary (and as we suspected), its organisation into a concentration of slightly disorganised but overall rectangular mounds reflects rather faithfully the first settlements in the region. Given the other neighbouring sites that date from the same period, to me it is more appropriately considered a modest 'classic' settlement, one that is dominated by its temple, is located in an area occupied since proto-historical times, and was already rather dense in pre-Angkorian times. Nevertheless, I stress that the test pits have also clearly shown that the density of the presently visible earth platforms in the region should be balanced with a diachronic perspective if we want to find the density of pre-Angkorian occupation.

The second site studied, the Bakong, is at the heart of the first Angkorian city and has been used for the past 50 years—and is still used—as a model to apprehend and explain the subsequent capitals (Stern 1951; Groslier 1979);

it has somehow become the counterpart of Angkor Thom, the other extreme of Angkorian urban history. But at Bakong, the initial construction of the main elements (*baray*, Preah Kô, Bakong) constituting this first city seems to contradict the established chronology, based on epigraphy, which attributes the foundation of all three elements to Indravarman I, who reigned in Hariharālaya from about 877 to 886 CE (Pottier 1996). On the other hand, detailed analyses of the architectural additions have suggested a chronological complexity that goes beyond the period of the reign of Indravarman I and the subsequent 12th-century transformations that were identified at the end of the 1930s (Pottier 2006). Work focused also on the overall development of the Bakong site, especially on the study of its organisation and chronology, and the occupation of the huge space between the temple enclosure and the external moat (approximately 840 x 800 metres). The detailed topographical survey we conducted between 1998 and 2000 helped us to define more accurately the configuration of evenly distributed elements (approximately 20 satellite sanctuaries made of bricks and sandstone, and a set of eight square ponds). It also revealed indications of prior occupancy. It was then necessary to ensure the contemporaneity of the various components of the geometrical master plan, which are characteristic of the beginning of the architectural design of the large temples with enclosure walls. Furthermore, it was vital to try to qualify this space: is it part of the religious foundation—a domain enclosure—or is it the first real urban space structured by religious installations? We could not consider this space *a priori* as urban without trying to link its formal organisation to the real distribution and specific activities of its occupants. It was, therefore, important to locate and evaluate the spread of activities in this organised and morphologically hierarchised space: areas for recreation, rituals, settlements, and so on.

Excavation campaigns organised in Bakong since 2004 have focused on this 'external' enclosure, particularly the southwest angle where an anomaly suggested a sanctuary constructed prior to the geometrical master plan. The first excavation campaign supported this hypothesis and also revealed—in apparent antinomy—the existence of huge volumes of earth embankment but few signs of occupation. It also stressed the need to acquire quickly an overall stratigraphic vision in order to distinguish properly between natural soils and anthropised layers. During the second campaign, a continuous cross-section of the studied enclosure was excavated, from the surrounding wall of the temple to the external moat—a length of 250 metres. Mechanical tools were used, although not near the monumental structures (the surrounding wall and satellite tower) and the domestic levels. Through this work we were able to confirm the contemporaneity of the structures (the surrounding wall, satellite towers, ponds, external moat) that shape the whole Bakong. The new data allowed us to see properly the real scope of the initial building program of the Bakong. For example, the stunning scope of the creation of earth embankments, following strict ritualistic guidelines, demonstrates completely the will of the inhabitants to deeply reshape their environment, and is on a scale that is completely different from modest installations like Trapeang Phong.

However, because I was still waiting for the results of the analyses, I remained cautious about the implications of the datings from such a huge program: collected artefacts showing an important evolution in the characteristics of the material culture of the Angkorian period will also have an impact on the dating of the site. These artefacts include glazed stoneware, ceramics imported from China, and Indian techniques of roofing that were abandoned with the introduction of new Chinese-inspired techniques. The dating of most of these elements is usually ascribed to the dating of the Bakong itself: the end of the ninth century. Although there is still a long way to go with dating the creation and the occupation of Bakong, the results of our 2004–05 research implies that its founding could have occurred a century earlier, at around the end of the eighth century, and that the site would have been inactive for a long time (Pottier et al 2006). This hypothesis is supported by the palynological study of a core taken during the Greater Angkor Project in the internal moat of the Bakong (Penny et al 2006). Although ephemeral in relation to the duration of Angkor, signs of occupation contemporaneous with the architectural structures of the Bakong were found in all of the excavation sites, although in varying densities. However, the scarcity of ceramic material and charcoal, in particular, in the areas of the temple wall and its enclosures, and around the satellite sanctuaries, has strengthened the hypothesis that these zones were not much used. On the other hand, some pits and densely anthropised layers suggest limited areas of habitation along the pond and by the dyke of the external moat, where no signs of any defence structure or even of fencing have been found, including on its external side. Although we should not generalise from a single diagnostic trench to the whole of the enclosure, this information suggests the presence of settlements concentrated on the periphery of the site. It has also led us to predict a specific (and probably planned) distribution of the occupied areas and settlements within this architecturally and symbolically structured space. The information also paves the way for deeper research into the hierarchical systematisation of the installations, the dissociation of the various spaces, and the density of housing. When emphasised, the diversity and distribution of usages—from the sacred to the profane—invite us to an understanding of how the space is connected to its pyramidal sanctuary.

To finish, although the above examples do not, of course, sum up all the 'new approaches' to understanding Angkor, they illustrate several possibilities that could be developed in order to broaden our understanding of other ancient religious sites in Southeast Asia. The 'traditional' approaches have proved their efficiency in identifying specific aspects of religious structures. Additionally, however, the findings in Angkor from these new methods—such as the study of the environment, and of the spatial organisation that characterised the temples and contributed to the ways in which they were shaped—stress the value of these methods and the resulting need to reassess the role of temples in these societies. Similarly, archaeological and paleo-environmental research reveals new information not covered in the available historical sources. As such, the Angkor region demonstrates how a comprehensive spatial approach can identify and stress the evolution of secular elements that characterise settlements and land use, beyond huge religious monuments and religious patterns. It also illustrates how interpretations of the research, informed by tangible and measurable stratigraphic data, can go beyond the classic 'dead end' which oppose urban patterns to rural settlements.

Acknowledgements

I would like to thank the French Ministry for Foreign Affairs and EFEO for funding the MAFKATA archaeological mission, the Australian Research Council for funding of the Greater Angkor Project, and APSARA. My sincere thanks go also to all 2004 and 2005 MAFKATA team members: Annie Bolle, Eric Llopis, Dominique Soutif, Jean-Baptiste Chevance, Cyril Tan, Peng Dara, Chea Socheat, So Sophearin, Kong Vireak, Sang Sun, Maartje Zwaneveld, Heng Than, Khieu Chan, Seila Yam, Tessa Simone Mah-Boer, Pin Vichear Sachara, Chhay Rachana, Rethy K Chhem, Fabrice Demeter, Caroline Souday, Mélanie Frelat, Nicolas Buchet, Anne-Marie Bacon, Christophe Gabillault, Alexandrine Guerin, Van Sary, Sin Sokchenda, Uong Savana, and the 60 workers from Prei Khmeng, Bakong and Trapéang Phong. Thanks also go to the Greater Angkor Project team members: Roland Fletcher, Dan Penny, Mike Barbetti, Damian Evans, Ian Johnson, Tous Somaneath, Terry Lustig, Andrew Wilson, Matti Kummu.

Chapter 3

Mysteries of Angkor revealed

Hydrology and the siting of Angkor

Bob Acker

Lecturer, Department of Geography, University of California at Berkeley

The theoretical setting

Introduction

Angkor was the first, largest and richest empire in medieval mainland Southeast Asia. Founded early in the ninth century around the Great Lake on the north Cambodian plain, it ruled an area that by the end of the tenth century comprised most of modern Cambodia, southern Laos, and northeastern and central Thailand; in the twelfth century, it created one of the wonders of the world, the gigantic temple complex of Angkor Wat. The fundamental question in Angkorian studies is to determine what factors enabled Angkor to become so large and so rich so early.

The first comprehensive theory of Angkor's greatness claimed that Angkor grew powerful through intensive rice irrigation based on gigantic, rectilinear water-holding devices known as *baray*, which permitted rice crops to be grown in the dry season as well as the wet, and so fed the army that supported its empire and the workforce that built its temples. In the second half of the ninth century, the first *baray*, the Indratatāka, was built just north of the first capital, Hariharālaya, on the north shore of the Great Lake. The Indratatāka measured about three kilometres along its east–west axis and 750 metres along its north–south axis; given a water depth of three metres, it could have held almost seven million cubic metres of water.

Toward the end of the ninth century, the capital moved from Hariharālaya to a new site on the banks of the Siem Reap River, about 18 kilometres northwest of Hariharālaya and 12 kilometres north of the shore of the Great Lake. The new capital, Yaśodharapura, was built around an elevation called the Bakheng, on which the state temple was constructed. A new and much larger *baray*, the Yaśodharatatāka, was built at around the same time, just to the east of the new capital. It measured 7.5 kilometres along its east–west axis and 1.8 kilometres along its north–south axis; with a depth of three metres, it could have held 40 million cubic metres of water. About 150 years later, in the middle of the eleventh century, the largest *baray* of all, the West Baray, was built just west of the capital district. With an east–west axis extending for eight kilometres and a north–south axis two kilometres in length, and a probable water depth of five metres, the West Baray was capable of holding around 80 million cubic metres of water.[1]

In short, these early capitals were from their very beginning associated with mammoth *baray*. For several decades beginning around 1960, the dominant explanation for Angkor's early rise to power and prosperity was based on irrigation and water control made possible by the *baray*. This was the so-called hydraulic thesis, chiefly promulgated by Bernard-Philippe Groslier of the École française d'Extrême-Orient (EFEO). Groslier hypothesised that water retained in the *baray* enabled a dry-season rice crop to be grown on the land down-slope from the *baray*, and also permitted a full wet-season crop to be grown even during years of abnormally scanty rainfall, in turn supporting Angkor's army and urban workforce. In short, the hydraulic thesis went far beyond agronomy, attributing every aspect of Angkorian society—its economic base, labour organisation, supposedly centralised politics, in fact its entire historical trajectory—to *baray* irrigation (Groslier 1966, 1979).

The hydraulic hypothesis, however, was never quantified or tested. Beginning in 1980, criticisms began to accumulate. The hydrologist van Liere published two papers, whose main thrust was that Khmer engineering could not provide the outtake structures needed to distribute water from the *baray*, and that in point of fact no trace of distributary canals could be found

---

[1] In an earlier paper (Acker 1998), I estimated the depth of the West Baray at around nine metres, with a proportionately greater water-holding capacity. But, while the titanic walls of the West Baray would have permitted it to hold nine or more metres of water, such a water depth would have submerged the West Mebon, the island-temple in the centre of the West Baray. I am indebted to Christophe Pottier, head of the Siem Reap office of the EFEO, for this observation.

downslope from the *baray* (van Liere 1980, 1982). In 1992, Stott restated van Liere's critiques and added criticisms of his own, first that there are no textual references in the very extensive Angkorian corpus to any irrigation works of any kind, and second, that the labour force that built the *baray* must have pre-dated them, and could not have owed its sustenance to irrigation from them (Stott 1992). Several years ago, I undertook quantitative tests of the hydraulic thesis and these indicated that the *baray* could not have irrigated more than a small fraction of the land downslope from the *baray* but above the northern shore of the Great Lake, and that the rice that could have been grown on the land thus irrigated could have fed only a minuscule fraction of Angkor's population. Thus, *baray* irrigation, even if it existed, cannot have been responsible for Angkor's rise to greatness. I suggested that the *baray* were part of the urban architecture of Angkor, and that Angkorian agriculture may have been based on another aspect of Angkor's geography, the very high water-table underlying most of the north shore of the Great Lake.

Recent research

Christophe Pottier of EFEO, in the course of an extensive exploration of the area down-slope from the *baray*, has discovered a network of canals near the southwest corner of the West Baray (Pottier 2001a); but, while these canals suggest the existence of some sort of hydraulic system related to the *baray*, they nonetheless surround no more than 600 hectares, an area utterly insufficient to have supported Angkor's labour force or to have played a decisive role in the Angkorian economy. In addition, remote sensing techniques used by Roland Fletcher of the University of Sydney have discovered canals to the north of the capital district (Fletcher 2000), but these very long canals, which have few distributaries, apparently served to connect the capital district with the northwestern spur of the Phnom Kulen range of hills, and so may well have been built for purposes of transportation rather than irrigation. In sum, these discoveries point to an extensive and well-engineered water system for the capital district, but, if anything, seem to argue against the hypothesis that irrigation was the main purpose of the water retention devices around Angkor, or that the *baray* played a decisive role in Angkorian agronomy.

Another discovery, having to do with the specific siting of Angkor, may contain a clue bearing on the basis of Angkorian agricultural wealth. While it was originally believed that the Khmer moved their capital from Hariharālaya, located near the small Roluos River, to take advantage of the larger Siem Reap River at Yaśodharapura, this has been recently disproved. Excavations carried out by Pottier have demonstrated that the Siem Reap River is not a natural river but a diversion from the Puok River at a point around ten kilometres north of the capital district; further work by the hydrologist Terry Lustig of the Greater Angkor Project of the University of Sydney has shown that the diversionary works were built at the end of the ninth century, at the same time the capital moved from Hariharālaya to Yaśodharapura. But if the Siem Reap River is a diversion created at the same time as the capital, it follows that the capital cannot have been relocated to take advantage of the river. To the contrary, the capital was moved from a riverside location to one of the few places on the north Cambodian plain that had no river, and a river was then brought to it. Thus, some other factor made the new location attractive, so attractive that even the mammoth job of diverting a river to that location was justified.

The present chapter proposes and tests the hypothesis that the decisive factor in the relocation of the Angkorian capital was the high water-table surrounding Yaśodharapura. Specifically, it is posited that the new capital was relocated to that part of the north Cambodian plain where the ground-water resources were the most plentiful, and that these water resources underlie the prosperity and greatness of Angkor.

The high water-table hypothesis

Basic hydrology and agronomy

The high water-table beneath the north Cambodian plain is caused by the combination of the plain's geology and climate. A substrate of ancient and largely impermeable sandstone is overlaid by a relatively thin layer of highly permeable Quaternary sedimentation; meanwhile, the region's average annual rainfall is about 1,400 millimetres (Rasmussen and Bradford 1977). Rainwater infiltrates into the permeable alluvium quite easily, but cannot infiltrate farther because of the impermeable sandstone just beneath it, so that ground-water, supported by the sandstone layer, is found close to the surface of the plain.

Contemporary Cambodian farmers make good use of the high water-table to supplement rainfall for their rice crops during the rainy season and to water their domestic animals during the dry season. Small tanks—artificial ponds dug into the water-table—are found next to almost every house in rural Cambodia (Garami and Kertai 1993), and farm villages are sited next to somewhat larger tanks (van Liere 1982). The historical record shows that this is no recent practice. Chinese travellers of the fifth century noted the presence of village tanks (Pelliot 1903), and Cambodian rural settlements of the eighth century were similarly located around natural and artificial ponds (Vickery 1986).

The combined water-holding capacity of large numbers of small and medium-sized tanks is enormous. According to Stargardt (1983), who studied the ancient agronomy of Satingpra, an area on the Tenasserim peninsula with a water-table similar to that of Cambodia, the average village tank contained 6,000 cubic metres of water during the wet season and 3,000 cubic metres during the dry season. These figures may seem insignificant compared with the large *baray* at Angkor, whose capacity was measured in tens of millions of cubic metres. But while the large *baray* were built by embankments resting on the land surface, tanks are dug into the water-table and so refill automatically. Thus, their annual capacity is much greater than their volume; an estimate of 500,000 cubic metres per year per tank is not implausible. If there were 800 such tanks in the vicinity of the capital district, to adopt a figure found in Higham (1989), the tanks in the capital district have had a combined annual capacity of 400 million cubic metres, much greater than the capacity of all the great *baray* combined.

Prior research on Cambodia's ground-water resources

Some early research on ground-water resources in Cambodia has demonstrated a correlation between high water-tables and the locations of Khmer settlements dating from the earliest times. In 1961, Rasmussen collected data on the level of the water-table in much of Cambodia, based on measurements of the water levels in tube wells, ordinary wells about a metre in diameter, bored into the earth and usually lined with concrete. Rasmussen's data demonstrates two things relevant to this inquiry. First, nearly all of central Cambodia has a high water-table, with water almost always within five or six metres of the surface. Second, four Cambodian provinces, Kompong Thom, Siem Reap, Svey Rieng, and Takeo, have even higher water-tables, with water found one, two or three metres below ground. Takeo is the home of Angkor Borei, the earliest seat of Khmer civilisation, Kompong Thom is the home of Sambor Prei Kuk, the capital of the Khmer kingdom in the seventh century, and Siem Reap is the home of the successive Khmer capitals between 802 and 1431, Hariharālaya, Yaśodharapura, and Angkor. Only Svey Rieng, located in the borderland between the Khmer and Cham kingdoms, was not the home of an early Khmer capital.

But, while Rasmussen's data thus contains clues to the importance of high water-tables in forming Khmer settlement patterns, his data is not detailed.[2] The number of data points in each province varies from fewer than a dozen to a few dozen, the data points are apparently closely grouped within most provinces rather than distributed across the provinces, and specific locations of the data points are not provided. Before reliable conclusions can be drawn correlating the height of the water-table and the location of Angkorian settlement centres, greater quantities of more widely distributed and specifically located data points, with precise information concerning water levels, are necessary.

Hypothesis testing

Consequently, between January and March 2005, I measured the subsurface water levels in 830 tube wells around Siem Reap province. Although I measured water-table levels in the middle of the dry season, the important consideration was how the water-table affected rice farming during the rainy season. To determine this, I interviewed farmers, virtually all of whom reported that the water level in their wells rises by two metres between the middle of the dry season and the end of the rainy season; these reports were verified by checking the water marks on the inside of the wells.

The data I collected are displayed on Plate 3.1, on which the locations and water-table levels of the measured wells are depicted. The levels are classified as 'very high', 'high', 'mid-level' or 'low'. These are classified as follows:

- **Very high water-tables** (blue dots) are those within 1.5 metres of the surface when measured halfway through the dry season. With the typical two-metre rise by the end of the rainy season, the water here will rise to the surface halfway through the rainy season and inundate the land.

- **High water-tables** (green dots) are those more than 1.5 but less than 2.5 metres below the surface when measured halfway through the dry season. With the typical two-metre rise by the end of the

---

[2] Rasmussen's survey of subsurface water resources, the first of its kind, was of course intended to create the groundwork for water-use policies in the present and not to conduct historical research in any sense.

rainy season, the water here will nearly or fully inundate the land by the end of the rainy season.

- **Mid-level water-tables** (yellow dots) are those more than 2.5 and less than 3.5 metres below the surface when measured halfway through the dry season. By the end of the rainy season, the water here will be approximately a metre beneath the surface by the end of the rainy season.
- **Low water-tables** (red dots) are those more than 3.5 metres below the surface when measured halfway through the dry season. Water here will remain well below the surface throughout the rainy season.

The data contained in Plate 3.1 is also presented in tabular form. Table 3.1 shows the measured water-table levels within a seven-kilometre radius of the Bakong temple at the centre of Hariharālaya; Table 3.2 shows the measured water-table levels within a 15-kilometre radius of the Bakheng temple-mountain at the centre of Yaśodharapura; Table 3.3 shows the measured water-table levels in the eastern part of Siem Reap province, east of the Roluos River; and Table 3.4 shows the measured water-table levels in the western part of Siem Reap province and more than 15 kilometres west of the Bakheng.

Data Tables

Water-table level	Number of data points	Percentage of total
Very high	14	19.4
High	42	58.3
Mid-level	14	19.4
Low	2	2.8

Table 3.1 Measured water-table levels within a seven-kilometre radius of the Bakong; n=72

Water-table level	Number of data points	Percentage of total
Very high	118	47.2
High	119	47.6
Mid-level	13	5.2
Low	0	0.0

Table 3.2 Measured water-table levels within 15-kilometre radius of the Bakheng; n=250

Water-table level	Number of data points	Percentage of total
Very high	25	10.0
High	101	40.4
Mid-level	62	24.8
Low	62	24.8

Table 3.3 Measured water-table levels in eastern Siem Reap province; n=250

Water-table level	Number of data points	Percentage of total
Very high	16	14.3
High	40	35.7
Mid-level	24	28.6
Low	32	21.4

Table 3.4 Measured water-table levels in western Siem Reap province; n=112

Groundwater resources and settlement locations

A comparison between the groundwater resources around Hariharālaya, the first capital, and those around the new capital at Yaśodharapura shows that:

- The water-table is on average significantly lower around Hariharālaya. There are 72 data points located within seven kilometres of the Bakong, the temple at the centre of Hariharālaya, of which 42 (58.3%) are high, 14 (19.4%) are very high, a further 14 (19.4%) are mid-level, and the remaining two, comprising 2.9% of the total, are low.[3] Across this area, approximately 154 square kilometres in extent, the average depth of the water-table is slightly greater than two metres below the ground surface halfway through the dry

---

[3] It is true that the water-table immediately around Hariharālaya is almost as high as the area around Yaśodharapura. There are 25 data points located within three kilometres of the Bakong, the main temple at Hariharālaya, of which 10 (40%) are very high, another 40% are high and the remaining 20% are mid-level. But the area of high or very high water-tables around Hariharālaya does not extend far. To the southwest, south and southeast, the Great Lake approaches to within three or four kilometres of the city during the rainy season; to the east and northeast, the very high water-table around the city gives way to a mixed region of high and mid-level water-tables within three kilometres. The only directions in which the water-table remains high are to the west and northwest, toward the new capital of Yaśodharapura.

season, so that this area, on average, would not be inundated during the average rainy season.[4]

- By way of contrast, the new capital of Yaśodharapura was situated in the centre of an almost perfect circle, approximately 30 kilometres in diameter,[5] within which ground-water resources are close to the surface. Of the 250 data points within this 30-kilometre circle, 118 are very high, 119 are high, and 13 are mid-level; none are low. The average depth of the water-table within this area is slightly greater than 1.5 metres below the ground surface in the middle of the dry season, so that virtually the entire region would have been inundated during the rainy season.[6]

- There is less variation in water-table levels around Yaśodharapura than around Hariharālaya. As noted, water-table levels around Hariharālaya varied widely, with as many mid-level data points as very high points. By way of contrast, almost all the data points around Yaśodharapura were high or very high, and the high and very high points were practically equal in number. In short, the average variance from the mean water-table depth was twice as great around Hariharālaya as around Yaśodharapura.

- The region of high and very high water-tables around Yaśodharapura was much larger than the corresponding region around Hariharālaya.

---

[4] This assertion obviously rests on the assumption that the amount of rainfall during Angkorian times closely approximates contemporary rainfall totals. Indirect evidence supports this point. The work of Kummu (2004) suggests that little, if any, sediment has been deposited in the Great Lake in the past 5,000 years; meanwhile, the locations of Angkorian and contemporary settlements along the shore of the Great Lake suggest that the shoreline has barely moved since Angkorian times. But the volume of water in the Great Lake is a function of precipitation and drainage in the Tonle Sap basin, on the one hand, and the volume of water stored in the Lake during the time of reversed flow of the Tonle Sap River from the Mekong mainstream in the second half of the rainy season on the other (Fisher 1963). If the surface area and the depth of the Great Lake, that is, the volume of water in it, have not changed significantly since Angkorian times, this must mean that the amount of precipitation over the Mekong drainage basin as a whole and over the Tonle Sap basin have not changed significantly since then.

[5] Measured from the Bakheng, the temple mountain at the centre of Yaśodharapura.

[6] The very highest water-table in Siem Reap province is in the area once occupied by the East Baray. Even in the middle of the dry season, the water-table is less than a metre below the surface of the ground. It is probable that this area was under water for much of the year even before the Angkorian capital was re-sited just to the west, and that only minor dredging and circumvallation was needed to convert this semiannual swamp into a *baray*.

The area of the 30-kilometre circle of high and very high subsurface water around Yaśodharapura measures approximately 700 square kilometres, over four times larger than the significantly lower region within seven kilometres of Hariharālaya, and around thirty times larger than the slightly lower water-table in the region immediately around Hariharālaya.

Moreover, a comparison between the area around Yaśodharapura and the far eastern and far western parts of Siem Reap province, where no capital was ever sited, shows much starker contrasts in water-table levels:

- The eastern part of the province has a much lower water-table than the regions around either Yaśodharapura or Hariharālaya. Specifically, while only 5.2% of the data points around Yaśodharapura, and 22.3% of the data points around Hariharālaya, reflected a mid-level or low water-table, 49.6% of the data points east of the Roluos River were mid- or low-level. Moreover, the concentration of low- and mid-level data points increases the farther east one proceeds. Between the east bank of the Roluos river and the road connecting Beng Mealea with the shore of the Great Lake, 53% of the data points (73 of 138) are very high or high; but between the road and the eastern border of Siem Reap province, 53% of the data points (59 of 112) are mid-level or low.

- The water-table in the western part of Siem Reap province is also much lower than around the capital, with especially low water-tables found in the area closest to the Great Lake. In all, 50% (56 of 112) of the data points in the area between the 30-kilometre circle around Yaśodharapura and the western boundary of the province show a mid-level or low water-table. In the area between National Route 6 and the Great Lake, 34 of 48 data points, or 70.8%, are mid-level or low. Meanwhile, there are 64 data points in western Siem Reap province to the north of NR 6, of which 22, or 34.3%, show a mid-level or low water-table.

- Moreover, while there are regions with very high water-tables in the western part of the province, practically all of them are found in two clusters. One of these is just northwest of the West Baray and so is on the verge of the capital district, while the other, in the far western part of the province, is suggestively located around a cluster of Angkorian sites,[7] and so was apparently a secondary settlement cluster to the west of Angkor.

High water-tables and Angkorian settlement patterns

The data presented here strongly confirms the hypothesis that Angkorian capitals were sited in the middle of regions characterised by high subsurface water-tables. The water-table around Hariharālaya is significantly higher than the water-table found further to the east in the area closer to the older Khmer centres. The new capital district at Yaśodharapura was in a large region of very high subsurface water, far surpassing the location of Hariharālaya in size, consistency, and, most importantly, proximity to subsurface water. More striking still, Yaśodharapura was in virtually the centre of that region. Finally, what may be the largest cluster of Angkorian sites outside the capital districts is found in the middle of the only region outside the capital district with very high subsurface water levels.

Why the capital was placed in the middle of the region with the highest water-table

This very strong spatial correlation raises the question of why regions with high water-tables were preferred centres of settlement. I will argue, first, that high subsurface water levels increase agricultural productivity in several ways, and second, that the labour requirements of Khmer urban development were most easily met when urban sites were placed in the middle of regions of high agricultural productivity.

The uses of high water-tables

Observation of contemporary farming practices indicates that high water-tables make three distinct contributions to Cambodian agronomy. First, high water-tables make rice culture more productive, especially in a region of poor, sandy soils such as central Cambodia. These poor soils can supply only modest amounts of nutrients to the rice plants. But rice, originally a swamp plant, can obtain nutrients dissolved in ambient water as well as from soil (Grist 1955). Rice farmers surround their fields with low dikes to prevent runoff, thus keeping water and the nutrients it contains in the rice field. But while dikes can prevent rainwater from running off horizontally,

---

[7] Prasat Don Ok, Prasat Loeuk Prey, Prasat Don Tuk and Prasat Laongieng. This is perhaps the densest cluster of Angkorian settlements outside the capital district.

they cannot prevent it from infiltrating vertically, down into the soil. During weeks of steady rain, when the amount of rainfall is greater than the amount of water that sinks into the soil, water remains in the rice field and the rice plants can receive nourishment. When the rain is intermittent, however, water sinks into the soil faster than it is replenished, and the field dries out; the rice plants can no longer receive nutrients from ambient surface water. Infiltration is particularly severe in Cambodia, with its highly permeable sandy soils.

Infiltration ceases to be a problem, however, if the water-table is close to the surface even before the rainy season begins. In this case, the soil between the water-table and the surface is quickly filled by infiltrating rain water; in other words, the water-table rises to the surface as the rainy season proceeds. Once this happens, the rice field becomes inundated and remains so throughout the rest of the rainy season, and even for some weeks after its end, so that ambient water continuously supplies nourishment to the rice plants. Moreover, the higher the water-table is to begin with, the sooner the rice field is inundated, the longer the inundation lasts, and the more nutrients the rice plants receive over the course of the growing season.

There are two additional ways in which regions with high water-tables are more productive than regions with lower water-tables. High water-tables enable domestic animals to survive the dry season more easily. As the dry season continues and many surface water features dry up, stored rainwater may allow human beings to survive, but their livestock need groundwater. Naturally, the closer the groundwater is to the surface, the easier it is to dig down to, especially with the few and poor tools available to traditional farmers. In addition, high water-tables make the cultivation of fruit trees and vegetables more productive. A high water-table means that more moisture reaches the roots of trees, leading to higher yields, and a very high water-table may enable farmers to plant a crop of vegetables in the still-wet soil after the rice harvest has been completed.

In short, relocating the capital from Hariharālaya to Yaśodharapura at the end of the ninth century moved the Khmer centre of settlement from a smaller, less agriculturally productive area to a larger, more productive one.

Agricultural productivity and urban location

The movement of the capital from Hariharālaya to Yaśodharapura required not only the construction of an entirely new city but also the diversion of a river, and creation of the gigantic, 15-square kilometre East Baray, all at roughly the same time. An enormous labour force was needed to build these gigantic works. Where did this labour force come from?

At one time, it was believed that the ancient Khmer used irrigation from the great *baray* to grow a dry-season rice crop that supported a large permanent urban workforce; but the *baray*, for all their huge area, were not very deep, and could not have provided the water to grow enough dry season rice to support tens of thousands of urban workers and their families (Acker 1998). Turning away from the idea of a permanent urban workforce, we see at once that, as elsewhere in mainland Southeast Asia, an available workforce could be assembled from rice farmers and other agricultural workers in the countryside, once the farmers had completed their rice harvest after the end of the rainy season. This rural-based workforce would have been available annually for the six months from December through June.

As was almost universally the case in traditional mainland Southeast Asia, the labour force that built the temples and *baray* of Angkor was likely divided into two halves, with one half put to work during the days of the waxing moon and the other half during the days of the waning moon; and, during the half-month when they were not employed on public construction projects, the workers in all likelihood returned to their home villages. This system of bi-weekly labour rotation would have worked efficiently only if the workers lived within one or, at most, two days' travel from their urban work place, not dozens or hundreds of kilometres away. In other words, the system worked best if the urban worksite were situated in the midst of a large, thickly settled agricultural zone. The relocation from Hariharālaya to Yaśodharapura was a move from a smaller, less productive and, therefore, less populated region to a larger, more productive and more thickly settled region—to a region, in other words, where the large labour force needed for the urban works of Yaśodharapura and, later, of Angkor was readily available.

Conclusion

This research, corroborating the work of earlier scholars, demonstrates a strong correlation between high water-tables and the locations of medieval Khmer centres of settlement, reflecting in turn the more productive agriculture found in areas of more abundant ground-water resources. This was the Khmer response to the problems posed by the nutrient-poor, permeable sandy soil characteristic of the Cambodian plain.

The peoples of mainland Southeast Asia each developed agricultural adaptations best suited to their environments. The Dai peoples in the hill country developed the weir and canal system. The Mon, in the meandering river valleys of the lower Chaophraya and the Khorat, developed moated sites around those river bends. The present research demonstrates that the Khmer, on the broad but relatively infertile Cambodian plain, developed their own characteristic form of agriculture, one that could take advantage of the strengths and counteract the weaknesses of their environment.

Acknowledgements

I would like to thank Dr Alexandra Haendel for giving me the opportunity to present these research results. I must also thank Dr Hang Peou and Mr Bun Sonnaroath of the Department of Water and Forestry of the APSARA Authority in Siem Reap, without whose help and co-operation none of this research could have been carried out. I also want to express my gratitude for the generous support of the Fulbright research program of the United States State Department, which made this research program possible.

Chapter 4

The dynamics of Angkor and its landscape

Issues of scale, non-correspondence and outcome

Roland Fletcher

Director, Greater Angkor Project, Department of Archaeology, University of Sydney

Damian Evans

Research Associate, Department of Archaeology, University of Sydney

The low-density urban complex of Angkor covered about 1,000 square kilometres, extending from the lake, the Tonle Sap, to the lower slopes of the Kulen hills, with the enclosure of Angkor Thom at its centre (Fig. 4.1). Also visible all over the landscape, both to aerial photography and to radar imaging, are a massive and elaborate water-management system, with canals over 20 kilometres long, and the fields whose rice sustained the inhabitants. The urban complex was apparently supported by extensification of rice production through the clearance of forest, while the water management system could have delivered water for a risk minimisation strategy that would have guaranteed the supply of rice in poor monsoon years (Fletcher et al 2003:116).

The key ecological significance of Angkor is that the settlement was extensive enough to have a substantial impact on its environment. The Greater Angkor Project is investigating this impact and the implications of altered water flow and sediment deposition rates for the stability and integrity of the water-management network. Today, river channels are several metres below the Angkorian ground surface. Some Angkorian canals, one to two metres deep and about 40–60 metres wide, are entirely filled with cross-bedded sands. Understanding this damage and its implications for the demise of urban Angkor requires an analysis of the potentially conflicting relationships between phenomena that operate across many different spatial and temporal

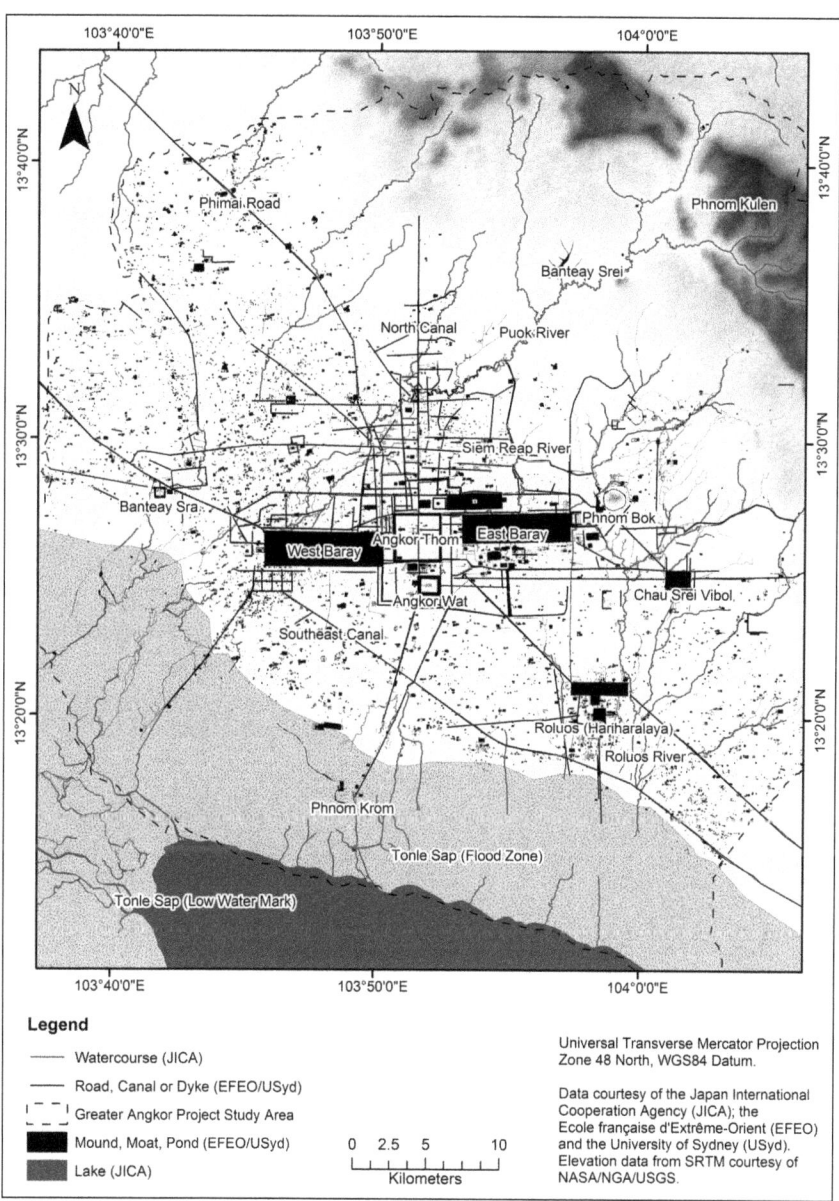

Figure 4.1 Map of archaeological features at Angkor, from the Greater Angkor Project
(After Evans 2007 and Pottier 1999)

scales. How might residential mobility have related to the settlement pattern? How did crop production interact with planetary climate change? Non-correspondence between the sociality of action and the material component of community life, and between economics and the environment may be of some significance for the history of Angkor.

Background

An archaeological approach to Angkor needs to encompass phenomena ranging from the small-scale, short-term event of a ritual deposit, such as the gold leaf placed under the floor of the eastern shaft of the West Mebon (Glaize 1936, 1937, 1942, 1943, 1944), through the larger magnitude and timescales of building the *mebon*, to the even larger scale of constructing and maintaining the West Baray (Fig. 4.2), up to the massive temporal and spatial scale of centuries involved in the staple crop economy and the water flow in and out of the *baray* from a catchment extending over 20 kilometres to the north. Finally, the operation of the monsoon cycle, the limit on the viability of the economy and the crop water-management system, have to be considered in the context of the millennium-long processes of planetary climate change that produced the rise and decline of temperatures in the Medieval Warm Phase between about 850–1000 and 1500–1600 CE.

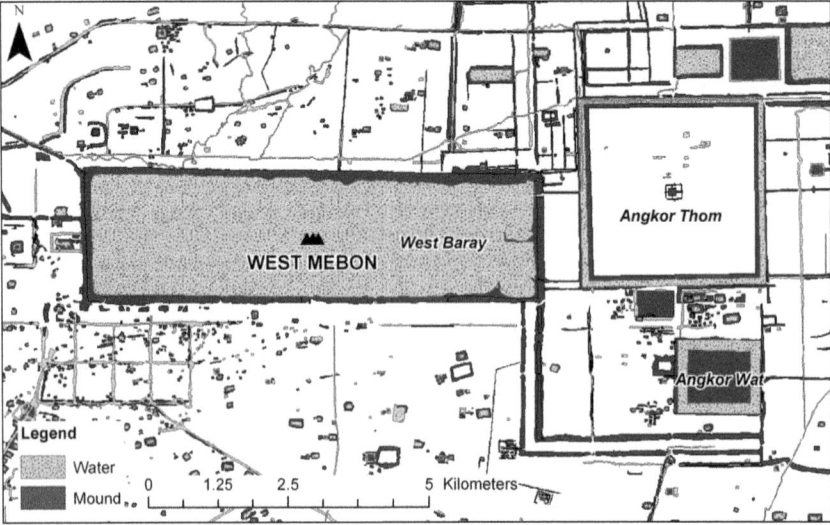

Figure 4.2 Map of the West Baray and vicinity, showing the location of the West Mebon (After Pottier 1999)

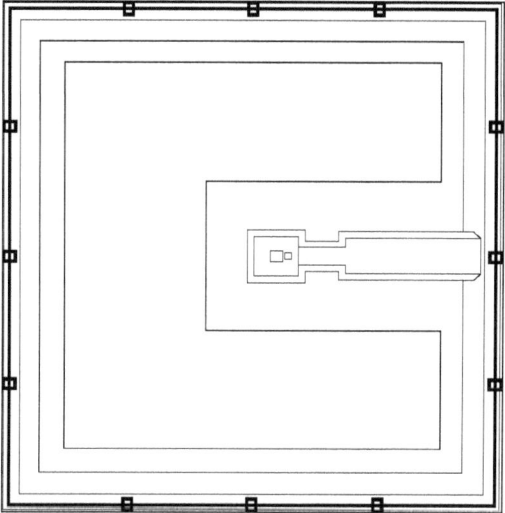

Figure 4.3 Plan of the West Mebon
Each side of the outer wall measures approximately 100m.

While social analyses and historical inquiry can opt to limit the spatial and temporal scale of their analyses, and studies of art and architecture can focus on specific creative works or on styles over time as phenomena in their own right, archaeology has to have the capacity for cross-scale analysis and interpretation. This is unavoidable once questions about viability are being asked. For example: how sustainable are patterns of behaviour like the expansion of forest clearance for rice fields, or the increasing complexity of a water-management system? These questions require attention to such phenomena as landscape ecology and planetary weather systems which have an impact on whether or not the behaviour of the community is causing ecological problems or can cope with changing circumstances, such as increasing, decreasing or oscillating monsoon rainfall over many centuries. The analytic necessity and its corollary, that humans may try to implement behaviour that is eventually damaging to their community, were recognised by Groslier in the 1960s and 1970s in his assessment of agriculture, environmental over-exploitation and water management in the Angkor region (Groslier 1979). The aim of this chapter is to introduce residential behaviour, the scale and inertia of the settlement pattern and the vast material infrastructure as additional factors, in their own right, in the demise of the Angkor urban complex. A reappraisal is overdue; in recent years, numerous conflicting views have been proposed (Coe 2003:196–7) and the standard explanation of a terminal sack of Angkor by the Thai in 1431 CE is increasingly problematic (Jacques and Freeman 1997:291–7; Pottier 1997; Vickery 1977).

Logical requirements

We are acutely aware today that dissonance exists within human community life and between the requirements of community life, such as infrastructure and economy, and the ecological balance of the environment. Words and actions do not necessarily connect. The material fabric of people's houses can be at odds with their community life. Housing conditions can actually be deleterious to health. Major infrastructure, such as sewer systems, can be inadequate for the needs of a community. Economic infrastructures, such as irrigation systems, can deteriorate and they can also damage the environment in which they are located, as when salination occurs. Unsustainable economies can severely destabilise regional ecologies, as has occurred with forest clearance in Brazil. We are now also acutely aware that such non-correspondence has occurred in the past and to differing degrees in different kinds and sizes of community. These dissonant or 'non-correspondent' relationships across many scales require the specification of an appropriate, logically consistent approach to ensure that cases in different regions and periods are treated in the same way and that confusions of scale are avoided (Diamond 2005). Otherwise, discussion inevitably becomes entangled in divergent and inconsistent explanatory preferences. For instance, are environments to be viewed as tests that push communities to innovation, or are innovations to be seen as products of human agency—a repetition of the old debates about deterministic as opposed to reductive causes in the natural sciences? Is a holistic, 'everything connected to everything else' view to be used, or is the strict primacy of the human personal scale to be applied? Unless assumptions about ways of explaining are examined, arguments about substantive cases are likely to be a futile exercise in mutual incomprehension.

The magnitude of the confusion is well illustrated by the problem in the humanities of the distaste, or liking, for environmental determinism as a causal explanation. The problem is that there should be no debate, because the presumed source of a concept of environmental determinism would have to be evolutionary biology. But the logic of Neo-Darwinian evolutionary theory precludes a deterministic relationship between different scales, for instance between the individual and the environment. The essence of Neo-Darwinism is selection—that only some individuals or populations are likely to survive in a given region. This means that some individuals and populations, for whatever reason, are not doing what would be necessary for them to survive. If environments do not determine what is necessary for survival, the concept of environmental determinism necessarily has no meaning. Once we make room in archaeology for the common-sense recognition that individuals and populations can behave in ways that lead to their death and extinction, we must, in turn, allow that the environment is not determining what they do; it is just reducing their chances of survival and reproduction when they do not do what is necessary. The pro- and anti-determinism debate in the humanities, therefore, is an essentially pointless discussion about a condition that simply does not exist in the relationship between individuals, populations and environments.

What then do we require to restructure our analysis across these different scales? A theoretical approach is required that incorporates operations at many different magnitudes and recognises the inherent potential for non-correspondence between these different scales of operation, while also recognising that this non-correspondence is not necessarily inevitable. A selectionist specification is required in which larger-scale, longer-term operations, for example, the boundary conditions of ecological systems, select against the persistence of phenomena that operate at smaller spatial and temporal scales, such as communities of individuals. The critical factor in the relationship between a community and its 'environment' is the amount of variation and the degree of inertia in the community's cultural behaviour, including the material form of its settlement pattern and infrastructure. The amount of variation is critical because it is the source of alternative behaviours that may assist the survival of individuals and communities.

Neither reductionist nor determinist explanations are adequate or valid. In the humanities the former over-privilege the level of personal action, while the latter infringe the liable human capacity for fatal errors. Nor can we opt for a rejection of either contextual, local perspectives or large-scale, cross-comparative analyses. The former are essential for understanding why a community does what it does and the latter are necessary to understand the factors that may select against the viability of that behaviour and to gain some comparative perspective on alternative ways in which human communities have behaved in similar environments.

Instead, we need to use a multi-scale approach that encompasses the personal and the global and everything in between—a hierarchy of scales. A 'hierarchy' is essential because the process of selection definitively precludes a holistic 'everything interacts equally with everything else in the best possible way'. What is required is to recognise many different phenomena and processes operating at many different spatial and temporal scales and constrained by the different kinds of boundary conditions that exist at different scales. For example, the boundary condition of ecological balance is what acts against a human community that over-exploits the landscape or a critical resource. The specifics of local environmental conditions or resource availability do not prevent humans from demolishing the landscape or from unsustainable exploitation of a food source. Rather, what happens is that the dynamics of ecological balance (or imbalance) set in motion processes, such as soil erosion or the reproductive collapse of the food source, that are ultimately disastrous for the dependent human communities.

In lieu of deterministic explanations of motivation and necessity, therefore, what is required is an analysis of outcomes—not a study of how the environment 'determines' what people do but an analysis of the particular outcomes that derive from human interaction with the environment. The dual application that is proposed here, of a hierarchy of scales and of outcome analysis, is consistent with the logic of Neo-Darwinian theory, but leaves us with the critical task of identifying the different operational parameters and replicative characteristics for culture. This approach combines contextuality, contingency and outcomes with a Neo-Darwinian logic for culture, just as the Neo-Darwinian Theory of Evolution does for biology (Gould 2002).

Issues of analysis

The phenomenon of non-correspondence is recognised in many different contexts and at many different scales, from the domestic through to the natural, regional and global environments. But the consistent occurrence of the condition has not been treated in an integrated manner under a single theoretical umbrella appropriate to the study of culture, despite the well-established logic of this mode of inquiry in biology. Interestingly, even in biology there is a dispute about the interpretative priority of the small, rapid scale of operation, especially genetic processes, over larger multi-scale analyses (Eldridge 2000:26–9). It is an irony that the strong preference in the humanities for the primacy of the small, familiar scale of human daily life is matched by the strong advocacy of essentially reductive, gene-based perspectives in evolutionary biology.

In the humanities, the negative consequences of choice, human action and social perceptions of reality are recognised, but the implications for theories of human behaviour over many scales of analysis have not yet been systematised in history and archaeology. As discussed below, the Annales 'school' has sought to create a scaled perspective, but its approach is problematic. The impact of the material structure of community life has also been recognised, but not systematically incorporated into the interpretations of history and archaeology (Fletcher 2004). The implications of non-correspondence have not been drawn out, especially the issue of the liable non-correspondence between the material and social action and verbal meaning (Fletcher 1996).

Non-correspondence allows both correlation and dissonance between material, action and verbal meaning, and also specifies that no consistent correlation between them can be expected either across communities or over time within a single community. This can only be formally recognised and theorised once the indeterminate relationships between operations on different scales are acknowledged.

There are, therefore, two key obstacles to a systematic theory of outcome. The first of these is an assumption that one scale of human activity—the short-term familiar scale of our daily existence and decision-making—is the proper scale at which explanation and meaningful interpretation resides. This perspective converts the material to an epi-phenomenon rather than allowing it be treated as an operator in its own right, capable of producing an impact in the longer term. In this view, material culture is analysed mostly under the epistemologically dim light of the human intentions that created it. The second obstacle to a systematic theory of outcome is the prevailing theoretical framework which, even while it recognises a multiplicity of scales of operation, treats those scales as a continuum rather than a hierarchy, strictly speaking. In the context of this chapter we will not examine in detail the reasons why this perspective, with its focus on connectivity and flow, tends to prevail in the humanities—suffice to say that it is consistent with a focus on cultural identity and the embedding of a community in its environment. Braudel's famous Annaliste 'Identity of France' (1990) illustrates the condition. The problem is that the interconnectedness involves a failure to rigorously define the magnitudes of the different scales of operation and the rates at which they operate, thereby obscuring non-correspondence and allowing no consistent analysis of scale relationships in different contexts (Fletcher 1992; Kinser 1981; Braudel 1981). The consistencies in the behaviour of human communities over time are not dualistic correlations, for instance between words and action or objects, or between material and social phenomena, or between economies and environments. Instead the consistencies are in triadic associations, over time, between operations, context and outcome. When operations and context are in synchrony, the outcome is the long-term persistence of the behaviour. When operation and context are not in synchrony, the outcome is a reduction in the persistence of the behaviour. In light of this, it is clear that Annales needs a profound redefinition in order to make it usable in the longer time-spans of archaeological enquiry.

Potential cases of scaled non-correspondence in Angkor: a theoretical overview

The analysis of behaviour in scaled terms requires recognising the material component of community life as slow behaviour, the specific class of material behaviour (Fletcher 1995:18–42), and as an operator in its own right. This is necessary because material features, such as constructions, possess an endurance and inertia that is itself a variable interacting with and forming the milieu for a community. A community's social life is composed of what people say and do—the rapidly transmitted verbal meanings they use and the actions they carry out. Actions and meanings change relatively fast because they are incessantly replicated. Because replication introduces slight differences, fast replication leads to more change over time than will occur in more slowly replicated features such as buildings. From an archaeological point of view, the most significant implication is that the building milieu, if it is durable, is an obstacle to social change and exerts selective pressure that should lead to some portion of the varied active and verbal behaviours that 'works' with material becoming more prevalent. But in transient domestic buildings that are readily replaceable, no such selective pressure is exerted. Because the building fabric can be readily replaced and the buildings do not last for a long time there will, somewhat paradoxically, be very little change in the structures as social actions and verbal meanings change (Fletcher 2004:135). The implication is that the flimsy structures of light timber, palm fronds and matting that were characteristic of Angkor would not have changed much as social action transformed. Nor would the material frame exert a strong selective pressure on some specific variants of social action that would lead to those variants becoming more prevalent, thereby creating a strong and simple directional trend in social change. Instead we should expect movement towards a wider variety of social options, none of which would be especially dominant, as well as a tendency for the spatial frame to change very little, because its flexible envelope can, in the short-term, 'tolerate' almost any social action and verbal meaning.

The smallest residential scale at Angkor was the simple, relatively transient, organic domestic structures. These were able to easily contain short-term problems of current social conditions by the addition of flimsy, temporary structures consistent with the existing design format. A domestic residence group could tolerate what would appear as temporary situations, to be dealt with when the building is next replaced in the easily foreseeable future.

Figure 4.4 Domestic space
From the Bayon bas-reliefs (late 12th century)
(Photograph: Catherine Wu)

Some indication of this capacity is given by the report of Chou Ta-Kuan in 1295–96 who remarked on the 'slaves' who lived under the houses (Chou 1992:21), in the spaces that are now, and presumably then, were normally used for cooking and the processing of raw materials, for storing carts and equipment and for sheltering animals. A distinct, specific social phenomenon was simply fitted into the existing, flexible spaces. In addition, we know that from the 12th–13th century onwards there must have been some gradual shift towards Theravada Buddhism, away from the Hinduism and Mahayana Buddhism associated with the great religious monuments. There is no indication that the domestic buildings changed significantly then or after (Dieulefils 2001:18–19; Giteau 1976:148). Present-day Cambodian traditional houses in the Angkor region do not look significantly different from their 19th-century and Angkorian predecessors. Stone-block footings for the posts of similar buildings have been found in the Tumnup Barang site (12th–14th centuries CE) (Fletcher et al 2003:109–10). In Angkor the ease of domestic structural replacement allowed continual gradual adjustments in social action and declaration, generating very slow overall social change in varied directions, because alternative social options had no distinct selective advantage or disadvantage. The slow transformations were cumulatively and almost imperceptibly profound.

In addition to the flexibility of the structures, the community had other flexible options open to it because of the dispersed nature of the urban landscape of Greater Angkor. In many areas land would not have been at a premium, so, even in a well-established settlement area, moving to a new building plot would have been a ready solution to new social demands. Since the community was also likely to have had distributed land holdings, as farmers do now, the family members could also shift to different localities within and perhaps even outside Angkor as social pressures arose. While this would have been applicable in most of Angkor, it is possible that crowding and the packing together or building could have occurred within Angkor Thom. If this were the case the flexible adjustment to change social stresses would have been more difficult within the walled enclosure. The work of Jacques Gaucher (2002b) is therefore critical to our understanding of social change in Angkor. We need to know whether housing was densely packed within Angkor Thom or whether the Khmer domestic spatial layout was so prevalent that a low-density format applied even there. In any event, the critical point to note is that not only was Angkorian domestic space generally stable in form, but there may also have been a habitual pattern of dispersal by domestic groups to deal with changing social pressures and social dissonance.

Settlement pattern

The layout of the more durable settlement space of Angkor is extremely simple, but at the same time substantial and inflexible. It consisted of house mounds around *prasat* (shrines) and *trapeang* (water tanks), in a landscape crossed by the long linear embankments of roads and canals along which houses were also located. These structures were enlarged or altered over decades. The distribution of the *prasat* (Fig. 4.5) and *trapeang* across the landscape (Fig. 4.6) is effectively near-random. Except to the southwest of the West Baray there is no clear clustering of house mounds and *trapeang* along the canals and roads (Evans 2007). Notwithstanding the apparent accumulation of residential features in a few areas (such as around Pre Rup or the Roluos group) that were central places and were inhabited for lengthy periods of time, there is little differentiation in the basic configuration of residential space (ponds, house mounds, bunded rice fields and *prasat*) throughout

Greater Angkor and no particular evidence that any other pattern was regularly employed. The layout of the settlement space appears, therefore, to have been remarkably consistent throughout the history of Angkor, from at least the ninth to the 15th–16th century CE, and quite possibly for some centuries before, as evidenced by the recent excavations undertaken by the École française d'Extrême-Orient (EFEO) in the MAFKATA program at locations such as Prei Khmeng (MAFKATA 2002). In turn, this almost certainly means that some dissonance was occurring between social change and spatial inertia. The gradual cumulative drift in social action and meaning makes the inertia of the layout of the settlement landscape problematic. It must be remembered that the engineered landscape of urban Angkor dwarfs the monumental constructions in terms of size and scope, and that this settlement network was using an extremely stable format with low levels of variation over time and across the landscape. At the larger scale of whole residential communities, such as those referred to in the translations of the 12th-century CE inscriptions as 'villages' (Coedès 1906), a spatial pattern that was both fixed and relatively inflexible may have meant that further dispersal across the landscape was the only means available to adjust to changing circumstances.

The material infrastructure was a massive, complex, delicately balanced and slowly transforming network of canals, road embankments, moats and *baray*, some of which were in use for several centuries. Gradients were shallow and numerous re-arrangements of the network channels are apparent, as are new supercessionary channels and barriers. This is particularly apparent just to the north of the Preah Khan. Some of the features are truly vast; the *baray* banks are 100 metres or more in width, while the great embankments that cross the northern half of Greater Angkor from east to west can be as much as 30 to 40 kilometres long. Canals were 40 to 60 metres wide and only one to two metres deep in the south, as can be seen at Kar Kranh on the line of the old canal south of Siem Reap (Fletcher et al 2003:115–17).The huge scale and interconnectedness of the network would largely have precluded any abrupt and easy alterations to the system. The system, therefore, suffered from severe inertia. What we are seeing is an inflexible, complex water-management infrastructure whose operation would have been at odds with long-term, extreme changes in the monsoon and the supply of water and sediment into the network. There was a potential for non-correspondence between the rigidity and the delicate balance of the system and the risks of abrupt changes in water-supply rate and sedimentation caused by changing monsoon intensity and trajectories.

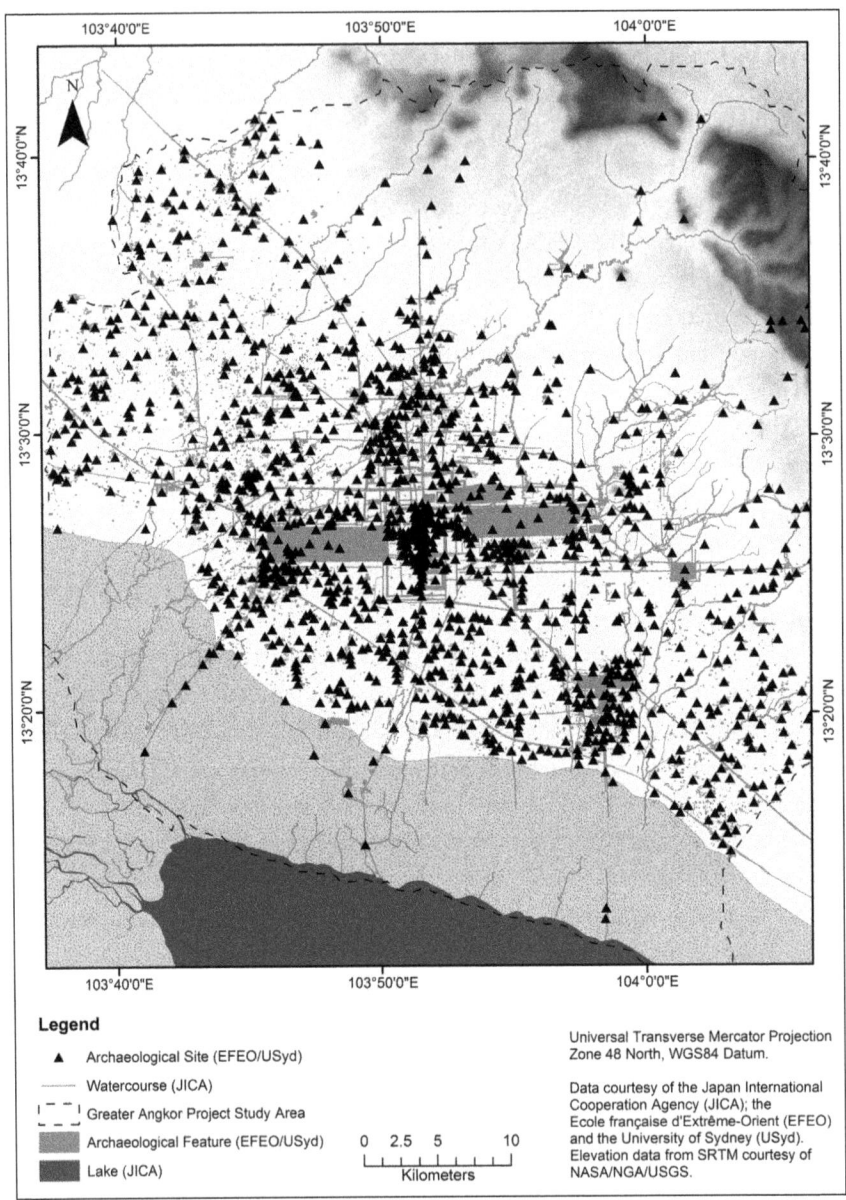

Figure 4.5 Locations of archaeological sites at Angkor, from the Greater Angkor Project
(After Evans 2007 and Pottier 1999)

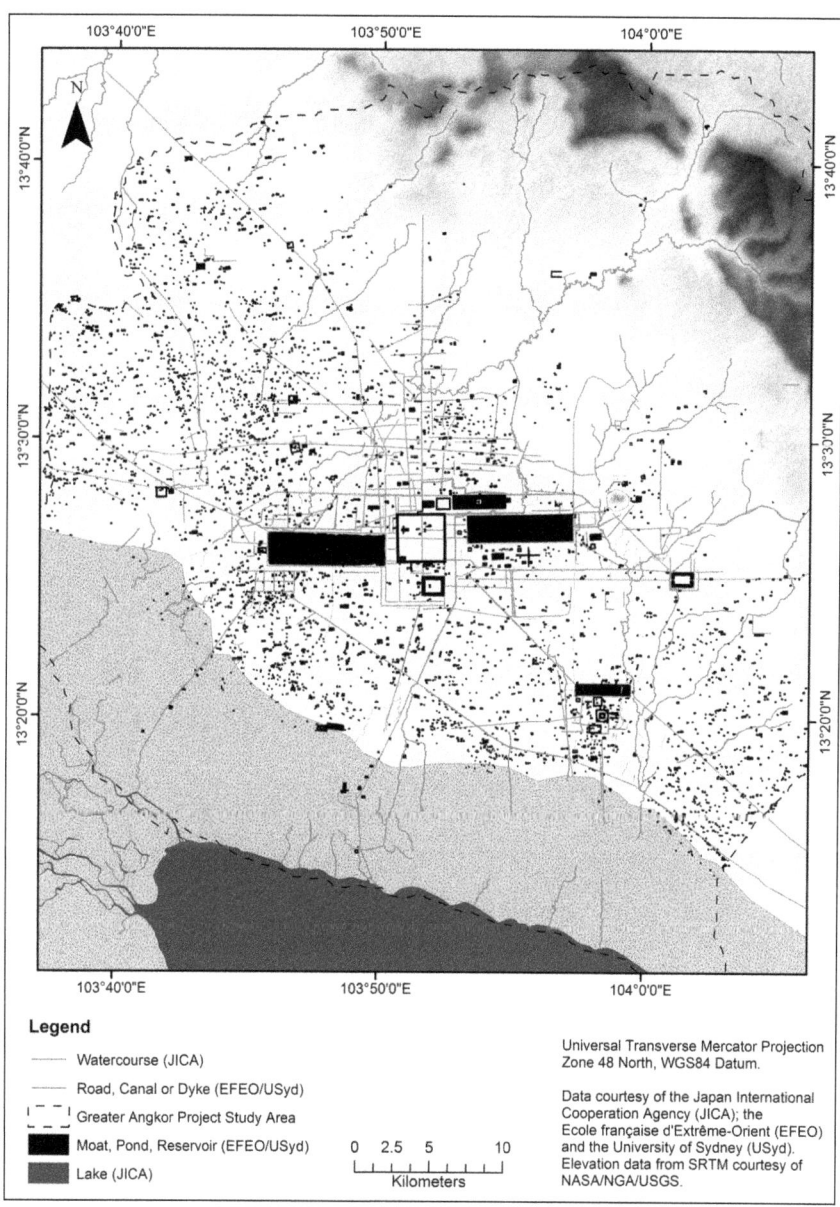

Figure 4.6 Locations of water storage features at Angkor, from the Greater Angkor Project
(After Evans 2007 and Pottier 1999)

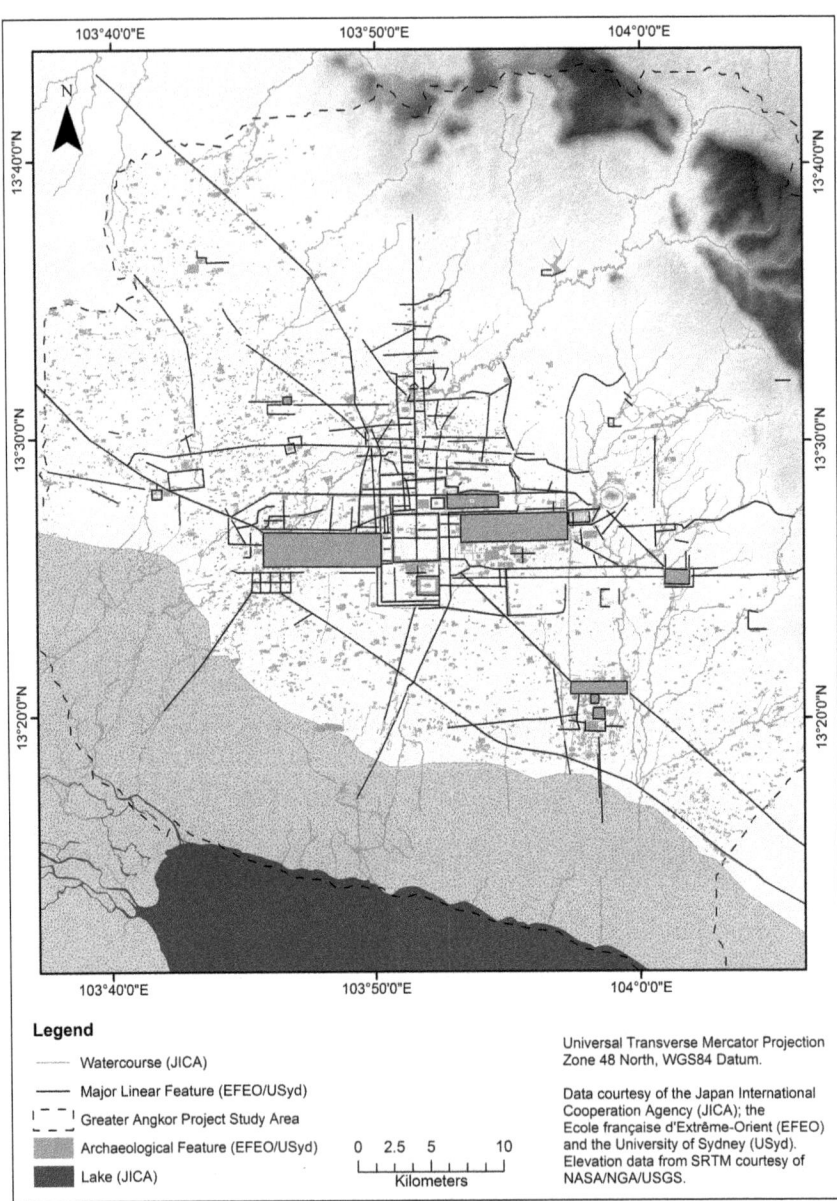

Figure 4.7 Map of linear archaeological features at Angkor, from the Greater Angkor Project
(After Evans 2007 and Pottier 1999)

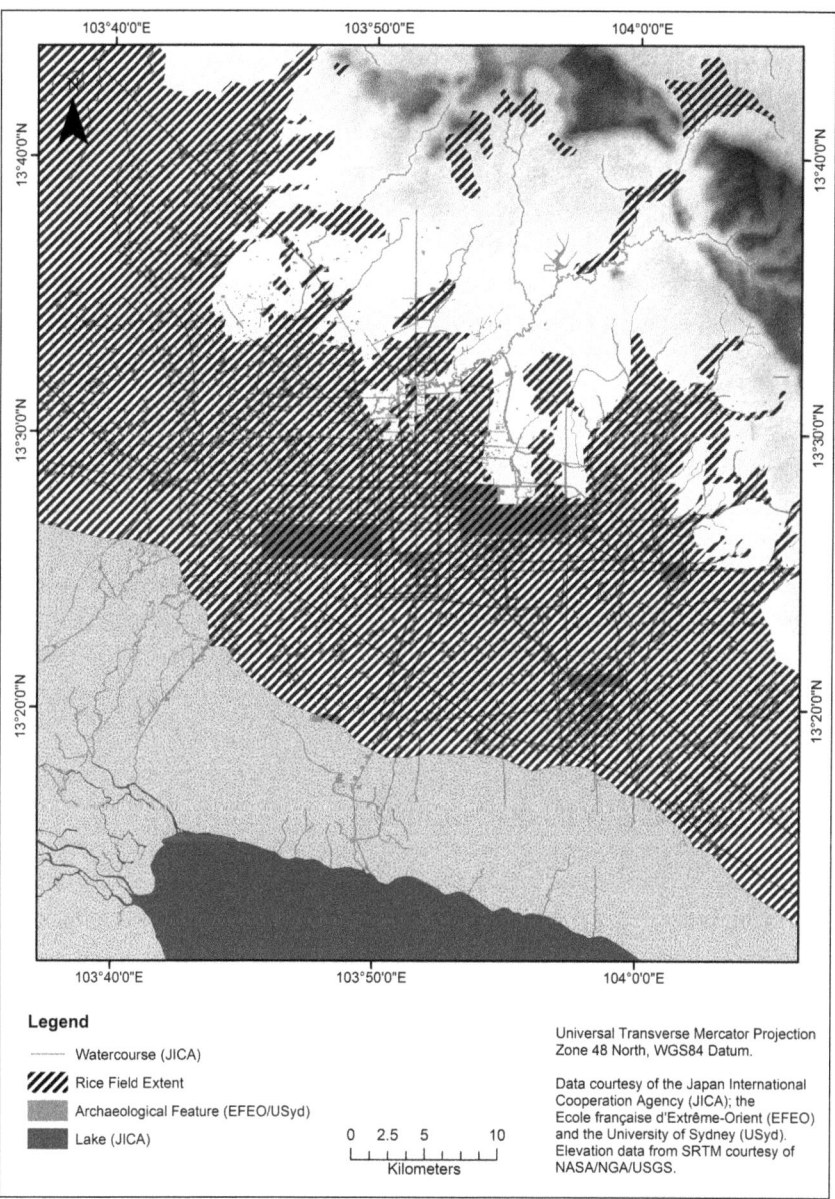

Figure 4.8 Approximate extent of medieval rice field distribution at Angkor, as interpreted from AIRSAR radar imagery acquired in 2000.

The system of bunded rice fields that can be seen in the Siem Reap area, which has long been assumed to be Angkorian by van Liere (1980, 1989) and others, now has a stratigraphic association (see the work of Pierre Baty at the Siem Reap Airport site in 2004 (Baty et al 2005)) and a horizontal–spatial association with known Angkorian features (Pottier 2001a). The spatial extent of this field network, which can therefore be taken as indicative of the maximum extent of wet-rice agriculture during Angkorian times, is extremely large and stretches across much of the landscape from the Tonle Sap to the Kulen hills (Evans 2007; Pottier 1999). The implication is that extensification was being practiced, clearing forest to expand the cultivation of rice as a way to increase rice yields in the region. This pattern of agricultural development is consistent with the water management system being used to mitigate risk and not to intensify yields.

Extensification of rice production to increase yields from the region would have resulted in non-correspondence with ecological balance. When forest clearance eventually reached the hill slopes in the north, it is likely that in the Angkorian period, as in the 1960s and 70s, it would have produced increased water flows and severe, rapid soil erosion. The habitual wet-rice agriculture of bunded fields, which was over 2,000 years old by 1000 CE (Bellwood 2005:130–4), may therefore have served to destabilise the landscape and the ecology of the urban complex.

Regional and global environment

The monsoon climate produces marked differentiation with large amounts of water impacting on the landscape in the wet season and marked long-term differences occurring over many centuries. While the Angkorian water-management system would normally have been able to control and disperse the huge water inflow of the monsoon season (Fletcher et al 2003:119–20), it would have had problems with longer-term climate change that led to erratic, high-intensity, episodic flooding and movement of sediment; this is because of the nature of the canals themselves, which, as noted, were extremely shallow and were generally only constructed with low embankments to contain the flow of water. Added to this, in the Angkorian period forest clearance, as noted above, would have resulted in increased run-off and sedimentation. Abrupt floods of water and sediment hitting the network would potentially lead to severe erosion and erratic extreme deposition, disrupting the water-management system and blocking channels. While the water-management system may have increased the resilience of Angkor's population to the usual annual variations in the level of rainfall, increasing dependence on the effective functioning of that system may, paradoxically, have exposed the population to increased risk from the combined impact of heavy monsoons and extended periods of drought, such as those recently identified in the late Angkorian period (Buckley et al 2010) (Fig. 9).

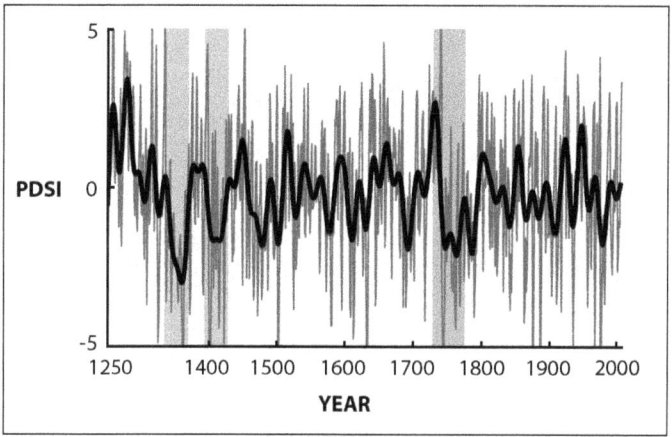

Figure 4.9 Long-term rainfall patterns and climatic instability, AD 1250 to 2000
Expressed as Palmer Drought Severity Index (PDSI). Data is derived from tree ring data in the mountains of Vietnam; periods of severe, prolonged drought are shaded.
(After Buckley et al 2010)

Severe non-correspondence is apparent between the scale, inertia and inflexibility of the water management system and the likely longer-term oscillations in the weather and climate. The network would have depended on stability, but, overall, planetary temperatures over centuries have led to large-scale changes in climate, particularly the Medieval Warm Phase. It is important to note that this is not a deterministic proposition. Rather, it involves an inquiry into the relationship between what a community is doing and its changing circumstances. After all, the start of the warm phase in the tenth century CE saw the demise of the Classic Maya cities of Yucatan (Petersen and Haug 2005), concurrent with the rise of Angkor. Planetary environmental change does not direct cultural change in any particular direction (Lieberman 2003), but it will tend to pick out the weaknesses in the way communities in a region are operating.

Environmental change and the material behaviour in Angkor: a theoretical perspective

The overall impression of the Angkorian settlement pattern and infrastructure is that they were stable, characterised by marked inertia and made up of similar components throughout Angkor. At the large end of the scale the water-management system was vast, cumbersome, hard to alter, complex and delicately balanced. It was therefore vulnerable to external change. By contrast, at the other end of the scale of magnitude, the domestic residence pattern was also largely unchanging, but it allowed relatively rapid *ad hoc* and specific solutions to changing social circumstances without introducing significant new variants in residential space. In addition, the domestic scale of residence would have allowed for adjustment to changing circumstances by dispersal within and therefore, potentially, beyond the area of Greater Angkor. In principle, an unusual situation could have existed in which large-scale rigidity in settlement patterns and infrastructure combined with ready access by the inhabitants to varied, short-term solutions, including a coherent social practice of episodic dispersal.

Altered external circumstances, such as climate change, combined with the ecologically damaging effects of consistent and persistent forest clearance produced by the staple economy, would have imposed severe stresses on the physical infrastructure of Angkor. The structure did not possess the flexibility or variability to permit the necessary *in situ* adjustment that could have coped with change. The physical nature of Angkor and the way the community replicated its structure should be considered as a significant variable in the way the inhabitants tried to deal with their situation in the period from the 14th to the 16th century CE. Critically, they may also have possessed a social mechanism for periodic relocation to deal with local problems, whatever those were. A cumulative tendency for more and more people to opt not to return to their primary residence location within Greater Angkor would have had a profound impact on its political and economic viability.

Implications and conclusions

The value of a multi-scale approach is that it allows non-correspondence to be identified and also formally specifies that inquiry can proceed at many complementary and different scales. Political interpretations and models of ecological failure are not oppositional alternatives—they are different explanations that are relevant to different scales of operation. The disputes between political and ecological interpretations are largely futile. A multi-scale approach also helps to separate a people and the community from its material assemblage. Neither can be reduced to the other, and they are not conterminous. A failure of the material infrastructure is not a failure of the community that is currently using it, since the seeds of that failure could lie centuries earlier than the breakdown. The hypothetical implications for how to interpret history are considerable, suggesting that the multi-scaled approach is a necessary tool of intellectual inquiry in the humanities. If it is the case that Angkor's physical structure became unworkable and rigid and the inhabitants had a sufficiently flexible social life that they were able to move away from it, then Angkor became a redundant mode of practice. The populace chose to move away to a new and different way of life. In this view, Angkor became redundant—no longer needed as the Khmer freed themselves from it. By contrast what is explicit in the story of the Thai sack is that Angkor was lost, stolen from the Khmer, and is a tragic loss to be mourned and regretted. The potent alternative implications of these two perspectives for contemporary Cambodian society suggest that the issues and the debate deserve intense attention, analysis and discussion.

Acknowledgements

Our thanks to Christophe Pottier of EFEO and to the staff of APSARA for the assistance, advice and support that have sustained the Greater Angkor Project. Our particular thanks to Ros Borath, the Director of the Department of Monuments and Archaeology, and to Ang Choulean, the Head of the former Department of Research and Culture and his deputy Im Sokrithy. In the field we have had an invaluable collaboration with Heng Than, Khieu Chan, Tous Somaneath, Chhay Rachna, Ea Darith, Chhay Visoth and Srun Tech—our special thanks for many long, hard days on research. The Greater Angkor team is large and we would not want to offend by omission. Many thanks to our colleagues within and outside the University, to the volunteers and to the staff in Sydney who establish the fieldwork facilities. Roland Fletcher specifically wishes to thank Martin King for his vital assistance. Thanks to Catherine Wu for the photograph of the bas-relief on the Bayon. The Greater Angkor Project is supported by the Australian Research Council (grants DP0211012, DP0558130 and DP1092663) and ANSTO/AINSE (grants 01/049, 02/042, 03/039,

03/091P, AINGRA05055, AINGRA05056, AINGRA05134). Thanks also to the University of Sydney, specifically the College of Science and Technology, the School of Geosciences, the College of Humanities and Social Sciences, the Faculty of Arts and the School of Philosophical and of Historical Inquiry.

Chapter 5

Religious architecture and irrigation in the plain of Phan Rang

William A Southworth

Curator of Southeast Asian Art, Rijksmuseum

The plain of Phan Rang was formerly the centre of a Cham polity or kingdom known as Pāṇḍuraṅga. This kingdom remained partly independent until the early 19th century (Po Dharma 1987), while the Phan Rang area (Fig. 5.1) is still the main demographic focus of the modern Cham ethnic minority in central Vietnam (Nakamura 1999). Two ancient brick temples remain in use today. The temple of Po Klaong Girai (Fig. 5.2) is situated on the crest of a hill rising 50 metres above the surrounding plain, on the left bank of the Dinh River; close to the main railway line and the modern settlement of Tháp Chàm named after it (Parmentier 1909:81–95). The earliest inscription found at this site (Finot 1903:643–6, 1915:39–49) records a date of 972 in the *śaka* era (circa 1050 CE),[1] but the present temple was probably only completed in the late 13th century.[2] The river-mouth port at Đông Hải and the main market at Phan Rang may also date back to this period.[3]

---

[1] This inscription, numbered C13 (C = Champa), was discovered by Henri Parmentier in 1901 and lies half-buried in the ground just to the north of the main eastern *gopura*, outside the perimeter wall. Two rock inscriptions (C119 and C120), containing dates in the same year, were found on neighbouring hills by Parmentier in 1908 (Finot 1909, 1915:40–1).

[2] The main shrine has both exterior and interior stone doorjambs, at the entrance to the porch and to the sanctuary; both are inscribed in the Old Cham language (C8–11). These inscriptions were partly translated and summarised by Étienne Aymonier (1891:67–82), who dated them to the 13th century.

[3] An inscribed doorjamb and lintel found at Phan Rang (C3 and C4) were first described by Aymonier at the end of the 19th century (1891:49–52), together with an inscription (C7) found at the mouth of the Dinh River (Aymonier 1891:52–3). A second inscribed

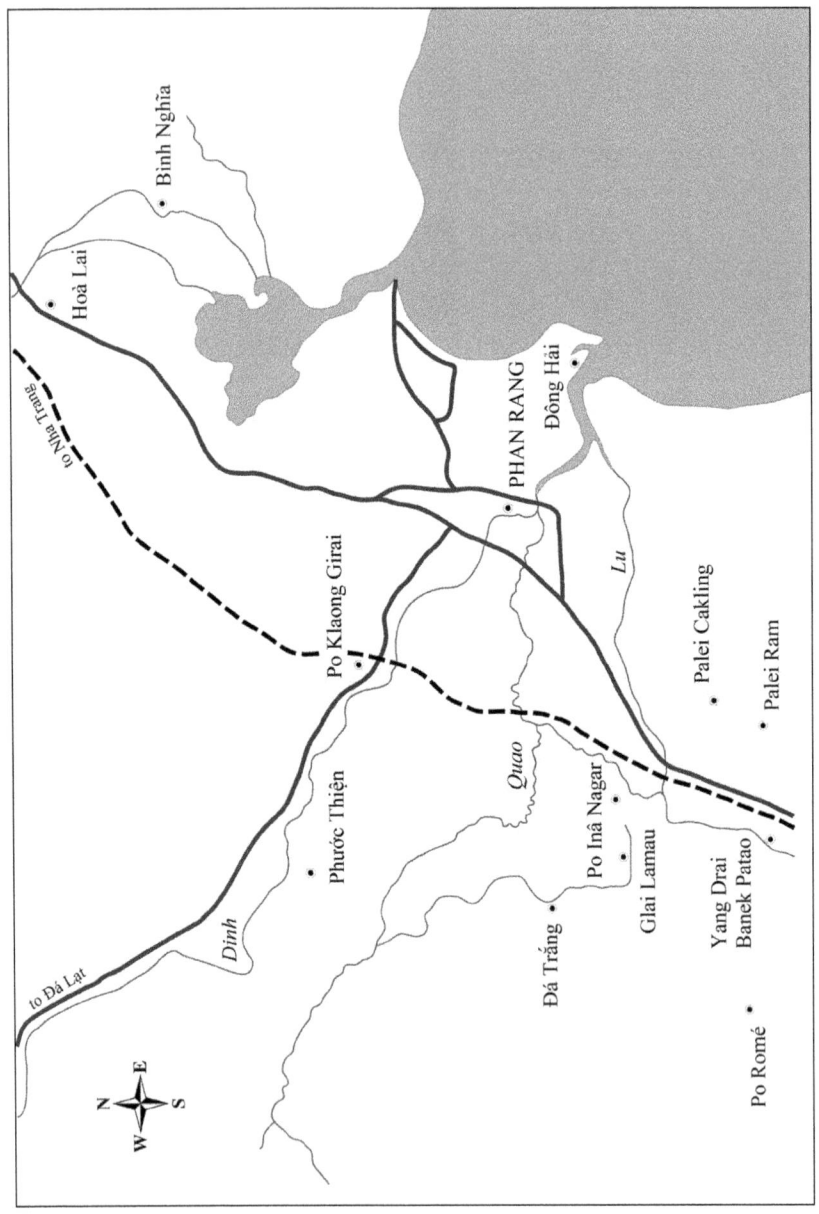

Figure 5.1 Map of the Phan Rang area

Figure 5.2 The main shrine of Po Klaong Girai

The temple of Po Romé, which enshrines an image of this king in the form of Śiva (Plate 5.1), is considered to be among the last constructed in traditional form (Parmentier 1909:61–71; Stern 1942:57). The entrance to the shrine is inscribed on both sides with 56 lines of text in Old Cham (C16), which were partly transcribed by EM Durand (1903:597–603), and appear to date from the 17th century. A further five-line inscription (C15) was found on a statue of one of the queens of Po Romé, named Sučih or Thu Chík (Parmentier 1909:71, Fig. 14), which was kept in a small shrine behind the main temple.[4] Despite the ethnographic and historical importance of

---

  doorjamb and lintel (C5 and C6) were reported from the same area of Phan Rang by Louis Finot (1903: 634–5, 646–8). All appear to date from the 11th to 13th centuries and are now kept in the National Museum of Vietnamese History (Bảo Tàng Lịch Sử Việt Nam) in Hà Nội (nos. B2, 14-18; LSb 21164, 21166-68 & 21178).

[4] This statue was damaged during an attempted burglary on 20 July 1991, and the head and upper torso were finally broken off and stolen on 11 March 1993. A new statue of Thu Chík was consecrated at the temple on 18 August 1999 (I am grateful to the Cham curator at Po Romé, Trương Đại Thợ, for this information). For discussion of the royal identity of the main image of Po Romé see Taylor (1996).

this region, very little archaeology has been conducted here. In particular, neither the geographic reasons behind the emergence of Pāṇḍuraṅga in the eighth and ninth centuries nor the relationship between the ancient temple buildings and the wider landscape have been discussed; they provide the focus of the present chapter.

Geographic location, climate and prehistory

Phan Rang is the provincial capital of Ninh Thuận province on the eastern coast of south-central Vietnam and is located approximately 270 kilometres north of Hồ Chí Minh City and 85 kilometres south of Nha Trang. The lowland plain of Ninh Thuận province is one of the driest areas in Vietnam. Japanese historian Shiro Momoki has noted that the average annual rainfall in Phan Rang is only 695 mm, compared to 1,441mm at Nha Trang and 2,890mm in Hue. In addition, there are only 49 days of rain, on average, per year, concentrated during the northeasterly monsoon between September and November (Momoki 1999:35). These climatic conditions suggest that the availability and control of water at Phan Rang was of particular historical importance.[5]

The extreme paucity of known prehistoric sites in the Phan Rang area is perhaps an indication of the difficulty of obtaining water for agriculture. So far, only a very small number of prehistoric sites have been recorded from the plain of Phan Rang. A single, shouldered, polished stone axe, similar to examples found at the coastal neolithic site of Bàu Tró in Quảng Bình (Higham 2002:37–8) was discovered by Olov Janse in 1939. However, this stone implement was found among fragments of later Tang, Sung and Ming pottery, at a site named Chau Re, located near the sea coast to the north of Phan Rang.[6] Janse also reported finds of local earthenware in lenses of blackish, compacted soil, together with fragments of charcoal, and suggested that this may have been the site of a former Cham village (Janse 1941:255–6, plates 19 (2, 3), 21 (1)).

---

[5] For an excellent survey of the geographic and agricultural basis of ancient Champa, including irrigation and water management, see the work of David Griffiths Sox (1972, especially 62–91).

[6] The precise location of this site remains uncertain. The village of Chau Re is not represented on modern maps of the region, and Janse's information is uncharacteristically vague. He states that the site was, 'close to the shore, near the village of Chau-re, about ten miles north of the town of Phan-rang' (Janse 1941:251) and also that: 'This locality is situated in a desert region, partly covered with dunes, close to the shore, about six kilometers from Phan-rang' (Janse 1941:255).

Two sites identified with the early metal-age Sa Huynh culture were discovered by Vietnamese archaeologists in 1979, in the territory of Nhân Hải in Ninh Hải district (Hà Văn Tấn 1999:305–6). This area is close to the sea, some ten kilometres northeast of Phan Rang, and may be the same region previously explored by Janse. Archaeologists from the Museum of Vietnamese History in Hà Nội excavated four test pits, covering a total of 72 square metres at the site of Mỹ Tường, and found two jar burials and numerous earthenware shards. This site was dated approximately to the second century BCE. The second site of Hòn Đỏ is situated on a natural promontory and is estimated to cover an area of about 8,000 square metres. The ceramics discovered here by the Institute of Archaeology, Hà Nội and the Institute of Social Sciences in Hồ Chí Minh City also included shards of square-stamped earthenware similar to those found in early historic sites in other areas of Vietnam (Hà Văn Tấn 1999:306). The site is considered sacred to the Raglai ethnic minority and a four-sided Cham inscription has also been found here, containing the date of 972 śaka (circa 1050 CE), the same date found on the earliest inscription from Po Klaong Garai.[7]

The emergence of Pāṇḍuraṅga in the eighth to ninth centuries

The earliest historical references to a kingdom of Pāṇḍuraṅga in the plain of Phan Rang date to the late eighth and early ninth centuries. The Chinese geographer Jia Dan (730–805 CE) recorded an itinerary by sea along the coast of Vietnam, which included references to a kingdom of Gu-da (Kuṭhāra) at Nha Trang, and to Ben-tuo-lang (Pāṇḍuraṅga) in the plain of Phan Rang. Paul Pelliot (1904:216–17, 372) has dated this itinerary to between 785 to 805 CE. It is notable, however, that the itinerary describes Kuṭhāra as an independent kingdom (*guo*), while Pāṇḍuraṅga is listed here and in three other contemporary Chinese references as a territory or province (*zhou*; see Southworth 2000:241–2, Griffiths & Southworth 2011: 288–291).

The Phan Rang region is also mentioned in the *ʾAhbār as-Sīn wa l-Hind* or *Account of China and India*, written in Arabic in 851 CE. This text describes a journey from Siraf in modern Iran to southern China, passing the coastal regions of India, the Malay Peninsula and Vietnam. After leaving the island of Tioman off the east coast of Malaya…

---

[7] A preliminary transcription and translation of this stela, based on photographs, has recently been published by Anne-Valérie Schweyer (2009:26–34).

the ships then sail to a place named Kadrang: [a journey of] ten days. There you can find fresh water, if you need it. As on the islands of India, if you dig a well, you will find fresh water.[8]

The translator of this text, Jean Sauvaget (1948:44 n6), identified Kadrang or Kandarang with Pāṇḍuraṅga. This identification is particularly appropriate to the area of Vĩnh Hảo, on the edge of the southern plain of Phan Rang, which is the site of the oldest bottled water factory in Vietnam. The factory is still in operation today, extracting natural underground mineral water reserves.

In addition, two temple groups in the wider region of Phan Rang can also be dated from the eighth and ninth centuries: the group of Hoà Lai (Fig. 5.3) in the rice plain to the north of Phan Rang and that of Po Dam on the edge of a series of low hills in the neighbouring southern district of Phan Rí. Both are associated with communication routes leading to the port of Phan Rang and are also linked to sources of fresh water. The group of Hoà Lai or Ba Tháp (Cham: *Bimong Yang Kran*) is located approximately 15 kilometres northeast of Phan Rang, on the main road linking Phan Rang to the port city of Nha Trang to the north.

The Vietnamese name of 'Ba Tháp' means 'three towers', and originally the group consisted of three east-facing brick shrines arranged in a row from north to south (Parmentier 1909:98–108). The central tower, however, collapsed in the mid-1970s and is now only visible as a low mound. The temple was not previously associated with any inscriptions, but was placed stylistically by Philippe Stern between the earliest surviving religious structure of Mỹ Sơn E1 and the Buddhist monastic complex at Đồng Dương (Stern 1942:46–8). Jean Boisselier (1963:84) agreed with this sequence and suggested that the complex could be dated to the mid-ninth century. From analysis of the elaborate motifs carved on the exterior of the buildings, both Parmentier and Stern argued that the South tower was constructed first, followed by the Central and North towers (Parmentier 1918:32–3; Stern 1942:91).

This architectural and art historical dating of the site has recently been validated by the discovery of a stone stela inscription between the Central and North shrines in 2006 (Griffiths & Southworth 2011). The stela is now kept in storage at the Ninh Thuận Provincial Museum (Bảo tàng Ninh

---

[8] 'Puis les navires appareillent pour un endroit appelé Pandouranga: dix jours. On y trouve de l'eau douce, si on en veut. – De même dans les îles de l'Inde: si on creuse des puits, on y trouve de l'eau douce' (Sauvaget 1948:9, author's translation).

Figure 5.3 South shrine of Hoà Lai

Thuận no. 1444/Đ.25). The two main faces of the stela (A & C) were originally inscribed in Sanskrit by a king Satyavarman and describe the consecration of an image of Śiva under the name Śrī Ādideveśvara in the year 700 of the śaka era (778 CE).[9] This inscription contains the earliest known occurrence of the name Pāṇḍuraṅga, under the slightly variant form of Pāṇḍaraṅga (Griffiths & Southworth 2011:285–288). A second inscription has been added at the bottom of face A, on one of the short sides, and on the separate base of the stela. This inscription lists new donations to the deity and includes the date of 760 śaka (839 CE).[10] It seems probable that the stela refers to the central shrine of the Hoà Lai group and suggests that the original structure of Satyavarman may have been rebuilt during the mid-ninth century.

---

[9] This king is well known from a similar stela inscription (C38) found at the temple of Po Nagar at Nha Trang, some 85 kilometres to the north. This stela was first translated by Abel Bergaigne in the 19th century (Bergaigne 1893:242–260, no.XXVI, 407) and is now on display at the National Museum of Vietnamese History in Hà Nội, no. B2,10; LSb 21157).

[10] The palaeography of this additional text matches that of the king Vikrāntavarman (see the stela of Po Nagar at Mông Đức, below), who also added inscriptions to the base and stela of Satyavarman from Nha Trang (C38B lines 15–16, c & d; Bergaigne 1893:254–258; Griffiths & Southworth 2007:355–360, 2011:292).

The remains of additional structures, including a columned hall, gate tower and surrounding wall, can be traced on the eastern side of the temple, and the religious structures at Hoà Lai were originally connected by a small river on the east to the Dầm Nai or Nai Bay. The water from this river has now been largely diverted by a concrete canal system northwest of Hoà Lai, but originally passed the Cham village of Bình Nghĩa, which is considered one of the poorest but most traditional villages in the Phan Rang area (Nakamura 1999:123).

The small, related group of Po Dam (Fig. 5.4) is located 40 km to the south of Phan Rang in modern Bình Thuận province, and consists of the remains of four small brick shrines on the slope of a hill near the east bank of the Lòng Sông River (Parmentier 1909:50–8). The group overlooks a natural passage through the surrounding hills which has been followed by the railway line from Nha Trang to Hồ Chí Minh City.

Despite the survival of these two temple groups to the north and south of the plain of Phan Rang, no ninth century architectural remains have survived in the central Phan Rang area. Nevertheless, a series of five Sanskrit and Old Cham inscriptions have been found in the district of Ninh Phước, to the south and west of Phan Rang, and can been dated between 783 and 854 CE; this is a period from which very little historical evidence has survived from other areas of the Champa culture (Finot 1903:633; Boisselier 1963:64–71).

Figure 5.4 The southern shrines of Po Dam

The Phước Thiện inscription

The first of these inscriptions is kept in the provincial museum of Ninh Thuận province (BTNT no. 1440/Đ.13) and was found in 1993 among rice fields belonging to the village of Phước Thiện, in Phước Sơn commune (Griffiths and Southworth 2007). The stela is 78.8 centimetres high, with an additional tenon of 14.4 centimetres (Fig. 5.5). It is inscribed on both faces, with 12 lines on each face, making 24 in total. The language throughout is Sanskrit and the text records the foundation of a *liṅga* named Śrī Satyadeveśvara by the king Satyavarman in the year 705 *śaka* (783 CE). The stela also includes the earliest known occurrence of the name Kuṭhāra, a kingdom based on the port of Nha Trang.

Phước Thiện is a small town situated about 12 kilometres northwest of Phan Rang in an agricultural area between the River Dinh and the River Quao. This area is of particular interest as it is the location of an ancient

Figure 5.5 The Phước Thiện inscription
Courtesy of the Ninh Thuận Provincial Museum

Cham canal system reported by the department of public works in Phan Rang to Marcel Ner in 1931 and investigated by Madeleine Colani in the late 1930s (Colani 1940:56–62). This canal system was intended to irrigate an area of approximately 7,000 hectares in the wide plain south of the Dinh River (Fig. 5.6). A large dam made of earth and wood, 13.7 metres high,

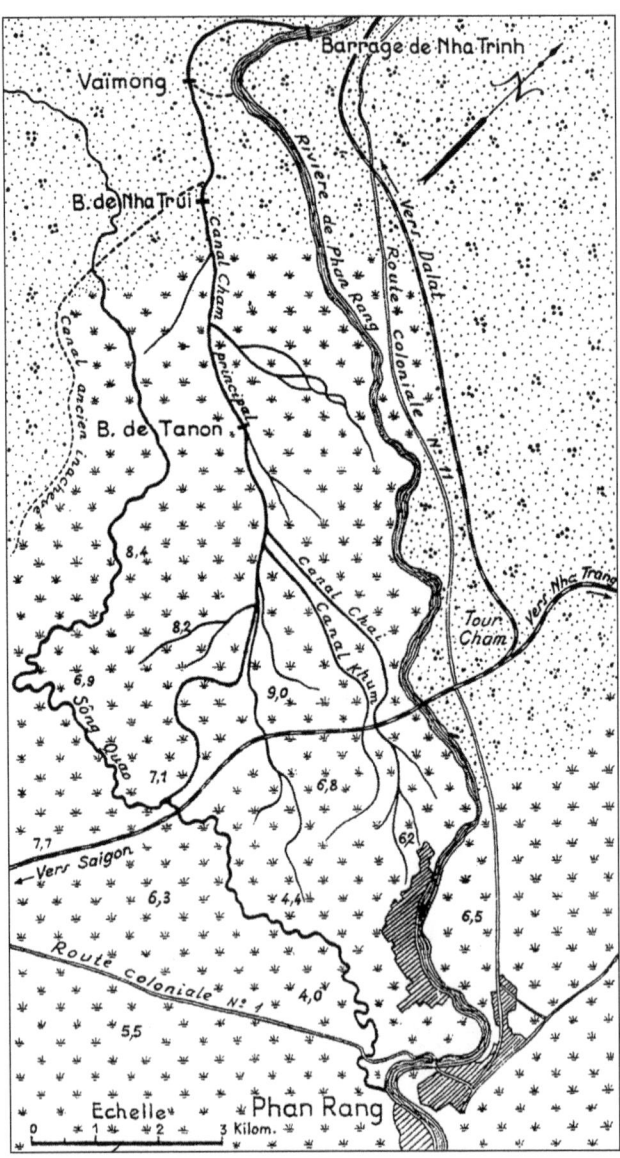

Figure 5.6 Plan of the main canal system in the plain of Phan Rang (Colani 1940: plate CXCV)

was constructed across the upper reaches of the Dinh River at Nha Trinh and diverted water into a main channel that flowed southeast to Ninh Chu, before joining a second channel flowing north from a dam on the Lu River above Po Romé. The water distribution was achieved entirely by gravity. These two main channels were estimated to exceed 30 kilometres in length, and supplied water for a network of smaller, arterial canals that fertilised the plain. By 1931, however, the canal system had already deteriorated and only about 500 hectares of land were still irrigated by it. Additional dams were also reported from the interior regions of the province where they were still used by the Rhade ethnic minority and often preserved the names of the Cham kings who had built them (Colani 1940:58).

Colani testified to the remarkable efficiency of the irrigation system, which allowed fertile areas of rice cultivation within an otherwise arid, desert landscape. She noted that the canals were not straight but followed a serpentine course, thus irrigating a wider surface area and slowing the progress of the water to allow greater penetration into the soil. She also reported that the Cham community of Phan Rang held a ceremony every seven years in honour of the inventor of the irrigation system, whom they referred to as King Lat. The ceremony was held in a forest clearing to the west of the dam at Nha Trinh, near the tomb of the king, and a few days later, on 15 August, it was followed by a second ceremony at the temple of Po Klaong Girai (Colani 1940:60–1).

Colani also recounts a local legend concerning the building of the canal. King Lat is said to have divided the workers into two teams—one of women and the other of men. Each team was to build a separate canal. The team of women began work on what is now the main canal system. During periods of rest, the women began to sing and sang so beautifully that all the male workers came to listen. Gradually, fewer and fewer men returned to work on their own canal and after ten years it was abandoned.[11] The main canal system was said to have taken 400 years to complete (Colani 1940:62). Despite this story however, three early stela inscriptions have been found recording religious foundations to the south of the river Quao, on the line of the abandoned canal system that was marked 'inachevée' on Colani's plan.

---

[11] Madeleine Colani (1940:62 n1) compared these women to the sirens of European mythology, adding: 'Les sirènes, la Lorelei, étaient malfaisantes; ces femmes cham, plutôt bonnes, n'occasionnaient aucune catastrophe'. A variation on this story has also been noted more recently by Ngô Văn Doanh (1998:178, 2002:176), in which the founding of the canal is attributed to King Po Klaong Girai. Ngô Văn Doanh also gives details of the annual repair of the southern canal, from the Lu River near the temple of Po Romé, to the River Quao (1998:195–6, 2002:193–4).

Đá Trắng and Glai Lamau

The first inscription (C 25), recorded by Aymonier under the Cham name of Yang Tikuh, was found in bushes close to the hill of Đá Trắng (Aymonier 1891:21). The Vietnamese name 'Đá Trắng' means 'White Rock', and the hill is in fact an outcrop of white, semi-translucent feldspar or quartz (Plate 5.2). The Cham name *Cek Yang Patao*, means 'King of the mountains' or 'the Mountain of the king'. The inscription is now stored in the Ninh Thuận Provincial Museum in Phan Rang, no. BTNT 1441/Đ.15 (Fig. 5.7). The Sanskrit text, in 37 lines, was engraved on two faces of the stela and was edited and translated into French by Bergaigne (1893:207-218, no. XXII, 397). The inscription records that a temple of Śiva, under the name of Bhadrādhipatīśvara, had been destroyed by the armies of 'Java' arriving by ship in 709 of the *śaka* era (circa 787 CE). It was subsequently rebuilt by a King Indravarman, the younger brother of Satyavarman, who installed a new *liṅga* of the god in 721 *śaka* (circa 799 CE) under the name of Indrabhadreśvara (Bergaigne 1893:208).

Figure 5.7 The Đá Trắng inscription
(Courtesy of the Ninh Thuận Provincial Museum)

Henri Parmentier investigated the Đá Trắng area in the early 1900s and found traces of two brick temple foundations in a clearing approximately 800 metres south of the hill itself (Parmentier 1909:78). During field survey in 2004, a site was found in this location, immediately to the west of the road leading north to Đá Trắng. The site occupies an elevated area of about 10,000 square metres (Fig. 5.8) and is surrounded by rice fields, with large granite boulders interspersed among them. It is raised on three levels, with the remains of what was probably a brick temple foundation at the highest point in the northwest of the site. The soil surface on the upper levels has a very dense coverage of low-fired, earthenware shards, with almost no later porcelain or stoneware.

The stela of Glai Lamau (C24) was first recorded by Aymonier (1891:21-2) in relation to a *bimong* or Cham shrine of that name and the remains of an earlier temple foundation were also noted. When Parmentier later visited the site, only a large pile of bricks and pebbles remained of this earlier

Figure 5.8 Site close to the hill of Đá Trắng

foundation, as well as a damaged stone image of a bull and a painted *liṅga*, which formed the main cult image of the later shrine (Parmentier 1909:77-8). The inscription in Sanskrit was edited and translated into French by Abel Bergaigne (1893:218-231, no. XXIII, 393), and is now on display in the courtyard of the Museum of Vietnamese History in Hà Nội, no. B2, 11; LSb 21170. The stela is engraved on two faces, with 45 lines in total. The inscription describes the dedication by King Indravarman in 723 *śaka* (circa 801 CE) of a sanctuary to Śiva under the epithet of Indraparameśvara, on the site of the former palace of King Satyavarman. The text also mentions two earlier foundations of King Indravarman: a temple to Indrabhogeśvara in the town of Vīrapura and a temple to Indrabhadreśvara, as recorded in the Đá Trắng inscription above. Side B also records donations made by Indravarman to Śankara-Nārāyaṇa, a form of Śiva and Viṣṇu combined (Bergaigne 1893:219).

The shrine or *bimong* of Glai Lamau described by Aymonier and Parmentier was destroyed by flooding in 1964 and a new shrine was constructed closer to existing Cham communities about 1.2 kilometres further to the northeast (Fig. 5.9). The new location of the shrine is also the original site of the Cham village of Palei Hamu Kraok. According to my guides, this settlement, and

Figure 5.9 Bimong of Glai Lamau

the former Cham village of Palei Hamu Muon, located some 800 metres to the south, were destroyed by the French colonial authorities under Vichy control in 1940 and the inhabitants were forcibly resettled further north. Both abandoned villages lie on the eastern side of a stone and concrete water canal built by the Japanese military in the same year and were probably moved for its construction. The site of Palei Hamu Muon is now marked by a line of 17 *kut* (memorial stones) (Fig. 5.10), with two others placed nearby. The shrine of Glai Lamau was formerly administered from these villages.

The shrine of Glai Lamau recorded in the earlier reports is now only a rough mound of bricks overgrown by thorns. The Cham term *glai* means a forest or thicket, but the surrounding plain is now mainly covered by rice fields and vineyards. About 100 metres to the northwest is a related site named Banau Yia Kyah or 'Brick Water', from where the bricks used to construct the former shrine are said to have been collected. This raised area of roughly 360 square metres had recently been cleared for a vegetable garden, and an extensive pile of brick fragments had been collected on the periphery, indicating that this was the site of the collapsed temple described by Parmentier. The site stands immediately beside an artificial watercourse named the Yeai Tra, and it is probable that part of the brick tower collapsed into the water, from where the bricks were later reclaimed. Numerous brick fragments and scatters of pottery were also clearly visible in the connecting

Figure 5.10 Comemorative kut at the site of the former Cham village of Palei Hamu Muon

paths around both areas of the site, suggesting that an area of at least 40,000 square metres may once have been occupied.

Po Inâ Nagar

In addition to the religious sites and canal system on the right bank of the river Quao, there are also three other inscriptions linking this network to the southern canal system fed by the river Lu. The stela of Po Inâ Nagar at Mông Đức (C14) was discovered at the foot of a tree on the left bank of a stream, some 50 metres from the *bimong* (shrine) of that name (Aymonier 1891:24–5) and a further 50 metres from the base of an earlier brick structure (Parmentier 1909:76). The shrine of Po Inâ Nagar contained three cult statues depicting the goddess and two of her daughters (Aymonier 1891:75–6). The stela is engraved with 16 lines of Sanskrit text on one side and was edited and translated by Bergaigne (1893:231–7, no. XXIV, 399). It describes the donation of lands by a King Vikrāntavarman to two temples of Śiva—the first dedicated to Vikrāntarudreśvara, the second to Vikrāntadevādhibhaveśvara. The date has been interpreted by Bergaigne (1893:232–3) as 776 *śaka* (854 CE).

The *bimong* of Po Inâ Nagar described by Aymonier was destroyed in the flooding of 1964 and was rebuilt in 1967 some 750 metres to the northeast, on the eastern outskirts of the Cham village of Hữu Đức (Fig. 5.11). The

Figure 5.11 Bimong of Po Nagar

inscription is now kept in a small enclosure just outside the boundary walls of the main shrine. The location of the former building is still known to the local Cham community, but now consists only of a low mound of bricks. The site lies on the northern fringes of the Vietnamese village of Mông Nhuận (Mông Đức), some 100 metres north of the main road. No traces of any other archaeological material could be found when I visited the site in August 2004.

Glai Klaong Anâk and Bakul

The inscriptions of Glai Klaong Anâk and Bakul were both found on the right bank of the River Lu, in the south of the plain of Phan Rang, but their exact provenance is now uncertain. According to Étienne Aymonier, the stela of Glai Klaong Anâk (C19) was found in a small grove of trees between the Cham villages of Ram and Pralau. It contained ten lines of text in Cham, from which Aymonier could distinguish only a few words and phrases (Aymonier 1891:23, no. 394). Henri Parmentier visited the site in the early 1900s and reported that the stela, broken into four pieces, formed part of the enclosure of a Cham cemetery located 250 metres east of 'la route mandarine' (now National Highway 1), in the territory of the village of Nhu Lâm. He also recorded a mound of bricks some 100 metres further south, which the local inhabitants identified as a former brick kiln. Parmentier (1909:72), however, suggested that these were probably the remains of a brick building.[12]

The Bakul inscription (C20), originally named Yang Kur by Aymonier and Bergaigne, was reportedly found near the ruins of a brick temple not far from the village of Chakling on the right bank of the Lu River (Aymonier 1891:25). The inscription consists of 16 lines of text engraved onto a rounded boulder and includes nine lines in Sanskrit and seven lines in Cham.[13] The Sanskrit text was translated by Bergaigne (1893:237–42, No XXV, 396) and the Cham section by Aymonier (1891:25–7). The inscription describes the donation of two *vihāra* (monastic buildings) and two temples to Jina and

---

[12] The stela has now been restored and is kept in reserve at the National Museum of Vietnamese History, Hà Nội, museum no.B2,12; LSb 21169. Although the date in this inscription was read as 73x śaka by Aymonier and Bergaigne, an examination of the stone itself by members of the Corpus des Inscriptions du Campā in September 2009 suggested that the century figure should not be read as 7, but as 9, thereby re-attributing the inscription to the early 11th century CE.
[13] This inscription is also kept in storage at the National Museum of Vietnamese History, Hà Nội, no.B2,13; LSb 21141.

Śankara (Buddha and Śiva) by a man named Samanta. The inscription was apparently commissioned by the son of the donor, named Buddhanirvāṇa, in 751 śaka (circa 829 CE; Aymonier 1891:238).

The site of the Bakul inscription could not be identified by Parmentier (1909:79), but investigation in this area in 2004 revealed a complex of small sites in the territory of the Cham village of Palei Ramgah (Nho Lâm), about 250 metres west of the present railway line and National Highway 1. The first of these sites, named Po Yang Nai, or the 'Queen', consisted of a small grove of trees about 80 square metres in area (Fig. 5.12), with a surface scatter of small fragments of earthenware pottery and brick. A second grove of trees, named Po Yang, or the 'King', was located about 150 metres further west, across a ploughed field with a similar scatter of pottery which included high-fired earthenware and porcelain. This site also consisted of a small copse or grove of trees, situated directly on the right bank of the Lu River. Again, about 120 metres further south, a third area was located with a modern platform supporting a row of seven *kut*, with a small grass clearing to the south.

The main site, however, was located about 250 metres to the northwest of Po Yang Nai, across a ploughed field and vineyard covered in dense scatters of pottery. The main area covers approximately 100 x 30 metres and is oriented from north to south. The northern part consisted of a large, walled

Figure 5.12 The copse of trees at Po Yang Nai

enclosure, with an iron gate on the north side, containing a second row of *kut*, arranged on a modern platform. Immediately to the south of this was the probable foundation of a brick temple, with surviving bricks measuring 24 centimetres in length and 6 to 7 centimetres wide. This area had recently been cleared for cultivation and a propitiation ceremony was taking place (Fig. 5.13) after a large stone fragment had been found. The bank of the Lu River is located only 80 metres to the west, at a point where much of the water is redirected into a modern, concrete canal. The area as a whole is called Yang Drai Banek Patao, and the pottery distribution indicates the use of at least 20,000 square metres. The range of surface pottery suggests that the area was a former Cham settlement, probably occupied until at least the 17th century.

Figure 5.13 Propitiation ceremony at Yang Drai Banek Patao

Conclusion

The discovery of the Phước Thiện inscription raises a series of questions regarding the relationship between water management and the early political and religious development of the plain of Phan Rang. The stela was found between the Dinh and Quao rivers in an area fed by an artificial canal, while five other inscriptions dating from the late eighth to early ninth centuries can also be linked to the water distribution system. The exact provenance of the Bakul inscription remains uncertain, but it was clearly discovered near a dam on the right bank of the Lu River. The Po Inâ Nagar inscription was found close to the left bank of the Lu River as it turns towards the east. The stela of Glai Lamau was found on the bank of an artificial canal linking the Lu River to the River Quao. The stela of Đá Trắng was found near the right bank of an artificial canal flowing south from the River Quao, which passes close to the sites of both Po Inâ Nagar and Glai Lamau. Finally, the stela and temple complex at Hoà Lai was situated on the right bank of a river running southeast to the Nai Bay.

The present canal system is clearly the result of centuries of adaptation, maintenance and rebuilding. Indeed, much of the water previously used for irrigation is now channeled through a modern, stone and concrete canal network that has its origins in the Japanese occupation of 1940. At present, the maps available to me are inadequate for tracing these alterations to the river and irrigation system and detailed field research will be needed to clarify the complex variations in water flow and water management. It seems to me highly probable, however, that the political development of the plain of Phan Rang in the late eighth and ninth centuries was dependent on the use of artificial water irrigation and canalisation. This process may have been initiated by a political elite from Nha Trang as a means of extending its limited agricultural base, but the Phan Rang region quickly became an important political centre in its own right.

Acknowledgements

This chapter is the result of approximately two weeks of fieldwork in the plain of Phan Rang between July and August 2004, conducted as part of a field survey sponsored by the Southeast Asia Committee of the British Academy, London. My research would not have been possible without the very substantial assistance of Dr Thanh Phần of the Anthropology Department of the Vietnam National University in Hồ Chí Minh City and of his son Thành Chế Phương, who introduced me to the Cham community in Phan Rang (Fig. 5.14) and helped to locate many of the sites described here. I am also grateful to the International Institute of Asian Studies (IIAS) in Leiden and to the Nederlandse organisatie voor Wetenschappelijk Onderzoek (NWO) in the Hague for allowing me to work on this material as part of a fellowship in 2004–05. Finally, many of the details were checked and updated in October 2009, during field survey with Professor Arlo Griffiths, Amandine Lepoutre and Thanh Phần as part of a project on the Corpus des Inscriptions du Campā sponsored by the École française d'Extrême-Orient. My sincere thanks are extended to all of the above.

Figure 5.14 Thành Chế Phương (far right) with local Cham guides at Palei Hamu Kraok

Chapter 6

Connecting the dots

Investigating transportation between the temple complexes of the medieval Khmer (9th–14th centuries CE)

Mitch Hendrickson
Assistant Professor, Department of Anthropology, University of Illinois at Chicago

> There is no real history if one does not account for the way a group has organised its natural space, just as a geographer must follow the birth of a civilization step by step in order to understand how it came about.
> (Groslier 1986[1973]:31)

> [Transportation] is an agency by which every part of society is brought into relation with every other, and interdependence, specialization, in a word, organization, made possible…
> (Cooley 1974:28)

The Khmer temples of modern day Cambodia, Laos, and Thailand have been the religious and iconic foci of the people who lived around these places for over a millennium. Not surprisingly, academic interest in the region has similarly been drawn to the vast array of architecture, art and epigraphy found at these sites. A consequence of this is that Khmer temples have been largely studied in isolation from each other and their regional geographic setting. B-P Groslier (1986[1973]) argued that any rational history of the Khmer and their temples must take into account the physical landscape, moving away from the local to consider patterns at regional and supra-regional scales. When viewed in this manner, the arrangement of these temples across the landscape provides crucial information about the nature, expansion and changes of the Khmer empire.

The approach used in this investigation is an examination of spatial relationships between temples through a theory of transportation and communication. The need for movement of goods, people and ideas is linked to every aspect of society, and, as with the historic and modern nation states, binds society (or societies) together (Cooley 1974:28). Thus, it is logically informative to examine how the Khmer temples were integrated into an 'empire' using principles of transportation as the means of connection. By using geographic information systems (GIS), preliminary models of how and where contemporaneous Khmer temples 'communicated' with each other and how the site selection is intricately linked to the need for transportation are examined.

The role of transportation theory

Transportation is one of the most pervasive components in society and can influence or be influenced by any combination of economic, religious, political, military and social factors. The study of transportation developed within transport geography and is specifically concerned with the movement of people, freight and information across the landscape. A transport geographer views the organisation and relationship of three central components—nodes (locations), networks (linkages between nodes) and demand (human need)— normally in relation to economic considerations related to infrastructure, logistics and specialisation (Rodrigue, Comtois & Slack 2009). For the purposes of this study, the role of transportation theory is limited to identifying actual and potential linkages (land or water routes) between a select group of nodes (the Khmer temples). If, as assumed, the Khmer temples are part of a greater cultural landscape under politico-religious control, an examination of connections at the regional and supra-regional scales will provide insight into the internal dynamics of the Khmer empire and its geographic history.

Evidence of Khmer transportation

Before analysing the transportation connectivity between temple nodes, it is worthwhile to outline the amount of land and river transportation information available from the archaeological and historical records. The Angkorians left significant evidence of their terrestrial transportation system, though it was not as substantial as the Roman road network. In the late 19th century, earthen road embankments and associated stone bridges were rediscovered during French reconnaissance missions (Aymonier 1900–01; Lunet de Lajonquière 1902, 1911). Artistic evidence of Angkorian mobility is also found on the bas-reliefs of the Bayon, Angkor Wat, and Banteay Chhmar temples with repeated depictions of different types of transport employed at that time (for example, elephants, chariots, horses and ox carts).

Perhaps the most important addition to our knowledge of the history and composition of land transportation came with the publication of Georges Cœdès' (1941) translation of the Preah Khan stela. Dated to the reign of Jayavarman VII (late 12th century CE), it describes three roads leading from Angkor to provincial centres and the construction of 121 rest-houses along these roadways. This information led to the rediscovery of many stone buildings, now referred to as rest-houses, placed at intervals of 12 to 15 kilometres along the roadways (Ittaratana 1998). More recently, a similar pattern was identified in the spacing of rectangular water tanks (*trapeang*) at four to five kilometre intervals along most of the Angkorian roads (Hendrickson 2004). This combined information points to an elaborate road network with a centrally-planned infrastructure to support the regular movement of people across the region.

Though it seems less visible in the archaeological record, water transportation played an important role in Khmer mobility. Rivers provide obvious natural routes of communication that would have been exploited long before the Angkorian period. Unlike roads and their associated infrastructure, which are highly visible archaeologically, rivers require little capital investment. It is also difficult to determine when, where, how and why they were used. The strongest evidence supporting the use of rivers as key transport routes is the placement of Khmer temples along major waterways (Groslier 1973:117; Im 1998:57–72). Hall (1985:173) argued that this pattern reflects the economic importance of rivers, in particular the Sen River in central Cambodia, as conduits for trade. Physical remains of water transport are currently restricted to the boats depicted in the battle scenes from temple bas-reliefs and landing platforms associated with the temple reservoirs, such as those at Srah Srang and Phimai. Interestingly, Paris' (1941b) study of these images concluded that the design of the boats is only suitable for riverine transport. While seemingly obvious, river transport must be considered to have had a significant role in day-to-day movement during the Angkorian period and must be thoroughly studied to understand past Angkorian societies. What is needed currently is to examine how the road and water routes were integrated into a regional transport network.

Transport theory in a Khmer context

While there is ample evidence of terrestrial transportation infrastructure to which transportation theory is readily applicable, the first stage of any such analysis is to understand the synergy between roads, rivers and temples. The primary aim of this chapter is to use transport theory to model potential locations of communication routes between the Angkorian temples. If our assumptions are correct these temples were integrated into, or influenced by, the developments at Angkor. Connections would have been required at the regional and supra-regional scales. Although there is unequivocal evidence that some of the temples were directly associated with the road systems, the majority of temples are not situated adjacent to known transportation routes.

In order to 'connect' the temples and reflexively conceptualise the development of the transportation system, we need to determine which temples were built, renovated and used during the reign of individual kings. In this approach, contemporaneously occupied temples can be integrated into a transport network that reflects the influence of kingly empires. The relationship between transportation and temples will be examined in three ways:

1. by using the location of Khmer temples as a means of identifying potential routes of communication between temples and settlement areas (land- or river-based);
2. by separating temporal sequences of temple construction on the landscape in order to assess when potential routes may have been established or most frequently used; and then
3. by using the known mapped roads and transportation infrastructure as a means of explaining temple placement.

Temple selection

Of the 2,450 pre-Angkorian and Angkorian period sites recorded in Cambodia (Bruno Bruguier, personal communication, August 2005), 22 temples outside of Angkor were selected for this study (see Fig. 6.1). The initial criterion for limiting selection of sites was based on BP Groslier's description of the Khmer heartland, which is associated with the zone of central cultural and political control:

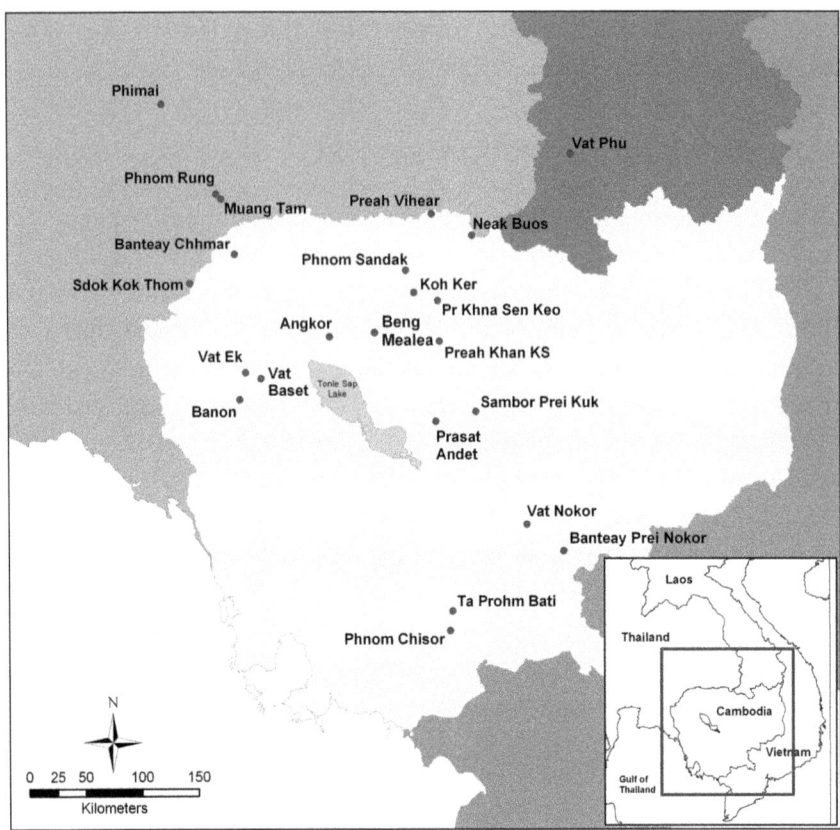

Figure 6.1 Location of Khmer temples discussed in this study

Although the Angkor plain prevailed, everything points to the fact that the Khmer really felt at home between the edges of the Lakes and the Se Mun valley, and more generally between the triangle of the Lakes and Tonle Sap to the southwest and middle Mekong to the southeast (Groslier 1986[1973]:39).

From a transport perspective, it is most likely that sites within this heartland had some form of intra-regional communication and a route to the capital. Four sites established during the pre-Angkorian period (Vat Phu, Sambor Prei Kuk, Banteay Prei Nokor, Prasat Andet) were included, as many of the Angkorian kings rebuilt or erected inscriptions at these older temples. Communication routes to these areas may therefore pre-date the Angkor period. The criteria used to further narrow the number of temples considered in this study were based on a combination of the following:

- *Proximity to the known Angkorian road system*. Temples located adjacent to known Angkorian roadways are most obviously included in this study. The majority of temples, however, are not connected to the mapped network.
- *Temple prominence*, specifically, the size and location of the temple or temple complex. Only large 'state' temples or temple complexes were selected following the idea that larger centres have more politico-religious interactions with the capital. Location refers to where a temple is situated; in particular, temples built upon hills which would have provided focal points of religious worship for the people and kings of Angkor.
- *Evidence of royal connection between temples and kings*. Presence of information about a temple's involvement in the greater political workings of the empire. This includes epigraphic and architectural data about the king who founded the temple, who and when modified the built structure, and any inscriptions written by or directly datable to specific kings detailing their involvement with the site.

Inscriptions are perhaps the most critical source of information for linking the provincial loci of the Khmer empire to the capital. The idea of using inscriptions to draw maps of the extent of the Khmer empire under each king was first adopted by Parmentier (1916). The temporal information used here to construct new maps is based on summaries of the original translations (Briggs 1951; Snellgrove 2004; Jacques and Lafond 2004). As with the selection of sites, the number of inscriptions used to construct the database are limited to those dedicated by, or associated with, a specific king. It is argued that this information indicates either direct influence by the capital or some form of communication between the sites. While an inscription might not have been directly written by the king to whom it refers, it is sufficient evidence to consider the temple linked to the greater communication network and the royal political milieu at that time.

Architectural style provides the other critical evidence of a king's involvement at a site. Dates for the temples are derived from a combination of the original art historical chronologies (Stern 1927; Parmentier 1939; Coral-Rémusat 1940; Briggs 1951; Boisselier 1966) and more recent summaries of the temples of the Khmer empire by Snellgrove (2004) and Jacques (Jacques and Lafond 2004). Ironically, the actual dates of these buildings are reliant on the inscriptions carved into their walls or on stela found in their enclosures.

Generating temple connectivity with GIS

The process of modelling potential transportation connections is greatly facilitated by integrating the historical information for each temple into a GIS platform (ArcGIS 9 and MapInfo). The value of GIS in addressing specific research questions is the relative ease with which comparisons between the temple data and a wide range of digital spatial data sets (topography, area of cultivable land, population density, etc.) can be made. To examine the relationship between temples and transport routes, the three operations undertaken through GIS are to:

1. connect each of the temples associated with a particular king;
2. create a maximum extent, or 'communication corridor', for each king by connecting the most distant temples of his reign; and
3. identify all areas of overlap between kings. For this last step the successive communication corridors of each king are layered and new zones extracted for every overlap that occurred (Fig. 6.2).

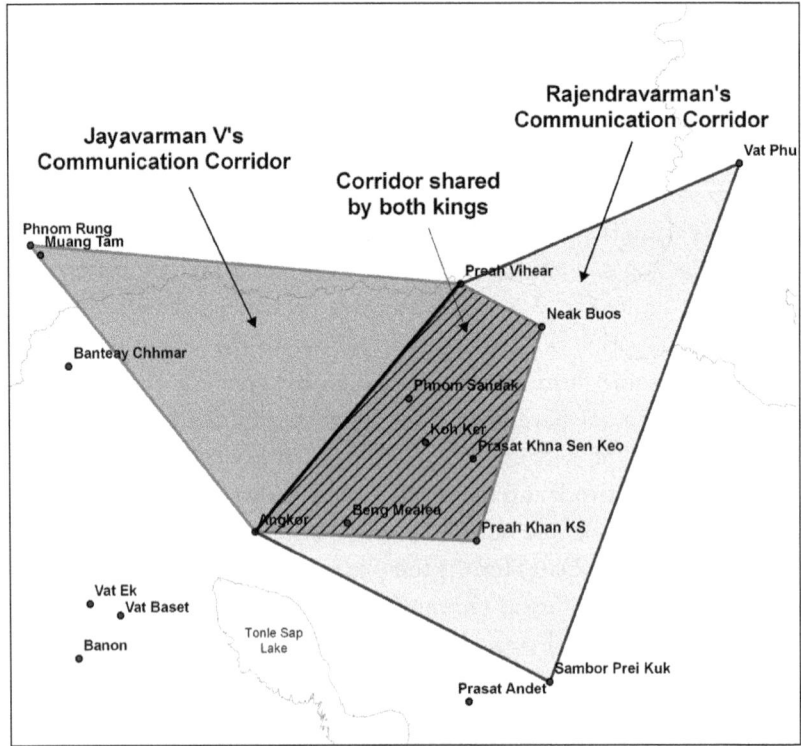

Figure 6.2 Example of the generation of shared communication corridors

These overlapping corridors are then organised according to the number of kings (one to 15) who shared influence over the area. Once the communication corridors are created, they are compared with digitised layers of the mapped Angkorian roads, rivers and watersheds, which consist of the tributaries and water catchment of a river. Topographic features (contours) are not included in this preliminary study.

Transportation analysis

The analysis of transportation routes involves three primary steps. The first is to establish the relationship of Khmer temples through time. The second step is to compare the GIS-derived information with the mapped roads to determine where other potential transport routes may have existed. Given the fact that transport is also an active agent in structuring settlement, the third step is devoted to examining the role of communication on the location of two Angkorian temples, Koh Ker and Banteay Chhmar.

Sites, Kings and Corridors

The results for the number of kings 'present' at a particular site are illustrated in Table 6.1. By making direct connections between the temples of each king in the GIS, a series of communication corridors is generated that relates to both the regional focus of the king and the potential transport routes between sites. Fig. 6.3 illustrates the change in the location of communication corridors for each king which influenced more than three temples between the ninth to 13th centuries. The first significant feature is the general bias to the northeast of Angkor. The importance of this region has long been recognised from the histories described in the inscriptions: 'Champassak (southern Laos), was to remain the mystical source of Angkorian power, the place erected by the Angkor kings for their pilgrimage, more important in a sense than the former patronage of the Fou-nan' (Groslier 1986[1973]:39).

The second significant feature is the restricted size of royal territories until the reign of Suryavarman I in the early 11th century. At this time the focus expands significantly to the northwest and south of the Tonle Sap Lake. Interestingly, the areas influenced by subsequent kings largely mirror the 11th century occupation, which suggests that regional communication was formally established at this time.

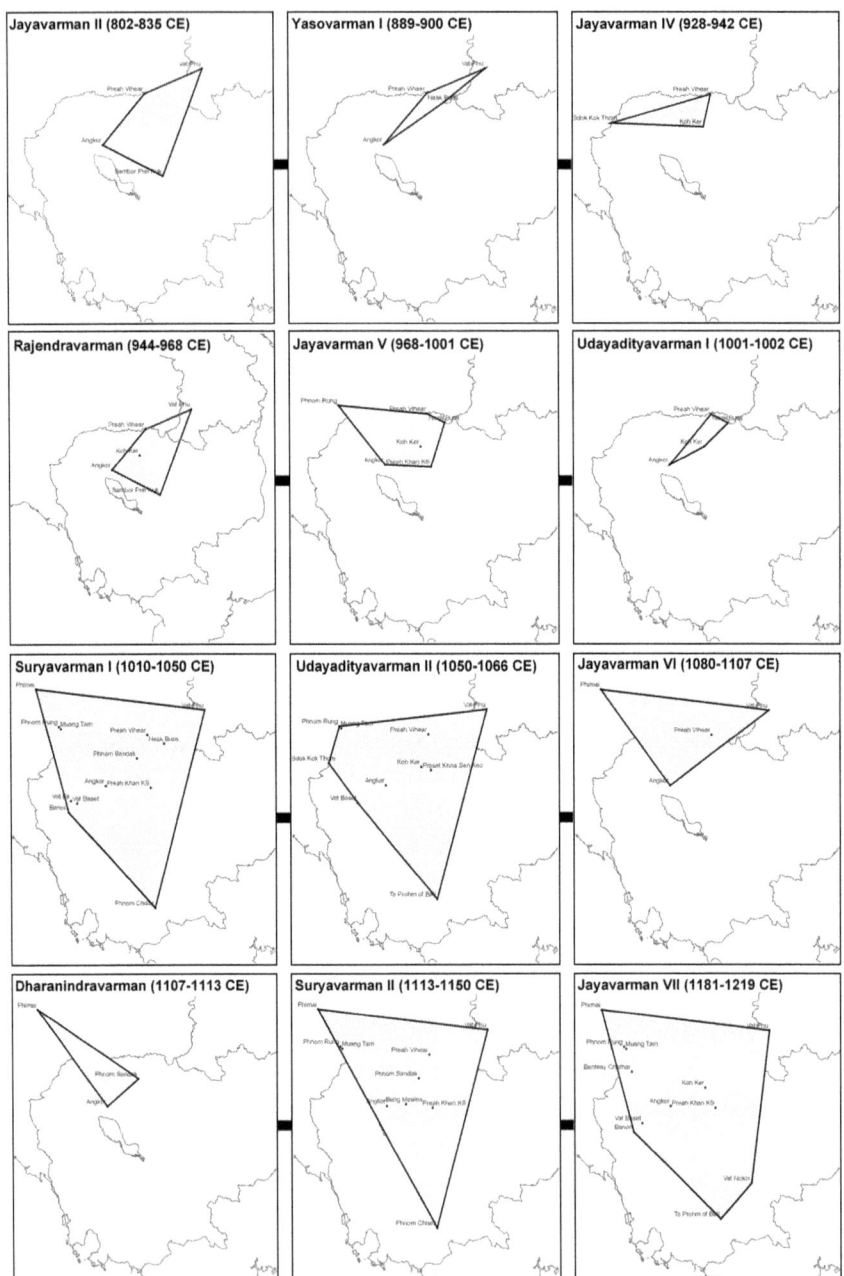

Figure 6.3 Communication corridors controlled by Angkorian kings between the 9th and 13th centuries CE

King	Reign	Temples
Jayavarman II	770–835	4
Yasovarman I	889–900	5
Isanavarman II	923–928	3
Jayavarman IV	928–942	3*
Rajendravarman	944–968	6
Jayavarman V	968–1001	6
Udayadityavarman I	1001–1002	2
Suryavarman I	1010–1050	13
Udayadityavarman II	1050–1066	10
Harshavarman III	1066–1080	3
Jayavarman VI	1080–1107	4
Dharanindravarman	1107–1113	3
Suryavarman II	1113–1150	10
Yasovarman II	1150–1165	2
Jayavarman VII	1181–1219	12
Indravarman II	1219–1243	3
Jayavarman VIII	1243–1295	2

Table 6.1 Number of Khmer temples 'influenced' by each Angkorian king
*Does not include Angkor

Shared corridors and mapped roads

The next stage in the analysis is to look at where and when corridors were commonly held by the Angkorian kings and how this information relates to mapped roads. Part of the GIS application, as discussed above, involved the identification of areas of overlap or commonly shared communication corridors. These communication corridors represent the shortest routes between two sites, which in effect mimic the role of roads to directly link two centres. These results are grouped into clusters of zones with one to five, six to ten, and 11 to 15 kings respectively (Fig. 6.4). Viewed temporally, these basic divisions provide some interesting clues about the expansion of the empire and where communication developed. Not surprisingly, the furthest areas from Angkor were controlled by the least number of kings, and almost exclusively by the pre-eminent rulers of the 11th to 13th centuries, Suryavarman I, Suryavarman II and Jayavarman VII.

By contrast, the most commonly shared region, located between Angkor, Preah Vihear and Neak Buos, was held continuously from Jayavarman II

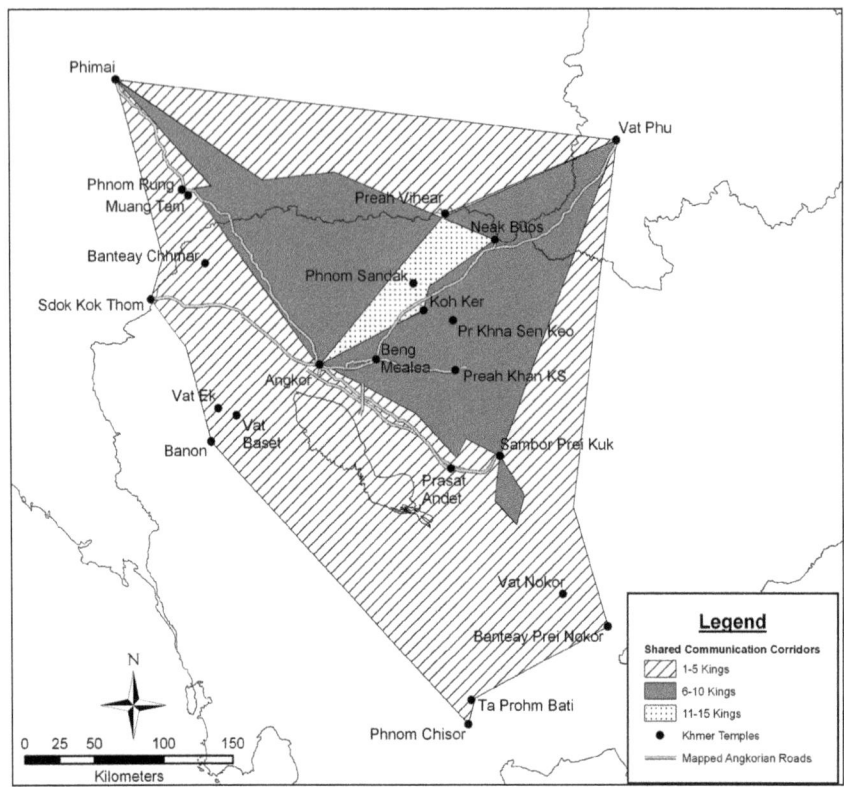

Figure 6.4 Location of commonly shared communication corridors and mapped Angkorian roads

(ninth century CE) through to Jayavarman VII (13th century CE). The potential longevity of interaction in this corridor strongly supports the need for a communication route within the area, and there is indeed one recognised road located within this zone. This confirms that the most commonly occupied Angkorian territory contained a formalised communication route. The implication for the age of the roads, in particular the route connecting Angkor to Vat Phu, is that they predate the Preah Khan inscription of Jayavarman VII (1181 CE).

Mapped roads, rivers and watersheds

Control of water has been a recurring feature in Southeast Asian culture since at least the early metal ages (Malleret 1959b; Moore 1989). Water management reaches its technical apogee during the Angkorian period with the construction of the great *baray*, embankments, canals, moats and

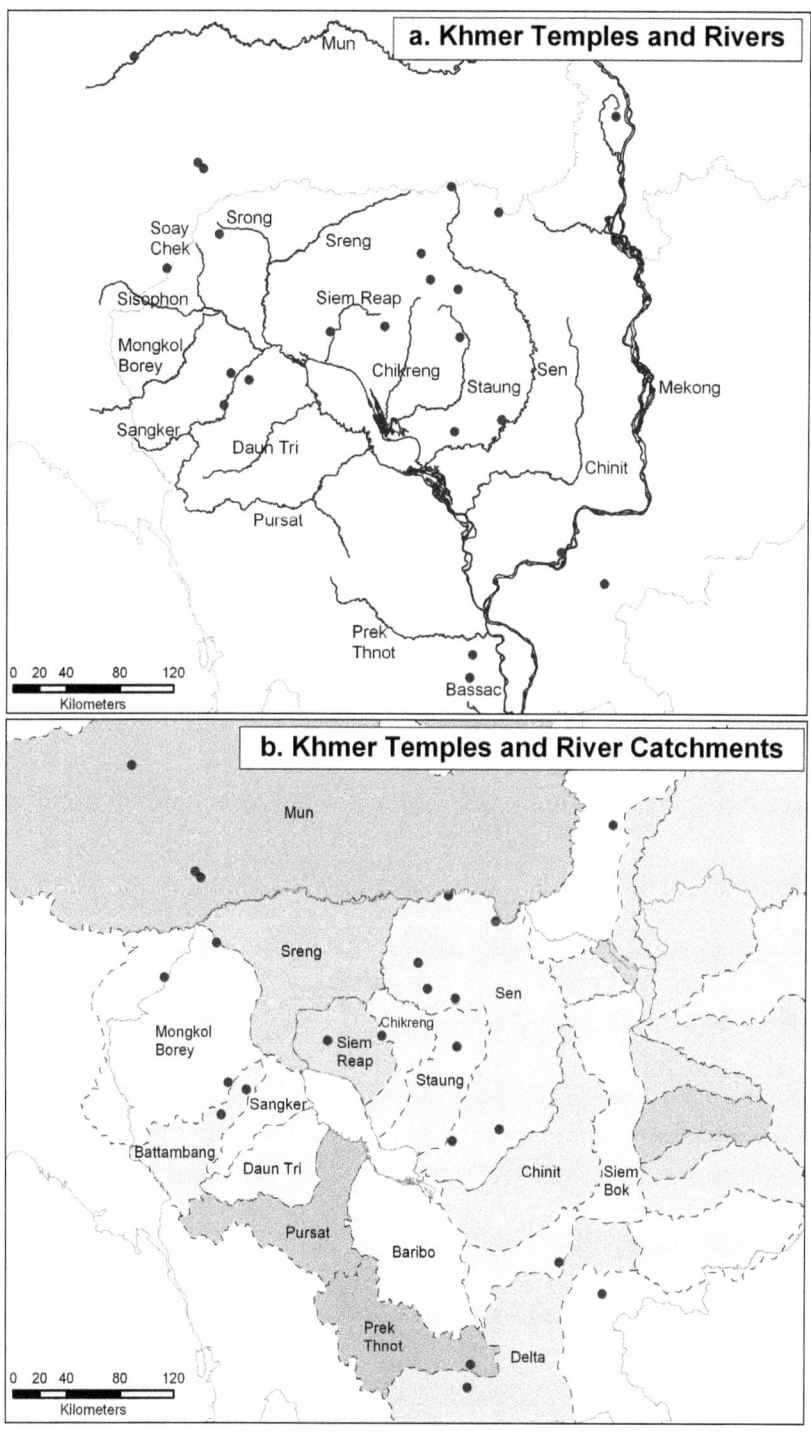

Figure 6.5 Location of Khmer temples relative to rivers (a) and river catchments (b)

bridges throughout the Khmer empire (Groslier 1979; Fletcher et al 2003). The concept that the Khmer actually controlled, or at least used, the rivers to facilitate movement has rarely been discussed in relation to transportation (Im 1998). Fig. 6.5 shows that the majority of Khmer temples are situated away from the main rivers (6.5a) or are located on the watershed (6.5b) between two catchments (Banteay Chhmar, Beng Mealea, Prasat Andet). Only Preah Khan of Kompong Svay and Banon, which is a hill temple, are situated on the main river. The reason for choosing to locate a site away from the main river may relate to avoidance of annual monsoon flooding, the tendency of large Cambodian rivers to meander, or the potential use of main rivers as a means of attacking settlements. The general settlement pattern, however, indicates that access to a natural waterway was a predominant factor in site placement.

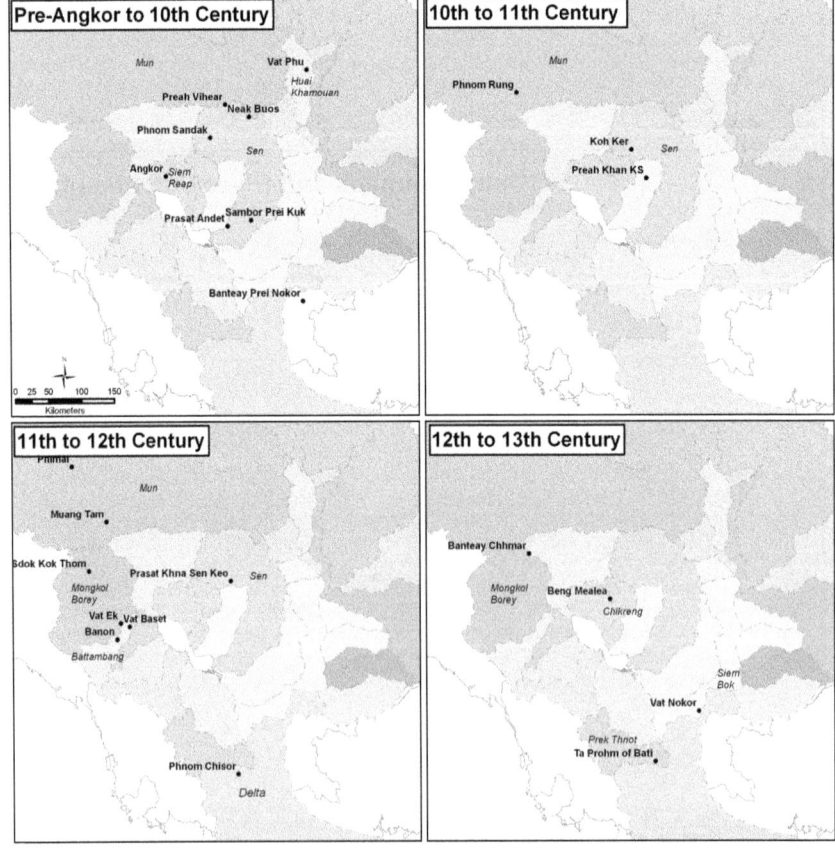

Figure 6.6 Comparison of the foundation date of Khmer temples and river catchments

The incorporation of river and watershed data is useful for clarifying the patterns of regional temple development discussed in relation to communication corridors. Comparing the position of temples and watersheds through time (Fig. 6.6) we see that the focus of Angkorian settlement for the first two centuries is the catchment of the Sen River, a fact previously noted by Hall (1985:173). It is not until the reign of Suryavarman I that other catchments, particularly the Nam Mun in northeast Thailand and Sangker around Battambang, become regularly incorporated into the empire.

An integrated transport network

From this discussion, both road and river networks appear to have facilitated communication between the Angkorian temples and settlements. The relationship between the roads and rivers, however, is only truly manifest when examined as an integrated network (Fig. 6.7). Without exception,

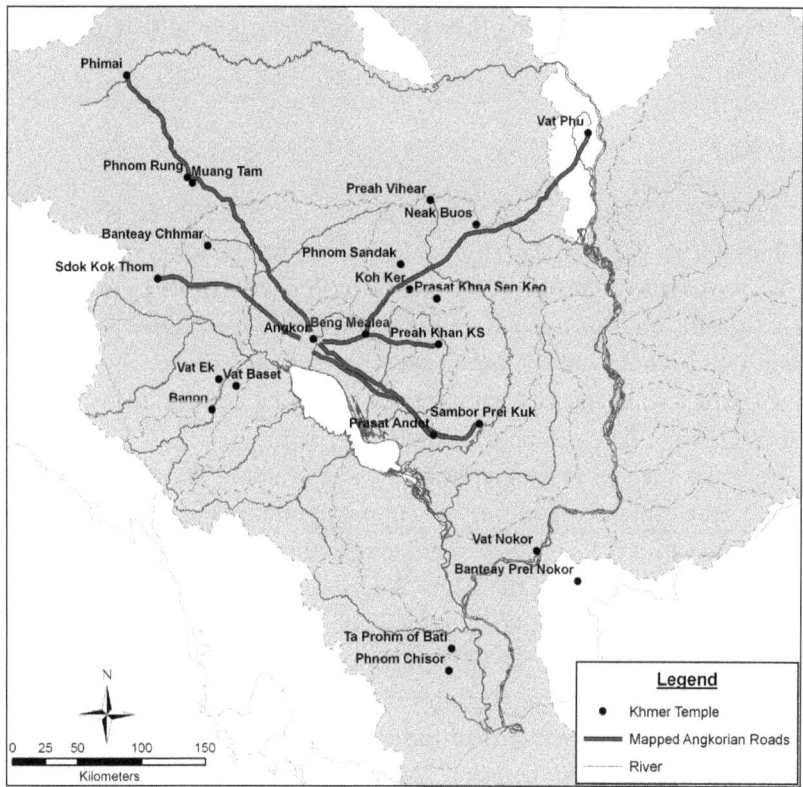

Figure 6.7 The terretrial and riverine communication networks during the Angkor period

roads bisect the space between the major rivers, running perpendicular to the flow of water in the watershed. While topography is not considered in this study, the shallow gradient across most of central Cambodia facilitates the development of these cross-cutting routes. These routes greatly expand the range of accessibility, both spatially and seasonally, in this region.

Towards a local historical geography of transportation

The dynamic relationship between settlement and transportation can also be applied to the debate surrounding site selection. Two temples whose positions on the landscape are enigmatic in Khmer history are Koh Ker, the temporary capital associated with Jayavarman IV (928–942 CE), and Banteay Chhmar, one of the temple fortresses of Jayavarman VII (1181–1219). The elaborate structures built at these sites suggest they were of great importance, but the environment in which they are situated has challenged rational academic explanation. A closer inspection of these two case studies will reveal that the selection of the sites is more purposeful than previously thought.

Koh Ker

In 928 CE, Jayavarman IV seized control of the Khmer empire and established his capital away from Angkor at what is now the location of Koh Ker (Cœdès 1968:114–115). Following Jayavarman IV's death in 944 CE, the site was 'abandoned' and the capital re-established at Angkor. Visitors and scholars to the area have long remarked on the apparent lack of geographic or economic benefit for selecting Koh Ker over the rice basket and fish bowl of Angkor and the Tonle Sap Lake.

From the analysis of geography and transportation, four relevant points emerge that can shed light on this curious location (Fig. 6.8). First, Koh Ker is situated in the Sen River catchment and on a tributary that connects to a significant number of the larger Angkorian temples. Second, it lies on the edge of the most commonly shared communication corridor (11 to 15 kings) and specifically on the edge of the corridor held by 11 kings, dating from Bhavavarman II (late seventh century CE) to Jayavarman VII (mid-13th century CE). Third, part of the road connecting the Angkor area to Vat Phu is located in this corridor, just to the north of Koh Ker. And lastly, besides the Jayavarman VII hospital built at Prasat Andon Kuk, no other evidence of architectural construction (other than that of the inscriptions) has been found at Koh Ker which can be attributed to Angkorian kings after the death of Jayavarman IV. While there has been limited fieldwork at Koh Ker, it is possible that this 'abandonment' is related to local environmental limitations for continuous, intensive agriculture. The landscape around Angkor, specifically its proximity to the Tonle Sap Lake, provides a much more tenable basis for supporting large populations.

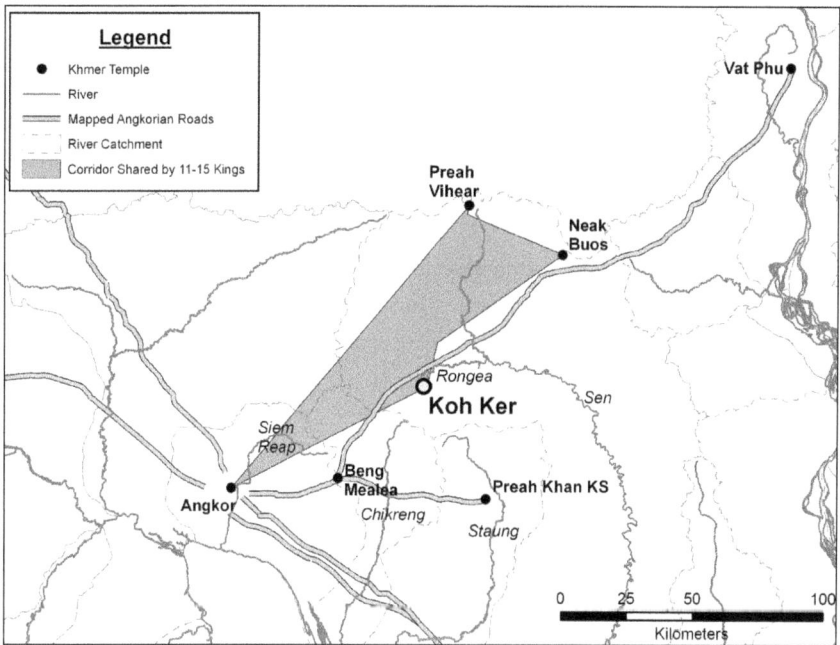

Figure 6.8 A transport geographic interpretation of Koh Ker

Using transportation as a guide, we can posit new interpretations for the selection of this site. Koh Ker is situated in the 'mini-homeland' of the Sen River valley which connects it via waterways to the major Angkorian sites in the region. More importantly, following Groslier's comment about the significance of the Champassak (quoted above), Koh Ker is located next to the road that connects Angkor to the pilgrimage sites of Vat Phu, Preah Vihear and Neak Buos. In fact, Koh Ker's close proximity to these religious sites would effectively cut off Angkor from the important religious centres, emphasising the significance of the new capital and isolating, and therefore diminishing, the importance of the old seat of power. The politico-religious implications of transportation may have overwhelmed the practical issue of sustainability in the area.

Banteay Chhmar

Like Koh Ker, scholars have long pondered the apparent isolation of the Banteay Chhmar temple complex. Even today travel to the site remains difficult and the surrounding landscape offers no obvious advantage to positioning a settlement in this region. Built by Jayavarman VII in the late 12th century as a tribute to his son, crown prince Indrakumara, who died during battles with the Cham (Cœdès 1968:176), Banteay Chhmar is one of the largest and most impressive temples in the Angkorian empire. From a transportation perspective the site appears to be dissociated from both the Angkorian roads and the major river routes (Fig. 6.7). The former is particularly interesting given that, as Jayavarman VII was a major proponent of road infrastructure and the indisputable importance of the route between Angkor and Phimai, the only immediate evidence that Banteay Chhmar is part of a greater transport network is the appearance of a rest-house in the main enclosure. The communication corridors associated with the site are only shared by three kings, Suryavarman I, Udayadityavarman II and Jayavarman VII, showing that influence in the region was late.

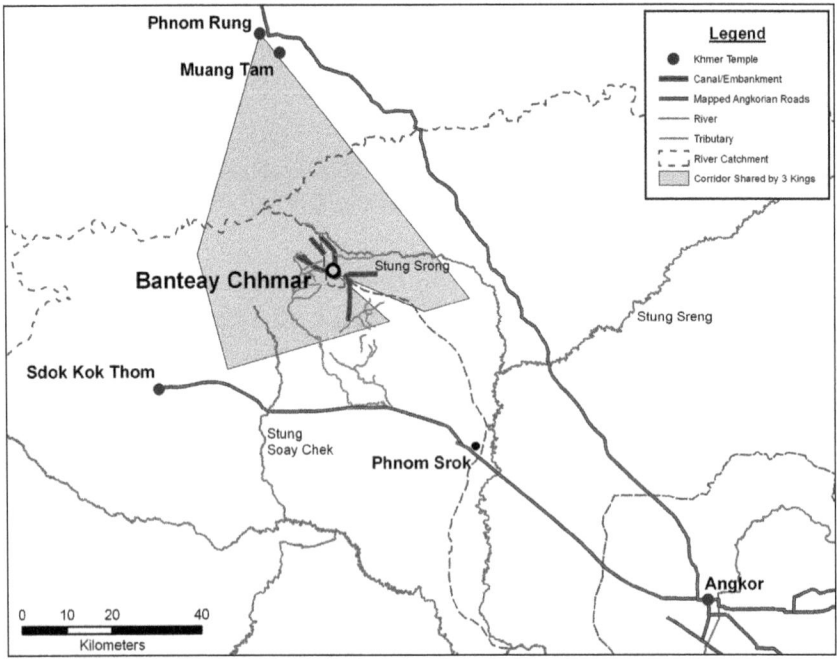

Figure 6.9 A transport geographic interpretation of Banteay Chhmar

The use of riverine transport is also questionable, as the site is not situated directly on the nearest tributary. Recent research by Pottier (2004), however, has identified the remains of an extensive canal network radiating out from Banteay Chhmar. When the location of these canals is examined in relation to watersheds, it becomes apparent that these man-made features could have connected the site to both the Mongkol Borey and Stung Sreng drainage basins and integrated Banteay Chhmar into a greater Angkorian transport network (Fig. 6.9). This would have significant military and economic advantages. Positioning Banteay Chhmar between these two catchments served to facilitate access to both the Chao Phraya and Mun River valleys in central and northeast Thailand. Travel to Angkor could therefore be undertaken to the south or east by river to the site of Phnom Srok and the beginning of the Angkorian road that connects to the West Baray. The construction of these waterways to increase local and regional mobility is yet another example of Khmer water-control practices.

A temple landscape connected

The focus of this chapter has been to introduce the concept that the 'isolated' Khmer temples were part of a dynamic communication network. The mapping of potential routes provides new insights into the relationship of temples and their geographic setting and, perhaps more significantly, identifies the significant role of transportation in the history of their development. By comparison with the preconceived notions of Khmer transport history, the GIS model offered here suggests that the 'classic' distribution of sites and terrestrial transport infrastructure dates back to the mid 11th century during the reign of Suryavarman I. These routes, however, were likely being exploited before this date, a fact attested to by the concentration of sites located along water routes, such as the Sen, from early in the pre-Angkorian and Angkorian periods. A final facet of this transport approach is that the need for mobility and communication can provide significant insight into understanding why sites are located where they are.

This study presents preliminary ideas on the role of transportation; it was not possible, nor was it desirable from a purely logistical perspective, to consider all of the available information, as we are interested in the physical limitations to transport through time. At the very least, this chapter offers a new path for investigating interactions in the Southeast Asian past. The application of transport theory must continue to utilise remote sensing, GIS and ground-testing data as a means of developing and verifying models.

These basic patterns of communication must be further examined in relation to topography, a more detailed analysis of the inscriptions, the location of road infrastructures (bridges, tanks, rest-houses), and the practicalities of river navigation.

Acknowledgements

Numerous people were involved in the process of translating this chapter from thoughts to reality. Eileen Lustig, Ngaire Richards and Damian Evans provided critical information, database set-up and GIS expertise. Critical editing and discussions were shared with Liz Holt, Dan Penny, Associate Professor Roland Fletcher, Dr Kyle Latinis, Martin Polkinghorne, Dr Christophe Pottier, and Andrew Wilson. I want to thank the Archaeological Computing Lab at the University of Sydney for providing access to the computer programs needed to undertake the GIS portion of this chapter. I am indebted to Larry Crissman at Griffith University who provided access to digital geographic resources. Lastly, I want to thank Dr Alexandra Haendel for organising the 'Sacred sites' conference in 2005 and inviting me to participate, and the Monash Asia Institute and Centre of Southeast Asian Studies for financial support for my attendance. This research was funded in part by the Social Sciences Humanities Research Council of Canada doctoral fellowship, the University of Sydney and the Australian Research Council. Any errors or omissions are mine alone.

Chapter 7

Journeys and landscapes

Some preliminary remarks on ancient Javanese perceptions of the environment

Peter Worsley
Emeritus Professor, School of Languages and Cultures, The University of Sydney

> Landscape in art tells us, or asks us to think about, where we belong.
> Important issues of identity and orientation are inseparable from the
> reading of meanings and the eliciting of pleasure from landscape.
> (Andrews 1999:8)

This chapter and the larger project it initiates are intended to be a contribution to the environmental history of Java. The chapter explores how the inhabitants of Java in the period before the 16th century apprehended the world in which they lived. More specifically, it sets out to describe the literary and mythic context in which works of epic *kakawin* represent the landscapes of Java. It is also a preliminary consideration of the extent to which these same works contain reliable empirical information about the Javanese environment prior to the 16th century.

The materials available for the larger project are manifold and include works from a variety of genres which have survived to us from before the 16th century.[1] They include epic *kakawin* poetry, a contemporary description of the eastern Javanese kingdom of Majapahit,[2] the corpus of legal documents

---

[1] As there has been no comprehensive study of genres in ancient Javanese literature, the generic categories listed in this paragraph are intuitive suggestions. Aoyama (1994) discusses the epic qualities of one 'epic' *kakawin*, the Sutasoma.
[2] This work, the Nāgarakṛtāgama, is hybrid; it is both a laudatory description (*praśasti*) of contemporary Majapahit and its ruler and a work that shares formal characteristics and

recorded in inscriptions on stone and copperplate which contain decisions of government made by rulers and other officials, a 16th-century history of religious communities in Java,[3] and travelogues.[4] The project presupposes that each of these genres has its own history and organises the world and the landscapes it describes in different ways.

The scope of the present chapter is more modest. It is based on representations of landscape from three courtly epic *kakawin* works: the early 13th-century Sumanasāntaka, the late 14th-century Arjunawijaya, and the mid 15th-century Śiwarātrikalpa.[5] The authors of epic *kakawin* were poet–priests and their literary works religious artefacts, intended as objects into which deities might descend and become manifest (Zoetmulder 1974:173–85). The poets who created these *kakawin* worked under royal patronage and their audiences were members of extended polygamous noble households which inhabited the courts of ancient Java. As Robson points out in this volume, their work betrays close links between the institution of kingship and the art of poetry.

In his pioneering study of the literature of ancient Java, Zoetmulder (1974) has noted the way in which epic *kakawin* narratives from the great Indian epics were relocated in a Javanese environment. For all the Indian personal and topographical names that characterise the poems, their authors situated their stories in what is clearly a Javanese seasonal, topographical, faunal, floral, and social space.[6]

---

imagery with epic *kakawin* works. See Pigeaud (1960–63), Zoetmulder (1974:Chapter 12) and Robson (1995).

[3] Tantu Panggĕlaran (Pigeaud 1967:122, 1924). This work narrates stories about the creation of Java, the creation of human society there, and then largely records the foundation and history of a variety of religious communities in Java.

[4] One, the Wargasari, contains an account of the journey of a young man from Wĕwĕtih in the provinces to the capital of Majapahit; another The Story of Bujangga Manik: a pilgrim's progress, is a late 15th- or early 16th-century Sundanese account of the journeys of the priest Bujangga Manik, who travelled from the Sundanese court of Pakuan through central and eastern Java and Bali, and records the locations of religious communities and sacred places. For a summary of the Wargasari see Robson (1979:313–5); for the text of the work, translated into English, notes and commentary, see Fletcher (1990). Robson suggests a date in late 14th or 15th century Majapahit for the work. See Noorduyn (1982) for a detailed discussion of the topographical information contained in The Story of Bujangga Manik: a pilgrim's progress, and Noorduyn and Teeuw (1999) for a discussion of the purposes for which this poem was composed. See Noorduyn and Teeuw (2006) for the text, translation and commentary on the work.

[5] For comment and summaries of these three epic *kakawin* see Zoetmulder (1974:298–311, 325–9, 342–9, 359–66). See Supomo (1977) for the text, translation and commentary about the Arjunawijaya.

[6] See Aoyama (1994:76–121) for a discussion of these aspects of the Sutasoma.

Day has taken landscape as an analytical concept to be 'a kind of representation of the natural world in temple (sculpture) and literary art' (Day 1994:175). I have followed Day in his use of 'landscape' as a form of representation.[7] However, landscapes are more than just what they represent. In the case of the three epic poems, we are considering landscapes that are an aspect of the hegemonic narratives that sustained the authority and status of the kings of ancient Java, their households and courts. The poet–priests who created them projected onto the space of landscapes certain social and cultural preoccupations about the nature and extent of royal authority and the nature of being beyond that authority.[8]

Religious odysseys

The immediate narrative context for the descriptions of landscapes in the three epic poems I have chosen to discuss are journeys: the journey of a hunter into the forest; that of a king and his royal entourage to the sacred River Narmadā; and that of a royal prince from Ayodhyā to the neighbouring kingdom of Widarbha, where he wins the hand of his bride before returning home to take the place of his father on the throne of Ayodhyā. The three journeys have a particular morphology. They link four quite distinct spaces— the royal palace at the heart of a kingdom's capital, the countryside, the seashore and the mountain forests.[9]

---

[7] Day's important essay was written for a conference on Orientalism. In it he takes as his starting point 'landscape' as 'a central mode in Western artistic expression,' 'a keyword in a Western discourse on human progress,' and a form of expression which moves 'toward or away from a representation of the real based on the visual truth of scientific realism.' He notes the realism of the description of landscape in ancient Javanese literary art and how it is constructed of accumulated details, each embedded in its own grammatical and descriptive unit. He points out how the temples, monasteries and villages serve as markers of the reach of royal authority in the landscape and describes the viewpoint from which the gaze is directed onto the landscape from above, as that of the gods or those who commune with them as they meditate on mountain tops. Finally, he notes how the landscape is organised on the model of a three-dimensional Indic cosmography.

[8] See Andrews (1999:Chapter 1) for a discussion of the idea of landscape in Western art and pages 15–22 in particular for comment on 'landscape' as 'a kind of cultural instrument'.

[9] In what follows, scant attention will be paid to the first of these locations. Instead, I focus on the idea of landscape in its most literal sense as representation of the natural world and examine countryside, seashore and mountain forests as they are described in the three works. We might question just how appropriate is the designation 'royal palace in a kingdom's capital', especially in the case of the hunter's journey. He, of course, lives with his family in a humble abode in the mountain forests. The hunter is, however, an exception

Journeys can also be metaphors and not just descriptions of travel from one place to another. The three journeys we are considering have religious goals. In the Śiwarātrikalpa, the journey of the hunter Lubdhaka, a worthless outcast from human society,[10] is a metaphor for the individual soul's search for the blessing of the god Śiwa. A serendipitous act of devotion wins the hunter's release from the punishments of hell and a place in Śiwa's heaven after his death.

The Arjunawijaya recounts the story of the journey of King Arjunasahasrabāhu and his court to the sacred Narmadā River. His stay at the river culminates in a display of kingly power. Priests of four religious orders, Brahmins, Śaiwites, Buddhists and Seers, perform a ritual in which the king is physically transformed and assumes the form of a giant with 1,000 arms, each wielding a weapon of some sort (Arjunawijaya 38.8–39.3). Having assumed this form, the king lies across the river and dams it. Here, in the sacred waters of the Narmadā River, perhaps we might take the transformed king to be a celebration of kings as the source of authority for initiating and maintaining irrigation works, which provide for the prosperity of their kingdom. The splendour of the king and, later, the king and queen lying in the riverbed calls to the poet's mind visions of the great god Śiwa—the first a vision of Śiwa's divine family and then, a little further on in the poem, the frustrated erotic play of the god Śiwa and the goddess Maheświarī (Arjunawijaya 40.9–10). These visions of the divine splendour of kingly power are placed strategically in the poem at a moment just before a sequence of events that culminates in a great battle in which King Arjunasahasrabāhu defeats the demonic ruler of Sri Langka, Rawaṇa.

In the Sumanasāntaka, the narrative of Prince Aja's journey to Widarbha has about it the character of a story of a life crisis.[11] The young unmarried Prince Aja departs from his father's realm in Ayodhyā with a large entourage. Before

---

as the hero of an epic *kakawin*. The story of his journey emphasises his separation from the social world of his fellow humans. In other epic *kakawin* the main protagonists inhabiting this space are kings and queens, princes and princesses, and their courtly households. In these cases the palace is the dominant feature in descriptions of this space. For these reasons I have retained the designation of 'royal palace in a kingdom's capital' for the space. One might be tempted to attach the term 'city' to this space. Because we have only an imprecise understanding of urbanisation in ancient Java at this time, I have avoided using this term.

[10] The poem describes Luddhaka's failed hunt. The link between the hunter's worthless character and his failed hunt finds interesting corroboration in the Nāgarakṛtāgama. There, in a description of a royal hunt in the forest, as the king Hayam Wuruk approaches the forest, the society of wild animals meet with the king of beasts, the lion, to discuss how they should behave. The point is made that if they are hunted by a virtuous person like the king they should submit to the slaughter; only if the hunter is evil should they evade death.

[11] The crisis is not altogether unlike that which Aja's grandson Rāma undergoes when his father, King Daśaratha, sends him to the aid of the priest Wiśwamitra, whose rituals

he finally returns home, married and in a fit state to replace his father, King Raghu, on the throne of the kingdom of Ayodhyā, Aja undergoes three trials: the exorcism on the banks of the sacred Narmadā River of the Gandharwa prince, Priyambada, from a curse which the priest Patangga had laid on him in anger; the winning of his bride, Princess Indumatī of Widarbha; and the armed challenge of his rival suitors as he returned home to Ayodhyā.

The social world of royal palace and countryside

It is in the context of these journeys that the palace and the landscapes of countryside, seashore and mountain forest take on the specific topographical, climatic, floral, faunal, emotional and social characteristics that determine the relationship between them. The textual moments of passage between royal palace and countryside, countryside and seashore, and seashore and forested mountains are clearly indicated in each of the three works we are considering. These four locations in fact form two categories of interrelated spaces. Palace and countryside together represent two aspects of human society, while seashore and mountain represent a wilderness, a world beyond human society designated in Old Javanese by the phrase *pasir wukir*.[12] In the three epic *kakawin* works, the moments of passage between society and wilderness are given an ambiguous character. They contain the ruined forms of human society in the process of being reclaimed by the wilderness. In one instance, however, in the Sumanasāntaka, the moment of passage from society to wilderness is marked by a trial undergone by Prince Aja in a place of pilgrimage and priestly ritual on the banks of the sacred Narmadā River.[13]

---

demons disturb. Rāma goes on to win Sītā's hand in marriage before he arrives back in Ayodhyā, his status enhanced, and fit to be consecrated as crown prince (see Worsley 2009).

[12] See Worsley (1986) for a discussion of this distinction drawn on the basis of analysis of the bas-reliefs illustrating the story of the Arjunawiwaha at the 14th-century east Javanese temple, Candi Surawana; and Worsley (1988) for discussion of the same distinction in Balinese paintings of the same narrative theme.

[13] A full discussion of the passageways in these poems between landscapes, and more particularly between the socialised space of palace and countryside and that of the wilderness of seashore and mountain forest, is beyond the scope of this chapter. In the Śiwarātrikalpa, when the hunter, Lubdhaka, loses the countryside from view and enters the wilderness, he passes by a large monastery and then the ruins of a large and isolated temple complex. The monastery is occupied and its religious life is a busy one (Śiwarātrikalpa 2.7–9); in contrast, the ruined temple complex is devoid of any sign of human presence and is being reclaimed by the wilderness (see Robson in this volume). In the Arjunawijaya, King Arjunasahasrabāhu and his party pass by a series of ruined temples, on which the king proceeds to stamp his authority by restoring them, as he had

The countryside is home to a rural population, which lives in the villages and hamlets close to the capitals of kingdoms and in more remote valleys. This is an ordered peasant society engaged in productive labour. These works provide us not just with random listings of places of habitation and agricultural and horticultural activities of the countryside; they also give us a sense of their distribution over the landscape. The rural population work wet and dry rice fields, plough them with oxen, and harrow them. They plant seeds in seedbeds before transplanting the seedlings to the fields and they harvest crops. There are dry fields, where root crops of various kinds grow, and stands of fruit trees and coconut and sugar palms. Cattle graze on uncultivated fields and the dykes between wet-rice fields and sheep and pigs are also mentioned. Salt is manufactured in saltpans, and fish, eels and crustaceans raised and fished from ponds. In remote areas of the countryside there is also evidence of extensive areas of forest which are also the site of agriculture, horticulture and cattle-grazing. The countryside is also the site of a religious order. A variety of religious institutions—temple complexes, monasteries and convents, hermitages, halls, retreats, and *maṇḍala*—are described. They are home to a number of religious orders—Brahmins, Buddhists, Śaiwites and Seers—who give instruction, conduct rituals and meditate on these sites. Kings rule over the countryside.[14]

Epic *kakawin* also describe seasonal differences in the countryside. In the Sumanasāntaka, Prince Aja is given an account of the passing seasons in a remote and poor region where he spends the night. Two seasons are described—a dry season from May to October and a wet season from October to April. During the dry season trees lose their leaves, the grass

---

been instructed to do by the priest in the Śaiwa–Buddhist complex which he has just visited. This episode is placed strategically in the narrative in order to draw attention to the nature of the relationship between the ruler and his subjects, just at the moment that he and his party were about to leave social life behind them and enter another mode of being in the wilderness of seashore and mountain forest. In the Sumanasāntaka, Prince Aja comes from the wilderness on his way to the city of Widarbha, passing by an abandoned hermitage before coming to a convent where a pious company of women of priestly descent live. However, it is not just the difference between the abandoned hermitage and the functioning convent that marks the transition between wilderness and countryside; rather it is the wretched condition of the countryside itself. Here, there are the trappings of society (wet and dry rice fields and rice barns), but the soil is dry, uncultivated and overgrown, the population forced by banditry to flee their homes, their rice barns tumbledown, and debts accruing on their fields.

14   See Arjunawijaya 22.5–32.4; Śiwarātrikalpa L2.3–9; and Sumanasāntaka 22.4–29.10 and 30. See Supomo (1977:57–68) for an excellent discussion of the palace, countryside and wilderness in the Arjunawijaya and Teeuw et al (1969: 45–51) for the countryside in Śiwarātrikalpa.

dries out, and plants wilt in the heat. It is a time when it hurts to travel over the sharp gravel on the roads, when the sap of the *lontar* palms is sweetest and when people remain at home to rest from the heat of the day and suffer from fever. The wet season is one of dark clouds, misty rain and heavy downpours when the roads are wet, house yards and cow pens are full of mud and trees and plants come into flower (Sumanasāntaka 28.15–26; cf Zoetmulder 1974:192–5).

Epic *kakawin* works give expression to a sense of political and religious interdependency, which unites palace and countryside. Much has been written about the manner in which taxes in kind and labour were drawn from the countryside for the support of royal households responsible for the administration and security of realms in ancient Java, and about how the right to these taxes was diverted to support the foundation and maintenance of religious communities, irrigation works and other projects sponsored by rulers. It is clear that extensive networks of markets also integrated centres of royal administration and countryside. However, it is not these aspects of the economic and commercial interdependence of palace and countryside that epic *kakawin* highlight.

We learn from inscriptions, and from the 14th-century description of Majapahit in Nāgarakṛtāgama,[15] of the ceremonial exchange of goods which took place on the occasion of great state and temple rituals, when the king redistributed wealth in the form of gifts to royal officials and retainers and to representatives of local village communities. It is this latter style of exchange which works of epic *kakawin* privilege in their accounts of the relationship between royal court and village. In the Arjunawijaya there is a description of a royal audience in the courtyard of a large rest-house. Village men come, formally attired, with their wives to pay their respects to King Arjunasahasrabāhu. To the rhythmic beat of drums, they make offerings of food; pyramids of rice and side dishes, a variety of alcoholic beverages, fruit, betel nuts and leaves, and seafood are presented to the king. Having accepted these offerings, the king redistributes the food to his entourage and to all the officials and commoners who wait upon him. At the end of the meal, before retiring, the king also presents the visiting local village dignitaries and the attending Śaiwite and Buddhist priests with gifts of cloth and other things (Arjunawijaya 31.6–17).[16]

---

[15] See, for example, Nāgarakṛtāgama 28, 30, 34.2–3.
[16] In the Sumanasāntaka there is reference to a similar event when Prince Aja spends the night in a village on his way from Ayodhyā to Widarbha. On this occasion, while food is offered to the royal visitor and his retinue and the host community and visitors share the

I have written elsewhere about the relationship between royal palace and religious communities in ancient Java and about the principles governing the relationship between king and priest in ancient Java and how these principles were acted upon (Worsley 2009, 1991). Rulers built and maintained temples, monasteries and hermitages, endowing them with the means to support the communities inhabiting them. It seems that these religious communities and the officials who governed them were on occasion powerful enough to remind kings of their responsibilities in this regard, and kings were prepared to act upon such protestations. In return, religious communities had the duty to provide doctrinal instruction and to conduct rituals designed to ensure the long life of rulers who supported them and to promote the stability and prosperity of the realms over which Javanese kings ruled. In arguing this point, I cited the description of the visit of King Arjunasahasrabāhu to a large Śaiwa-Buddhist complex in the Arjunawijaya (26–31).[17] The priest who welcomes the king on this occasion lectures the king at some length on his duty to provide in perpetuity for the upkeep of temples. He informs the king of the difference in law between classes of religious foundation and points out that the merit that comes to a ruler who carries out his obligation to provide for the welfare of religious communities is no less than that which comes to one who dies a warrior's death in battle. Both the account of the royal audience, which we have just discussed, and the second episode set in the Śaiwa–Buddhist temple complex are situated strategically in the narrative of Arjunasasrabāhu's journey. It would seem that the poet has chosen to draw attention to the nature of the social relationship between the ruler and his subjects at the moment that he and his party were on the point of leaving social life behind them and entering another mode of being in the wilderness of seashore and mountain forest.

The wilderness of seashore and mountain forest

The seascapes described in epic *kakawin* poems commonly refer to the sea, the sky, the coastline with its beaches, rocky cliffs and reefs, islands dimly visible in the mist off the coast, storms, mists and fogs, the fall of heavy rain, rainbows, and ships and fishing boats. In the Sumanasāntaka, for example,

---

meal, there is no explicit reference to the royal visitor giving gifts to officials of the host village (Sumanasāntaka 28).

[17] See Worsley (1991), and Robson in this volume.

Prince Aja and his retinue arrive early one morning at the seashore. There, they view skyscapes of thunder and lightning, clouds and rainbows, the estuary of a river with its reefs, a rugged coastline of rocky cliffs, a waterfall, 'elephant' rocks, promontories and headlands, dark woods close by the sea, a dead pandanus and a solitary ivory coconut palm. The remains of a pavilion and a statue of Gaṇeśa fallen in the sands amidst the ruins of a temple are also to be seen. And then there is the sea and the waves and an island just visible in a veil of gentle rain. There is also mention of hawks and herons, *dhwatala* fish, wrecked ships and torn sails, and fishing boats. This is a remote area, where humans have been and left traces of their presence in the form of poems and paintings on the beams of pavilions. Aspects of the landscape also recall the presence of the poets, lovers, ascetics and fishermen who frequented this landscape (Sumanasāntaka 33.3–36).

In the Śiwarātrikalpa, the moment is clearly signalled when the seaside passes from the view of the hunter, who now finds himself entirely in his own domain surrounded by the mountain forests. The description of the mountains and forest about him takes on an immediacy not evident in the earlier descriptions of rural countryside and seashore which he had viewed only at a distance. Now, he journeys over the rugged terrain of the mountains, past steep cliffs and ravines to a lake where he halts as night falls. The landscape is forested and flowering trees of various kinds grow there, as do palms, bamboo and *jangga* vines. The area is covered by thick undergrowth. This was the habitat of birds, particularly of male and female cuckoos. Insects, particularly bees and dragonflies, are also found there and the hunter has come here in the expectation of finding wild animals: rhinoceroses, wild bulls, lions, tigers, wild boars and elephants.

In the case of the Sumanasāntaka, Prince Aja and his party come across a hermitage in the mountain forests (Sumanasāntaka 37, 3–8). There is no question that the hermitage here formed part of the rural society of the countryside. This community of ascetics is clearly categorised by the poem as a feature of the mountain forests. The hermitage is situated in a ravine overlooking the sea, and on the slopes of the ravine above it are its fields, ploughed by oxen, and its gardens, planted with millet as well as some kind of tuberous plant, perhaps yam. The hermits offer the prince fermented palm sugar to drink, so it seems likely that sugar palms were cultivated or exploited too.

It is worth noting here that the seashore is categorised as wilderness, despite the reference to fishing boats and, in the Sumanasāntaka, to a population whom Princess Indumatī observes on one occasion to have no respect for rank or for poets. Even the waves—nature itself—she says display more respect (Sumanasāntaka 50–51). The story of the hunter Lubdhaka in the Śiwarātrikalpa also reminds us of the presence of another population that inhabited remote areas of Java beyond the ken of courtly elites and the reach of royal authority, whose way of life was based upon arboriculture, root cropping and the hunt as in parts of eastern Indonesia.

Here we might also note what could be described as the topographical juxtaposition of the wilderness of mountain forests and the heavens, which are home to the gods and other divine beings, and the traffic between them. In the Sumanasāntaka, we read of damned souls cursed to wander the world in human or animal form until they are exorcised and free once again to return to their divine existence.[18] Nor were the seashore and mountain forests only places where displays of royal power evoked divine visions, as we saw in the case of King Arjunasahasrabāhu's ritual transformation in the Arjunawijaya; they were also considered to be the site of great cosmic events, such as the Churning of the Milk Ocean and the Erection of the Śiwa *liṅga*, as is made clear in a debate about the comparative merits of the landscapes of seashore and mountain forest between Princess Indumatī and one of her ladies-in-waiting on the eve of her choice of husband (Sumanasāntaka 50–51).

The wilderness is a disaggregated world. There is no authority to integrate those who frequent this world into a harmonious order as royal authority does in the case of the social world of palace and countryside. Hunters and fisherfolk were not the only ones to frequent the wilderness. There were also refugees from human society seeking freedom to give expression to their erotic emotions—lovers escaping the control of kin groups, or poets and their paramours seeking an ambience and place to contemplate nature's beauty and turn their ecstasy into poetry. Kings and queens on leisurely tours also sought and found sexual pleasure there. Then there were ascetics who meditated in their search for an existential freedom from the human condition—an exercise that required suppression of their erotic nature so that they might temporarily or permanently achieve apotheosis with their chosen godhead. There were other denizens of the natural world of seashore and mountain forest who provoked fear: angry priests who laid dreadful curses on those who threatened their dignity; wild animals who

---

[18] Note the case of the Gandharwa prince, Priyambada, cursed by the priest Patangga, and of Princess Indumatī, who was a nymph sent from Indra's heaven to seduce the priest, Tṛṇawindu, whom Indra feared was preparing to usurp his rule as king of the gods. Patangga curses her to an existence as a human until she is exorcised by a *sumanasa* flower.

might kill even experienced hunters;[19] and a demimonde of violent demons who knew no constraint to their emotions and violently threatened gods and mankind alike. Here, warring kings filled with anger also wreaked violent havoc on enemies.

Emotional ambience and the landscapes

We have just seen that epic *kakawin* associate emotions with the different landscapes. Landscape is not simply an appropriate space for certain kinds of emotional display on the part of the narrative's protagonists. Emotional moods are written on to the landscape.[20] Unsurprisingly, the poetic countryside is a space where emotions are subdued under the harmonious influence of kingly rule. It is with the passage from countryside into the wilderness of seashore and mountain forest, however, that the emotional tenor of the text is heightened. Certain emotions hold sway here. Anger and fear heighten the mood of the poem, as does eroticism, the sadness of an abandoned and lonely lover (love-in-separation) or the delight which comes with love-in-fulfilment.[21]

In the Arjunawijaya for instance, the emotional tenor of the description of the rural countryside is quietly busy. Here the king, having set out on his journey to the Narmadā River, provokes wonder and those who witnessed the passage of the royal party, basking in the king's regal glory, are described as lovely to behold. The king's own state of mind was tranquil (*līlā*). However, with the passage of the royal party into the landscapes of

---

[19] See the account of the royal hunt described in the Nāgarakṛtāgama (50–54) and the fear of the hunter, Lubdhaka, in the Śiwarātrikalpa that he would be killed and eaten by wild animals.

[20] We cannot always be sure of identifying the emotional mood represented in *kakawin* poems. Often they contain simple descriptions of landscape and we are left to guess the emotional connotations they might have had for poet and audience. Some descriptions incorporate designations of charm and beauty which we might assume indicate the emotional connotation the description evoked in poet and audience. On other occasions the text explicitly indicates the emotions, for example, 'delight', 'wonder' or 'terror', that overwhelmed the sensibilities of witnesses to the scene. Then there are figures of speech, metaphors or similes that clearly inscribe particular emotional moods on features of landscape.

[21] Works of Sanskrit dramatic and literary aesthetics distinguish between nine *rasa*, or flavours: romantic, comic, sorrowful, violent, heroic, terrifying, repulsive, marvellous and peaceful. Among the characteristics required in Indian *kāvya* and ancient Javanese *kakawin* are vipralamba, the sentiment of love-in-separation, and *wiwāha*, the concluding of a marriage (see Keith 1920:372–3; Hooykaas 1958:13, 17, 44).

seashore and mountain forest, the erotic sensibility of the narrator and reader is incited by what is seen. In a series of similes vines, blossoming flowers and waterborne lotuses, clouds in the sky and the pale moon, for example, are likened to the image of a young woman aroused by passion and deflowered (Arjunawijaya 22.9–11). Here, nature's beauty calls to mind a woman's beauty. Interestingly, a later description of the seashore reverses the direction of the imagery: the beauty of a young woman from the royal party is likened to the beauty of the natural landscape of the seashore in what is a portrayal of feelings of unrequited love. The young woman, described emerging from the sea, her hips curved like a wave, her breasts as firm as coral reefs and her whimpering like the rolling thunder, composes a *kakawin* in which she sings of her loneliness as she awaits a lover who has not kept a rendezvous (Arjunawijaya 32.10–13). In this instance, the seashore is associated with the erotic emotion of love-in-separation.[22]

In the Sumanasāntaka, the mountain forest is inscribed with a distinctly erotic character. It is entirely in keeping with the portrayal of a hermitage, which is home to an ascetic, that we find a description of the single-minded meditation of a hermit who is challenged by erotic emotion. As Prince Aja approaches the hermitage, the fragrance of ferns and the carpet of fallen leaves, which welcome the prince to the forested mountains, assail him with the perfume of a bed on which he has made love, filling his heart with a wistful longing. The young nubile women whom he sees in the hermitage call to mind heavenly nymphs who await their satisfaction before slipping back to the world of the gods. Even the remains of a painting of a princess in the demure company of nuns rouses the prince's emotions. So deeply moved is he when he sees the painting that he believes the women in it are asking to join him on his journey. In contrast to the prince's emotional turmoil, the poet presents us with the vision of an aged hermit, meditating and beyond temptation.

Conclusions

The discussion above has said something about the way in which the inhabitants of pre-16th-century Javanese courts apprehended the environment in which they lived, how they thought, imagined and felt about their environment. These works of epic *kakawin* were not written with the purpose

---

[22] Compare with Robson in this volume.

of providing an empirical description of Java's climate, topography, flora and fauna. Rather they were works intended to shore up the grand myths that underpinned the power and status of Javanese kings and priests and the courts and religious communities in which they lived. The authors of these works were nourished by, and in turn maintained, traditions of knowledge they had inherited about the world in which they lived; traditions of literary criticism shaped the form and determined the content of the poems they composed, and they worked within systems of classification and description which we might easily put aside because they are quite different from and even alien to modern forms of scientific knowledge. Nevertheless, Zoetmulder has been able to recognise Java in their descriptions, rather than India. The realism of the descriptions, which Day insists upon, means we cannot deny them any empirical value.

The landscapes we have been examining contain information about climate and weather patterns, topography, species of animals, birds and plants which belong to the realities of a Javanese environment. They are not totalising, bringing all that they describe within the framing sweep of the eye. Rather they are, as Day says, itemising descriptions which focus on the details in landscapes.[23] They present us glimpses of different aspects of the landscape. However, they do not give us the impression of random listings. Rather they give us a sense of how different species of plants and animals were distributed over the topography of different landscapes. There is still much work to be done to test the consistency or randomness of the information about the distribution of the species across the landscape in these works. This might be done by examining other works of the same genre and the descriptions contained in the other genres of writing mentioned at the beginning of the chapter, and by comparing what we learn from epic *kakawin* with later Javanese and European botanical and zoological knowledge and, of course, with the findings gleaned by botanists and zoologists from archaeological excavations.

Acknowledgements

I would like to thank Dr S. Supomo, Professor Mark Hobart and Dr Anthony Day, who read and commented on this chapter.

---

[23] See also Aoyama (1994:76–121).

PART TWO

SITES AND GROUPS OF BUILDINGS

Introduction to Part Two

David Chandler

Adjunct Research Fellow, Monash Asia Institute, Monash University

The four chapters that follow introduce us to some of the exciting archaeological work taking place nowadays in Cambodia and Indonesia. All of the chapters demonstrate a range of new interpretations that spring from recent findings, and will encourage readers to make interesting comparisons between the cultures and archaeological methods being discussed.

Veronique de Groot's chapter takes us to south central Java, where she discusses the intimate relationships that existed in classical times between the local landscape and the orientation of Hindu temples, showing how local notions of 'cardinal points' often overlapped with canonical Indian ones, and sometimes differed from them, a pattern that made the temples Javanese as well as 'Hindu'. This conclusion has implications for Angkorian Cambodia as well, where Indian architectural and artistic influences often took on distinctly Cambodian forms.

In her chapter dealing with the 15th century central Javanese temple complex of Sukuh, Jo Grimmond argues that priests and artists working at Sukuh 'transformed a sacred locality into a religious setting'. Here, as at Angkor, water was infused with sacred power, connected with its importance to life itself. Grimmond examines the art motifs at Sukuh to show how the natural environment was sacralised by the people who came to worship there.

In his chapter about the city of Rowallan in East Java—once the capital of the last great pre-Islamic kingdom in Indonesia, Majapahit—archaeologist John Miksic discusses classical Javanese patterns of urban settlement that have been revealed by recent scholarship. Miksic persuasively takes issue with earlier scholars who had claimed that Javanese cities like Trowulan were laid out in a consciously cosmological fashion.

At the end of the section, Heng Piphal's chapter explores the uses to which the landscape was put in the pre-Angkorian kingdom of Sialaporia, some hundred kilometres south of Angkor, which flourished in the sixth and seventh centuries CE.

All of the authors in this section owe debts to the colonial-era pioneer archaeologists from France, Great Britain and the Netherlands whose work provided the outlines for much of early Southeast Asian history. Their work also shows how scholars since the 1990s have moved beyond some of the concerns of earlier work to explore a range of other issues that bring us closer to the everyday lives and cultures of the region and that honour the descendants of the people who built the settlements, cities, roads and temples under discussion.

Chapter 8

Temples and landscape in south Central Java[1]

Véronique Degroot
Archaeologist and Researcher, Ecole française d'Extrême-Orient, Jakarta

By the fifth century CE, the maritime route passing through the Strait of Malacca had become the main trade route between India and China. Contacts between civilisations, particularly between India and Southeast Asia, intensified, allowing what scholars have called the 'Indianisation' of Southeast Asia—the appropriation by local societies of the Indian language, script, religions and political system and the re-articulation of Indian culture to fit Southeast Asian realities.

On the island of Java, the first traces of an Indianised kingdom are the rock inscriptions of King Pūrṇavarman of Tārūma dating from about 450 CE,[2] with most of the remains of early Javanese kingdoms to be found in Central Java. From the eighth to the early tenth century the region around Mount Merapi and Mount Sumbing in Central Java was a centre for powerful kingdoms which built monuments as prestigious as Borobudur or Loro Jonggrang (Prambanan) and influenced large parts of Southeast Asia. Nevertheless, the history of Central Java is still largely unknown. No literary texts have survived from this period. Early Javanese society can only be studied and understood through its archaeological remains and through its inscriptions, of which there are roughly 200 from more than two centuries of history. The epigraphic data helps to sketch in broad lines of political events, although there remain many gaps and uncertainties.

---

[1] This paper is based on my PhD research, published in 2010 under the title *Candi, space and landscape*.
[2] The inscriptions of Pūrṇavarman use an archaic form of the Pallava script which was in use in South India from about 400 to about 750 CE. Paleographical comparisons with Indian records make a dating around 450 CE probable (Kern 1917:9, 131; Sarkar 1971: I,4).

The first Central Javanese king to leave an inscription is King Sañjaya who, in 732 CE, consecrated a *liṅga* at Canggal.[3] Within 50 years, inscriptions ceased to mention Hindu princes, but praised the glory of Buddhist rulers, referring to the Śailendra kings.[4] It was formerly thought that the Śailendra formed an almighty Buddhist dynasty and ruled Java for about 70 years before they were ousted from power by the descendants of the Sañjaya dynasty. This picture, however, has been questioned by the discovery in 1983 of the Wanua Tengah III inscription, which mentions a continuous series of Buddhist and Hindu kings without making any allusion to their belonging to two different dynasties.[5] What may still be held as certain is that, around 838 CE, a conflict between two potential heirs (one Buddhist, one Hindu) resulted in the flight of the Buddhist prince to Sumatra. A new impulse was then given to Hindu architecture and a vast program of building was undertaken. It is to this period that Loro Jonggrang is usually ascribed.[6]

In 928 CE, the epicentre of the Javanese civilisation moved to the eastern part of the island. After this date, kings resided and built their temples in East Java for more than four centuries. In comparison with Central Java, the East Javanese period is relatively well known, since it left not only inscriptions but also manuscripts of historical character. Central Java was to become powerful again centuries later through the impetus of Islam.

Given the scarcity of the epigraphic data and the difficulties of its interpretation, archaeology and art history are essential for understanding the emergence and development of Central Javanese culture. Up to now, most of the archaeological studies have focused on specific temples, so that a general overview of the area is lacking. Following the pioneer work of Mundarjito (2002), I have tried in my own research to fill this gap and to reconstruct the use of landscape during the Central Javanese period, focusing on the distribution, organisation and spatial arrangement of Hindu/Buddhist temple remains (Degroot 2009).

---

[3] Inscription of Sañjaya (also named inscription of Canggal or Gunung Wukir).
[4] Three kings present themselves as belonging to the Śailendra dynasty: Pañcapaṇa Paṇaṃkaraṇa/Indra Sanggrāmadhanañjaya (inscriptions of Kalasan, 778–779 CE and of Kĕlurak, 782 CE); Dharmmotunggadewa (Abhayagiriwihāra inscription/Ratu Boko I, 792–793 CE); and Samarattunga (inscription of Kayumwungan/Karang Tengah, 824 CE).
[5] Concerning the Wanua Tengah III inscription and its importance for Central Javanese history, see Kusen (1988), Wisseman Christie (2001) and Sundberg (2009).
[6] The dating of the Loro Jonggrang temple complex is not precisely known and scholars have different opinions. It is, however, never ascribed to the period before 828 CE. It is, for example, dated 832–856 CE by Dumarçay (1993:74), tenth century by Krom (1923:I,441), 898–928 CE by Vogler (1953:271) and around 856 CE by Williams (1981:38).

In the first part of this chapter, I concentrate on the plain of Prambanan, in the southern part of Central Java, and show how the natural landscape played an important role in the choice of sites and in temple orientation. In the second part, I focus on inscriptions. I demonstrate that the epigraphic data makes use of two conceptual systems to organise space and to list the cardinal directions, suggesting that two different traditions co-existed at this time, one of Indian background and the other probably of local origin.

Temple distribution in south Central Java

Almost all of south Central Java, apart from the south coast and the extreme east, is scattered with temple remains (Fig. 8.1). However, the ruins are unevenly distributed. They are far more numerous in the Prambanan plain along the southern slope of Mount Merapi, where there are 101 temple sites (91.8% of the total number of remains), than anywhere else. Furthermore, none of the sites located outside this area of high concentration can match the size of the remains of the Prambanan plain, except perhaps Candi Risan in Kabupaten Gunung Kidul.[7]

As Mundarjito (2002:96) has already noted for the district of Sleman, most of the temples of south Central Java are located at an altitude of 100–200 metres, corresponding to a particularly rich agricultural zone. The volcano enriches the soil with its deposits, and dozens of small- and medium-scale watercourses ensure a continuous water supply, but without any risk of the flooding that happens in the lower plain. Furthermore, the gentle slope makes it easy to control water and to irrigate rice fields without developing large hydraulic systems.

In the Prambanan area, however, there is a group of temples that seems to avoid fertile ground, gathered together on the dry limestone hills around Gunung Pegat and Gunung Ijo (Fig. 8.2).[8] This peculiar location, as well as the unique character of some of the remains (for example, Ratu Boko), leads us to think that they were of a different category than the temples of the plain. They were most probably hermitages and monasteries rather than state temples or city shrines.

---

[7] Candi Risan, also known as Candi Rejo, is located in the village of Candi (Kecamatan Semin, Kabupaten Gunung Kidul, province of Yogyakarta). It is composed of two structures, both badly damaged. The main temple is 13 metres square and still bears some decoration, including floral design, *kāla* and *makara*. A sculpture, which is probably the *bodhisattva* Avalokiteśvara, was found near the temple (Bosch 1915:25).

[8] These remains are Tinjon, Barong, Arca Ganeca, Dawangsari, Gupolo, Ijo, Miri, Sumberwatu, Sumur Bandung, and Ratu Boko.

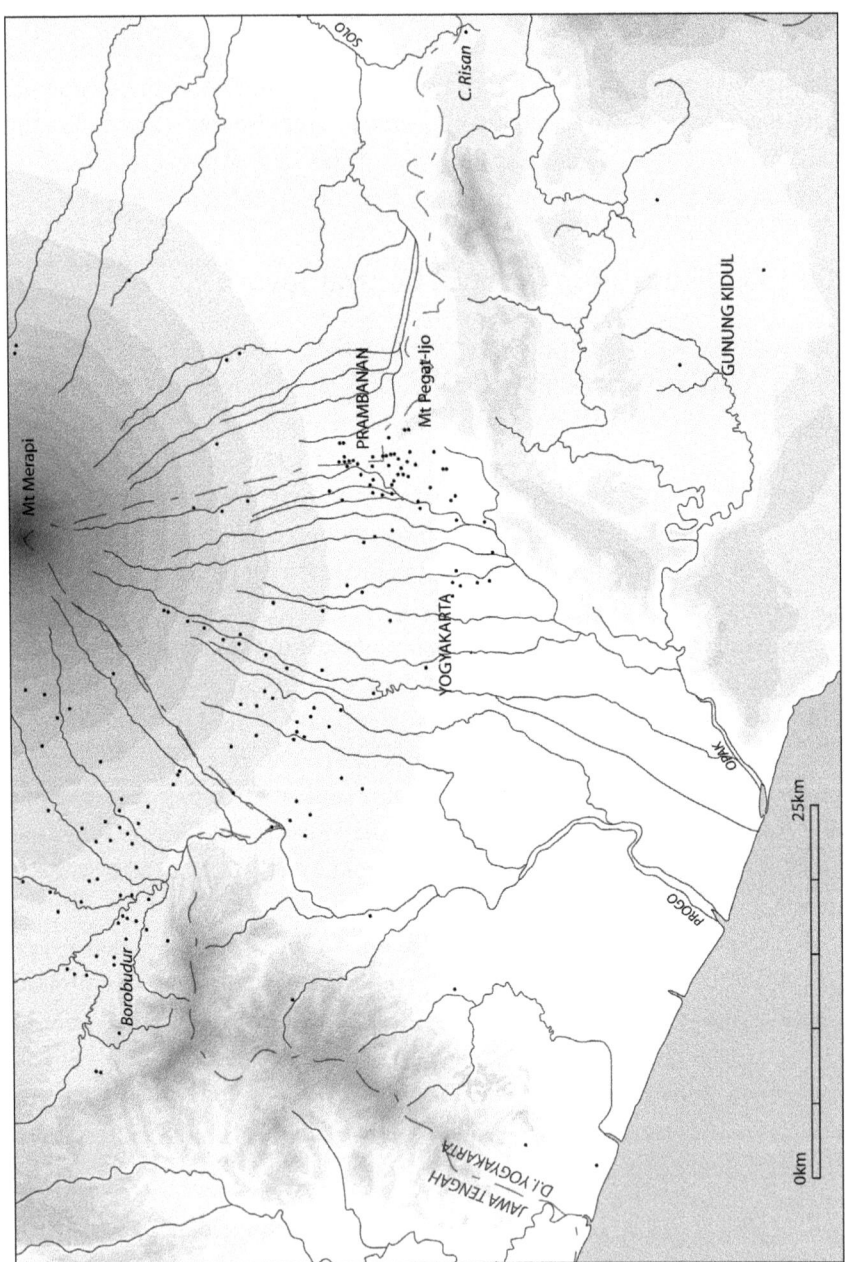

Figure 8.1 Distribution of temple remains in south Central Java
(Image: Véronique Degroot)

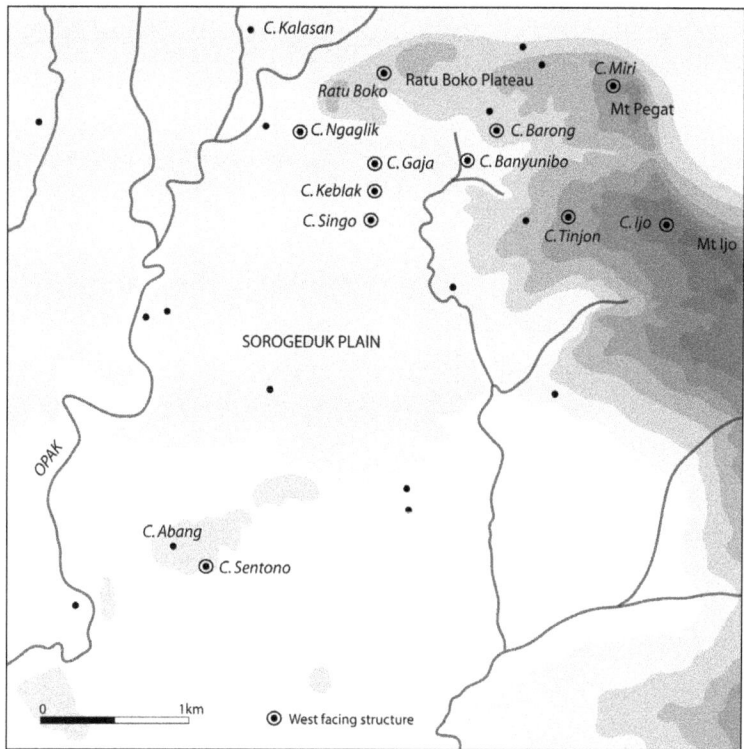

Figure 8.2 Temple remains of the Sorogeduk plain and Pegat-Ijo hills
(Image: Véronique Degroot)

The highest temple density is around the modern town of Prambanan, which can be seen as a transitional point in the natural landscape of the region (see Fig. 8.1). Prambanan is distinguished by a landscape of contrast, with both a fertile plain and dry steep hills. It is also situated where the plain is at its narrowest, constrained by Mount Merapi to the north and the northern tip of the Gunung Kidul hills to the south. Anyone travelling from the plain of Yogyakarta to the plain of Solo has to pass Prambanan. But Prambanan is not only a staging post on the Yogyakarta–Solo road; it is also a gate for the northern coast, as well as for East Java. That these roads, heading north and east from the Prambanan plain, were already well-established before the invention of modern means of transportation is testified by sources dating back to the 17th and 18th centuries, when the centre of Javanese power was located in the Yogyakarta/Solo region, as it had been in the heyday of the early kingdoms (Fig. 8.3).[9]

---

[9] See, among others, van Goens' account of his trip in 1656 (Goens 1856).

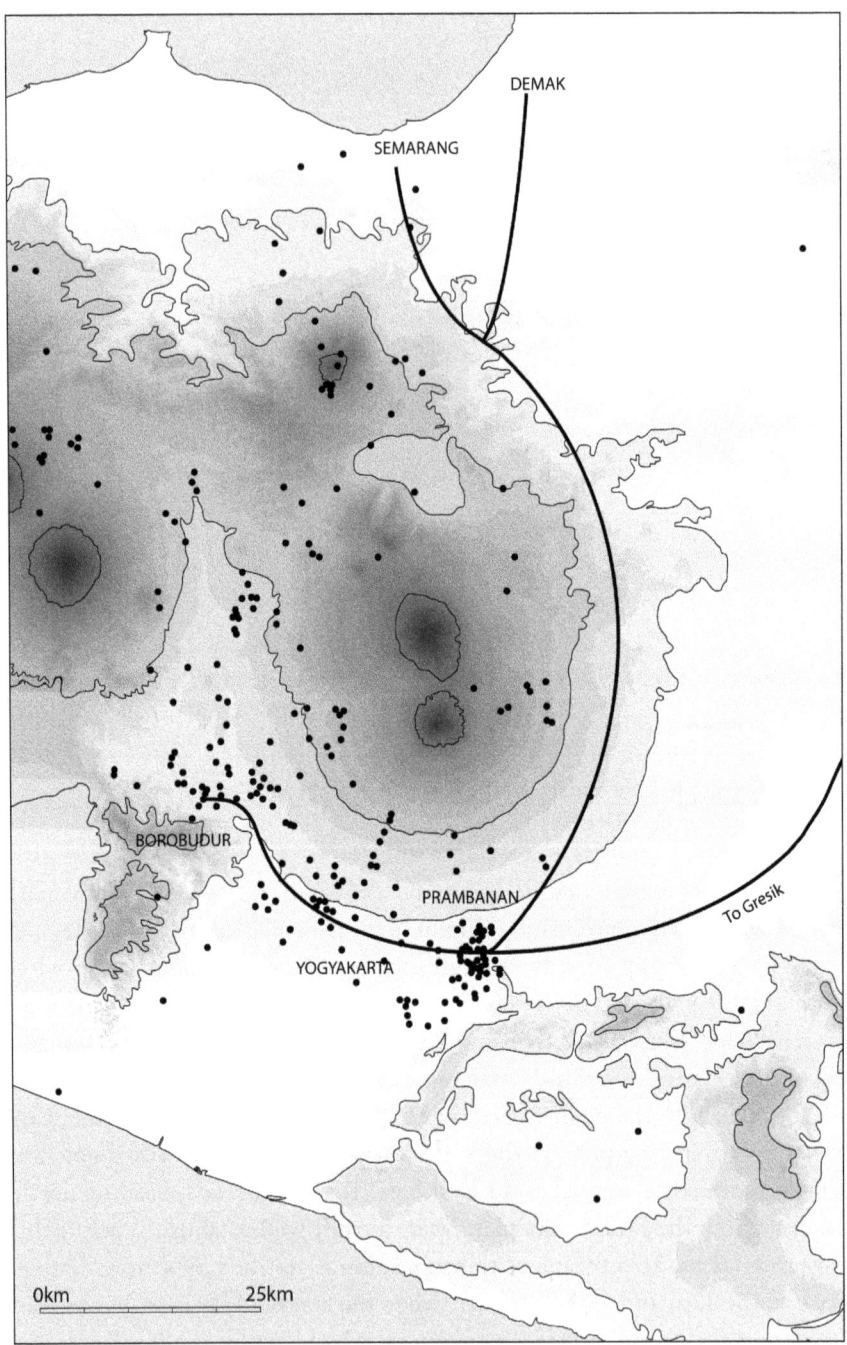

Figure 8.3 Main routes leading out of the Yogyakarta plain in the 17th and 18th centuries
(Image: Véronique Degroot)

Prambanan also occupies a specific place in terms of hydrography. Being located near the northwest tip of the Gunung Kidul hills, Prambanan marks the limit between the Yogyakarta plain and the Solo plain—in other words, between the Opak/Progo River system and the basin of the Solo River (see Fig. 8.1). A few hundred metres west of Prambanan, the rivers form tributaries of the Opak River which flows into the Indian Ocean. Immediately to the east of Prambanan, rivers join with the Bengawan Solo River, crossing the eastern part of the island and reaching the Java Sea near Gresik. Prambanan appears thus as a location of strategic and symbolic importance. Its proximity to the Solo basin is of the highest commercial importance; the Solo River could easily be used to ship goods from the east to the Prambanan area (and from Prambanan to the east) and constituted an alternative to road travel. In ancient times, the river seems to have been navigable even for larger ships, and in the 18th century the Solo River was the main trade route between Mataram and the coast (see Fig. 8.3). It was because of its location at the Solo River's mouth that Gresik developed as an important trading post (Jonge 1878:90).

Temple orientation

A close analysis of the surrounding landscape may help not only to get a better understanding of temple distribution, but also to provide a new insight into their orientation. In Southeast Asian archaeology, there is a tendency to assume that the natural orientation for religious buildings is for the entrance to face east. However, Central Javanese temples do not follow the pattern. It is true that Central Javanese temples tend to be oriented almost exactly around the cardinal points and that their entrance is always located on the east–west axis. The east is not particularly favoured, however; in fact, in south Central Java west-facing temples (22) considerably outnumber east-facing ones (12). There are probably many reasons for architects to opt for east or west. Some are already mentioned in Indian treatises on architecture, which do not consider the east as the sole possibility. According to these treatises, temple orientation may indeed be influenced by the position of the building within the settlement, or by the divinity to who the temple is dedicated.[10]

In south Central Java, it appears that temple orientation was also influenced by local topography and by the river courses. Here, local

---

[10] Mānasāra, IX:85; Mayamata, IX:85; *Agni-purāṇa*, 41:36.

topography seems to have played a key role in the orientation of some of the temple structures; those located on the northern tip of the Gunung Kidul and most of those dotting the Sorogeduk plain are indeed all facing west.[11] In this area, the hills form a sort of crescent encircling the eastern half of the Sorogeduk plain (see Fig. 8.2). Furthermore, the eastern façade of the Gunung Kidul is a steep cliff that offers little natural passage and the easiest access to the hills dominated by Gunung Pegat-Ijo is via the west. It is clear that, for topographical reasons, temple compounds were most easily approached from the west and it is, therefore, no surprise that they faced west.

This natural determinism does not mean that the western orientation was without symbolic value. First of all, although they realised that temples built there would have to face west, Javanese architects considered the location suitable for temple construction. This may indicate that, in their eyes, east and west were roughly equivalent symbolically. It may also mean that physical settings had more influence than other prescriptions and that temples were deliberately oriented with their backs to the mountain. As a matter of fact, temples are not built on the summit of the mountain, but on its western slopes, which means that the devotee praying in front of the temple is actually facing the mountain.[12] Outside the area of the Sorogeduk plain and of Gunung Pegat-Ijo, temple orientation is not as homogenous. East- and west-facing temples are found in equal number and without any clear reference to topographical features.

Keeping in mind the idea that, in south Central Java, temple orientation could have been intimately linked with the surrounding landscape, I started to study temples not on their own, but as part of a larger landscape, especially in relation with the river system. Temples built outside the Sorogeduk valley and the Gunung Pegat-Ijo hills seem to entertain some kind of relationship with the river system. Whatever the temple orientation

---

[11] The west-facing temples in the area of Gunung Pegat-Ijo and in the Sorogeduk plain are: Ratu Boko, Ijo, Miri, Tinjon, Arca Ganeca, Barong, Banyunibo, Gajah, Singo, and Sentono. The orientation of the following remains is unknown: Ngaglik, Watugudig, Keblak, Polengan, Polangan, Abang, Krapyak, Sawo, and Grembyangan. No east-facing temple has ever been reported from this area.

[12] Mountain worship might have been an important element of Central Javanese Hinduism. According to Wisseman Christie (2002–2004: no 4), line 2 of the Blado (Kepokoh) inscription (mid-eighth century CE?) may relate to this issue. A clear reference to mountains as dwelling places of spirits is found in the Kuṭi inscription. The inscription was found in East Java and dates from the Majapahit period, but it appears to be a reissue of a Balitung inscription (898–910 CE) (Sarkar 1971: I, no 12).

(east or west), in 17 out of 22 remains the river is located at the back of the building.[13] In only five cases, does the temple face the river.[14]

The fact that temples are located near rivers but that the river tends to be at the rear of the temple seems to suggest that rivers were not directly—or not solely—used by devotees for their ritual ablution. Just as a temple backed by a mountain could indicate a certain form of mountain worship, the placing of a religious building in front of a river could suggest that the water played a more significant role. The identification of a local watercourse with the sacred river Ganges is a frequent phenomenon in Hindu thought and ritual. Traces of it are clearly attested in Central Javanese inscriptions. The inscription of Canggal (732 CE), for example, states that 'there is a great island called Yava ... where there is a wonderful place dedicated to Sambhu, a heaven of heavens, surrounded by the Ganges' (Sarkar 1971:I,20). Although no similar inscription has survived from the area of Yogyakarta, the number of temples located along the *kali* Opak/Gendol should make us consider the possibility of its identification with the Ganges.

But the temple–river relationship is two-fold. A temple can benefit from the presence of purifying water, but a river can also acquire religious efficacy from the presence of a shrine on its bank. Such a situation is expressed in the short inscription of Pabaikan (early to mid-ninth century?) found near Ungaran in Kabupaten Semarang. The text reads: 'the hermitage of Pabaikan shall bubble forth well-being into the rivers' (Wisseman Christie 2002–04:no 29). Through this intimate relationship, natural and constructed landscapes mutually strengthen their religious power and are perceived by early Javanese society as an undivided and inseparable whole.

Indeed, the dichotomy between civilisation and wilderness is not explicit in the epigraphic data from Central Java. Although temples often have enclosures that firmly separate the inner, sacred space from the outer sphere, it is clear from the inscriptions that the natural environment remains within the religious realm and obeys the rules of the gods. In the curse formula that concludes numerous commemorative inscriptions, it is stated that the person who violates the charter will be punished by wild animals; if he goes into

---

[13] Karangnongko, Kaliworo, Plaosan Lor, Plaosan Kidul, Kalongan, Jetis, Kadisoka, Palgading, Morangan, Mantup, Sewu, Bubrah, Lumbung, Kedulan, Jetis, Prambanan, Gampingan.

[14] Merak, Sari, Kalasan, Gebang, and Sambisari. Of these five temples, Gebang is exceptional in that, although the nearest river is located east of the temple (thus in front of it), the site is close to a confluence, so that there is also a river to the west (at the back of the temple).

the river he will be eaten by crocodiles, and if he enters the forest he will be devoured by tigers or bitten by snakes.[15] It is striking that wild animals are seen as instruments of the deities to impose their will. The natural environment is not a mere setting, but an active supporter of *dharma*, whereas men themselves are viewed as possible wrongdoers and as disturbers of the world order.

Lists of cardinal points in inscriptions

As we have seen, temple orientation in south Central Java may be influenced by landscape markers (either hills or rivers), but buildings still must face either east or west; in spite of the importance of Mount Merapi for the local landscape, not a single temple is oriented towards it.[16] The preponderance of the east–west axis and the exchangeability of these two cardinal points may suggest that the Indian tradition is here being superimposed onto a pre-existing local concept. These observations, made on the base of the architectural remains, led me to take a closer look at the epigraphy in order to try to understand more deeply the concept of space in ancient Java. Unfortunately, this concept is not directly mentioned in the inscriptions. It is, however, present in the form of lists of directions usually given when delimiting the boundaries of donated fields or in the curse formulae concluding some inscriptions.

As in India, *pradakṣiṇā* (clockwise circumambulation) was part of Hindu and Buddhist ritual in Central Java. This fact is testified to by the reliefs and in the epigraphic data.[17] The inscription of Air Kali (928 CE), referring to the creation of a freehold, mentions that the people involved in the ceremony 'circumambulated the boundary, marking out the *sīma*' (Wisseman Christie 2002–04:no 206). Furthermore, in numerous inscriptions where cardinal points are mentioned, either in the body of the text or in the curse formula, the directions are listed in *pradakṣiṇā*. The inscription of Gaṇḍasuli II (810 CE?), for example, states 'throughout the kingdom, that he protects – in as many regions that there are in all the directions, in the east, south, west and north, all around – they praise the virtues of the *dang karayan partapān*'.[18]

---

[15] Curse formulae that include wild animals occur in the following inscriptions: Tru i Tpussan II (842 CE), Kañcana (860 CE), Wuatan Tija (880 CE), Mantyasiḥ I (907 CE), Sangsang (907 CE) and Sangguran (928 CE).
[16] According to the present state of knowledge, there are no south- or north-facing temples in south Central Java.
[17] The narrative reliefs of Borobudur and Prambanan must be read clockwise.
[18] English translation based on the transcription and Dutch translation of de Casparis (1950: 61-65). 'Het rijk, dat door hem beschermd wordt – zoveel streken als er zijn in alle

In all these inscriptions, the terms used for the various directions are of Sanskrit origin: *pūrwwa* (east), *dakṣiṇā* (south), *paścima* (west) and *uttara* (north), or Yama (south), Waruna (west), Kuwera (north) and Waśawa (east).

It is notable that directions are not always mentioned in *pradakṣiṇā* order. In the inscriptions of Mamali (878 CE) and Taragal (881 CE), freehold boundaries are even listed in *prasavyā* (counterclockwise, from east to south for Mamali and from north to east for Taragal). It may be deduced that, although the *pradakṣiṇā* was a well-known and important ritual, it was not automatically applied in every circumstance; directions could be listed in other ways, even in *prasavyā*. It seems that the latter was not especially connected to funerary rituals, death and destruction.

The inscriptions of Haliwangbang, Mamali, and Taragal belong to the same series of charters. The three inscriptions commemorate *sīma* made for the benefit of the same temple (Gunung Hyang). However, in the Haliwangbang inscription, the *sīma* boundaries are given in *pradakṣiṇā* order, while in the other inscriptions they are given in *prasavyā*. It is therefore not possible to maintain that the use of *pradakṣiṇā* and *prasavyā* relates to two different types of temple.

In fact, as it was the case for temple remains, the explanation might be that the Indian idea of *pradakṣiṇā* was being challenged by a local concept of space and directions. The clockwise circumambulation, although part of numerous rituals, had not been totally integrated into Javanese culture and was therefore somewhat inconsistently applied—hence the use of *prasavyā* in two of the inscriptions. Indeed, in Central Javanese inscriptions, there are already signs of the dualistic vision of the world that has characterised numerous traditional societies of the archipelago. These traces are visible in the inscriptions of Wuatan Tija (880 CE), Wanua Tengah III (908 CE), Sugih Manek (915 CE), Lintakan (919 CE), Gilikan (923 CE), Sangguran (928 CE), and Kampak (928–929 CE), where directions are listed in pairs—north–south and east–west. The terms used are no longer of Sanskrit origin, as employed when the directions are listed in *pradakṣiṇā*, but they are clearly Javanese (Klokke 1995: 82): *lor* (north); *kidul* (south); *wetan* (east); *kuluan* (west).

Sometimes, both lists are found in the one inscription, as is the case with the inscription of Wuatan Tija. In the first part, the gods of the directions are listed in *pradakṣiṇā*:

---

richtingen, in het oosten, zuiden, westen en noorden, dichtbij en verweg – zij prijzen de deugden van Z.H. Partapān' (Casparis 1950: 65).

> Be gracious, you gods Baprakeśvara [holy spirits of all directions] (...) Yama [south], Varuṇa [west], Kuvera [north], Vāsava [east] (...) you all deities who are known to protect the *kraton* [palace] of the illustrious great king [śri mahārāja] in the country of Mataram (Sarkar 1971, I: 257).

In the curse formula, however, the cardinal points are mentioned in pairs:

> When he goes to [dry] fields (...) may he be torn to pieces by titans [rakṣasas] summoned by ye holy spirits (...) guardians of the north, south, west, east (adapted from Sarkar 1971, I: 258 and Wisseman Christie 2002–04: no 108).

We may conclude that, as early as the second half of the ninth century, two perceptions of space were challenging one another among the elite of Central Javanese society. One was the imported *pradakṣiṇā* concept, which relates to space, time and the sun. The other was of Javanese origin, probably ancient, and was conceived in relation to a dualistic world. The apparent reticence about using *pradakṣiṇā* might come, as suggested by Klokke (1995:75–6), from the fact that the path of the sun is not as straightforward in Java as it is in India. Java is located in the southern hemisphere but near the equator. This means that for two thirds of the year the sun seems to be moving from east to west via the north (and not via the south as in the *pradakṣiṇā*). Hence, the association between the *pradakṣiṇā* movement and the path of the sun loses its relevance and becomes meaningless during most of the year. As the Javanese could not rely on the sun as a fixed point of reference they had to search for it elsewhere, and the most obvious source was their natural environment.

The notion of space as being fixed by two axes, a primary one relying on landscape markers and a secondary one based on the rising and setting sun, is quite common among traditional Indonesian societies. This suggests that the organisation of cardinal points into pairs, as in certain inscriptions, should probably be regarded as local in origin.

Conclusion

In south Central Java, both the location and the orientation of the religious buildings were influenced by the natural landscape. This relationship was not only economic and strategic, but also religious. Nature was perceived as an essential element within the divine order and, according to inscriptions, wild animals could be turned into divine weapons to punish those among humans who did not obey the gods' rules. This peculiar relationship between wilderness and the religious world can most probably be considered as a local trait.

The penetration of Indian traditions into Central Javanese culture did not mean the abandonment of local beliefs and concepts. Evidence for this is given in the lists of directions mentioned in Central Javanese inscriptions, where cardinal points are sometimes arranged according to the Indian *pradakṣiṇā* and sometimes organised in pairs according to Austronesian tradition. It is impossible, therefore, to maintain the idea that Central Java relied exclusively on Indian principles, in contrast to an East Javanese society that would have then re-introduced a local element. Indigenous concepts were already an essential part of Javanese civilisation in Central Java during the peak of the Indian influence. These concepts included a strong relationship between sacred sites, space and landscape.

Chapter 9

Mountains, forests and water

A new approach to the study of the Javanese temple complex of Sukuh

Jo Grimmond

The Graduate School, University of Queensland

The temple complex of Sukuh is situated on the western foothills of Mount Lawu, about an hour's drive from the city of Solo in Java. In 2004, the cultural heritage significance of Sukuh was recognised officially when the Indonesian government indicated it was considering the temple for nomination to the World Heritage List (UNESCO 2004:Annex 3,4). Today, the Sukuh temple complex is frequented by mystic groups and is an important pilgrimage site and ritual space during Javanese New Year celebrations. Significantly, the complex is one of the last remaining monuments constructed prior to Java's cultural transition to Islam. The enigmatic architecture and large corpus of statuary and reliefs at Sukuh provide invaluable insights into the religious beliefs and ritual practices of a rural community in Java during the 15th century, for which sources are rare. The Sukuh artwork communicates from the past a highly distilled form of meaning and provides a unique visual record of the physical, social and spiritual connections that one Javanese community created with its lived environment.

The site upon which Sukuh was built was a place of power in the landscape. The site exploits the most dramatic features of the surrounding countryside and demonstrates an appreciation of nature's beauty, a Javanese aesthetic (Patt 1982:469). Shrouded continually in mist, the top of Mount Lawu in the west provides a backdrop for Sukuh's large pyramid. Constructed on a hill at 910 metres, the site provides an aerial view of the lush river valleys of Karanganyar in the east, extending to a horizon framed by the volcanoes

Merapi and Merbabu. Connecting the site with the river valleys below is the water that cascades over the cliffs at Sukuh after monsoon rains, together with spring water emerging from the rock. Water is fundamental to the Sukuh monuments, which were designed to channel water over and through the architecture. The entire site was claimed from the forest, which frames the complex with its unique atmosphere. The rustling of the wind through the casuarinas creates a ghostly whistle and condenses the fog that forms at this altitude. During the 15th century, the forest was a refuge for herds of deer, wild cattle and large predators, all of which appear in the artwork of Sukuh. The mountain, water and forests emerge as significant aspects of the spirituality of the Sukuh community.

Eleven stone inscriptions at Sukuh, which date from 1416 to 1459 CE, provide evidence that this sacred place was utilised as a prime religious site for more than 60 years. It is feasible that ascetics who traditionally travelled the countryside visiting sacred springs sheltered in caves in the vicinity of Sukuh and later in structures made of bamboo, palm-leaf or wood. In time, the natural gradient was transformed into three terraces that are arranged like wet-rice fields up the side of the mountain. Causeways and three gateways provided access to the terraces, in addition to steps to the third terrace on the northern, southern and eastern sides. In the years 1437 to 1443, a growing

Figure 9.1 View of the third terrace at the Sukuh complex
(Photograph: Brian Graney)

repertoire of rituals led to the construction of more permanent stone structures, mostly on the third terrace (Fig. 9.1). These include the main temple (Fig. 9.2, D), a subsidiary temple that functioned as an offering place (Fig. 9.2, G) and two stone platforms—the southern platform (Fig. 9.2, E)

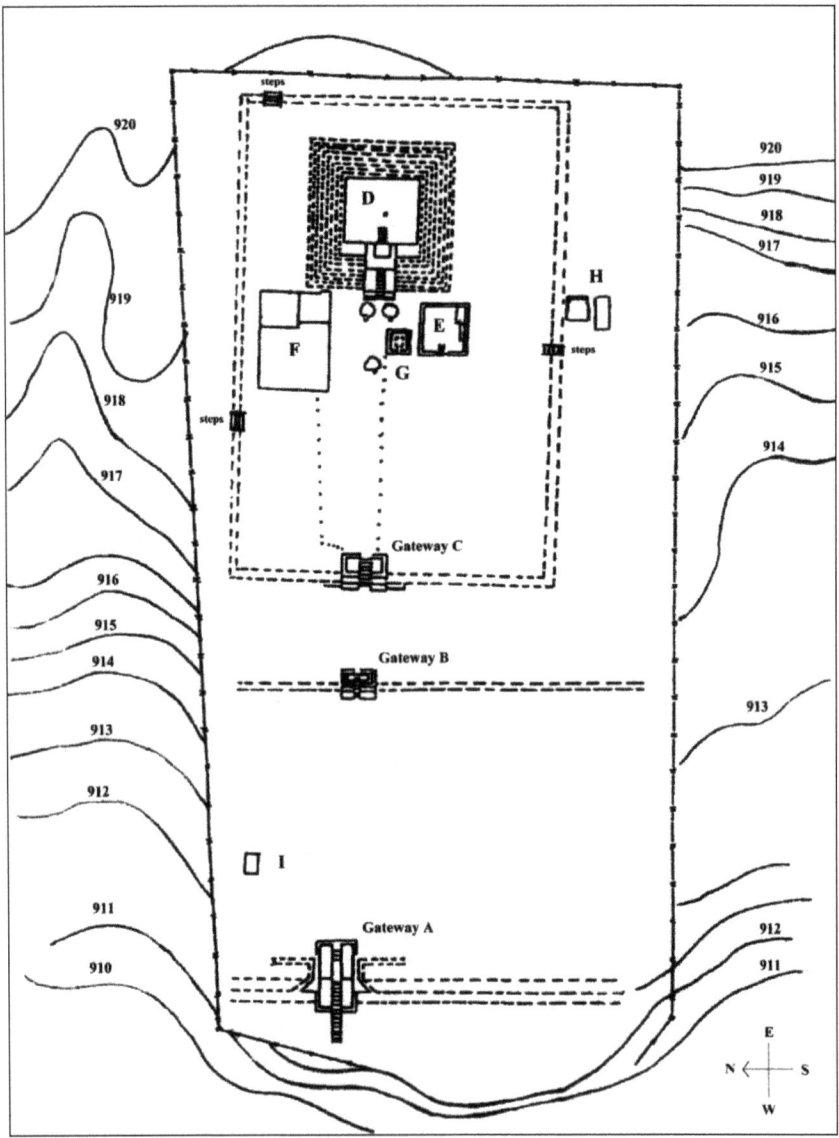

Figure 9.2 Site Map of the Sukuh complex
(Drawing: Jo Grimmond after Henri Cholis, 'Ulas rupa dan lambang pada kumpulan Candi Sukuh', Tesis Magister, Instituut Teknologi Bandung, 1998, 136.)

and northern platform (Fig. 9.2, F). A sacred pool or *tirtha* was constructed in 1439. The combination of temples, bathing place and hermitage in the vicinity of an important water source supporting a village was characteristic of a number of sites during the Hindu–Javanese period (Resink 1968:33).

Old themes and a new approach to Sukuh

Sukuh has received little scholarly attention since its rediscovery in 1815 by Major Martin Johnson, the British Resident at the court of Surakarta. The temple came to the attention of European scholarship in 1817 with the publication of Thomas Stamford Raffles' *History of Java* (1965:45–51). A more detailed survey of the antiquities by CJ van der Vlis appeared in 1843 (Vlis 1843). Before the Second World War, the Commission for Archaeological Research on Java and Madura in the Netherlands East Indies and its replacement organisation, the Dutch East Indies Archaeological Service (Oudheidkundige Dienst in Nederlandsch-Indië), produced inventories of the site at intervals (Verbeek 1891; Knebel 1910; Hoepermans 1913). NJ Krom, then head of the Archaeological Service, provided a summary in *Inleiding tot de Hindoe-Javaansche Kunst* (1923:v1,372–81). Since 1953, the Indonesian Archaeological Service (Dinas Purbakala) has administered the Sukuh temple. It was not until 1975 that Riboet Darmosoetopo (1976?) published a more up-to-date survey of the temple with an inventory of its sculptures, which remain on site or are housed in the Jakarta National Museum, Kraton Mangkuncgara in Solo and the Rijksmuseum in Amsterdam.

From the very first interpretation, Sukuh was considered different from other Hindu–Javanese temples. Basing his argument on its terraced design, truncated pyramid and obelisk shaped stones, Robert von Heine Geldern (1945:148,153) postulated that Sukuh was the product of a megalithic cultural complex which had produced stepped pyramids, assemblages of large stones, stone-cist graves and stone steps throughout Southeast Asia and Polynesia.[1] Heine-Geldern (1945:149) argued that these megalithic structures functioned to facilitate 'rites destined to protect a soul from the dangers believed to threaten it in the underworld and to assure its eternal life'. As a result, Sukuh gained a reputation as a megalithic monument which reflected indigenous religious practices devoted to mountain spirits, fertility cults and ancestor worship. In his 1930 guidebook to Sukuh, WF Stutterheim (1930:27–32) concluded that

---

[1] Heine-Geldern's theories were expounded in a series of articles dating from 1928 to 1966. A first summary was published in English in 1945.

the art at Sukuh was concerned with liberation from curses and the release of the souls of ancestors, although he admitted this was a broad view, as he had not examined the visual evidence in detail. Without supplementary analysis of the temple's visual components, AJ Bernet Kempers (1959:101) and, subsequently, Claire Holt (1967:30) presented Sukuh as a medium for the deliverance of the souls of ancestors from earthly bonds and a derivative of prehistoric art respectively. Based on these preconceived notions, misinterpretations of the inscriptions and inappropriate contextual sources, the leitmotiv of the liberation of souls became standard in the literature on Sukuh.

This chapter draws on new research that is based on the detailed description and analysis of the artwork at Sukuh on its own pictorial and intra-visual terms, complemented by literary sources (Sbeghen 2005). The research incorporates new directions in the field of Indonesian art history, including an interpretation of images in relevant geographical and architectural contexts, with consideration given to codes of representation and visual metaphor, the process of scene selection and cultural traditions. This new approach to the study of Sukuh produces fresh meanings and a more viable interpretation of the complex decorative program and religious functions of the site between 1437 and 1443. Evidence indicates Sukuh was not one temple, but a complex of sacred places that facilitated ritual practices concerned with a process of purification and spiritual empowerment. These rites were undertaken by a community drawn from the elite classes of Javanese society, who were motivated by an ideology centred on keeping the world in balance. The principal didactic model presented to this audience was the journey of warriors into the natural world of mountains and forests in order to meditate, to undergo ordeals, to summon gods for assistance, to bathe at sacred springs and do battle with demons. This religious ideology is consistent with what is known of Hindu–Javanese culture. Despite its differences, there is enough evidence from a close reading of the images to remove Sukuh from its peripheral context of megalithic art and position it back in the mainstream of Hindu–Javanese art to which Sukuh is related both thematically and iconographically.

Links between the Sukuh complex and the landscape

Javanese mountains play a vital role in agricultural productivity, as they trap clouds and increase rainfall which is fed into rivers draining the high regions with their bountiful volcanic nutrients (Wisseman Christie 1992a:8,11). According to Tony Day (1994:196), the water that descended from Javanese mountains was inscribed with symbolism, particularly if the water 'had first passed through a sculptured representation of the sacred Mahameru and descended to earth, no longer as mere water but as *amṛta*, the elixir of life'. The mountainous site upon which Sukuh was constructed was considered by the Sukuh community to be imbued with high concentrations of sacred power. The Sukuh *liṅga* inscription refers to this power as the 'quintessence of life'. The 'quintessence' embodied divine male and female essences and is symbolised as a *liṅga-yonī*, which is carved on the floor of gateway A (Fig. 9.3). This divinity, imbued with the power of purifying, revitalising and protecting life, was concentrated in the rain and spring water that flowed over and through the Sukuh temples. The Sukuh sculptors made numerous references to Javanese legends concerning *amṛta* flowing from Mahāmeru.[2] The production of *amṛta* was the principal function of the main temple, northern and southern platforms, and sacred *tirtha*. By partaking of the power of the springs, in conjunction with yogic practice, the adept believed this divine energy could be generated from within to gain liberation in the present lifetime and to achieve magical power. The images present exemplary models in the attainment of *amṛta* and the use of its power to maintain world order.

The main temple

The main temple at Sukuh is a representation of Mahāmeru. According to Hariani Santiko (1989:v2,316), Sukuh may be compared to other pyramid temples in Southeast Asia that are known to symbolise the cosmic mountain and the abode of god Śiva. The main temple, with its distinct pyramid form, is the focal point of the complex. The pyramid measures 20 metres square and consists of a coarse wall construction of roughly hewn rocks over a core of rubble. The upper part of the pyramid is an altar-shaped form constructed of seven courses of regularly faced stones. Access to the open-air platform on the top of the pyramid is via a set of steps on the western side. From the bottom, the visitor ascends fourteen steps and stands below a lintel created by a jetty before ascending a further ten steps to the top.

---

[2] Two accounts of the *amṛta* story survive in Old Javanese literature. In the Adiparwa version, which is based on the Indian Sanskrit story, *amṛta* emerges from the ocean after it had been churned using Mahāmeru as a stick. A later version that appears in the *Tantu Panggĕlaran* explains that Mahāmeru itself produced poisonous water which was transformed into *amṛta* by god Śiva.

The jetty is constructed of seven courses of worked stones and is shaped as a cornice. Entwined decoratively on top of the jetty are two serpents whose open mouths are spouts for a water channel that runs beneath the top layer of stones. The hydraulics of the waterworks on the main temple is presently not understood. It is possible that the pyramid functioned as a surface area with which to collect up to 3,000 litres of rainwater that flowed over the temple each day.[3]

Figure 9.3 *Liṅga-yonī* on the floor of Gateway A, Sukuh
(Photograph: Coffin Collection, National Library of Australia)

---

[3] This was calculated on 20 x 20 metres square and translates into 70,000 litres per month or one million litres per year. The steps may have dissipated the water flow into a channel that fed catchments.

The Sukuh pyramid may be identified as Mahāmeru using internal evidence, including its overall configuration and the iconography of its carvings. The main temple is orientated to the four cardinal points which are related to Mahāmeru, the centre of Hindu–Javanese cosmology. On the western side, three turtle sculptures mark the terrestrial world and may signify the waters that surround the mountain. The narrow staircase on the western side invokes the symbolism of ascent from the terrestrial world to a more purified realm in the celestial region. A band of alternating lotus-flower motifs forms a decorative band around the perimeter of the altar and demarcates the purified realm. Although the lotus has its roots in muddy waters, the lotus flower is raised above the water and is therefore a symbol of purity. Just below the lotus band, the jetty over the staircase creates a dark space that may signify passage through a cave. The two serpents on top of the jetty are water deities and protect the flow of water in the celestial realm. The symbolism of two serpents, a cave and water are reminiscent of the Adiparwa legend in which two fierce serpents with blazing eyes guard the *amṛta* stored in a cave on the sacred mountain (Phalgunadi 1990:83). The image of water flowing over the main temple, a representation of Mahāmeru and descending down the sides of Mount Lawu to transmit divine benevolence to the soil refers also to *amṛta*.

Connected with the main temple are a number of free standing sculptures of the mythological bird Garuda. The representation of Garuda is conventionalised at Sukuh—five erect tail feathers, a large wingspan of layered feathers, a long beak and the loincloth of an ascetic. Garuda is well known from the Adiparwa to have overcome enormous obstacles on his journey to Mahāmeru to procure *amṛta* (Phalgunadi 1990:73–85). The Garuda statues functioned in a similar way to Javanese Gaṇeśa statues, which were positioned in fields or at crossroads as the remover of obstacles and to control natural forces (Sedyawati 1994:251). Garuda statues were positioned along the causeway leading to the main temple as protectors of the flow of *amṛta* to the world. In one example, Garuda carries a pole across his shoulders (Fig. 9.4). A number of agricultural products are attached to the pole with strings. On the left, five coconuts, or possibly mangosteen, hang with a few bananas. On the right, two woven baskets are depicted, conceivably full of ripe fruit. At the bottom of one basket there are freshly picked rice stalks that have been tied into bundles. Garuda carries fruits of the earth and objects of human endeavour: coconuts and bananas picked from trees; rice grown in the fields; pottery and basketry made by human hands. These symbolise a prosperous and peaceful life based upon a fertile land and an obliging natural world, free from calamity.

Figure 9.4 Back view of a Garuda statue at Sukuh
(Photograph: Jo Grimmond)

On the northern platform is a stone upright, carved on two sides with images of Garuda. On one side, Garuda transports god Viṣṇu across the celestial realm (Krom 1923:v1,379) (Fig. 9.5). Viṣṇu sits on the shoulders of the gigantic bird with his *dodot* hitched, wearing ornate body decorations and a bejewelled headband with a flat-topped cap. The image portrays movement across the skies. The enormous bird 'with the wind protecting his wings; the moon, his back; and fire and air, his head' transports Viṣṇu across the heavens (Phalgunadi 1990:75). Viṣṇu's left hand is placed backwards on his hip, a confident riding posture, and he grasps the handle of an enormous weapon, raised in a sign of aggression. The normally benign face of Garuda manifests as a demon, a trait that Pauline Lunsingh Scheurleer (2000:202) argues signifies a divinity's destructive aspect and readiness to attack. The image demonstrates Viṣṇu and Garuda's roles in fighting obstructions to the flow of *amṛta*, which guarantees the prosperity of the world.

Figure 9.5 Garuda transports Viṣṇu across the celestial realm, Northern Platform, Sukuh
(Photograph: Jo Grimmond)

The northern platform

Contiguous with the main temple is the northern platform, 11.6 metres long, 7.8 metres wide and 0.85 metres high. It consists of eight courses of worked stones with cornices that are corbelled. The north side of the platform is severely damaged and, if there were stairs on that side, none remain. The tower on the southeast corner contains waterworks designed so that water flowed through the tower before exiting along a channel on the south side which ends with a gargoyle shaped like a serpent's head. Although the hydraulics of this waterworks is presently unknown, it is certain that the channel could deliver only a small amount of water, perhaps a few litres per minute. The water that flowed from the conduit was probably collected in pots for ritual purposes.[4] The

---

[4] Raffles (1965:43) reported a stone water-jar on the northern platform that is no longer in situ.

images that decorate the stonework on and around the conduit were designed to communicate the properties of this water. These include a set of reliefs carved on top of the tower and a large relief that leans onto the base of the tower.

The reliefs on top of the tower are carved on the western and southern faces only. On the western face are three rows of reliefs that depict Garuda in a version of the Adiparwa story. The surface area of Rows 4 and 5 has been extracted level with Rows 1–3. Row 3 depicts *bagawan* Vṛhaspati, preceptor to the gods, informing Viṣṇu and Bhatara Guru that Garuda will overpower them and obtain the *amṛta*. Row 2 depicts five forest trees that signify Mahāmeru. In Row 1 Garuda is depicted in profile perched outside a closed building on stilts, which has a tiled roof (Plate 9.1). It is the place where the *amṛta* is stored (Stutterheim 1930:23). The building faces outwards and is surrounded by thick earthen walls, on top of which are sharp metal fortifications. On the left is an entrance, across which is a wheel or *cakra*. According to the Adiparwa, at the entrance to the cave where the *amṛta* is stored is 'a wheel of sharply pointed iron, revolving incessantly, so that whosoever dares to enter would be cut into thousands of pieces' (Phalgunadi 1990:83). The Adiparwa relates that Garuda makes himself small and passes through the *cakra* to procure the *amṛta*.

The reliefs on top of the northern platform tower are carved relatively high above the ground and it would have been difficult for the adept during rituals to view the narratives at close range. The positioning of sculptures outside the normal viewing range of an audience was not uncommon on Hindu–Javanese temples. One example is the *jātaka* reliefs at the Borobudur temple which are difficult to see without crouching. Robert L Brown (1997:100) argues that the *jātaka* reliefs were not intended to be read as narratives, but functioned instead as icons in order to manifest the presence of god in the temple. The northern platform tower at Sukuh is a representation of Mahāmeru; thus it is feasible that the images around the top of the tower functioned as icons which transformed the water flowing though the tower into *amṛta*, a manifestation of the divine.

At the base of the northern platform tower is a large stone slab which would have been clearly visible to anyone partaking of the water. The slab, measuring 2.23 metres, leans onto the western side of the tower directly beside the water channel and serpent-headed gargoyle. The image is in four parts, with a *kāla*-deer head motif enclosing three rows of reliefs. The reliefs are to be read vertically from bottom to top, which emphasises progression through a series of stages. The reliefs concern the journey of the warrior hero Bima to obtain *amṛta*. In the bottom relief, Bima is a prisoner in his caul in Setra Gandamayu, the abode of the demon goddess Durga. Stutterheim

(1956:126) interprets the symbolism of the caul as Bima's performance of asceticism. Thus, rather than referring to physical birth, the relief signifies Bima's purification and spiritual empowerment. The middle row depicts the second phase in Bima's journey, in which he acquires a spiritual guide in the form of *ṛṣi* Narada (Stutterheim 1956:123). Above the relief on the middle row is a scaly two-headed serpent whose body, shaped not unlike the letter W, is similar to the rainbow bridge illustrated in Balinese manuscripts (Bosch 1931:486). The rainbow was considered to form a link between the earth and sky, and it seems Bima has journeyed to the heavens via the rainbow bridge.

The top row takes up over half the available space inside the *kāla*-deer head frame and was, therefore, designed to be the focus of the audience's attention. The relief represents the upper world, where the gods jealously guard the *amṛta*, which ensures their immortality (Fig. 9.6). On the left, on a pedestal, is Bhatara Guru who is given multiple arms and a hermit's headdress and is surrounded by an aureole filled with a spiral design that alludes to clouds or water. On the right stands Bima who is given traits that signify his supernatural qualities, including a *poleng*-patterned loincloth, tamarind-pod earrings, a *nāga*-shaped sacred cord and a long thumbnail (Stutterheim 1956:122). Bima has journeyed to the abode of the gods to obtain *tirtha amṛta*, which he considers the only means of obtaining release for his father Pandu and his wife Madri who are suffering in hell as a consequence of killing a brahmin (Stutterheim 1956:123).

Figure 9.6 Bima and Bhatara Guru, Northern Platform, Sukuh
(Photograph: Jo Grimmond)

Stutterheim maintained the relief was concerned with the liberation of Pandu and Madri, which reinforced his belief that Sukuh was an ancestor temple concerned with the release of souls. To the Sukuh community, as for all Javanese communities, ancestors remained a part of life and fulfilled a vital role in ensuring prosperity and fertility. Although Bima's motivation was to liberate his father, the Sukuh relief depicts Bima beseeching Bhatara Guru for *tirtha amṛta*. The relief is juxtaposed with the tower reliefs that depict the god's apprehension at Garuda's proximity to the elixir of immortality and Garuda perched outside the place on Mahāmeru where it is stored. In the Bima and Garuda reliefs, the visual emphasis is on obtaining *amṛta* from the gods. Garuda must fly through the *cakra* and Bima must convince Bhatara Guru that he qualifies to take the *amṛta*. Bima's traits signify his spiritual power, obtained through progressive stages of purification, as presented in the lower reliefs. The signs embedded in the Garuda and Bima reliefs indicate that the water that flowed from the conduit on the northern platform was considered transformed into *amṛta* and was associated with the attainment of liberation in the present lifetime, a goal of all asceticism. The water may have been regarded as having high medicinal value through which physical weakness was cured and direct entry to heaven procured, as in the case of Pandu and Madri, which is equivalent to the immortality of the gods.

The southern platform

The third waterworks on the upper terrace at Sukuh is on the southern platform. At the top of the attenuated tower on the southeast corner are two lotus motifs, symbolising the purified realm. Three quarters of the way down the north side of the tower is a water channel, similar to the conduit on the northern platform. The water appears to have exited on the south side through a gargoyle in the shape of a demon's mouth. The figure is possibly a *guhyaka*, who live in mountain caves and are among the demonic host of god Śiva (Raven 1988:112). The waterworks could not work in its present configuration. The channel could deliver only a small amount of water, however water may have been collected for ritual purposes.

On the western face of the tower is a medallion, four blocks high, framing the figure of a deity (Fig. 9.7). The god wears an ankle-length *dodot* secured by a waistband and girdle. His ornate body decorations include upper-arm bands, bracelets, a double necklace, earrings and jewellery worn over his ears. The headdress is a high crown that consists of a series of crescent moons. His arms are bent symmetrically and in each hand is a weapon—either a double-headed trident or a long-stemmed *bajra*, a symbol of lightning and thunder. The pedestal has the form of a crescent moon, beneath which is a rectangle and five verticals that drape down. With no standard iconography incorporated, identification of this deity is difficult. The deity is highly ranked, as he is the only god at Sukuh depicted entirely *en face* with feet turned outwards. It is unlikely to be Bhatara Guru, as he is depicted at Sukuh with head in profile, multiple arms and a hermit's headdress. The deity in the medallion is extremely powerful, for his elbows radiate *teja*. The medallion may function as a luminous halo, or to separate the god from all other beings. The crescent moon headdress and pedestal appear to drip with fluid, alluding to an association with water and *amṛta*, of which the moon is a repository. Whichever god this icon represents, the water that flowed through the tower must have been considered potent, as it was imbued with the powers of this deity, who may have been considered the source of *amṛta* or, at least, to control its flow.

Figure 9.7 Deity on the Southern Platform tower, Sukuh
(Photograph: Jo Grimmond)

The Sukuh *tirtha*

The construction of a *tirtha* at Sukuh is memorialised in an inscription dated 1439, but all that remains are nine stone slabs carved with reliefs. The inscription describes the *tirtha* as *sunya*, that is, a place of quiet, a peaceful retreat away from the noise and activity of the social world. The term *tirtha* refers generally to water in a pool, river or sacred bathing place (Zoetmulder 1982:2019). Ritual bathing is described in most *kakawin* and sacred *tirtha* are admired for their purifying and salutary powers (Klokke 1993:150). The word *tirtha* embodies the idea of passage from one state to another (Kramrisch 1976:I,3). It is within the architectural context of a *tirtha* and the conceptual context of individuals entering water as a form of passage from one state to a more purified state that the nine reliefs must be interpreted.

The nine bathing-place reliefs depict the actions and ideological agenda of *kṣatria*. A *kṣatria* in the wider literary context of court poetry is a leader whose duty it was to use his spiritual strength and heroism in battle to maintain world order. In Javanese art *kṣatria* embody 'the dual nature of princely heroics and spiritual obligations' (Levin 2000:250). The bathing-place reliefs present the *kṣatria* Sadewa and Nakula, Bima and Arjuna as didactic models (Sbeghen 2005:170–91). The sculptor selected images that portray the *kṣatria* outside the social world in the liminal world of forests undergoing ordeals and confronting gods and demons. As the adept entered the waters of the *tirtha*, they could ponder the arduous mental combat confronting Sadewa in the place of the dead, be inspired by the determination and power of Bima to destroy a ferocious demon, a manifestation of his desires (Duijker 2001), and celebrate the strength and skill of Arjuna in his role as maintainer of world order. This journey of *kṣatria* into the mountains and forests belies a deeper meaning of engaging with the spiritual world to acquire divine power (Worsley 1986:349). Thus the reliefs mirror the journey that members of the Sukuh community had themselves taken to reach the relative isolation of the temple in the mountain forests to undergo their own purification and empowerment.

One relief of the Sukuh *tirtha* depicts Sadewa and his twin Nakula (Fig. 9.8). The sculptor has depicted the stronghold of the Pandawa family in an episode from the Sudamala story. This compound signifies the social world, the boundary of which is marked by a high masonry wall. Inside the compound is an open pavilion, its six-pillars signifying everyday use, and is possibly sleeping quarters, an area for food preparation or assembly (Galestin 1936:121). On the right is a pavilion with a three-tiered *meru* roof, wooden floor and four posts set in pillar bases, possibly a sacred place. Areca nut and coco palms beautify the ordered grounds. By presenting a bird's eye view of the compound, so that the details of its interior are visible, the sculptor creates a dichotomy between the world inside the compound, where established gardens and pavilions for routine life engender an atmosphere of safety and order, and outside the compound, which is the natural world. Sadewa and Nakula stand outside the social world heading towards the forest, a dangerous world where wild animals and innumerable demonic spirits create disorder, as illustrated by the demon lying dead in the foreground.

Sadewa, who turns to face Nakula to discuss their return to the social world, encapsulates the meaning of this relief (Stein Callenfels 1925:137). Two peacocks in the upper part of the relief mirror the behaviour of the two brothers. The first peacock sits on top of the jackfruit tree; its body faces left, but its head faces right in the direction of another peacock that flies towards the compound. In *kakawin*, the peacock is a motif of the social realm and identified with gateways (Zoetmulder 1974:200). Their depiction in the relief away from the gateway reinforces the message that the *kṣatria* must return to the social world. This episode communicates the idea that the journey into the liminal zone is not a singular event but one of many a true *kṣatria* must undertake in order to fulfil his spiritual obligations and demonstrate his heroics on the battlefield. Members of the elite class in Javanese society who journeyed to Sukuh to be purified and empowered understood they too must return to the social world to uphold their duties as *kṣatria*.

Figure 9.8 Relief belonging to the sacred tirtha at Sukuh
(Drawing: Jo Grimmond)

Conclusion

During the 15th century, the Sukuh complex transformed a sacred locality into a religious setting. The Sukuh community believed that the universe was impelled by a divine power and that this power was concentrated in the water that flowed over and through the architecture at the site. Transformed into *amṛta*, water is the reason Sukuh was a place potent with magical power; it is the purifying power that the *kṣatria* who journeyed to Sukuh were in search of, and it gave the mountain rains at Sukuh the power of revitalising and protecting life, which benefited the lowland communities visible from the complex.

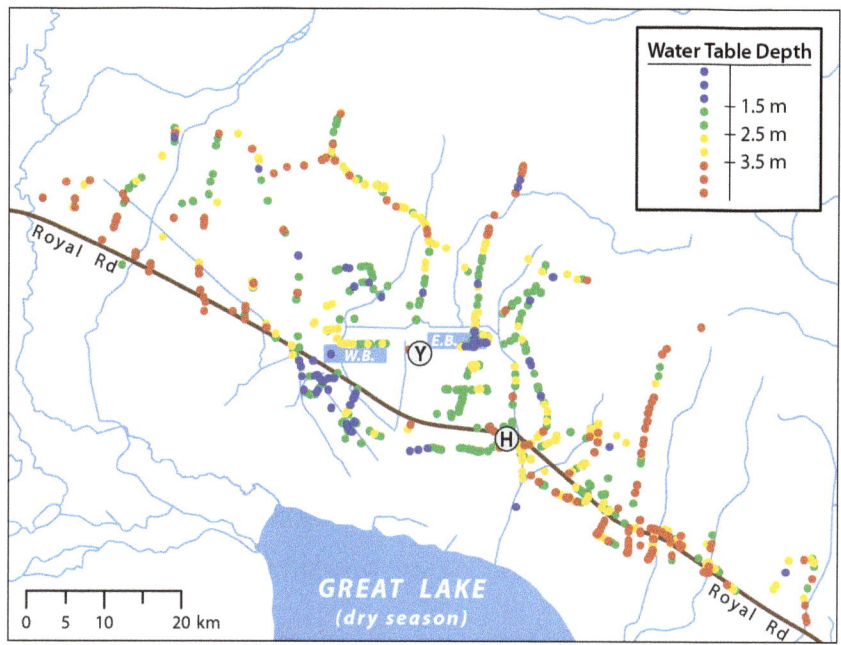

Plate 3.1 Locations and water-table levels of measured wells in the southern Siem Reap province

This map, prepared by Cameron Reed, University of California at Berkeley, depicts most of Siem Reap province. The location of the first capital, Hariharalaya, is shown by a capital H, and the location of the second capital, Yasodharapura, is shown by a capital Y. The ninth-century East Baray and the eleventh-century West Baray are the two rectangles to the east and west of Yasodharapura. The Great Lake is shown at its smallest, dry-season extent.

Blue dots represent very high water-tables—those within 1.5 metres of the surface when measured halfway through the dry season.

Green dots represent high water-tables—those more than 1.5 but less than 2.5 metres below the surface when measured halfway through the dry season.

Yellow dots represent mid-level water-tables—those more than 2.5 and less than 3.5 metres below the surface when measured halfway through the dry season.

Red dots represent low water-tables—those more than 3.5 metres below the surface when measured halfway through the dry season.

Plate 5.1 The central image in the temple of Po Romé, in which an image of the king is enshrined in the form of Śiva

Plate 5.2 Hill of Đá Trắng
Children playing on the semi-translucent feldspar or quartz rock that makes up the hill of Đá Trắng. The Vietnamese name 'Đá Trắng' means 'White Rock'.

Plate 9.1 Garuda outside the place where the amṛta is stored on Mahameru, Northern Platform tower, Sukuh

(Photograph: Jo Grimmond)

Plate 10.1 At Trowulan, the two-metre difference in elevation between irrigated rice land (*sawah*) and the original land surface enables farmers to grow two crops per year

Plate 10.2 Topography of Trowulan

White:	low-lying irrigated land
Green:	dry land, village, roads, etc approximately two metres higher
Brown:	foot of Anjasmoro volcanic complex
Red lines:	survey transects of 1991
Blue lines:	survey transects of 1992
Orange lines:	survey transects of 1993

Plate 13.1 A rendering of Banteay Srei temple
(Reproduced with permission of the digital artist, Bruno Truffert)

Plate 13.2 Screenshot from Philip Day's *Lost Worlds: City of the God Kings*, showing the centre of Angkor Thom. The trees shown appear to be date palms.
(Reproduced with permission of Philip Day)

Plate 13.3 An image captured from a 3D animation of circling around the east of Angkor Wat, with Phnom Bakheng in the upper right of the image

Crowds of tiny animated figures walking the paths can be discerned on the lower right quarter of the image.

(Image and model: Tom Chandler and Michael Lim)

Plate 13.4 A view of the northwest corner of Angkor Wat's moat in the virtual model

The layout of settlement is based on cartographic layers in the Greater Angkor Project map. Here, the position of the virtual camera is placed not far from the location of the tourist balloon in the Angkor Archaeological Park.

(Image: Tom Chandler and Michael Lim)

Plate 13.5 A set of three village shrine models, each row of images showing a left to right progression, working from geometric outlines to textured and coloured renders

The first row represents a seventh-century shrine type based upon Prasat Andet. The second row represents a tenth-century shrine and the third row approximates a 12th-century shrine.

(Modelling: Tom Chandler and Carol Merlo)

Plate 14.1 Pilgrims worshipping the tree planted by Mahmud Kashgari, located near his mausoleum (*mazar*)
(Photograph: AA Di Castro)

Plate 14.2 Threads and ribbons tied to the tree planted by Mahmud Kashgari
(Photograph: AA Di Castro)

Chapter 10

Life among the ruins

Habitation sites of Trowulan

John Miksic
Associate Professor, Southeast Asian Studies Programme,
National University of Singapore

The village of Trowulan (anciently called Antarasasi), 55 kilometres southwest of Surabaya, east Java, is the site of the 14th-century capital of Majapahit. Raden Wijaya, founder of Majapahit, established his capital at Trik, now Tarik, 20 kilometres to the east, and probably moved to Trowulan in 1294. Since we have no information on the principles according to which premodern settlements in Indonesia were laid out, we cannot determine whether Trowulan evolved from earlier patterns or whether it constituted a radical departure from an older pattern. Attempts to reconstruct the spatial organisation of Majapahit's capital began in the early 20th century. Ir H Maclaine Pont, who was in charge of the Trowulan sugar plantation in the 1920s, explored the site and published some of his conclusions, but, unfortunately, without much supporting data. His work is interesting, nevertheless, because he had extensive local experience.

He composed an elaborate reconstruction of Trowulan based on the *maṇḍala* concept. How much is based on observation and how much on imagination is impossible to estimate. According to oral tradition, he exposed buried ruins with high-pressure water hoses; the villagers took advantage of the opportunity to carry off the bricks. Pigeaud (1960–63:IV,12) found that his town plans 'do not carry conviction, [but] his idea that the town covered a considerable area of land no doubt is right'.

Archaeological data may be biased by the destruction of huge portions of the site of Trowulan, but available information does not support Maclaine

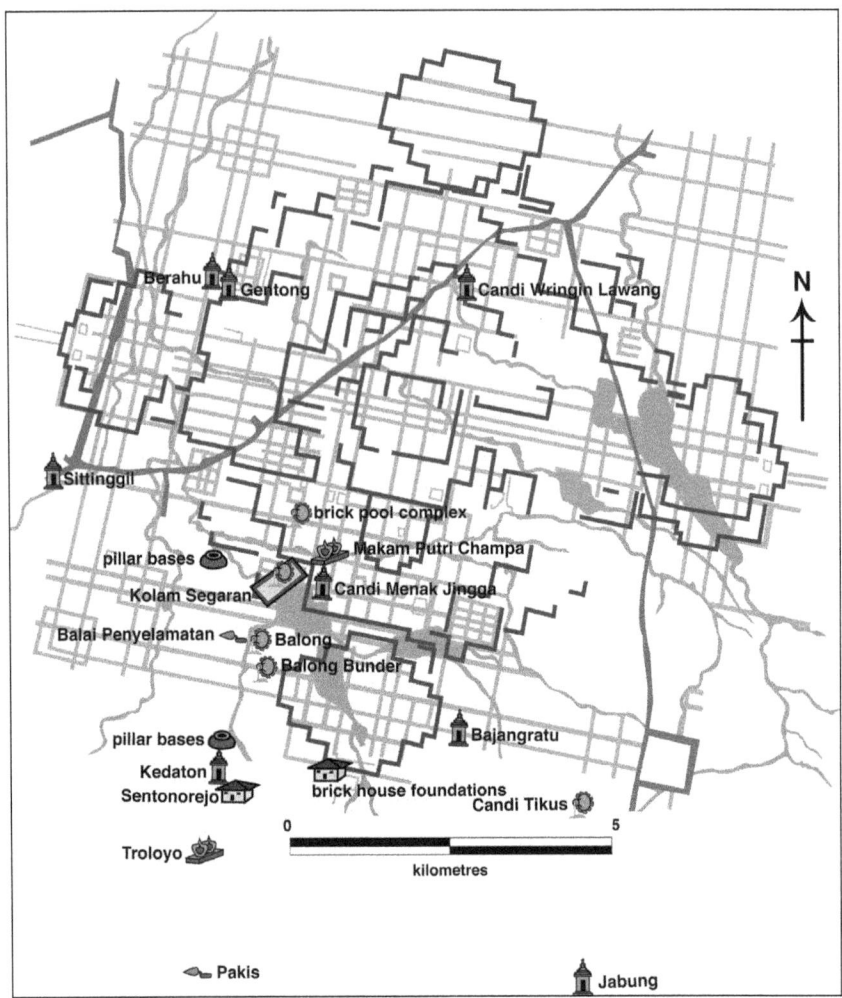

Figure 10.1 Maclaine Pont's 1926 reconstruction of Majapahit's capital as a *maṇḍala*

Pont's vision of a huge urban *maṇḍala*. *Maṇḍala* concepts were influential in central Java's sacred places, such as Loro Jonggrang and Candi Sewu, but there are no comparable temples in east Java. The word *maṇḍala* was used often in east Javanese inscriptions, but in references to religious communities rather than to ground plans. Trowulan's remains display patterns suggestive of a predetermined layout. Unlike the *maṇḍala*, the Majapahit capital was not defined by a rectilinear wall. Indonesian cities were not walled until the Islamic period. If the *maṇḍala* was not the concept underlying Trowulan's plan, then what was?

Paul Wheatley wrote two influential books on Asian cities. He argued that 'traditional' non-Western cities evolved as ceremonial rather than economic centres (Wheatley 1971). Religious rather than economic factors would have been the critical variables determining urban ground plans. He later argued that the origins of Southeast Asian cities lay outside the region—in China for north Vietnam, in India for the rest of the region (Wheatley 1983).

Two major objections may be made to the general approach to conceptualising early Southeast Asian cities typified by Wheatley. First, they conflate different sets of variables into one analytical category, assuming a perfect correlation among them, and second, they present an image of the city as a discrete category. While some sites, such as Angkor, were no doubt laid out mainly according to ceremonial principles, they show no signs of dense populations. Other sites, such as Oc Èo, may have had dense populations, but centres of ceremonial activity do not seem to have dominated them, either symbolically or economically. The way out of this conundrum is to reformulate the question. A multilinear, polythetic definition of settlement patterns is needed, rather than an ethnocentric assumption that the modern Western city is the most advanced example of a single evolutionary progression (Miksic 2000). In a multilinear model of settlement pattern evolution, one dimension of variation consists of a spectrum from one pole, consisting of cities with ground plans completely dictated by religious concepts, to the opposite pole, in which all is determined by economics. Most settlements probably contain differing combinations of these factors; individual cases can be ranked on a scale, according to the relative influence exerted by praxis versus idealism.

If Southeast Asian cities were imported from India, and if Indian cities evolved on the basis of ritual principles, they should conform to certain criteria. The Arthaśāstra, an influential Indian text, provides instructions for city planning. The ideal ground plan is a grid, of which each square is allocated to a specific occupational or status group. *Brahmins* should live in the north, *kṣatriyas* in the east, *vaiśyas* in the south and *śūdras* in the west. The palace should stand in the centre.

One archaeological correlate for such a pattern would be a segregated distribution of occupational specialisation. A test of this theory at Anuradhapura in Sri Lanka indicated a uniform distribution of various craft activities throughout the site instead, from the Iron Age (ca. 900 BCE) to the 11th century CE. Anaradhapura's layout incorporates some cosmological imagery, but:

such imagery was only one of a number of contesting 'texts' present within the urban form. Even at that period, as we have seen with the case of Anuradhapura, economic dynamics are clearly visible within the 'artefactual' record, forming a 'contestational' reading (Coningham 2000:354).

Christie (1992b) believed that Majapahit's capital bore little resemblance to a modern city. Evers (1984:146) concluded that 'the early Indonesian or Javanese capitals do not seem to have matched an urban image…The spatial perception is centrifocal, and the centre is the kraton or istana of the ruler rather than a capital city.' Javanese literature, the source of these generalisations, focuses on political and religious aspects of capitals, with some information about the economy. Residential areas, whether large or small, dense or dispersed, are ignored. This omission may be significant, but what does it signify? Does it indicate an absence of dense habitation, or lack of interest on the part of the authors? These questions should be tested with data, rather than simply made the subject of assumptions.

Figure 10.2 Fourteenth-century temple relief
This relief depicts a mountainous landscape with a road leading to a distant cluster of walled pavilions, perhaps a *maṇḍala* community

Trowulan, the axis of the world, and the four quarters

Indonesian cosmological thought includes the *axis mundi* and the four-fold division of the world. In Balinese cosmology, the southwest and northeast quarters are auspicious, while the intersection of two axes is powerful and dangerous. Rather than being marked by structures, crossroads were left empty until recent times, when the government began to erect large statues in them, interfering with processions.

Roads have been neglected as a potential factor in the spatial organisation of temples and settlements in Indonesia. Enough information is now available to establish that Trowulan's plan was dictated by two axes oriented approximately 14 degrees southeast of true north–south and east–west. The site was originally oriented to a mountain, Penanggungan, 30 kilometres southeast of Trowulan. Later buildings are oriented further southeast, toward Mount Arjuna. The east–west axis was the key direction which determined the orientation of the north–south axis. The chthonic mode of thought has been acknowledged as a significant criterion in the design of temple plans in east Java (Baskoro 1993). It was probably used in the design of Trowulan as well.

Figure 10.3 View of Mount Penanggungan from Jabung, five kilometres southeast of Trowulan

Trowulan has been severely altered in the past 100 years. Generations of farmers have lowered much of the original land surface by approximately two metres (see Plate 10.1). In the process, they have ground to dust much of the ancient capital—its bricks, its artefacts, its bones. Ironically, some of the brick dust has been added to soil in local brickyards, or *bengkel bata*, to make new bricks, which are sold in Surabaya and other large towns. Despite this distortion, one can still see an axial pattern in the modern roads and water features, which, it is logical to infer, reflects a 14th-century situation (see Plate 10.2).

The centre of the site was neither a temple nor a palace, but an intersection. The Deśawarṇana, Canto 8, in its description of the 'awe-inspiring royal palace', refers to 'the crossroads, other-wordly in its elegance' (Robson 1995:29). Pigeaud (1963:V, plate II) gave particular prominence to this feature in his reconstruction of the palace. This crossroads probably corresponds to the intersection near the hamlet of Nglinguk, just north of Pendopo Agung. The north–south road runs from Pakis past Troloyo, Kedaton, Sentonorejo, and Segaran, to the east of Berahu. The east–west road, aligned with Mount Penanggungan, runs from Mojoagung, the largest town in the vicinity about five kilometres to the west of the crossroads, to Bajangratu and Candi Tikus.

Figure 10.4 Candi Berahu

Figure 10.5 Bajangratu

Figure 10.6 Candi Tikus

These two roads divide the site into four quarters, conforming to the Arthaśāstra, but the allocation of space in the Deśawarṇana makes no reference to *varṇas*. The four quarters thus formed probably expressed the fundamental design principal governing the layout of the capital. As at Loro Jonggrang, where the centre of the site was occupied by a small shrine to the local gods of the soil, the centre of Majapahit was probably also perceived as dangerous. Again, contrary to the Arthaśāstra's advice, but consistent with Balinese cosmology, the royal quarter was in the southwest, where Kedaton ('palace') and a number of other hamlets are found, including Sentonorejo (*sentana*, an official rank), Kemasan (*mas*, 'gold'), where gold has been found, and Sumur Upas ('well of poison'), probably where oaths of loyalty were taken. Most religious edifices that have survived lie along the north–south axis.

One reason why Trowulan has not attracted much interest from either the public or from historical preservationists is its dearth of monuments. The city's plan dictated the placement of religious structures rather than the reverse. The city was not a major centre of religious life. The Deśawarṇana describes official places of worship around the palace in Canto 8, stanzas 3 and 4, but most major religious complexes lay not in the capital; they were scattered through outlying districts, which the court visited on royal progresses. The Deśawarṇana describes these processions, which in some years travelled hundreds of kilometres, filling the breadth of the royal highway with carriages, oxcarts, elephants and horses. Important nobles had carriages with their own symbols, such as a sun, a bull or a flower. Travel by road seems to have been a regular form of transport. It is not surprising, therefore, that roads dictated the form of the royal capital. Canto 86, stanza 2, states that the field of Bubat, where public spectacles took place, was the north of the city. Bubat was bounded on the east by 'the royal road' and on the north by a river. The royal road ran from the city to some other location, perhaps the bank of the Brantas River or beyond. That there were ferries at rivers to assist overland transport is proven by the Ferry Charter of 1358 (Pigeaud 1962:IV,399–411), which regulates ferries in the Brantas and Solo rivers, and another charter from the upper Solo River, dated 903.

The 15th-century Chinese text Yingyai Shenglan said that the country of Java had four unwalled towns. Majapahit, 'where the king lives', was a royal residence 1.5 days' walk from the nearest place accessible by river (Groeneveldt 1960:46). Thus, the capital was linked to the nearest waterway by land; it was not directly dependent on water transport for provisioning.

The kingdom's interest in land transport is further manifested in the Deśawarṇana, Canto 88, stanza 2, where the prince of Wengker, one of the principle nobles, orders local officials to make their districts prosperous by constructing and maintaining bridges, main roads, *waringin* trees, houses and other useful public works (Robson 1995:89).

Figure 10.7 Wringin Lawang

Alfred Russel Wallace passed through Trowulan in 1861 (the main road between Surabaya and Jakarta still runs through Trowulan):

> On our way we stayed to look at a fragment of the ruins of the ancient city of Modjo-pahit, consisting of two lofty brick masses, apparently the sides of a gateway. [This must have been the site of Wringin Lawang, which is near the main east–west road which still runs near the ancient gateway.] The extreme perfection and beauty of the brickwork astonished me. The bricks are exceedingly fine and hard, with sharp angles and true surfaces. They are laid with great exactness, without visible mortar or cement, yet somehow fastened together so that the joints are hardly perceptible, and sometimes the two surfaces coalesce in a most incomprehensible manner. Such admirable brickwork I have never seen before or since…Traces of buildings exist for many miles in every direction, and almost every road and pathway shows a foundation of brickwork beneath it—*the paved roads of the old city*. (Wallace 1869:I,101–2 [emphasis added])

Unfortunately, the preservation of Wringin Lawang, the brick gateway in the northeast sector of Trowulan that Wallace saw in 1861, is an exception. In 1939 the archaeological report *Oudheidkundig Verslag* published warnings about 'roving collectors' at the site. Between 1975 and 2005, a vast area of brick ruins mixed with millions of artefacts was consumed by local *bengkel bata*.

Archaeological research

The Indonesian National Research Centre for Archaeology (Puslit Arkenas) investigated Trowulan from 1976 to 1990 (Pusat Penelitian Arkeologi Nasional 1995). The site was defined as a single 'cultural unit', one urban system consisting of habitation clusters. This conforms to the image of Trowulan as a set of discrete walled compounds containing residential quarters similar to modern Balinese *banjar*. The Deśawarṇana refers to them as *kuwu*. It should be possible to discover discrete characters and functions of these habitation clusters by analysing artefacts discovered within them. These should include the king's palace, other royal residences, residential areas of the general population, ceremonial centres, and industrial zones.

The Centre's research began with a survey to determine the limits and nature of the distribution of archaeological remains on the site. The survey covered an area of 100 square kilometres. Over 15 years, the Centre excavated the Pendopo Agung (Great Pavilion), Pandan Sili, Klinterejo, Sentonorejo, Nglinguk, Sumurupas, Kejagan, Kedaton, Batok Palung, Wringin Lawang, and Blendren.

Pendopo Agung

Excavations in the Pendopo Agung sector sought to determine the form of Majapahit-period residential structures. Forty-seven squares measuring two by two metres were dug with the aim of exposing the floor plans of brick buildings. A wide variety of artefacts was uncovered, including many forms of local earthenware, as well as stoneware and porcelain from China, Thailand, and Vietnam. Metal objects found include tools and Chinese coins. Dietary remains, including bone and shell, reinforce the inference that this area formed a residential sector. Brick features and dense remains of clay tiles were interpreted as foundations and roofs of houses.

The Pendopo Agung sector was occupied during more than two phases; it had probably been inhabited for several centuries before Majapahit was established. This conclusion is based on the presence of several layers of foundations made of bricks of different dimensions, foreign ceramics and Chinese coins. Chinese ceramics dated from the Song (tenth-13th centuries), Yuan (13th-14th centuries) and Ming (14th-16th centuries) dynasties. Thai stoneware from Sawankhalok and Sukhothai, and Vietnamese ware (14th-16th centuries) were also present.

Segaran

Another habitation zone was excavated by the Faculty of Letters, University of Indonesia. Excavation about 400 metres southwest of the Segaran Pool revealed foundations of buildings floored with cobblestones, interior partitions, and a well. A foundation measuring four by two metres, of which the long sides were oriented about 12 degrees northeast, lay upon a disturbed layer of fill containing fragments of brick and earthenware. The building was provided with a brick drain.

A room measuring 4.5 by 2.6 metres, parallel to the rectangular foundation, adjoined the north side of the well. Three of the room's four sides were marked by a single layer of brick, the exception being the south side, where a doorway once existed. Thus, one residential pattern in Trowulan included a well to the south, in front of the house, and a drain in the rear.

Figure 10.8 Segaran Site
Square I-10 spit 3, July 26, 1986, cobblestone floor with brick foundations

Sentonorejo

Sixteen large pillar bases of stone on a brick foundation, arranged in two rows running east–west, lie 500 metres south of Pendopo Agung. Excavators found fragments of earthenware, porcelain, stoneware, metal, Chinese coins, charcoal and faunal remains. Imported ceramics included Chinese wares of the tenth to 16th centuries and Thai and Viet wares of the 14th to 16th centuries. Imported ceramics declined suddenly in the 17th century. This supports historical sources stating that Majapahit flourished during the 14th and 15th centuries, then disappeared during the 16th century.

Nglinguk

Aerial photography suggests that the Majapahit-period city was divided into rectilinear wards by water channels parallel to roads (Karina Arifin 1983, Mundardjito et al 1986). One of the north–south channels crosses the Nglinguk sector. Research in this sector was intended to discover whether the channel had brick walls. Excavation pursued buried linear brick structures running north–south or east–west, but it was impossible to determine whether these were enclosing walls or foundations of buildings.

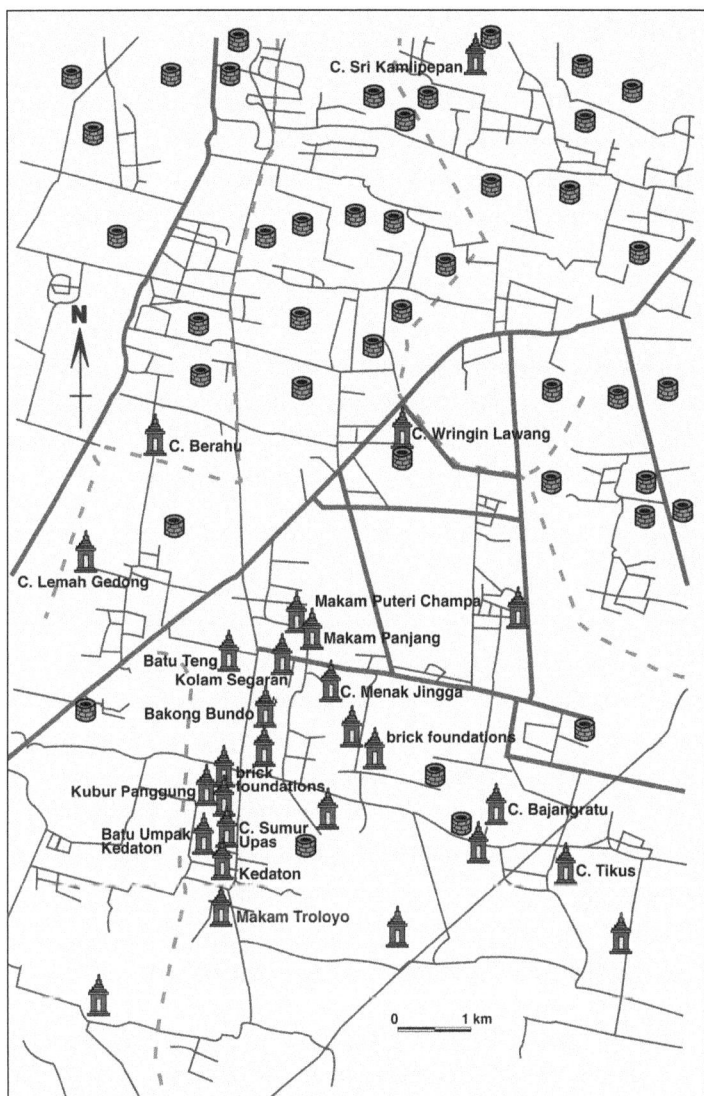

Figure 10.9 Sumur – sacred sites and water features
(Based on Karina Arifin 1983 and Mundardjito et al., 1986)

Nglinguk was found to have been a multiphase habitation cluster, with several superimposed brick structures with different orientations. The habitation areas contained dense concentrations of domestic refuse: earthenware, stoneware, porcelain, other household utensils and numerous wells. Many shards of high-quality Chinese ware imply that Nglinguk residents were members of the elite.

Batok Palung

Excavations revealed a layer of animal bone, approximately one metre thick and extending over an area of about one hectare, containing remains of buffalo, cattle, chicken, pig, goat and rat. Some had been boiled or roasted. Among the faunal remains were fragments of earthenware, stoneware and porcelain.

Kejagan

Surveys yielded terracotta figurines and moulds for making them. Excavations imply that Kejagan was a multiphase ceremonial site, based on the discovery of miniature buildings, probably used for ceremonies, and large earthenware containers, probably used for offerings.

Blendren

Remains of a brick-lined artificial spring-fed pool and the mouth of an underground channel distinguish this site. In the rainy season, a quantity of water sufficient to inundate the nearby rice fields flows from this channel; in the dry season, residents use the spring for bathing and washing. The channel exploits a source of ground-water at a depth of 375–425 centimetres, beneath an impermeable stratum. Neither its length nor its possible connection with the Segaran Pool and the network of canals covering Trowulan have been determined.

The Indonesian Field School of Archaeology

In 1991 the Indonesian Field School of Archaeology (IFSA) was instituted with a grant from the Ford Foundation and matching support from Puslit Arkenas. The project aimed to determine the borders of the urban area and to obtain some idea of the density of occupation remains within those borders. The results demonstrated that remains of densely settled clusters of the 14th and 15th centuries were spread over 100 square kilometres. Seventeenth-century Mataram covered only 41 square kilometres (Reid 1993:74). At the same time Thang-long (Hanoi) covered only 22 square kilometres. Estimates of its population varied from 130,000 to one million. It is now possible to designate 14th-century Trowulan a heterogeneous city.

Although the boundaries of the site have now been approximately determined and dense areas of habitation have been detected, the population of the site cannot be estimated because large areas of it have been destroyed. Probably an appreciable portion of the site was devoted to reservoirs, open fields, as described in the Deśawarṇana, and religious sanctuaries. Descriptions of these mention flowers and trees, which grew around them. For example, the Kanuruhan inscription, found near Malang in east Java, dated 856 *śaka*, records the presentation of land to be made into a flower garden (Sedyawati 1994:121). If only 50% of Trowulan were devoted to habitation, rough calculations based on expected density of inhabitants per square kilometre yield a minimum population of 200,000.

The IFSA survey recovered 100,000 artefacts, including Chinese wares mainly of the 14th century, together with ninth and tenth century examples in the Kejagan sector and late Ming shards near Mojoagung. The Alasantan inscription, dated 6 September 939 CE, proves that, in the pre-Majapahit era, the area had been a *sima*, where residents were freed from taxes in return for rendering services to a religious institution.

Figure 10.10 IFSA survey in progress
A student (in white hat) gathers artefacts near a *bengkel bata*

Settlement pattern

Neither literary sources nor archaeology describe the use of space in Majapahit's capital—the density of buildings, the proportion of space devoted to various types of uses, etc. Temple reliefs do not depict urban scenes, but they do contain sketches of settlements, including groups of pavilions surrounded by walls. Prapañca mentions several *kuwu*, walled compounds in which lived a noble, his family, servants, slaves and others attached to him by various forms of clientship. How large and how far apart were these *kuwu*? How was the ground between them used? Were they separated from the *nagara* by rice fields, and thus outside of it? We can only speculate on these matters.

Figure 10.11 Gold pendant with semi-precious stones
Found at a brickyard in Kemasan and surrendered by the finder

Figure 10.12 Repoussé gold cover for a small container, crushed as if in preparation for recycling
Found in the same cache as the pendant in Figure 10.11

Majapahit's capital was wealthy. Many pieces of gold jewellery have been discovered on the site, but unfortunately most have found their way into private collections and have little relevance to archaeological reconstruction. Although Java has no large sources of gold, Majapahit's connections with islands such as Sumatra, Borneo, and Sulawesi, where ancient mines existed, made it possible for many goldsmiths to find work in Java. At Kemasan not only have gold ornaments been found, but also tools such as small anvils and clay cups used as crucibles for melting gold for use in lost-wax casting. Not far away, at Pakis, a large number of clay crucibles for melting bronze have been excavated. Some of the bronze was used to make *uang gobok*, large coins or amulets, stone moulds for which have been found.

A 14th-century source (The *Nawanatya;* Pigeaud 1960–63 vol.3:122) mentions a court official whose duty was to protect the markets: '[e]ight thousand cash every day from the markets is the share', which this official received. The 'cash' referred to are Chinese coins. In about 1300, Majapahit adopted Chinese coins as its official currency for use in paying fines, taxes and other obligations, in place of Javanese gold and silver coinage, which had been in use for centuries. Chinese coins were preferred because they were available in small denominations, suitable for use in markets.

Pottery forms one of the most important sources of information about early civilisations. Pottery products found at Majapahit's capital indicate that this craft was an important activity here too. The range of clay objects found at Trowulan is wide and further research will undoubtedly uncover yet more types. Some of the more elaborate items must have been made by professional potters. Terracotta figurines were produced in large quantities. They represent many subjects: gods, humans, animals, buildings, and scenes. We do not know what they were used for; perhaps they had several functions.

Colonies of foreigners resided in Majapahit for varying lengths of time. Archaeological evidence for foreigners at the capital of Majapahit comes in two forms: written inscriptions and other documents; and depictions of foreigners by Javanese artists. The Chinese were probably the most numerous. In the early 15th century, 20,000 Chinese lived in four communities in Java, one of which was Trowulan.

The data, although not enough to provide detailed information on the distribution of activities with precision comparable to Anuradhapura, show that a wide range of economic activities were conducted on the site and that money was a familiar aspect of everyday life. Economic factors were certainly a significant influence on life in the city and probably on the urban ground plan as well.

Figure 10.13 Half of a terracotta image depicting a bird-man, perhaps Garuda, found during IFSA survey

Majapahit temples

Few temples in Trowulan have been preserved. There are probably several reasons for this; however, it seems that religious structures occupied less space in Trowulan than buildings for habitation. Javanese society during the Majapahit period preferred to locate its religious structures and activity centres in rural areas. The locations of temples and their plans was probably not a significant factor in determining Trowulan's ground plan.

Majapahit rulers were *didharmakan* (memorialised) at certain places. In 1365 CE, there were 27 religious domains where religious sanctuaries were set up in the names of particular rulers. Prapañca describes his visit to the abbot of a religious complex to collect information about King Hayam Wuruk's lineage and religious domains set up in the names of the king's ancestors. For example, Raden Wijaya, founder of Majapahit, was portrayed as a Buddhist image in the palace, and as Śiva in Simping, 150 kilometres southwest of Trowulan.

While the royal cults produced some great statuary, many subjects of Majapahit were more attracted by the worship of hermits, or *ṛṣi*. The west slope of Mount Penanggungan, southeast of Trowulan, is dotted with over 50 *punden berundak* (sets of terraces), averaging one metre wide and about ten metres long, which ascend the mountain slope like stairs. Other *punden* were constructed on Mount Arjuna, Mount Lawu, Muria and Wilis. These sites, rather than temples in the *nagara*, were the most significant religious centres of Majapahit. The complex of Panatāran, the largest ceremonial centre of the kingdom, was about 150 kilometres from the capital.

Water and settlement patterning

Water supply was one of the most critical factors facing an ancient city. A large reservoir, the *segaran* (ocean), occupies a site quite close to what must have been the centre of Majapahit's capital. Wells lined with bricks or clay rings have been found in several parts of the site. A 14th-century bathing place, Candi Tikus, has been preserved on the southeast edge of the site. Traces of what may have been canals for water circulation have been found on aerial photographs. They form a grid pattern.

One of Maclaine Pont's most useful contributions was his study of the hydrology of the region between Trowulan and Tarik (Maclaine Pont 1925, 1927). His engineering expertise was put to good use in identifying various canals and dams, which had probably been in use for centuries. He was able to show how they were connected with remains of reservoirs in the Trowulan area. Waduk Kumitir seems to have been Trowulan's main reservoir in ancient times, providing water for the canals of the city, as well as for rice fields. Later, other smaller reservoirs were built.

Figure 10.14 Brick-lined well in process of being dismantled for building material

It is difficult to date hydraulic features, such as canals. This is especially true in Trowulan, where it seems that the grid pattern observed by Karina Arifin (1983) may be very old, but the canals themselves have been widened and converted into rice fields, making their original size and age difficult, if not impossible, to ascertain. Several sites on the slopes of the Arjuna/Penanggungan massif have remains of dams and dated inscriptions, which support the conclusion that Majapahit's capital was supported by an elaborate water management system. At Kutogirang, 175 metres above sea level, is an inscription dated 1432 CE. At Juju, ten kilometres away, are four inscriptions, two from 1485, one of which mentions a dam (Ferdinandus c. 2000).

A comparison of the locations of wells and religious structures at Trowulan reveals an interesting pattern. The distribution of the two types of remains is quite different. The wells have been dug in certain places where the water table is closest to the surface of the ground. Temples were situated in other areas. Perhaps this was done in order to maximise the water resources of the site to support a dense population.

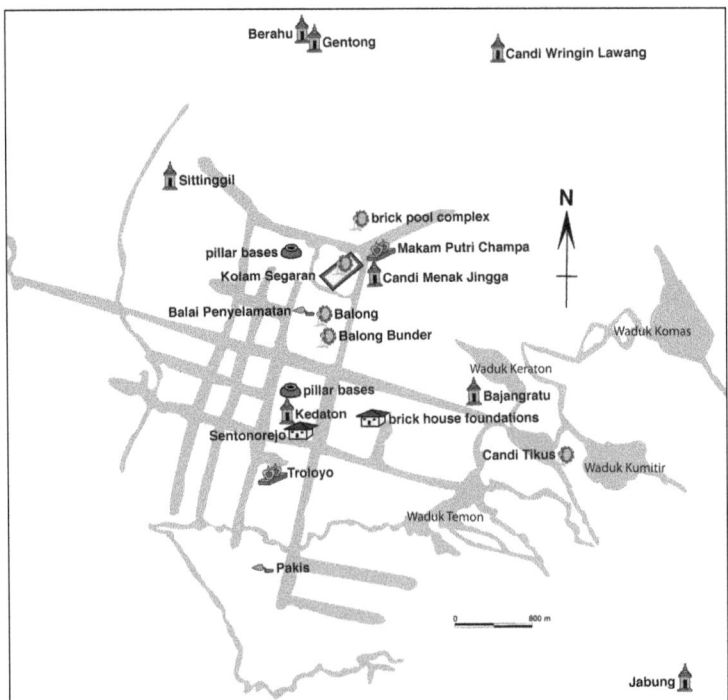

Figure 10.15 Hypothetical system of canals and reservoirs (waduk) in 14th-century Trowulan
(Based on Karina Arifin 1983 and Mundardjito et al 1986)

Conclusion

Trowulan has been more intensively investigated than any other large urban site from the pre-Islamic period in Southeast Asia. The significance of the accumulating data from Trowulan to assist in the clarification of early urbanisation in Indonesia can now be explicated more clearly than previously.

Neither the Javanese nor any other Southeast Asian culture had a concept exactly equivalent to the modern Western 'city'. It seems that there are many paths to urbanisation and that the present situation, in which all countries in the world now possess entities that are superficially alike, is the result of a process of convergent evolution in which analogous, rather than homologous, structures have formed (Miksic 1989).

The 14th-century Javanese did have the idea of an urban area marked by the absence of agriculture. The *Nawanatya*, selections from a primer of court etiquette, contains the rhetorical question, 'what is called the *nagara*? All where one can go out (of his compound) without passing through paddy fields' (Pigeaud 1960–63:III,121). Literary sources from Southeast Asia should be exploited, in conjunction with archaeological data, to gain further insight into human spatial behaviour. Much variation between areas is to be expected. The types of settlement units recognised by the people of Java, for example, are likely to have been significantly different from those of Sumatra or Cambodia. Many archaeologists assume that modern concepts of urbanisation can be directly applied to the past and to any part of the world. A moment's reflection will serve to illuminate the absurdity of this notion. The nature of cultural evolution in Southeast Asia will only be clarified if each part of the region is viewed in its own terms rather than as an example of a larger regional identity.

According to Veth (1896-1907), writing in the second half of 19th century, a study of the remains of Majapahit that conforms to the demands of archaeology was lacking. Sady,Veth's lament is still relevant today. Despite the considerable amount of research that has been accomplished, we are still far from understanding much about the society of this early city. The chance that such a study can ever be performed diminishes with every passing year.

Acknowledgements

The illustrations in this article were prepared by Ms Goh Geok Yian, whose contribution is gratefully acknowledged.

This article was originally published in a slightly modified form in *Arts Asiatiques*, Tome 64, 2009.

Chapter 11

Speculation on landscape use in and around Sambor Prei Kuk

Heng Piphal

Department of Anthropology, University of Hawaii at Manoa

Background

Based on the interpretation of ancient inscriptions, on art history and on historic architecture, the seventh century is assumed to mark the beginning of the political dominance of the city of Isanapura. Researchers believe that the city and political centre encompassed the Sambor Prei Kuk temple complex in Kampong Thom Province. The city is thought to be the capital city of the Chenla polity during the reign of Isanavarman I. However, with the exception of preliminary accounts from Groslier's unfinished work, no archaeological evidence addressing urbanisation and settlement has been recovered to assess the validity of these speculations. Chenla was a prominent polity and Isanapura, located at Sambor Prei Kuk, was its most likely capital.

Groslier's excavations in 1962 (Groslier 1962) shed light on a continuing occupation that spanned periods beyond what inscriptional evidence suggests. Chenla is consistently assumed to fit conveniently within the seventh to ninth centuries. As with Groslier's work, unpublished assessments indicate that it is likely that Sambor Prei Kuk had a significant and interactive population well before and after its definitive period.[1] Thus,

---

[1] Chenla is a periodisation created by historians who have based it on Chinese accounts. However, Chinese and Vietnamese continued to refer to Cambodia as Chenla until the 20th century, demonstrating the continuation of this polity until the modern period.

preliminary evidence indicates that the 'Chenla Period' as it is commonly defined by many researchers may not fully portray the true history.

The political and state-controlled economic centre may have shifted to Angkor after the eighth century, but significant populations and urban centres in the Sambor Prei Kuk region continued to engage in commercial and agricultural activities after the eighth century. The degree to which a network of related centres interacted with each other before, during and after Chenla's political pinnacle, remains obscure.

Many temples have been documented in the Sambor Prei Kuk area; these, together with inscriptions and a few historic documents, are what currently define Isanapura. It should be noted that many new structures are being discovered within the core area and outside the main complexes in the Stung Sen drainage area. Also, many Isanapura-period structures are found throughout present-day Cambodia, northeast Thailand and southern Vietnam. Isanapura is much more extensive than is often assumed, and may have been part of broader and more complex political, cultural and economic systems. Chenla did not merely comprise its city-state and the immediate periphery; it was larger and more complex. The concept of a self-contained city-state is not used as a straw man in this case. Rather, in order to understand broader interactions, the following essay is focused on moving beyond the concept of isolated and bounded systemic polities that have a central capital.

Past settlement territories and settlement patterns have been under-researched because studies of the art and architecture at temple complexes in Cambodia have taken precedence. Also, the relationship between temples, settlement, economy and many other general aspects of life is unknown. Most of the social institutions entwined with the temple complexes remain enigmatic at best. The following discussion explores landscapes from the past (including human usage and modification) in relation to the scattered brick architecture and historical records within and surrounding the temple complexes that currently define Isanapura and Chenla. This provides a better understanding of why pre-Angkorian kings may have chosen the Sambor Prei Kuk area as the place for a capital.

Geography

Sambor Prei Kuk is located on the northwestern side of the Sen River, one of the longest rivers in Cambodia. It lies northeast of the present provincial capital of Kampong Thom. The area is strategically located between the Tonle Sap lake (approximately 40–60 kilometres to the southwest, depending on flood levels), the mountainous area of Phnom Santuk (approximately 20 kilometres to the south), the plateau of Kampong Cham and Kratie to the east, and the highland area of Preah Vihear to the north (continuing from the Dangrek Mountain range). The Sen River has a rapid flow, especially in the wet season, and is five to 15 metres deep depending on seasonal change. There are no large tributaries in the Sambor Prei Kuk area and most contributing drainage is from small creeks. Sambor Prei Kuk lies between numerous resource environments, but its immediate environment is not necessarily the best for supporting a large agriculture-based urban population. Currently, Sambor Prei Kuk is isolated from the main communication routes (Fig. 11.1).

Sambor Prei Kuk rests near higher elevated topography to the north, west and east, and the lowland area to the southwest. This geographical condition results in significant amounts of water in the rainy season to the floodplains, but heavy rains can cause unwanted destruction. In the dry season, there is much less water anywhere other than in the central river channels. River and adjacent stream levels decrease dramatically during the dry period. The floodplain areas of the Sen are not particularly broad until the river passes Kampong Thom to the southwest.

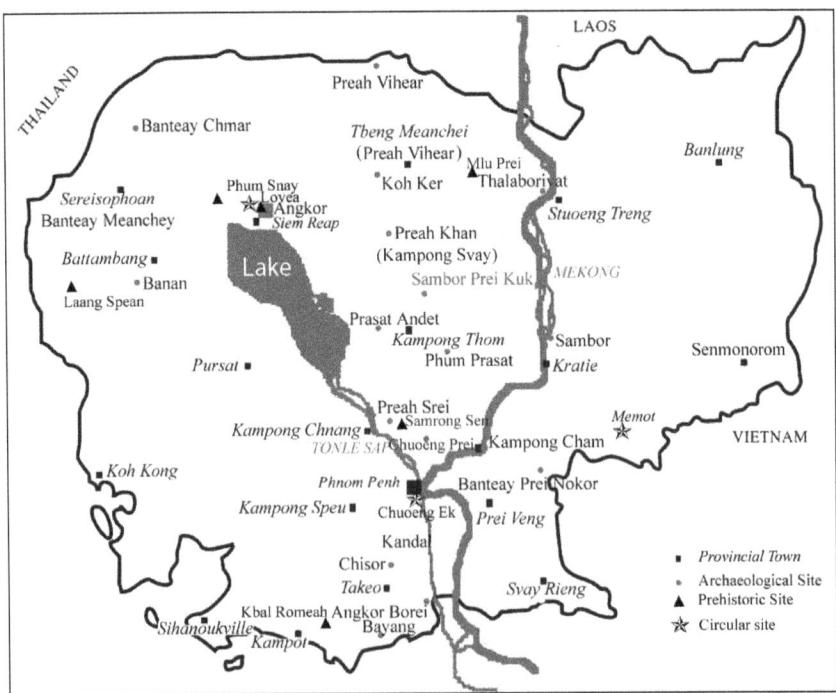

Figure 11.1 General map of important archaeological sites in Cambodia

Settlement is denser at the upper and middle sections of the Sen River and decreases to only a few scattered farmsteads west of Kampong Kou (approximately ten kilometres west of Kampong Thom), where flooded forest, shrub and grasslands dominate. Areas within a 20 kilometre radius of Sambor Prei Kuk are dominated by swidden agriculture, generally between five to 20 metres in elevation. Grassland, shrubland and forest are common, mostly above ten to 20 metres. Rice fields dominate the river surroundings, although, according to a 1998 Japanese International Co-operation Agency and Ministry of Public Works and Transport map, there are few irrigated or flooded fields. With the exception of a few hills reaching approximately 100–200 metres in height, elevation rarely exceeds 30 metres (Fig. 11.2).

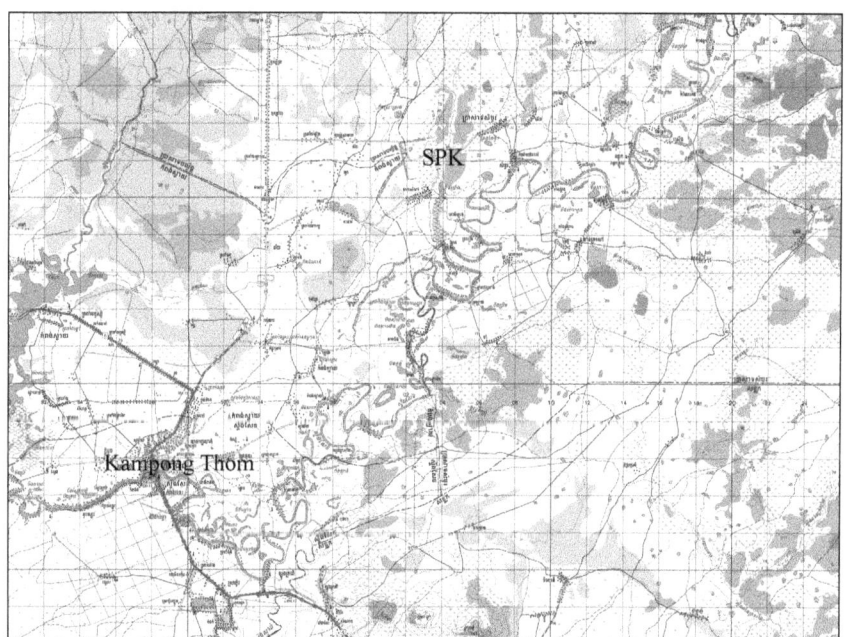

Figure 11.2 Topographic map of the Sambor Prei Kuk area, produced by the Japanese International Co-operation Agency, 1998

Geologically, Sambor Prei Kuk contains sandy and silty soils, mostly formed from eroded sandstone formations and alluvial flooding. This soil condition extends to the swamps along the Sen valley, and eventually to the great lake (Tonle Sap). Conditions provide limited potential for intensified wet-rice irrigated agriculture. Agroforestry and collecting and hunting for forest resources may have greater potential.

Thus, the landscape contains relatively fewer productive areas for intensified agriculture and aquaculture than other areas in Cambodia, such as Battambang, Takeo and several floodplains around the Tonle Sap. The productive areas located along the river floodplains are not particularly large and, presumably, would have been unlikely to have supported a significantly large urbanised population who relied solely on wet-rice agriculture and aquaculture yields.

Existing archaeological evidence

The data sets of only four archaeological features have been given adequate attention. These are temples, statuary, water features and inscriptions. Inscriptional evidence is covered thoroughly by Cœdès, Vickery, and others (see Vickery (1998) for a thorough review) and further discussion is not needed. Groslier's excavations can be considered a fifth set, but most of the data gathered by his research has not been published.

Temples

Over 250 towers have been identified in Sambor Prei Kuk. They are divided into seven major groups combining towers and basements: North; Central; South; Trapeang Ropeak (main complex); Khnach Tol (located west of the main complex); Srei Krup Leak; and Robang Romeas (to the north of the main complex) (Parmentier 1927; SCP 2004) (Fig. 11.3).

Of these groups, only the North, South, Srei Krup Leak and some isolated towers are dated to the seventh century on the basis of inscriptions at the sites. Others probably date to pre-Angkorian and Angkorian periods. This suggests a significant amount of activity after the presumed economic and political decline of Chenla/Isanapura (Heng 2005).

Most inscriptions were recovered from the main complex and Robang Romeas (see Finot 1928:42–6; Cœdès 1952:3–35). Most inscriptions list various donations from previous kings and officials, rather than information about daily activities in and around the temples, including the population centres and less populated but connected areas. Even though there is no direct record of the relationships between the common population and the temple complexes, inscriptions provide information concerning the range of occupations from the seventh to 11th centuries. Fortunately, this data allows us to build a better understanding of these relationships.

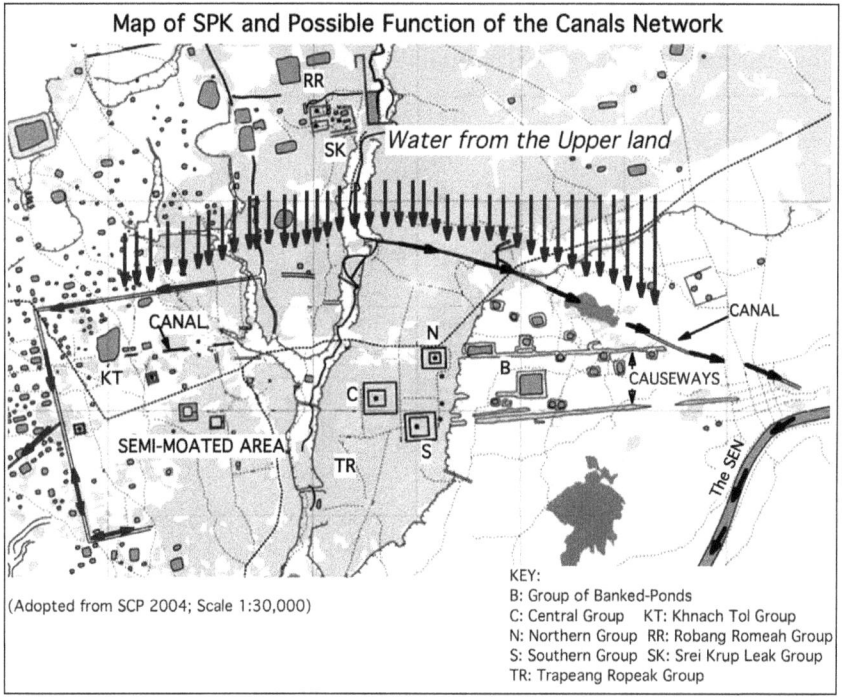

Figure 11.3 Possible hydraulic system(s) in Sambor Prei Kuk

There is little need to detail past architectural studies here (see Parmentier 1927; Coral-Rémusat 1940; Boisselier 1966; Bénisti 1970). It is noted that recent surveys have resulted in many new finds. For instance, approximately ten kilometres to the northeast of the main complex, a possible ancient road has been identified. The road is probably contemporary with the main complex. There is a collapsed brick structure and a pool next to the road. After interviewing a local villager who recently dug a pond behind his house, it was revealed that 50 centimetres beneath the surface an archaeological deposit, about 70–100 centimetres thick, exists. It is filled with potsherds and the remains of a brick structure. The top 50 centimetres contain few remains. This may indicate that the site was abandoned for a period of several hundred years. The brick structure might possibly serve the function of a rest-house, often located along Angkorian roads mentioned in Jayavarman VII inscriptions. Thus, road and rest-house planning and engineering may have existed before the Angkorian period.

To quickly summarise, it is evident that interconnected and intricate relations existed before and after the classic Sambor Prei Kuk/Isanapura period. With the exception of Sambor Prei Kuk Conservation Project

(SCP)'s, Groslier's and our preliminary research, almost nothing is known. Most current work and speculations still remain unpublished.

Water control systems

One problem in need of attention is how people managed their landscapes. Past hydrological technology has always been a central concern in Cambodian historical research. Were Angkorian models derived from earlier technology and engineering? In Angkor, massive hydraulic systems and networks are still visible. Most are connected to large temple complexes. What about Sambor Prei Kuk?

Sambor Prei Kuk has no visible large-scale systems outside the temple complexes. There are few recognised large-scale hydraulic features. The only features prevalent in the area are a large number of undated small ponds and a few canals around the temple complex. Why are there no large *baray* or massive hydraulic networks? Did the hydraulic systems in Angkor evolve from Isanapura or other earlier settlements? Could it be possible that the inhabitants did not have the hydraulic technology, did not need the technology, or could not use it because of other conditions? On the other hand, did they have hydraulic technology that we have yet to discover?

As mentioned previously, the geographical and geological conditions in Sambor Prei Kuk were not the most productive for wet-rice farming. It is known that people farmed rice. However, we do not know how they farmed rice and if rice surpluses fulfilled all needs, including social needs such as a desire for status- and wealth-enhancing trade items, beginning at least in the Neolithic and Metal Age periods throughout Cambodia. Agricultural potential may not have been sufficient for this. What other economic activities could have enhanced Sambor Prei Kuk's ability to develop to its comparatively high socio-economic position at that time, with its surplus labour and capital to build monuments and cities and, presumably, to exert control over a large population?

Ponds and reservoirs

Angkor Borei has two large artificial reservoirs termed *lboek* (derived from *loek*, to raise or elevate). They lie outside the city walls to the east and south. The eastern feature is currently used as a fish farm. The owner reported that the pre-existing east and south banks are higher than those to the north and west. Because of various conditions, it is possible that the north and west walls functioned as a water intake feature during the wet season. The east and south banks may have been used to retain water in the reservoir during the dry season. The southern reservoir is just a rectangular pond, not a *baray*. The reason why this feature does not need an embankment may be related to flooding during the rainy season and its topography, where water-trapping is not necessary. Sufficient water flows in from the southwest and north (Fig. 11.4).

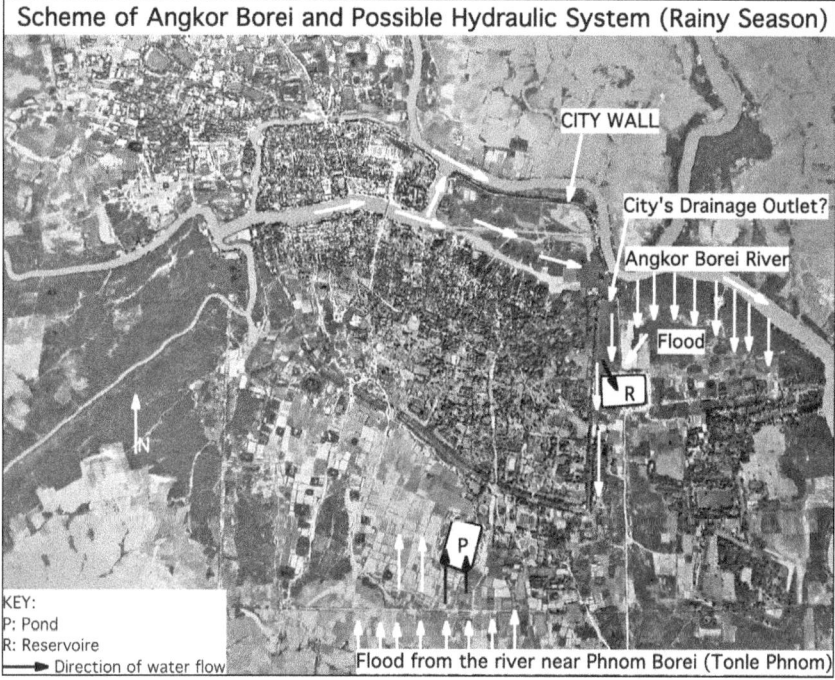

Figure 11.4 Possible moats, walls and reservoirs in Angkor Borei

In Sambor Prei Kuk the majority of ponds in the area are rectangular in shape and, therefore, are probably artificial. Some still function in the dry season for water storage, because they are deep enough. Most have low elevated banks made from inner soil excavation and have no outlets. These were possibly used for household and animal husbandry purposes. Ponds are mainly concentrated to the northwest, north and northeast of the temple complex—the higher areas. These areas may have been heavily populated. This does not mean that other areas were not populated, but it may mean that people in other areas did not need to rely on excavated ponds, especially in settlements along the river where people could access water more easily.

Ponds can be classified into two groups: banked and 'unbanked'. Those with banks are in highland areas, and those without banks are commonly located in lower areas. Ponds without banks are more likely to result from the excavation of soil used to build terraced and/or mounded house platforms. This technique is prevalent throughout modern Cambodia.

Banked ponds might be used to retain water, particularly in highland areas where house platforms are probably unnecessary. Some of these ponds (more likely reservoirs in the Cambodian context because the inner areas are not very deep) exist in the lowland area east of the main temple complex. They have inlets or outlets, depending on exterior seasonal water levels. Unfortunately, none of the structures in Sambor Prei Kuk has been studied (Fig. 11.3).

It could be hypothesised that an evolution of hydraulic engineering from reservoirs without inlets/outlets, noted in the earlier Angkor Borei (Funan) period, could have influenced hydraulic engineering at Sambor Prei Kuk and, eventually, Angkor. However, Sambor Prei Kuk shows a development in inlet/outlet technology that possibly influenced the massive hydraulic networks and technology of the *baray* systems in Angkor.

Researchers have seldom pursued topics that might lead to an understanding of the evolution of pre-*baray* water-control features in earlier sites, such as Angkor Borei and Sambor Prei Kuk; they have not compared them with the large *baray* and other hydraulic systems found in Angkor. That is, Angkorian hydraulic systems have seldom been examined from the perspective of an external, rather than internal, evolutionary process. What were the technological and social evolutions that led to developments in Angkor, and were they functionally or symbolically similar? Fortunately, these are becoming more popular research topics in Angkor with large projects led by the École française d'Extrême-Orient (EFEO) and the University of Sydney.

Canals

Another type of water control system in Sambor Prei Kuk is the use of canals, although we have little archaeological evidence on the history of canals in the region. Most of the recognised canals (all undated) are connected to the O Krou-ke natural stream and the Sen River. They were possibly used to channel water that flowed from the upper environs to the

Sen, perhaps to avoid flooding the temple complex and habitation areas. One canal, possibly contemporaneous with Sambor Prei Kuk's earlier period, is located to the north of the temple complex. It links O Krou-ke to the Sen River. It is plausible that this canal was used as a device to trap water flow from higher areas and to divert unwanted excess to the Sen River,[2] thus protecting the temple complex and access routes from damage and periodic inaccessibility.

The other known canal is a 'semi-moat' located to the west of the main complex. The northern course of the moat links to another natural stream, a tributary of the Sen. The southern course probably links to the lower part of the same stream or possibly ends after a short turn from the west course where it reaches the edge of an elevated area to the east. In the centre of the western course there is an outlet canal running northeast–southwest to the lowland area. The moat and canals were probably designed to protect part of the city from flooding rather than serving symbolic or defensive (militaristic) purposes (Fig. 11.3). This seems somewhat similar to Angkor Borei where moat(s) are presumably needed to avoid major destruction from flooding. During the rainy season, Angkor Borei is an island of non-flooded habitable land. There is very little evidence so far that moats were intended for militaristic protective purposes. Another structure that may not have been used in Sambor Prei Kuk is the long-distance canal, presumably used for transportation. Pierre Paris (1941a) and Louis Malleret in 1931 (Malleret 1959a) identified canals in the region of Angkor Borei and Oc Èo. Today, the Lower Mekong Archaeological Project (LOMAP) (Stark 1998, 2004; Bishop et al 2004) is conducting surveys of the canals identified by Paris around Angkor Borei. The canals seem to link various archaeological sites, including Oc Èo, with Angkor Borei.

In Angkor similar canals are seen in the pre-Angkorian city of Wat Khnat (West Baray), linking Angkor Wat to the Tonle Sap Lake, and a huge canal in Damdek linking the Kulen region to the Great Lake (Groslier 1979; Pottier 1993a; 2000). In Sambor Prei Kuk similar structures might not have been necessary because of its physical location, adjacent to the Sen River, and its geology. The Sen River already served the purpose for sustainable communication and transportation. Sambor Prei Kuk is also not suitable for long distance canals, because there are no highland water sources to sustain water in the canals.

---

2   There is a significant difference in elevation between the highland area to the north and the Sen valley.

Relationships

Evidence is available to clarify topics related to multiple variables. We can sample the dispersal of brick structures, ponds, settlement and habitation sites, as well as the inscriptions, oral history, historical linguistic patterns and environmental data within the area to collect holistic data sets. Questions do not need to be limited to understanding the conditions of Sambor Prei Kuk, but need to be extended to understanding why and how Sambor Prei Kuk evolved and what the relations were to different spatial, temporal, environmental, economic and cultural factors. We need to understand the relationships among many variables and how they changed through time. An important spin-off beyond understanding historic patterns is the ability to discern reasons for past successes and failures.

We do not know precisely where the population centres were. It is assumed that they are defined by the location of the temple complexes. This is a plausible assumption, but it is not supported by multiple archaeological data sets. Were the people living there, nearby or in more distant areas? We also have few clues to understanding the nature of connected settlements, including their interactions and changes through time and space. Further studies, other than architectural and epigraphic histories, can provide the necessary data.

Landscapes and population

Based on his 1962 excavations, Groslier assumed that the earliest occupation of Sambor Prei Kuk began in the Bronze Age. However, he did not widely publish evidence to support his hypothesis. Nonetheless, along the upper stream of the Sen River in Preah Vihear Province, there is a prehistoric (Bronze Age) site, Mlu Prei (see Lévy 1943). The Stuoeng Slab[3] River, which was possibly once connected to the Sen, runs near another prehistoric site, Samrong Sen (see Mansuy 1923; Ly 1999). It is obvious that the area along the Sen River and its tributaries has been inhabited since prehistoric times. Groslier's hypothesis is reasonable and it is possible that significant populations existed in and around Sambor Prei Kuk in the preceding Neolithic and Funan periods.

---

3   Stoeng Slab means the dead river, or the river that is not functioning. Technically, the upper end of this river, where it splits from the Sen, was blocked.

Features

The distribution of the Sambor Prei Kuk style of monument is a good aid in understanding the influence of Chenla/Isanapura. Contemporaneous monuments in the same style exist all over Cambodia. It is clear that Sambor Prei Kuk had extensive regional influence. The distribution, inscriptions, statuary and stylistic traits indicate that it is likely that Sambor Prei Kuk was a cultural and political centre.

The area to the west of the main complex contains many temple bases which are marginally datable. One exception is Khnach Tol, which bears octagonal towers and Sambor Prei Kuk lintel styles, and also includes a newly found eroded inscription which links it to the pre-Angkorian period. Most of the mounds west and east of the main complex are moated, whereas those in the main complex are not. This implies that they possibly belong to periods outside of the seventh century. It could also be evidence of differing methods of temple construction between highland areas and lowland areas, with lowland areas needing higher terraces to avoid flooding. They may have mined soil to build the terraces which created moat-like features. The upland area did not need this type of technology because of its topography.

Inscriptions in this area almost always eulogise kings from the period in which they were inscribed. Some describe donations by kings and officials to the temples. However, the inscriptions do not provide clues to specific locations of settlement areas, particularly economic centres where the core city might have been located.

In another case, the SCP assumes that the citadel of Isanapura was originally located in the semi-moated area to the west of the temple complex. However, the date of the moat is still questionable. The moat was more likely used to protect the area from flooding, in preference to creating a *maṇḍala* concept of supernatural protection. Today this area is flooded in the rainy season.

Were all cities in the past always created with moats and/or *maṇḍala* conceptual layouts as suggested by researchers? This question requires an appropriate answer. Most researchers treat ancient cities in Cambodia as belonging to the Indic model of *maṇḍala*, in which cities have to be strategically moated, walled, square or rectangular. However, it is noted that many circular prehistoric (Bronze and Iron Age) sites, such as the circular earthwork noted by Malleret (1959b), have been discovered throughout Thailand, Cambodia, and Vietnam. Circular earthworks, especially those found in Siem Reap and northeast Thailand, are also moated/ditched, walled and circular in shape. Were those sites based on Indic models? Could it be that this local prehistoric moated concept influenced later settlement and temple designs in Cambodia?

Another question is why many prehistoric sites in Cambodia have walls, moats and ditches (for example, sites found in Siem Reap and Memot) and other sites do not (such as those in Mlu Prei, Samrong Sen and Phum Snay). There is limited research on circular prehistoric sites west of Angkor. We do have research results on some sites in Memot (Dega 2002). Nevertheless, the walls and ditches may not have been for defensive purposes. In Memot, the term 'ditch' may be more appropriate than the term 'moat' because the area has no water source or geology to support true moats. These sites are commonly located on hill slopes and hilltops and are surrounded by walls at the outer edges and a ditch between inner platforms and walls. Many test excavations show traces of habitation along the edges of the platforms, but not at the centres or outside the walls.

If circular earthwork walls were designed for protection, why would the slope of the wall be located at the outer edge rather than the inner? The environs of this area might always have been forested, lacking large permanent water resources. Thus, supporting sizeable agriculture-based settlements may have been difficult. Inhabitants were possibly targeting forest resources rather than intensively farming rice, although rice chaff in ancient pottery indicates some form of rice cultivation (Dega 2002). The rice, however, might have been traded from somewhere else in the lowland area. Thus, the location and design of the sites may have been chosen to adapt to the environment. Settling in circular sites surrounded by walls with slopes at the outside edges on the natural hills may have allowed the sites to be camouflaged or to blend into the natural setting. If hunting were prevalent, this design might not have frightened animals away so easily, thus increasing rates of prey capture. Hunters could collect resources, hunt and process their products without disrupting the distribution of animals. Hunters could also live and work in the same place rather than constantly having to move. In a sense, the sloping walls may have acted as something similar to a duck blind or camouflaged deer-hunting locale, but on a larger scale. On the other hand, moats and walls at other sites may serve different purposes. Viewshed analysis would provide more information regarding the distribution of these circular earthworks.

At Angkor Borei, numerous areas within the wall are built up with millions of potsherds, approximately three metres deep, suggesting dense population. It might result from geological and topographic conditions in the area. Extensive flooding always occurs during the rainy season. This forces people to aggregate in higher places, like Angkor Borei and Phnom

Borei, to avoid flooding. The walls and moats of Angkor Borei might not have been used for military defence but for water defence. Flooding could devastate the entire city.[4] Also, the layout of Angkor Borei's wall does not show any relationship with the *maṇḍala* ideology.

In comparison, within the semi-moated area of Sambor Prei Kuk, low density scatters of artefacts occur,[5] suggesting a low population density in the immediate area. The SCP concept of a populated citadel defining the Isanapura city within the moated area may be insufficient.

On the other hand, there are significantly more ponds and other water features outside the semi-moated area. This is suggestive of greater occupation in the surrounding areas. After surface artefact inspection in Sambor Prei Kuk, a picture emerged of low population density within a large area, but in which Angkor Borei and the delta area had pockets of high density settlements; these may relate to geological and topographic conditions. In Sambor Prei Kuk, people did not need to aggregate because they could disperse without major threat from flooding. However, it is likely that the core centre of each urban and political centre might have been more densely populated. The question remains—what was the core area in Sambor Prei Kuk?

The causeways from the north and south complexes to Kampong Chuoeteal seem to demonstrate some kind of special connection between these areas. It is possible that this area was an important centre in Sambor Prei Kuk's dominant period. It is still heavily populated today and is a lucrative trade node in the region. Both of these causeways connect Kampong Chuoeteal directly to the main east entrances of the north and the south temple complexes.

Conclusions and hypotheses

Preliminary results of current Sambor Prei Kuk research highlight a complicated mystery. One of the main problems is to understand the shift of power from the south, most probably from Angkor Borei, to Sambor Prei Kuk. Is there any evidence of changes in urban planning, temple engineering, hydraulic system engineering, political institutional changes and economic evolution from the previous centre of Funan to Isanapura and then to Angkor?

---

[4] Dr Michael Dega and Dr Kyle Latinis, who worked in this area in 1995, raised the same idea that the wall and moat of Angkor Borei were used for defence against unwanted inundation (Dega & Latinis 1996).

[5] This is based on recent observation of small amounts of surface findings and new road construction activities in the area.

Previous scholars imagined that warfare or political and religious chaos occurred in the past (Cœdès 1968; Briggs 1951) and they used these factors to explain power shifts. This perception may have arisen from colonial-centric, or even Sino-centric, ideas of the rise and fall of civilisations. It should be noted that the Chinese documented shifts in Southeast Asian empires throughout the first two millennia CE and that their chroniclers were influenced by concepts of militant conquest and that many of them rewrote earlier records and had no direct experience of the places and times they were chronicling.

Though there may have been warfare and political and religious chaos, these factors are insufficient to explain shifts in power. In the past, Cambodian warfare, and Southeast Asian warfare more generally, might not have been similar to East Asian or European warfare. Warfare in Southeast Asia may have occurred to control cities and gain citizens rather than to destroy them. A similar concept can be seen in the Khmer–Cham war of the 13th century and the Thai–Khmer war of the post-Angkorian period. Warriors were more concerned with capturing and controlling human resources rather than destroying competitors.

The question of why people chose to build a significant polity in the narrow Sen River valley, which seems to have had little productive agricultural land, is still unresolved. Why did a major city and capital arise in the area during the Chenla period? Nevertheless, an hypothesis other than one relating to the political factors of warfare and conquest could also explain the shift. The magnet pulling the ancient Cambodian capitals from south to north, north to south, and so on, was charged by dominant economic variables.

Most scholars assume that the ancient capitals of Cambodia were based on proximity to the most productive agriculture areas, as particularly proposed in *La Cité Hydraulique Angkorienne* (Groslier 1979). However, Sambor Prei Kuk and Angkor were located in similar landscapes (somewhat upland areas characterised by sandy soil), which probably did not have immediate potential for high-surplus production. Sambor Prei Kuk and Angkor might not fit a theory of agricultural surplus alone as providing the catalyst for becoming central and large cities. Why did Sambor Prei Kuk and Angkor become powerful centres in the past? Why did kings move their political and economic dominance, and perhaps even their cities, to Sambor Prei Kuk and then Angkor (especially the areas north of Roluos and Siem Reap) instead of to other areas with greater potential for agriculture and aquaculture?

It is noted that the rich hydraulic network in Angkor was possibly used for irrigation and water control to supplement the demands of agriculture and aquaculture. Others have theorised that the hydraulic works served a more symbolic function (van Liere 1980). Sambor Prei Kuk, on the other hand, has very few known hydraulic structures compared to Angkor. Sambor Prei Kuk and the 'City of Angkor' may not have had immediate access to the agricultural and aquacultural resources needed to sustain large populations.

Sambor Prei Kuk is rather centrally located among the known contemporaneous archaeological sites, such as Thala Borivat in Stoeng Treng, Sambor in Kratie, Han Chei in Kampong Cham, and further sites in the south, including Angkor Borei, Kampong Chnnang and Battambang. A newly found inscription from the seventh century suggests that Battambang belonged to the city of Bhimapura. Sambor Prei Kuk could easily communicate with these areas via river systems, such as the Mekong, Tonle Sap, Sen, and other rivers linking several archaeological sites, and possibly roads that are yet to be identified (see Hendrickson's chapter in this volume). It is likely that the agricultural and aquacultural surpluses would have come from neighbouring areas with differing or more productive ecosystems. This may imply that production and trade were important variables regarding the development and maintenance of the urban centres.

It is possible that surrounding areas may have functioned as smaller economic nodes by collecting and producing local resources to support the macro-economic centre in capital cities. For instance, it is clear from the non-militaristic panels of later period bas-reliefs on the Bayon, a 13th-century temple, that market trade and hunting were prominent, which supports any suggestion that agricultural production played a lesser role in the city.

Furthermore, Sambor Prei Kuk seems to have been inhabited and important long before the time of Isanapura. Archaeological evidence found along the Sen River, which includes the evidence of the Bronze and Iron Age sites at Mlu Prei and Samrong Sen and Groslier's inferences from Sambor Prei Kuk, suggests contemporary sites buried underneath the temple complex at Sambor Prei Kuk.

Recent archaeological research in areas such as Phum Snay, Krasang Thmei, Prei Khmeng, Koh Tameah (West Baray) and Samrong Sen indicate that large settlements or civilisations may have existed in this area before the definitive Funan period. Absolute dates from these sites generally go back to before and inclusive of the third century BCE. However, absolute dates produced from sites in southern Cambodia, such as Angkor Borei and Phnom Borei, and sites in southern Vietnam, such as Oc Èo, frequently are no earlier than the third century BCE. This might suggest that the earliest intensive occupation (urbanisation) of the lower Mekong delta started around the end of the first millennium BCE in the Metal Age. It is an interesting contradiction that many absolute dates deduced from sites in north Cambodia and northeast Thailand are before the third century BCE. Materials found at these sites, such as Phum Snay, Krasang Thmei, Koh Tameah, Mlu Prei, Samrong Sen, Laang Spean, and other looted sites in Banteay Mean Chey and Pursat, indicate a possible rich, interactive and vast civilisation which existed in the north before Funan. Furthermore, similar material culture found throughout early sites in northern Cambodia demonstrates that well-connected societies and trade relations existed in areas around the Tonle Sap Lake.

It is clearly evident that a more complex and interactive history existed throughout Cambodia and neighbouring countries before the Funan period and that this history is supported by a growing corpus of archaeological data that indicates:

1. possible concentrated populations defined by 1,500–3,000 year old burial sites in places like Angkor and Angkor Borei;
2. pre-Angkorian to post-Angkorian temple construction or modification in many sites;
3. industrial activities (kilns, for example) in areas such as Angkor, Sambor Prei Kuk, Angkor Borei and neighbouring Phnom Penh (such as Cheoung Ek and Sre Ampil which span many periods); and
4. post-Angkorian burials in places such as the Cardamom Mountains.

Inscriptional evidence found so far has never described urbanisation. Archaeological research has hitherto not focused on understanding the nature of urban planning at Isanapura. Most comments about it have been purely speculative. The city's core centre may be located in the modern villages of Kampong Chuoeteal and Sambor, because of causeways linking this area to the main temple complexes. It is probably no coincidence that villagers in Sambor still maintain an annual ceremony honouring the spirit(s) of the northern temple complex (Fig. 11.5). In addition, it is likely that the existence of ponds explains a vast area of habitation around Sambor Prei Kuk, rather than a concentrated dense city in a small area, such as what is likely to have existed in Angkor Borei. This pattern of large dispersed populations is similar to the pattern of urbanisation in Angkor, as described by Roland Fletcher (Fletcher et al. 2003).

Figure 11.5 Ceremony in Sambor Prei Kuk (February 2005) honouring the village spirit and the northern temple complex spirit.
In the background is the ruin of the eastern gate of the northern temple complex.

The preliminary analysis of hydraulic systems in Sambor Prei Kuk demonstrates that structures such as canals, ponds and moats might not have been used for irrigation or transportation. It is more likely that they were designed for water control, especially to prevent flooding. This technique could have allowed people to divert water flow away from populated areas (cities) to the Sen River. Some pond structures in Sambor Prei Kuk also show a possible earlier evolution of the *baray* network later seen in Angkor.

Hydraulic technology seems to have existed since the prehistoric period, as evidenced by the circular sites in Angkor, northwest Cambodia and northeast Thailand. The Funan period may have witnessed a boost in similar technology because of the environment of the area. The southern area is low and often flooded, which may have encouraged people to dig ponds and moats and to mine soil for habitation mounds and the construction of temple terraces. Archaeological evidence indicates that the earliest temple construction possibly started in the south during the classical Funan period and that the builders of these temples used their understanding of the immediate environs, as is demonstrated by the formation of moats and pond structures attached to temple and habitation mounds. However, when the capital was moved to Sambor Prei Kuk, from archaeological evidence it can be determined that there were pond structures, but no trace of moats can be seen in the main temple complex. This might result from topographical differences between southern and northern Cambodia, especially at Sambor Prei Kuk, where moats were not needed for the temples. It is also possible that moats became significantly more important structures in the early Angkorian period, as seen in large-scale temples such as Bakong (Siem Reap).

Lastly, since the prehistoric period, moat and water feature construction seems always to have been prevalent in Cambodian and neighbouring societies. Water features and urban designs may have evolved locally, and later been incorporated into designs which some researchers claim are examples of Indic technological diffusion. This claim is questionable. However, if a dedicated multi-disciplinary research project were to be conducted in this area, it would help to fill the gaps in our knowledge.

PART THREE

LIVING THE SITES
THE COMMUNITIES AROUND

Introduction to Part Three

Stuart Robson

Adjunct Associate Professor, School of Languages, Cultures and Linguistics, Monash University

So far, we have presented a number of chapters that have looked at the ancient religious architecture of Southeast Asia in its natural environment, and we have seen that a great deal of good work has been done describing the monuments and the sites. Without doubt, much progress has already been made in this area.

In Part Three we offer some further contributions that are intended to open up the subject to new perspectives, both theoretical and descriptive. Once sites have been discovered, documented and (sometimes) restored, and once we have formed an idea of their symbolic interpretation, we move on and ask ourselves what kind of relation may have existed between the monuments and the human communities that inhabited the surrounding region. These were the people who saw the buildings on a daily basis, may have had a hand in constructing them, will have entertained certain ideas regarding their purpose, and may well have used them on special occasions. After all, it is obvious that the great expenditure of effort required to build such monuments—many of them magnificent achievements—must have been inspired by motives more than mere obedience to royal commands.

In this way we introduce the concept of *functionality*, that is, a social dimension in the interpretation of the 'use' of a religious building. An investigation of what people actually did within or around a temple complex will help, for example, to explain the presence or absence of certain types of building there, and at the same time we may be able to point to shifts in the way that monuments were used over time. There is no need to assume that understandings of function were static, and we also do not need to imagine that functions were identical in different parts of Indianised Southeast Asia, such as Angkor, Java, Champa and Burma. See, for instance, the chapter on this subject by Alexandra Haendel.

In order to visualise an Angkorian temple within its surrounding urban and agricultural landscapes, it is no longer necessary to rely solely on our imagination—visualisation can be assisted by using digital reconstructions, even down to figures and animals. Such an exercise can serve as an interpretive tool for both researchers and the general public, as clearly demonstrated in the chapter by Tom Chandler and Martin Polkinghorne. Perhaps eventually a musical or linguistic dimension can be added.

It is worth recalling that sacred sites are not restricted to areas containing constructed stone or brick monuments: trees and graves can also mark sites as sacred. Here again the question is what their relationship was (or is) to the community that used them. We can observe that these sacred sites are perceived as the abodes of powerful spirits, such as ancestors, local heroes or guardians of sacred places. The function of the sacred space is to provide a channel for the community to make contact with and access the spiritual power believed to be available there, as can be seen in Angelo Andrea Di Castro's chapter.

The temples and hermitages that in some places lay scattered across the plains and mountainsides became a familiar sight to the population, and in this way also entered into the mental landscape. As a result, the poets who wandered the hills and shores of Java seeking scenes of beauty to inspire them termed their works 'monuments of literature'—not only because they were elaborate constructions, but also because they shared a function of the temples as a receptacle of the divine power of deceased royal ancestors. These are some points explored in my own chapter.

Then we are fortunate to have the chapter by Tran Ky Phuong and Rie Nakamura: the authors examine a particularly interesting example of the link between a royal cult and the monuments, as provided by the kingdom of Champa. Is it suggested that the Cham principle of cosmological dualism was applied in order to unify the northern and southern parts of the realm, representing Siva and the goddess of the state respectively, as enshrined in ritual and symbolism.

An exploration of the functionality of the ancient monuments of Southeast Asia has to take into account the ideas that were (and to some extent still are) held by the local populations, whether these relate directly to the great world religions or to local cults, and it also has to take a sufficiently broadly based view of the region, to include comparative or contrastive data from the better known traditions of the Khmer and Javanese, as well as others such as the Mon and the Cham.

Chapter 12

Incorporating the periphery

The classical temples of Southeast Asia and their social context

Alexandra Haendel

Adjunct Research Fellow, Monash Asia Institute, Monash University

> Whatever space and time mean, place and occasion mean more. For space in the image of man is place, and time in the image of man is occasion. (Aldo van Eyck, quoted in Lawson 2001:23)

What imbues space and time with significance and transforms them into meaningful place and occasion is human activity happening at that node of space and time—the usage of that 'location'.[1] The happening of that activity, the bodily experience of the location, results in knowledge; embodiment of space is necessary for familiarity with space and for its transformation into place. In order for this process to happen successfully, synomorphy, the congruence between a setting and people's actions, has to exist. Synomorphy can be achieved through various means, most significantly the physical setting, social forces and learning (Barker 1968:18ff, 29ff). At temples, a combination of physical and social factors is necessary because of the abstract nature of activities undertaken at those locations. In terms of the physical aspect, it is important to remember that 'an architecture of complexity and contradiction has a special obligation toward the whole: its truth must be in its totality or its implications of totality' (Venturi 1977:16). That is, for totality to be reached, the significance of individual elements

---

[1] The term 'location' is used as a neutral term. *Space* is filled with the possibility of becoming a meaningful *place*, whereas 'location', as it is used here, does not necessarily have either connotation.

has to transcend those elements. With an increasing number of parts, we deal with an increased complexity which 1) makes the architecture increasingly difficult to understand, and 2) offers more scope for the usage of that space by people. This means that, physically, architecture has to accommodate those activities which, in turn, are socially determined and learned.

If synomorphy exists, architecture can induce behaviour patterns that would not be displayed otherwise; through the architecture, the building(s), this behaviour is also bound to the place where it happens. In a religious context, worship, embedded into the temple, takes place at the *axis mundi*, which determines the placement of the temple and is, in turn, expressed through the temple. It would be easy to assume that the existence of synomorphy indicates a successful, 'working' space, revealed by spatial continuity. This would place increased significance on interruptions of the existing spatial arrangement. However, this is not necessarily so and discontinuity can occur, even when spaces are used in an appropriate way.

Why is this approach, with its focus on the appropriation of temples, needed? Hitherto, the historiography of most ancient and/or classical sacred sites in Southeast Asia has been characterised by a discourse of cosmological representation, with a concentration on the (central) shrines, galleries and enclosure walls and, if present, on moats and other water management structures. When we consider the magnitude of the temples the early researchers encountered, in terms of both size and number, this focus is not surprising. The sites had to be freed from centuries of overgrowth and excavated, the remnant sculpture and other fragments had to be catalogued and, finally, all of the material had to be interpreted—a tremendous task!

What has largely been missing from research undertaken so far is a step beyond the symbolic interpretation. Central issues, which still need examining, concern the social factors of temple compounds—that is, the functionality of the sites—as well as an interpretation of the temporal dimension and changes occurring over time (architecturally and in terms of usage), and a consideration of how the information gathered about one civilisation might relate to others in Southeast Asia.

The present chapter is a first step within this analytical approach and will discuss the issue of the functionality and usage of sacred sites, which is immediately relevant for the integration or non-integration of the temple compounds into the everyday life of the surrounding community. What has to be remembered is that, even though the temple compounds are structurally complete entities in themselves, they need people to display their full meaning and functionality; there is a reciprocal relationship between buildings and people (Arnheim 1977:217). The temples,[2] although complete in themselves as representations of cosmology, are only made whole through the presence of humans with rituals and worship—through the usage of the site. Examples discussed in this chapter will mainly be drawn from Cambodia and Java.

Temples in Southeast Asia and sources for studying temple functionality

Before examining the functionality of sites, a few general points have to be made. The temples of classical Cambodia and Java were Brahmanic or Mahāyāna Buddhist, with their layout based on the regulations given in the Indian treatises, the *vāstu śāstra*s,[3] which are, in turn, determined by cosmological principles. Despite the large number of descriptions of the cosmos in Brahmanic and Buddhist texts, they are similar overall; at the centre is the cosmic mountain, Mount Meru, which is surrounded by landmasses, oceans and mountain ranges.[4] Therefore, the temple layout is similar for compounds of differing religious background and, with regards to the Southeast Asian foundations, it is often only the decoration or still extant pedestals that allow conclusions as to the dedication of the site. For example, at the central Javanese Candi Barong only the finials indicate that it is a Hindu foundation. This similarity in layout also results from Brahmanism and Mahāyāna Buddhism having comparable spatial requirements with regards to activities taking place inside temples; both focus on individual *pūjā* rather than large congregations.

---

[2] When the term 'temple' is used in this chapter, it is in the sense of temple compound, rather than of an individual building.
[3] The *vāstu śāstra*s are an extensive body of texts spanning hundreds of years. They contain extremely detailed regulations as to the elements of architecture, for instance dimensions of parts of a building, the exact size and layout of building sites, or particulars regarding icons. The Indian treatises on that subject, such as the Mānasāra (Acharya 1934) and Mayamata (Dagens 1970–76), were known and in all likelihood applied in ancient Cambodia and quite likely in classical Java as well. Therefore, India can be drawn upon in two regards as a cultural reference: firstly, in terms of architectural features with these texts in mind and, secondly, for an analysis of ritual practices, as the historical continuity evident in India allows inferences to rituals practised in classical Southeast Asia.
[4] See Kirfel 1967 for a meticulous research.

Figure 12.1 Candi Barong
(Photograph: Alexandra Haendel)

Figure 12.2 Candi Barong courtyard
(Photograph: Alexandra Haendel)

The necessities following from the symbolic representation of temples also mean that differences between Brahmanic and Buddhist compounds can be insignificant, whereas the differences between compounds of the same religious background can be quite considerable. For instance, the tenth-century foundations of Prasat Bei, a Śivaite foundation, and Bat Chum, a Buddhist temple, at Angkor are virtually identical, both having three sanctuaries on a common platform, oriented east, with the lintels showing Indra on Airāvata and, at Bat Chum, one lintel with a lion disgorging an elephant. On the other hand, the foundations of Pre Rup and the Baphuon, both Brahmanic sites at Angkor, show widely differing layouts. Pre Rup has a quincunx of towers on top of a three-tiered pyramid, on the lowest level of which are an additional 12 shrines, whereas the Baphuon only had one *prasat* on top of its pyramid.

In all this, the degree of complexity of a site is not indicative of qualitative improvements over time to the temple layout; rather, increases in complexity can occur in all temples, regardless of size, significance and the period in time. For example, at Angkor complex temples were built from the late ninth through the tenth centuries, followed by almost two centuries of sites of comparatively low complexity, followed in turn by extremely complex compounds in the late 12th and early 13th centuries.

On Java, the situation is somewhat similar, although overall there is a 'simplification' of temple compounds discernible over time. While the central Javanese temples can be large and complex, foundations of the East Javanese period tend to be smaller and consist of fewer buildings. As in Angkor, though, this is a rather generalised statement and exceptions do exist.

How can we examine the social significance of sacred sites? Sources seem to be numerous and varied: contemporary epigraphy and later texts; sculpture; the architectural remains themselves; and contemporary uses in India and Bali.

Epigraphy

A most valuable source is epigraphy contemporary with the temples. In Cambodia, hundreds of inscriptions were found, which can be extremely detailed as to the usage of the compounds. On Java, significantly fewer inscriptions were found than in Cambodia, with many of them badly damaged and not necessarily discovered near the temples they were composed for, which can create considerable problems with regards to their interpretation. Generally, their content is similar to the Khmer-language inscriptions in Cambodia: secular details, such as the land attached to temples; tribute and taxation matters; some give genealogical information; and, by and large, only a little information about the temples themselves is related. These inscriptions do not necessarily mention the name of the foundation and, even if they do, it is of limited value as the original names of the sites are largely unknown. Possibly, in parallel to classical Cambodia, shrines were named after their central icon.

Later texts

Particularly for classical Java, later chronicles, such as the Nagarakṛtāgama or the Pararaton, and religious texts, such as the Sutasoma,[5] are most useful because of their numerous references to earlier sites. It is problematic, though, that frequently it is unclear which sites these texts refer to, again because of the name issue. In Cambodia, the situation is somewhat different and later texts contain hardly any information relevant to the interpretation of Angkorian sites, mainly because of the dramatic change of religion to Theravada Buddhism in the 14th and 15th centuries.

Sculpture

Icons of deities, the heart of the temple, have been found in large numbers at most sacred sites in varying degrees of preservation. Some statues are still more or less intact; of others, only small fragments, such as hands or feet, remain. Despite being numerous, only few references to the icons can be found in the inscriptions. Usually, only the central icons are mentioned, without, however, much additional information, especially about their placement. Nevertheless, drawing mainly on regulations in religious texts and also, in some cases, on the location that these icons were found within compounds, one can use these sculptures as most valuable indicators of the spatial arrangement within temple compounds.[6]

---

[5] Nagarakṛtāgama (Robson 1995), composed in 1365 by Prapañca under King Hayam Wuruk, traces the lineage of East Javanese kings back to divine origins and gives details regarding the usage of sites. The Pararaton (Phalgunadi 1996), written in the early 16th century in Kawi language and covering the period from the early 13th until the late 15th century, does not specifically mention religious foundations, but it does refer to the temples where deceased royals were commemorated and gives some information about religious practices at the time. The Sutasoma (Santoso 1975) dates from the 14th century and was written by Tantular; it does not give much information on usage of temples, but deals with religious issues.

[6] See Haendel (2005) for a detailed study of the sculpture, its placement and the significance of this for the usage of the sites of the tenth century East Mebon and Pre Rup at Angkor.

For classical Java the situation is somewhat more complicated than at Angkor. Firstly, only a few inscriptions mention specific icons; often not even the central ones are named. And secondly, most sculptures, or fragments thereof, were not found *in situ*, which makes it difficult to discern where the icons would have been placed originally. Moreover, it seems that not as many icons were established as in the Cambodian temples.

Architecture

At most historical sites in Southeast Asia, physical remains are limited to shrines and other structures connected to religious activities. This is only to be expected, given that these buildings were the only ones constructed from permanent materials such as stone or brick; and even within religious compounds, especially the early ones, only the shrines were built from these materials and all other buildings from wood, bamboo and other perishable supplies. Since not even the palaces of the kings were deemed worthy enough for permanent materials, no trace of them remains and their locations are still open for discussion. In ancient Java, not even the location of the capital of the central Javanese period has been found. Inscriptions refer to a place (*Meḍang*) and it is assumed that the site changed several times, but nothing can be said with certainty. Nevertheless, the remaining buildings can give invaluable evidence as to the usage of the temples, if studied closely, as will be discussed below.

Contemporary usage of sites in India and Bali

One further important source is the contemporary usage of temples in India and Bali. The religious continuity in these places is both a blessing and a curse for a researcher of classical Southeast Asia. On one hand, it allows inferences as to former practices because

> [w]hat may be observed of rituals and ceremonies in present-day Hindu Asia indicates that they have not basically altered from what was practised in the earliest periods of Hinduism, even though the ancient rituals have doubtless become greatly simplified (Michell 1988:63).

On the other hand, though, this very continuity means changes have taken place since the decline of the classical period which have to be taken into account. Therefore, parallels have to be drawn with caution.

Nevertheless, the social integration of the Balinese temples, for instance, might to a certain degree reflect the organisation in Java, as temples for certain groups of society seem to be referred to in various earlier inscriptions. For example, the inscription of Candi Perot, dating from 850 CE, mentions a temple of the merchant guild, indicating temples for specific social groups for their own worship (Soekmono 1995:61).

Temple functionality and social context

Fundamentally, the function of the temple is to enable contact between humans and the divine, to dissolve the boundaries between the two realms, and to assist humans in their quest for unity with the divine. The focus of activity in the temple is rituals and worship, *pūjā*, which are similar in temples dedicated to different gods. *Pūjā*, 'conceived as an evocation, reception and entertainment of the god or goddess as a royal guest' (Michell 1988:63), is strictly regulated in various Indian *śāstra*s. However, in addition to this 'core' function, temples served various other purposes as well. Intellectually, they were centres of learning. They housed schools for mainly Brahmanic pupils studying such subjects as grammar and astrology and the sacred texts. The same activities can still be witnessed in temples in India nowadays. This function also demanded space for living quarters for some of the students who stayed inside the temple compound. More popular education took place inside the compound as well, for instance the recital of the Vedas, the epics and Purāṇas, performances with dance and music as part of the rituals, and the singing of hymns (Michell 1988:58). Another communal activity was the meals distributed in the temple not just to priests, but also to pilgrims, regular worshippers and the poor. These meals were not necessarily simple and were prepared daily for lunch. Furthermore, the temples were economic centres, integrated in a temple network spanning the entire kingdom, binding the local elites to the central power through the exchange of material and immaterial goods. This function as economic centre entailed significant administrative tasks which needed to be housed, as did the goods traded within the system.

Given these varied and manifold purposes the sites fulfilled, it becomes obvious that, for a discussion of usage, a focus on the central shrines is not very helpful. Firstly, their purpose needs no further definition; secondly, they represent a fairly stable element within the compounds, in terms of architecture and decorative program; and, thirdly, in a significant number of compounds they constitute the minority of buildings. Instead, what needs to be focused on is the subsidiary buildings, mainly the long halls and *pendopos*, of religious compounds in Southeast Asia which diverge the most between different compounds and change the most over time.

As stated before, Southeast Asian temples were based on the prescriptions of the Indian *vāstu śāstra*s, some of which give extremely detailed rules as to the usage of subsidiary buildings in relation to the cardinal directions and their associated deities (see Table 12.1).

Cardinal direction	God associated with direction	Building
SE	Agni, Gandharva	Kitchen, with open yard with well
SW	Pitṛ	*maṇḍapa* for keeping *vāhana*s
W	Mitra, Śōṣa	Temple of principal *devī*s; can also be location of *garbhagṛha*
WNW	Vanhi	Kalyāna *maṇḍapa*
NW	Rōga	*maṇḍapa* for keeping dresses and ornaments of deities
NNW	Bhallāṭa, Danta	Yāgasāla for performing *homa*s
N	Bhāskara, Bhūdhara	Surrounding deities
NNE	Bhujaṅga	Hall for keeping objects for everyday use, garden, tank
NE	Īśa	Grain store

Table 12.1 Overview of the cardinal directions, their associated gods and subsidiary buildings
(After Sastri and Gadre 1990:xxxix, lxiv–lxv; Kramrisch 1976:I,32; Chakrabarti 1998:68–74.)

Because of the reciprocal relationship between 'visual properties and functional characteristics' (Arnheim 1977:205), it is possible to draw conclusions regarding the intended purpose of a building from its architectural features. However, it is not only the buildings themselves that determine usage, but also the space around. According to von Meiss (1998:101[emphasis as in the original]),

> [a]rchitecture is the art of the hollow; it is defined both from the interior and from the exterior; *walls have two sides*. We penetrate it with our body and not only with our mind. Any critique of architectural

history must take account of this double aspect of hollow and solid in buildings. A work of architecture which is designed or considered only from the exterior ceases to be architecture and becomes a stage set. Conversely, the reduction to just the spatial characteristics eludes the concrete signs and symbols underlain by its material nature.

In other words, in order to analyse functionality, not only the built material has to be considered in our interpretation, but also—maybe even more so— the space created.

When looking at temple compounds in Southeast Asia with the regulations in mind, tentative conclusions can be reached as to how individual buildings might have been used. Naturally, the architectural features of the buildings, such as the degree of openness or closedness, have to be taken into account as well. Thus, buildings with open portals were certainly not suitable for use as storage space of valuable items, such as ornaments of the deities or ritual paraphernalia.

Conclusions as to the usage have to remain slightly hypothetical, although to some extent there is evidence for usage of these halls and *pendopos* when examining the various sources in conjunction. For example, the Randuskari II inscription, dating from 885 CE, mentions *padewāharān*, which, originating from Sanskrit *devāhāra* (divine food), seems to mean 'place for the preparation of food offerings to the gods' and could denote a whole temple, but at least one building for the preparation of food offerings. This is still being practised in Bali, where food offerings are being prepared in a designated building (Soekmono 1995:68). In classical Cambodia, the Lolei inscription mentions in stanza LXIX that outside the dance hall, etc., they [the worshippers] should not eat anything else than betelnut (Bhattacharya 1999:37 line 45). This is a clear indication that dances were performed inside the compounds and that at least one building was designated especially to this purpose.[7]

As already stated above, with an increasing degree of complexity of temple layout, the scope for different activities was increased as well. Given the information contained in the Lolei inscription stanza LXXIII/LXXIV that

---

[7] The Lolei inscription is a special document as it gives a long list of rules and regulations, not just with regard to behaviour and codes of conduct in the temple, but also access and activities. I am very grateful to Professor Bhattacharya for allowing me to use his unpublished translation of the Lolei inscription, which he did during a project organised and directed by Professor T S Maxwell at the Lehrstuhl für Orientalische Kunstgeschichte, Universität Bonn in 1999.

every pious devotee was allowed access to the temple, and current practices in Bali and India, we can assume that the compounds were busy places, full with devotees undertaking *pūjā*, attending recitals, and dance and music performances.

What, then, happens at sites with few or none of these subsidiary buildings, like Ta Keo in 11th-century Cambodia? Generally, the transition from Pre Rup/Banteay Srei to Ta Keo is said to be a shift in building materials from brick to sandstone temples.[8] However, this is not the main change. Instead, what is more significant than the building material is the change in layout, from a compound with a large number of subsidiary buildings to one with only four. From the late ninth century up until Pre Rup and Banteay Srei in the mid-tenth century we can see a continuing development,[9] which changes dramatically with Ta Keo. From the temples of King Indravarman of the ninth century onwards, temple compounds contain a large number of buildings and halls built parallel to the enclosure walls, which have certain architectural features in common (for example, building materials or their overall design). In the temples of subsequent reigns, both in Koh Ker and at Angkor, the number of halls increases, as does the elaborateness of their execution. At Preah Ko, six halls were built; at Bakong, three. At the main temple of Koh Ker we find 12 halls; at the East Mebon, 16. At Pre Rup we find 17 in two enclosures (nine in the inner and eight in the outer enclosure), and Banteay Srei contains 11 of these long halls, albeit in a slightly different arrangement. The next temple, Ta Keo, however, only contains four of these halls, two in the eastern section of each enclosure.

This dramatic change in layout between Pre Rup/Banteay Srei and Ta Keo has far-reaching implications with regards to the functionality of the temples and their social significance.[10] With only four halls, no space was

---

[8] This is not quite correct. Two large earlier temples whose central elements (that is, the stepped pyramids and sanctuaries) were in large part constructed from sandstone are Bakong and Bakheng. Nevertheless, when the compound as a whole is taken into account, Ta Keo certainly is the first temple for which brick was not used at all and laterite was used in only limited quantities.

[9] Development here is used in the sense of changes over time, not in the sense of evolution or progression. We are concerned with the neutral tracing and examining of changes which occurred over a period of a good 100 years, with no intention of evaluating them.

[10] Incidentally, this shift in layout and building material coincides with a dramatic change in the epigraphy. After the mid-tenth century, the Sanskrit inscriptions, giving long eulogies about their founders and other valuable information, are no longer an integral element of the temple compounds. Instead, inscriptions now are more scattered—

provided to undertake many of the activities detailed above. The available space for those activities was not only reduced because of the limited number of halls, but also because of an overall reduction of space inside the compound. What had happened? In contemporary epigraphy no explanation is given as to either a formal religious change or a shift in religious practices. Nevertheless, it seems that the role of the temple changed dramatically with Ta Keo. If the temple had previously been very much part of the everyday life of the surrounding community, indeed of the kingdom as a whole, it had now assumed an exclusively religious role with a strong focus on the 'core' activity of worshipping icons inside the five central *prasat*s and two subsidiary shrines. Whether other activities, such as recitals of texts or dance performances, were relocated to buildings made from perishable materials outside the temple cannot be said with certainty.[11] But it seems clear that a separation of the temple from the everyday life of the people took place, moving it from being the social centre of the community to being predominantly a sacred place of worship, which it would remain until the reign of King Jayavarman VII.[12]

The question is, therefore, why did this change take place? Was the notion of the temple as a social focus, as well as the religious focus, of the community not seen as successful? Was the large number of people visiting the compounds on a daily basis for numerous activities seen as disturbing the worship of the icons at the centre? Or was the shift more a reflection of the personal likes and dislikes of the founding king?[13]

Turning our attention to the temples of classical Java, the situation seems to be a somewhat different one, as indications for the social integration of temples are not only provided by *pendopo*s and their more 'practical' functions, but also by subsidiary shrines. There only exist a few temples nowadays with foundations of subsidiary buildings nearby, for example the Arjuna group on the Dieng Plateau and Candi Barong on Gunung Ijo. The remains of the *pendopo*s at these

---

fewer in number and much shorter. This only changes again under the rule of King Jayavarman VII.

[11] For this to be determined, archaeological excavations would have to be executed around the temple sites and, regrettably, this has not happened so far.

[12] The very detailed inscriptions from that reign (late 12th to early 13th century) indicate that temples once again became the focus of the community and were very much part of their life. The inscription of Ta Prohm mentions 12,640 people living inside the enclosure, and Preah Khan served as a university.

[13] One reason for this change that we can discard is the availability of building materials. Usually, these halls were constructed from laterite, which was readily available locally, and were covered with wooden roof constructions and ceramic tiles, which were also readily available.

temples consist of stone foundations and stone bases for wooden posts, which give clear evidence of the number and size of these buildings.

Subsidiary shrines can only be found in a limited number of temples, most significantly Candi Loro Jonggrang, Candi Sewu and Candi Plaosan. As is stated in the Śivagṛha inscription (856 CE), these auxiliary shrines were founded not only by nobles but also by commoners. At Candi Plaosan, little inscriptions on these small shrines even mention the name of the founder (Soekmono 1995:62ff). Because of a lack of evidence, we can only guess whether worship was undertaken on a daily basis, as it is still practised in India, or whether temples were only visited on festival days, as is customary in present-day Bali. Whichever was the case, though, the sheer number of shrines meant that the temple was frequented by large numbers of devotees on a regular basis. Nevertheless, the focus within these temples seems to have been on worship of icons, as there is no indication of space provided for dance performances or recitals. An exception seems to be Candi Plaosan Lor. Here, we still find the base of a large stone foundation in an enclosure, adjacent to the main temple enclosure on its northern side, which might have been used for assemblies or performances.

Figure 12.3 Candi Loro Jonggrang
(Photograph: Alexandra Haendel)

Conclusion

The temples of classical Southeast Asia, the Brahmanic as well as the Buddhist foundations, are characterised by a variety of layouts and degrees of complexity which are not related to their religious background or foundation date; there is no 'evolution' of temple plans. The conceptualisation of sites seems to have been quite variable and adaptable to the requirements of a specific temple.

In addition to their main function, to facilitate *pūjā*, the temples of classical Southeast Asia served an array of other functions, as evidenced in the various sources. Activities related to these functions can tentatively be assigned to particular subsidiary buildings. With all these activities undertaken inside the compound and the increasing familiarity with it, the temple gains significance as a lived space and becomes an integral part of society.

At Angkor, the change in temple layout in the mid-tenth century does not seem to suggest the preference of the founding king, because the more simplified layout remained in use for two centuries. Rather, it seems to denote an underlying shift towards a concentration on *pūjā*. Both the fact that there were fewer buildings, most of which are now shrines, and that only a small amount of space was provided in between these shrines suggest a channelling of devotees through towards the central *prasat*s. This, in turn, reduces exposure of devotees to the site and the time they spent there, which removes the temple from the experiences of everyday life of the surrounding community and turns it more into a distant place of exceptional activities rather than a place of habitation.

In Java, the focus of most temples seems to have been on activities connected immediately to *pūjā*; even in those compounds that have numerous subsidiary buildings, they are in most cases auxiliary shrines. At those sites, other activities, like recitals or performances and even the preparation of offerings, apparently took place outside the confines of the temple. Notably, those sites which include *pendopo*s within their enceintes or immediately adjacent to them are located in somewhat isolated areas, for example, the Arjuna group on the Dieng Plateau or Candi Barong on the slopes of Gunung Ijo. This leads to the assumption that the location might have necessitated shelters for pilgrims to stay there. This very restricted functionality of classical Javanese temples also means that they have only limited continuity with the temples of present-day Bali. The sequential courts of Balinese temples are only hinted at at Candi Jeto, where courtyards lead up to the central sanctuary.

Figure 12.4 Candi Jeto
(Photograph: Alexandra Haendel)

Overall, temples appear to have been very much the centre of the religious life of the people, and it appears that their integration into more social aspects of the community was more the exception than the rule. It is for this reason that the temples of the early Angkorian period and those built under King Jayavarman VII are remarkable, because they facilitate an array of activities not immediately connected to *pūjā*. It is interesting to note that these periods coincide with what Stern has termed the 'four great reigns' at Angkor (Stern 1934, 1951), which are characterised by a very structured, sequential building program, and long and complex inscriptions; the further exploration of this relationship, however, would go beyond the scope of this chapter. Nevertheless, the phenomenological study of temple layouts reveals related activities and usage patterns which indicate the degree of integration into the everyday life of the community and the social significance the sites had—and partly still have.

Chapter 13

Through the visualisation lens

Temple models and simulated context in a virtual Angkor

Tom Chandler
Lecturer, Faculty of Information Technology, Monash University

Martin Polkinghorne
Honorary Associate, Asian Studies Program, The University of Sydney

In recent years, the shift away from the temple-centric approach of Angkorian studies has become well known (Evans et al 2007; Fletcher et al 2008; Pottier 1999). However, in the short history of the three-dimensional (3D) computer modelling of Angkor, there have been many studies of temple models (Cerezales 1997; CyArk 2006; FOKCI 2007; Visnovcova, Zhang and Gruen 2001; Kenderdine 2004; 3DreamTeam/Vizerra 2008–10; Levy 2001a; 2001b), but little consideration of the environment around the monuments. While the architectural drawing and scale modelling of Angkorian temples has a long history (see Dumarçay 1971a and b; Dumarçay and Courbin 1988; Nafilyan 1969), the modelling of these structures in the virtual world has so far followed a tradition of appraising the temples as isolated exhibition pieces and symbolic artefacts. It is argued that the narrow focus of such studies misses great opportunities in harnessing the power of the medium of 3D visualisation.

This study seeks to introduce the space *between* the temples and to produce the simulated historical, cultural and ecological landscapes that once surrounded them. The future of virtual Angkor can now move beyond digital reconstructions that are defined in only architectural terms. Knowledge about the landscape around the temples has until very recently received significantly less attention. 3D visualising of landscapes cannot reference the relative certainty of the interlocking stone assemblages but must deal with the large, unexcavated (and therefore apparently empty) spaces where the door is open to considerable conjecture. However, while some researchers might fret about committing digital images of reconstructions to relative permanence of a printed publication, we should be mindful that virtual reconstructions remain dependably ephemeral. Physical reconstructions inevitably draw criticism[1] because they are more or less permanent, but the comparatively transient and provisional nature of a virtual reconstruction presents an underexploited contribution to scholarly investigation and debate.

Within *animated* 3D models, the permanence of a reconstruction is doubly transient, especially if the process of prototyping the model means that each time the model is rearranged, so too is the resulting image. Multiple versions are made available through the medium of 3D animation and no one view is presented as correct and peremptory. 3D animation is perfectly suited to dealing with conjecture because it patently is not real. In coloured virtual models with a roving camera, walking figures, echoing sounds and consistently alternative visions, there can be no harm in weighing historical or archaeological evidence to visually experiment with possibilities. Armed with exactly such an impermanent and malleable virtual model, it is into this breach between evidence and conjecture at Angkor that 3D animation can venture.

At Angkor, the ruins of temples have long served as focal points of scholarly interest and investigation. Even in a ruinous state, their obvious size and extent, though not their decoration is still clear today (Polkinghorne 2008:22). But what the Angkorian temples constitute today is only a 'skeleton without a body' (see Groslier 1958:108), for the wooden architecture of the humble peasant dwellings and the richly decorated pavilions of the kings have long since rotted away.

There is an established tradition of illustrated temple reconstruction in the literature (Cunin 2007; Dumarçay 1973; Dumarçay and Courbin 1988; Dumarçay and Royère 2001; Dumarçay and Smithies 2003; Parmentier 1914, 1927, 1939). The conversion of architectural drafts and plans into virtual models is also predicated on customary methodologies. The mathematical geometries used for modelling architecture are an inherent function of most all-purpose 3D programs, and many 3D applications build upon a long lineage of software evolution with roots in Computer Aided Design (CAD) programs for architecture, engineering and construction industries (Fallon 1998; Myers 1998). As architectural remains hold a natural appeal for architects, it is

---

[1] Among the most infamous monumental archaeological reconstructions are the various projects commanded by the late Saddam Hussein in Iraq (Vale 1999) or by Mussolini in the 1930s (Galaty and Watkinson 2004).

unsurprising that they are attracted to modelling such structures with computer software. Conversely, there is also the mathematical attraction of running the iterative architectural patterns and designs of Khmer and Indian temples through computer-generation procedures among computer scientists. Writing more than 20 years ago, Trivedi demonstrated the procedures of self-similar iteration and fractalisation in the construction of Hindu temples (Trivedi 1989) and Datta and Beynon (2005) described a computational technique for reconstructing the surface geometry of Hindu stone temple superstructures based on information derived from textual canons (*śāstras*). More recent still, Pheakdey Nguonphan's detailed study in his thesis 'Computer Modelling: Analysis and Visualization of Angkor Wat Style Temples in Cambodia' places the endeavour of modelling Angkorian temples in computational architecture, a field that combines historic architecture, computer science and applied mathematics (Nguonphan 2009). All of these approaches produce finely grained and detailed visual results and their methodologies are necessary components of visualisation studies; however, they remain intrinsically architecturally specific.

Like the computer models of Angkorian temples, scale models of Angkor are reproductions of an already created monument in miniature. The model of Angkor Wat in the Royal Palace grounds in Bangkok is a much photographed example. In 1860, following a failed attempt to relocate an existing temple (Prasat Ta Prohm) from Angkor to Thailand, the Thai King Rama IV had to settle on a much smaller scale model of Angkor Wat, crafted in the Thai capital at Wat Phra Sri Ratanasasadaram (the temple of the Emerald Buddha) (Kasetsiri 2003). Curious stylistic embellishments in the modelling of this replica of Angkor Wat (Fig. 13.1A) lend it a uniquely Thai interpretation and hint at deeper conceptions of what the heritage of Angkor means to Thailand's historical identity (Ünaldi 2008). Similarly, in the late 19th and early 20th centuries three-dimensional replicas of Angkor's art and architecture were used to promote the wealth and curiosities of France's colonial assets. Casts of artworks made by Doudart de Lagree were shown at the Exposition Universelle in Paris in 1878. In 1889, a replica of Angkor Wat's central tower was erected in the Palace des Invalides and an almost life-size expanded model of the temple was shown in Marseilles in 1922, and again in Paris 1931 for the Colonial Expositions (Fig. 13.2B) (Dagens 1995:104; Edwards 2007). Recently, numerous cement models have emerged in the gardens of Khmer families of Siem Reap (Fig. 13.2A).[2]

---

[2] Scale models of temples are becoming increasingly common in the Angkor area today. Examples can be found at the Bakong temple and the Banteay Srei Rachana workshop on the banks of the Siem Reap River. Miniature replications abound in the markets in the form of key rings, paperweights and clocks.

Figures 13.1 The model of Angkor Wat in the grounds of the Royal Palace at Bangkok
(Photograph: Juliette Truffert)

Figures 13.2A and 13.2B On the left, a scale model of Angkor Wat near the Bakong temple site, Siem Reap. On the right, a photograph of the reconstruction of the central towers of Angkor Wat at the 1931 Paris Colonial Exposition.

The computer models of Angkorian temples are similar to the real-world models in that they mimic the sharp orthogonal views of the architectural draftsman into the 3D computer drawing space. The models are marooned in a digital space and entirely cut off from their cultural context. If the analogy of the temples as the 'religious skeleton' of the city can be extended, these visions equate to the bones of the skeleton having been removed and each displayed in separate glass cases.

While recent restoration studies suggest that parts of the temples were brightly coloured and variously decorated (von Plehwe-Leisen and Leisen 2005, 2008), most digital reconstructions of temples remain decidedly coy about such uncertainties. Levy's observations on rebuilding a virtual model of the temple of Phimai are relevant here:

> Creating an accurate surface treatment is both an art and science. If the goal is to show the monuments as they existed centuries ago…current photos of surface detail must be renewed or reversed in age. Samples of cut quarry stone can help in establishing the colour and luster of materials as they once appeared in the past (Levy 2001b:7).

Interestingly, both the Phimai (Levy 2001a, 2001b) and Heidelberg (Interdisciplinary Center for Scientific Computing 2007) studies situate their reconstructions against a background of finely manicured lawns.[3] Whether this is intended to be the historical context is not clear, but both studies seem to suggest that they use 3D space solely as a kind of digital anastylosis,[4] where the computer assists in visualising the original form of the ruined architecture by reassembling its constituent parts. Aside from the stones being cleanly cut, redressed and reset in the appropriate place, such reconstructions venture nothing more about how the temples might have actually appeared when operational, or what their environs might have looked like.

While surviving stucco features on numerous *prasat* are well known (Fig. 13.3), researchers have also drawn attention to evidence of painted decoration and plastering (von Plehwe-Leisen and Leisen 2005; Uchida et al 2005; Falser 2007). Von Plehwe-Leisen and Leisen (2008:367) argue that the stone and brick surfaces of the temples were covered by paint layers with or without washes, plaster, and stucco. Polychrome decorations were applied directly onto the surface of the stone or over a thin lime wash, and microscopic analyses have yielded pigments of gold, cinnabar, red and white lead, iron red and ochre (von Plehwe-Leisen and Leisen 2008:368).

---

[3] A reconstruction of one of the libraries of Angkor Wat on the University of Heidelberg website features snow-capped mountains in the background.

[4] Anastylosis is a method of architectural conservation pioneered at Angkor in the 1930s by EFEO Conservator Henri Marchal on the temple of Banteay Srei. The method involves the de-assembly of the monument and its re-erection using its own materials.

Figure 13.3 Stucco rendering laid over brickwork amidst a sandstone representation of a *dvarapāla* at Preah Kô

Zhou Daguan refers to 'gold towers' (gilded towers) at the Bayon and Phimeanakas and accounts of Portuguese and Spanish visitors in the 16th century suggest that the towers of Angkor were covered in gild and crowned with globes, banners and bronze tridents (Groslier 2006:71). Such decorations, however minor, were no doubt strategically placed and would have lent considerable visual impact to the temple as a whole. Given the opportunities for suggesting possible reconstructions within the 3D medium, it is surprising that so many Angkorian temple reconstructions have stubbornly stuck to monochrome visions. Indeed, colour is one archaeological reality of Angkor that is seldom expressed in visual descriptions, though a *National Geographic* article featuring paintings by Maurice Fievet (Moore 1960) is a well known exception. In this widely published vision of Angkor as a vividly coloured living city, the illustrations paint lively scenes full of rich red, green and blue fabrics in technicolour, and a great deal of gold ornamentation. Intriguingly, these colours adorn everything but the temples which remained relegated to a uniform cement grey.

Though Zhou Daguan mentions gold towers and faces at Angkor, and there are obvious remains of plaster stucco, the physical evidence for the colouration of the temples is scant. Very little paint work or stucco has survived the centuries of the tropical climate. There is evidence of polychrome decoration and plastering *inside* some of the ruins, but to date no clear evidence of colour has emerged on the many thousands, if not millions, of tumbled stones in the Angkor area. In the words of Carl Sagan, absence of evidence is not necessarily evidence of absence. As a broader analogy, we might consider the field of palaeontology, where renderings of dinosaurs have gradually evolved over the years from grey-green Victorian 'iguanodons' that haunt the grounds of Crystal Palace on the outskirts of London. Today popular science literature depicts dinosaurs as brightly coloured bird-like creatures, despite the lack of hard evidence.

Some experimentation with temple colours has taken place at the fringes of 3D representation. The Siem Reap-based artist Bruno Truffert, on his website Angkor Planet, has used the 3D medium to trial one extreme of possibilities in temple decoration by bringing to bear a wider palette of colours. Citing examples of the highly coloured and decorated original forms of Greek and Roman temples, the colours of Indian temples and the evidence of painted architectural forms in present day Cambodia, Truffert's visions of Angkor suggest fantastic temples rendered in dazzling colour combinations passed by bicycles, cars and aeroplanes (Plate 13.1).

The visualisation of Khmer temples would benefit from a reappraisal of a 'grey' Angkor to one that includes even partially painted attributes. The recent painstaking research into one possible colouration for the central enclosure of Angkor Wat, published as a fold-out supplement in the July 2009 issue of *National Geographic*, is an inventive elaboration of this issue.[5]

Computer-generated images (CGI) in archaeological documentaries have also experimented with colour—for example, Philip Day's 2002 documentary *Lost Worlds: City of the God Kings* (Plate 13.2). Using a mix of live-action footage and CGI sequences, the digital animations set a precedent in composing the first computer vision of a living, medieval Angkor. Colour played a valuable part in image production; the *prasats* were decorated in fringes of red, green and blue, and the tentative reconstruction of the Royal Palace was washed with an imperial red. Wide-ranging renders of Angkor Thom (Yaśodharapura) were cloaked in smoky sepia tones, suggesting the composition as somehow archival. In addition to the decorated stone temples, the images in Day's *City of the God Kings* also depict cultivated vegetation and wooden buildings.

The environment around the temples provides the most exciting opportunity to speculate about the 'look' of a living medieval site. Angkor Wat forms a rectangle of about 1,500 by 1,300 metres, and covers an area—including its 190 metre wide moats—of nearly 200 hectares. Some telling descriptions of Spanish and Portuguese travellers in the 16th century

---

[5] The magazine illustrations were by Bruce Morser. The magazine researchers consulted widely with members of the Greater Angkor Project and also referenced selected visualisations created by Tom Chandler and Michael Lim at Monash University (see Stone 2009).

describe it as an operational temple with gilded statues. To the 3D visualiser and animator, even more valuable are the descriptions of the temple's decorations, which illustrate features no longer in evidence today.

The Portuguese traveller and trader Diego do Couto described the five towers of Angkor Wat as gilded and topped with globes and banners; further accounts by Antonio da Magdalena and Christoval de Jaque also mentioned details of bronze- or copper-gilded balls (Groslier 2006). Groslier points out that the Khmer inscriptions often refer to tridents and banners which decorate the temples. Gifts of decorative banners are mentioned in 17th-century texts. Furthermore it was highly likely that the towers at Angkor Wat were gilded, including metal finials (Groslier 2006:17). For the animator, the addition of windblown banners and pennants to an otherwise motionless structure holds obvious appeal. It may not be a representation of Angkor Wat, but a graffito discovered and outlined at the Bayon by Japanese archaeologists (Nakagawa, 2003) suggests wispy, tapered textiles fluttering from a spire atop a *prasat* as if sketched from a European fairytale (Fig. 13.5A). The July 2009 fold-out illustration of Angkor Wat in the *National Geographic* magazine resulted from considered consultation with Angkor researchers[6] and also conveys a series of decorated towers and banners.

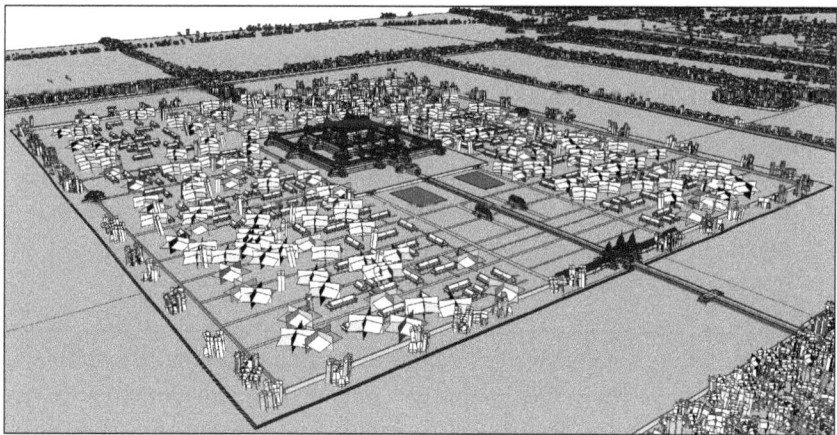

Figure 13.4 A view inside the workings of the model of Angkor Wat. Although the areas approaching the horizon are empty, they have been made invisible to save processing power.
(3D model: Tom Chandler and Michael Lim)

---

[6] Including the present authors and Christophe Pottier. The visualisations are used here as reference pieces.

Figures 13.5A and 13.5B On the left, the chalked outline of a graffito in the Bayon temple, clearly indicating a windblown pennant attached to the top of a spire (Nakagawa 2003). On the right, an image showing the preparation of virtual physics for the banners in the 3D model. Here, the fabric looks as if it is being buffeted in gale-force winds, but this is because the subtleties of the flowing cloth are only realised once the model is rendered in an animation.

When we move beyond the intricacies in detailing the edifice of Angkor Wat to the enclosure around it, we encounter problematic issues in the visualisation of Angkor's medieval urban form. While the walls of some temple complexes, such as Preah Khan and Angkor Wat, enclosed immense spaces, the temples themselves occupy a comparatively small fraction of this area. Groslier attempted to describe the operational city:

> In the middle of the city the temple formed a separate town of its own. Between the sanctuary and its surrounding wall rose a labyrinth of buildings which housed a whole population of priests and assistants (Groslier and Arthaud 1966:162).

If the temptation to see the walled temples of Angkor enclosing self-contained urban centres like the walled towns in China or Europe is hinted at in the excerpt above, very few illustrations or images have attempted to imagine it. The inscriptions offer little information about how many people lived within the major temple enclosures. For example, the Ta Prohm inscription refers to 12,640 'staff', but only states that the total includes those residing in the temples (see Cœdès 1906:11–52 K273).

Angkor Wat has been continuously operational since its construction and, when colonial visitors arrived in the late 19th century, a community of monks was living in front of the central enclosure. As part of France's colonial 'restoration', the wooden buildings of the *sangha* were considered an eyesore and were removed in 1909 to satisfy the tourist desire for the 'picturesque' (Edwards 2005:17–18, 2007:125–143; Winter 2007:32; see also Glaize 2009:57) (Fig. 13.6). Interestingly, the set for the movie *Tomb Raider* in 2000 seems to have had wooden houses and structures temporarily reinstalled in a mock village in the same position.[7] Just as there are several Theravada complexes within the outer walls of Angkor Wat today, it is likely that the temple walls also enclosed an array of wooden buildings.

Figure 13.6 A photograph of thatch dwellings near the north side of the galleries and porticos of Angkor Wat in the early 1900s
(Dieulefils 2001:39)

It is uncertain that Angkor Wat was a temple and a walled city. Jacques (1999:49–50), however, suggests that the roads leading from both sides of the causeway are a grid of streets of 'the original city'. Similar layouts revealed within Angkor Thom (Gaucher 2007; 2002a) and at Banteay Sras in western Greater Angkor by Sonneman and Fletcher, suggest more than empty space. While future archaeological investigations may reveal what was within these walls,[8] visualisation experiments can explore the possibilities. Dozens, if not hundreds of illustrations and 3D models of

---

[7] See Figure 2 in Winter (2002).
[8] Results are anticipated from the mid-2010 Greater Angkor Project excavations within the enclosure walls of Angkor Wat.

Angkor Wat (both scholarly and popular) can be gleaned from a search on the internet. The majority of these graphic depictions present renditions of the same stone architecture, walls, ponds, causeways and moats that remain in place to this day. Although there is no obvious trace of a city or a palace within the boundaries of the great temple, Jacques writes that there is little doubt the outer walls enclosed a capital, including a royal palace placed north of the temple (Jacques 2005:152). Jacques argues that Angkor Wat may have been originally accessed not primarily through the front, western pavilion, as it is today, but along wooden bridges which connected with the cart ways crossing the north and south entrance pavilions. (Jacques 2005:156). These connecting bridges are apparent in the Japanese plan of Angkor Wat drawn in the 1600s, though Péri (1923:126) argues that the three additional bridges can be accounted for by the desire for symmetry in the unknown draftsman who redrew Shimano's rough plans from notes and interpretation.[9]

Little information about the possible contents of the enclosures has been gleaned from archaeological surveys or from historical accounts; however, it is likely that Angkor Wat contained an array of structures and habitation.[10] These matters may be resolved through further invasive archaeological research, but, in the meantime, 3D visualisations offer the utility to test possibilities with visual experiments. For example, did the empty spaces contain large wooden storehouses and official residences or only a scattering of more modest abodes? Could perhaps a proportion of the land inside the precinct have even been cultivated? As a foundation for the 3D visualisations, architectural plans of Angkor Wat are abundant.[11] One possibility considered by our visualisation was to populate the open areas of the Angkor Wat enclosures with a set of wooden buildings patterned along the grid roads within the outer enclosure. Clusters of trees were scattered in a similar manner, with large, solitary and presumably considerably aged types being most visually apparent. The placement and swapping of larger wooden structures and tree models generated new combinations each time the computer was directed to visualise the scene. In attempting visualisations of the entire enclosure of Angkor Wat in the

---

[9] It would be interesting to test the inclusion of these wooden bridges in the virtual model, but this will have to wait for a later study.

[10] The remains of *prasat* bases have been revealed in ground-penetrating radar analysis by Till Sonneman and excavation by the Greater Angkor Project in 2010.

[11] There is no shortage of general top-down plans of Angkor Wat to model against, but for illustrated profiles of the temple as a reconstructed edifice, undoubtedly the best source was Nafilyan (1969).

medieval period, we can venture the possibility that it was something other than a lonely monument in a featureless green lawn and can also distinguish it from walled medieval European or Chinese cities with densely crowded wooden buildings.

In addition to a visual speculation of the contents of Angkor Wat's enclosures, 3D models can position the great monument in the cultural landscape which lies beyond its moat.[12] Our visualisation depicts dense settlements along the outside banks of the moat, the rising bulk of the Bakheng hill (capped with a model of the Bakheng temple) and the road leading to the south gate of Angkor Thom.

The image of Angkor Wat (Plate. 13.3) captured from one of the animations supplied to *National Geographic* (Chandler 2009) followed a classic archaeological documentary format of a flying semi-circular arc, approaching from the south and swinging around to the northeast. The space between the temple and the moat is patterned with modular sets of varied representation—large trees and sizeable wooden structures—which regenerate in slightly different places each time the animation is rendered. Colour and lighting effects have been applied in successive layers and we can see the water of the moat, the dark green of the trees and the gilded towers shining through a tropical haze. Sounds also accompany this animation.

In addition to the totality of the temple complexes, the trees and vegetation of medieval Angkor have similarly not been adequately articulated in 3D visualisations. Though there is substantial evidence in palynological studies (Penny et al. 2006, 2007), epigraphy (Jacob 1978), historical accounts (Loti 1989; Mouhot 1868), historical illustrations (Delaporte and Garnier 1998) and the contemporary landscape, the inclusion of trees in virtual visions of Angkor is usually used as a device to indicate decay and abandonment.[13]

Originally bound to a 19th-century concept of revitalising a culture in decline (Edwards 2007:125–43), the earliest interventions of the École française d'Extrême-Orient (EFEO) at the turn of the 20th century considered clearing of the Angkorian monuments as the best approach to recognise the architectural and artistic legacy of Angkorian civilisation.

---

[12] Cartographical information is provided from the Greater Angkor Project map (see Pottier 1999; Evans 2007).

[13] The image of the silk cotton tree strangling the galleries of Ta Prohm has become not only a photographic cliché but a literary one as well, prompting 'more writers to descriptive excess than any other feature of Angkor' (Jacques and Freeman 1999:136).

The necessity of French researchers to 'clear' the structures, which, on first inspection must have appeared impossibly chaotic in their foliage-covered state has transposed into virtual reconstructions where the trees are removed and replaced by the manicured lawns. Particular species of trees maintain religious and utilitarian associations with Buddhist pagodas in Cambodia, Thailand and Laos (Fig. 13.7). Dumarçay and Royère (2001:52) suggest that *hopea odorata*, commonly known as Koki trees, were planted within temple environs, corresponding to the necessity to renew beam work. Sugar-palm leaves used for temple manuscripts and *ficus religiosa* trees are considered sacred because of their associations with the narrative tradition of Siddhartha Gautama. Pollen samples dating to the medieval period at the Bakong and Sras Srang sites indicate temple grounds were deliberately planted with stands and groves of trees.[14]

In a study on gardens and Hindu–Buddhist architecture in Java, Satari (2008) notes numerous references to the establishment of temple gardens in temple reliefs and epigraphy. These sources distinguish between plants cultivated near a hermitage and around the royal palace ground. The density of vegetation in central Angkor during the medieval period is not known, but by considering the historical and palynological evidence we can begin to hypothesise a living context around the stone structures. Figures 13.8A and 13.8B show Angkor Wat from the north; while the temple itself has faded from view, the landscape in the foreground is in sharp relief. Each image patterns the model clusters with different densities, allowing us to experiment with the intersection of the mapped landscape and the features that are patterned over it.

There are many examples of digital visualisations that consider monumental 'state' architecture, but none that reflect on the local shrines and their context where the majority of the medieval Angkorian population lived and worshipped. In the 1950s Groslier (1958, 1959a, 1979) began to hypothesise that Angkor was a 'hydraulic city', where a large-scale system of canals, embankments and village ponds was integral to the operation of the 'city'. Embraced by Pottier (1999) and Evans (2002, 2007; Evans et al 2007), remote-sensing techniques and substantial ground survey confirmed key aspects of Groslier's thesis and revealed a vast urban settlement characterised by village shrines constructed in both durable and 'temporary' materials stretching across nearly 2,000 square kilometres.

---

[14] Dan Penny (personal communication, July 2010)

Figure 13.7 A 19th-century rendition of the environs of the Royal Pagoda in Bassac in Southern Laos showing large trees shadowing the foreground of the image

(Drawing: E Tournois, based on a watercolour by Louis Delaporte)

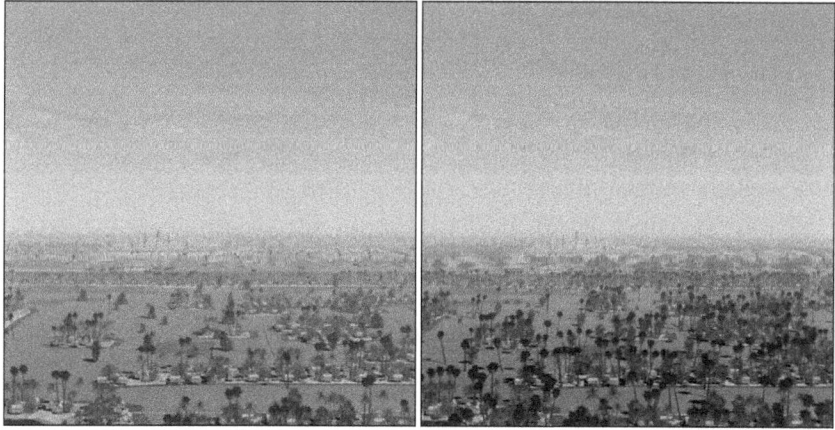

Figures 13.8A and 13.8B Two contrasting views from the north of Angkor Wat in the virtual model. The image on the right has twice the number of clusters of trees and dwellings as the one on the left. These two images show the result of random repatterning of model clusters both inside the compound of Angkor Wat and in the landscapes surrounding the moat.

(Images: Tom Chandler and Michael Lim)

As a relatively contained village settlement on the Angkor plain, the site of He Phka just to the north of the Tonle Sap lake was considered as a potential location for a 3D visualisation of a village shrine *in situ*. It appears distinctly on the Pottier's (1999) archaeological survey of the south of Angkor as a U-shaped moated temple site surrounded by a conglomeration of mounded areas and ponds (Fig. 13.9). Today, the site is scattered with brick fragments and laterite blocks, but, based on a survey conducted by Pottier, we can envisage that the central mound once housed three towers, open to the east, with one *gopura* and one brick enclosure wall passing 12 metres north of the north tower.[15]

Figure 13.9 A visualisation of the village of He Phka as drawn from Pottier's archaeological mapping (1999). Colours were matched with samples from contemporary photography in the area.
(Image: by Tom Chandler and Michael Lim)

When considering an animation of the Greater Angkorian landscape, it was necessary to include numerous local shrine sites. Corresponding to the ability to represent variation in settlement clusters of trees and houses, we can provide nuanced interpretations of the 'styles' of village shrine models. Seen from afar in the virtual model, the 3D village shrines partially obscured by trees appear to be one of the three architectural models, but they are agglomerations of additional stylistic layers and colour schemes overlaid in a modular fashion.

---

[15] Christophe Pottier (personal communication, June, 2010).

Greater Angkor developed as a dispersed low-density city over a period of roughly 600 years (see Evans et al. 2007) during which architectural and artistic styles changed considerably. The artistic genius of the medieval Khmer was an ability to change, modify and invent temple forms in a multitude of combinations. Inconsistency in temple design and form is related to last-minute decisions, reversals, recombinations, medieval restorations, deconsecrations, demolitions and the successful execution of 'inconsistent' plans. The temples we see today can be regarded as cumulative monuments that underwent numerous and different transformations. 3D visualisation of the village *prasat* has the ability to represent the actual diversity and variation that pervades the material culture. To represent the inherent variation in the architectural landscape, a series of three *prasat* were produced broadly corresponding to the artistic 'styles' of the seventh, tenth and 12th centuries.[16] Additional variation is integrated within each designated 'stylistic' period and the *prasat* are divided into another three subsets that distinguish building materials. For example, a shrine of the tenth century might be rendered as either brick, sandstone, laterite, or a combination of these materials. Supplementary variations of colouring, plastering and decoration compose these models differently again resulting in nine nominal combinations of *prasat*.

With an interchangeable array of 3D settlement, landscape and *prasat* models, we can create a non-specific local shrine and village scene. The ability to vary the modular components of the scene allows us to apply the model to nearly any location in medieval Angkor. While the moat, mound and the shrine model serve to define the layout of the site (Fig. 13.10A), it is crowded with many other modelled components (Fig. 13.10B). Pandanus plants fringe the banks of the moat containing scattered lotuses. The shrine is decorated with brightly coloured lintels and its entrance flanked by wooden stands with baskets and parasols. In the background are stands of large trees that shade the entire scene. When we apply light and colours (Fig. 13.11), the vivid red flowers of the *bombax ceiba* tree accent the dusty green canopy and we can see dappled sunlight upon the trodden red soil where a number of figures stand. As well as the animation of the walking figures and waving pennants, the visualisation is layered with atmospheric sounds that fade in and out of earshot to suggest an added spatial dimension to the scene portrayed.[17]

---

[16] These categories do not correspond to the artistic 'styles' designated by French art historians of the early 20th century to describe the broad characteristics of Khmer art over more than 700 years (see Coral-Rémusat 1940; Stern 1927), but are generalised architectural composite models representing periods of approximately one-hundred years.

[17] See Chandler (2009).

Figures 13.10A and 13.10B Two images showing the geometrical underlay behind the 3D render of the shrine in Figure 13.11. On the left, the moat, causeway and architectural model of the shrine. On the right, a wide range of vegetation models crowd the background and foreground of the image, together with wooden religious paraphernalia placed around the shrine's main entrance and a draped pennant on long bamboo poles.

Figure 13.11 A 3D image of a village shrine. A pair of Theravada monks walk towards the viewer, while other figures can be seen sitting in the shade of the nearby wooden shelters, conversing on the causeway and in the foreground. The air here was 'thickened' with a tinge of yellow to mimic humid air permeated with dust or smoke.
(Image: Tom Chandler and Brent McKee)

Figure 13.12A, 13.12B and 13.12C The camera is at ground level, emphasising talking human figures. Each image appears superficially similar, but in the background, the shrine models have been interchanged between the three distinct architectural 'styles'.
(Images: Tom Chandler and Brent McKee)

The scene can be augmented by interchanging the modular shrine 'types' and vegetation models. For example, swapping the hulking, shading mass of a *ficus religiosa* for the slender stands of areca and sugar palms changes the effect of light. The employment of generic shrine 'styles' is distinguished from the meticulous techniques of computational procedural architectural grammars (see Müller et al. 2005, 2006); however, these visualisations place a new and augmented importance on the cultural and environmental landscapes.

When Angkorian architectural models are considered in their historical landscapes, archaeological visualisations can be refocused from the geometrical phenomena of architectural structures to the pluralities and uncertainties of 'living sites' populated with wooden architectural models, colours, vegetation and animated forms. Creating these models inevitably involves extrapolation from incomplete and inconsistent epigraphic, archaeological and art history sources. However, 3D visualisation offers scholars the unique opportunity to hypothesise with plural reconstructive possibilities. At Angkor, where the landscape between the temples was previously rendered merely as 'jungle' or 'white voids' on the printed page, we can begin to address archaeological uncertainty with shifting patterns of wooden buildings, trees, settlements and village shrines. And, finally, in this space of interchangeable elements, moving figures and simulated sound, we can begin to explore the wider potentials of what a historical 3D computer model might offer to scholarship in the digital age.

Acknowledgements

The authors are indebted to the 3D modelling and animation expertise of several research assistants at Monash University who ensured the quality of the digital images reproduced in this chapter: Michael Lim, Brent McKee, Chandara Ung, Janet Saw and Carol Merlo. Unless otherwise indicated, photographs were taken by the authors. Martin Polkinghorne wishes to acknowledge the support of the Greater Angkor Project, the Authority for the Protection and Management of Angkor and the Region of Siem Reap, l'École française d'Extrême-Orient and Heritage Watch. Research was conducted with funding from an Australian Postgraduate Award, the Carlyle Greenwell Bequest and an Endeavour post-doctoral fellowship.

Chapter 14

Graves, trees and powerful spirits as archaeological indicators of sacred spaces

Angelo Andrea Di Castro

Assistant Lecturer, School of Philosophical, Historical and International Studies, Monash University

> We find that what connects all the cases of comparing is a vast number of overlapping similarities, and as soon as we see this, we feel no longer compelled to say that there must be some one feature common to them all. What ties the ship to the wharf is a rope, and the rope consists of fibres, but it does not get its strength from any fibre which runs through it from one to the other, but from the fact that there is a vast number of fibres overlapping.
> (Wittgenstein 1965:87)

In this chapter an outline of selected indicators is presented that can help in investigating and understanding various perceptions of primary factors of experience associated with sacred spaces. The liminal sacredness of spaces is taken into consideration in an attempt to define a limited framework of inference for the archaeology of religion.[1]

Sacred spaces are often characterised by the presence of graves (including cenotaphs and memorials) and/or sacred trees. These are generally perceived as abodes of powerful spirits—ancestors, founders of villages, initiators of

---

[1] For the archaeology of religion see Renfrew (1994) and Insoll (2001, 2004); see also the alternative model proposed by Verhoeven (2002:233–6). For a theoretical approach to the phenomenology of landscape archaeology, see Tilley (1994). On liminality see, for instance, Kelleher (2009:32–6, 49–50).

lineages, chiefs, or local heroes—and can be identified with the *genii loci*, the local guardians of sacred places. These powerful spirits related to tombs of heroes, kings, saints and sacred trees are foci of rituals meaningful for social cohesion. Memorials of heroes and village founders signify important aspects for the identification of the current living group with the land. Local people can see themselves as belonging to and as active elements of the land they live in; this is reflected in the worship and rituals they perform at sacred trees or at their ancestors' graves.[2]

A selection of various Southeast Asian examples will be used to compare the worship of holy trees, which are at times associated with the memorials of deified heroes in the Indian subcontinent,[3] as well as the worship and prayers performed at particular sacred places of Islamic Central Asia. This will provide an opportunity for an assessment of preliminary categorisation based on the theory of family resemblances, adopting the polythetic classification as formulated by Rodney Needham (1975).[4] The analysis through family resemblances of the various religious phenomena and evidential material—textual, iconographic, or symbolic—may well be advantageous when carrying out an investigation in religious contexts, such as the study of popular practices performed around trees, tombs and so forth in Islam, Buddhism and Hinduism. In fact, using monothetic classes would be too reductive, because by definition the entire range of constituents has the same features and is, therefore, characterised by identity and exclusivity. In a polythetic categorisation, the constituents do not necessarily have the same characteristic features, but the majority of them generally have a range of features in common. Their relation is defined by similarity and is characterised by inclusivity. Because of this inclusivity, when polythetic classification is applied as an open-ended method for comparative analysis, it possibly will result in more complexity and, at times, reveal unfeasibility. However, the reward is that it brings in broader and more meaningful data and a limited risk of arbitrary exclusions (Needham 1975:358).

---

[2] In anthropological research this relation between sacred space and cultural landscape is well established; to cite only few works on Indonesia, see Forth (1998), Wessing (1988) and Hefner (1985:65–103).

[3] On the funerary practices in tribal and rural India, and on graves and memorials of ancestors, village founders or deified heroes, see Settar and Sontheimer (1982), Archer (1947) and Singh (1970:151–70).

[4] On family resemblances and polythetic classification in regards to the study of the archaeology of religion, see also the remarks about the categorisations of religions by Insoll (2004:143–5). For an early attempt to redefine religion following the method of polythetic classification applied to Singhalese Buddhism, see Southwold (1978). On polythetic classification of spirits in Flores, see Forth (1998:323–48).

Figure 14.1 Sacrificial tree outside the *mazar* of Sultan Setoq Bogra Khan at Stachi, near Artux, Kashgar
(Photograph: A A Di Castro)

Even terms such as 'Hinduism', 'Buddhism' and 'Islam' are, by their basic definitions, rather problematic because each of these terms implies a wide disparity and variability in practices and beliefs. Looking at the Islamic religion we find that the basic tenets, the Five Pillars, are particularly simple.[5] Nevertheless, there are many blurred zones when it comes to defining the Islamic nature of some rituals, such as the sacrifice of fowl or goats, a common practice in many Islamic societies (Insoll 1999:23, 44, 89, 114, and plate 2.4), and the votive offerings for obtaining protection, healing, good luck and for a vow or a thanksgiving (Lymer 2004:164–6;

---

[5] The Five Pillars, *Arkān Al-islām*, are considered duties for every faithful Muslim: *shahādah*, the profession of faith; *salat*, the prayer performed five times daily; *zakat*, charity, or alms tax, for the benefit of the poor; *sawm*, fasting during the month of Ramadān; and *hajj*, the pilgrimage to Mecca.

Sakai 2002:109–12), as well as the offerings at particular graves on specific occasions and for the performances of life-cycle rituals.[6] For instance, the 'sanctification' of particular places under the broad definition of 'holy grave' is a widespread practice that might also comprise the recognition of pre-Islamic sacred sites and their transformation and assimilation into the Islamic sacred landscape. This process of Islamisation, or the creation of new sacred places *ex novo*, is a common practice in Islamic societies, especially when these places are associated with remarkable figures, such as Sufi saints, founders of schools and preachers. Some people believe certain tombs possess particular powers, and they visit these miraculous tombs of saints, thus following the Islamic tradition of pilgrimage. Local and regional places of pilgrimage at times can also attain a national or super-national importance. Along these lines tombs, mausolea and cenotaphs are essential elements of a spiritual geography, functioning as sacred markers within the physical and metaphysical landscape.[7]

Last century, unorthodox practices and beliefs were generally considered a sort of religious 'contamination' and 'pagan survivalism'; however, understanding the process of integration of various religious substrata of tribal and/or local cults within the Islamic world has become a more significant issue.[8] Exemplificative in this regard is the change of perceptions and reinterpretations of *slametan*, the Javanese communal feast, considered by Geertz a ritual preserving some forms of animism, as, for example, when food is offered to the tomb of the guardian spirit of the village. For Woodward, *slametan* incorporated pre-Islamic elements interpreted in Islamic terms. However, if one follows Woodward's line of reasoning, one can understand the ritual redistribution of food (to people as well as grave spirits) which characterises the *slametan* as a form of *zakat*, the Islamic injunction of charity (Geertz 1960:82; Woodward 1988:55; Hefner 1985:104–17). This will be even more apparent when ritual offerings of food and ritual meals at cemeteries and memorials are compared with similar practices outside Indonesia.

---

[6] See, for instance, the practices described by Heringa 1997.
[7] On pilgrimage to holy places, or *ziyarat*, see, for instance, Insoll (1999:113–14, 183–84) and Lymer (2004:161).
[8] See, for instance, the work of Westermarck (1933), dealing mainly with religion and magic in Morocco. Bausani (1966, 1984) has tackled the problem of cultural integration in Islam, distinguishing three levels: the primitive phase of Muhammad; the second phase of the caliphates; and the third phase, of integration of the Umayyad-Abbasid Islam with the local elements of the various cultures from Africa to Southeast Asia.

Trees and tombs

In the late 1970s, limited excavations were carried out in the proximity of the village of Jurang, about ten kilometres north of Kudu, in central Java (Satari 1981:1). Decorated fragments of terracotta miniatures and pottery dated to the transitional phase of Majapahit/Islamic kingdoms of late 15th century were found on the slope of a hill called the *pundhen* of Pundisari, on the edge of a burial area (Satari 1981:7). The term *pundhen* indicates a place where a local guardian spirit is worshipped (Chambert-Loir 2002:133; Sukunda-Tessier 1997:339). Apparently, the place is considered to be sacred and people still offer pots containing coins and flowers, which with time has caused the formation of a massive deposit of vessels under a tree (Satari 1981:1). The miniatures mainly represented mountains, caves, elephants and other figures. The association of trees, pots full of offerings and mountains can be found on numerous friezes of Borobodur with figurations of the cosmic tree with vases full of riches placed at its foot and with *kinnaris* and other mythical figures at the sides (Nou and Frédéric 1994:figs 101–2, 126, 137, 143, 147, I a 28, 364, 371). The Borobodur itself represents the cosmic mountain, Mount Meru (Nou and Frédéric 1994:39–40; Mabbett 1983), and in this case the Indian symbolism merged easily in the Javanese culture where the cosmic mountain plays an important role in the ancestral narration and imagery. The sacred tree and the cosmic mountain are also fundamental symbols still covering an important role in the Javanese tradition of the *wayang*, the shadow play. In fact, the *gunungan*, decorated with the design of a tree on a mountain surrounded by birds and other animals is one of the main figures of the traditional Javanese puppetry (Bosch 1960:178–86; Mair 1988:64–6). In Burmese Mon's narrations of the lineage of the chiefs originated with the union of a male hero (a wizard, a foreigner) and a chthonic goddess (a snake-woman, an ogress). The notion of this mythic dyad, widespread in different variants in Southeast Asia, is reflected in the cult and the symbolism of the sacred tree and the cosmic mountain, and is generally connected to matrilineal descent (Shorto 1967:140).[9]

Tree and mountain are ancient Indian cosmogonic symbols. The complex symbolism of the cosmic tree alludes to the Vedic sacrificial stake, the pole of Indra, the *axis mundi* separating and joining the underworld and the

---

[9] For the matrilineal descent of power and for foundational myths, see Shorto (1963:574, 585–91) and Brown (1921:89–96). For the mythic origin of Funan, see Mabbett (1977:146) and Hall (1985:48–77).

heavens. The Vedic tree, *Indrakhīla*, or sacrificial post, is also Vanaspati, the Lord of the forest, the tree of the knowledge and life; the symbolic polarity of the tree, implying the coincidence of the opposites, is clearly evident by the snakes coiled around its roots and the birds among the branches.[10]

Trees are important symbolic element in major events of the Buddha's life; in specific circumstances they also mark the sacredness of the place, such as in the case of Lumbinī or Bodhgayā. The symbol of the tree was also used to indicate the Buddha himself in the early artistic representation (Dehejia 1997:ch 2, 4–6). The chthonic element of the tree might be connected to the primordial funerary association as can be inferred from the *Atharva Veda* (XVIII. 2. 25; 3. 70), perhaps referring to the fact that the corpses were sometimes buried in hollow trunks or near the roots of a tree (Stutley & Stutley 1980:494; Crooke 1978:II, 85).[11] In various Southeast Asian islands the shamans' corpses were left on the branches or on a platform on a tree or in a hollow trunk; the Orang Laut, the Sea Gypsies, who lived in boats around the Southeast Asian coasts used to bury their dead in trees (Winstedt 1961:12–13; Rivers 2003:101).

On the other hand, sacred trees are also connected with fertility; Burmese women worship *nats* dwelling in sacred trees to obtain a child.[12] Ancient Indians used to ask progenies to be granted by *yakṣas*, the tree spirits (Coomaraswamy 1971:I, 32–3; II, 11–12, 33n3).[13] Dravidian hunter-gatherers in central India worship Vanaspati/Bansatti, or Bansuri, the goddess personifying and presiding over the forests for protection and fertility. Uncut triangular stones called *śakti*, decorated with red ochre are placed on platforms at the foot of particular trees.[14] The association of divinities connected to the vegetal realm and fertility and female energies is already manifest in the *Atharva Veda* (Di Castro 2008:25). The worship of the Indian village goddesses (*grāmadevatā*), characterised by votive offerings such as terracotta figurines, food and rags, is typically connected to a tree on the edge of the village.

---

[10] For the tree symbolism, see Bosch (1960:65–98), Coomaraswamy (1979:7–12), Eliade (1958:265–330; 2004:259–87) and Crooke (1978,:II, 83–121). For the symbolism of tree in association with pillars and the stupa, see Irwin (1973:716–17, 20; 1976; 1979:825–43) and Snodgrass (1992:153–7, 180–4, 256, 320–8). For the snakes and the birds, see Zimmer (1946:72–6).

[11] John of Plano Carpini (Roux 1990:207) also records a similar tradition among the Mongols.

[12] For a contraposition between Burmese *nat* cult and Buddhism, fertility and contraception, see Brohm (1963:164).

[13] On the association of *yakṣas*, trees and fertility, see also Sutherland (1992:24–9).

[14] Palaeolithic populations of the area also used similar votive stones as the excavations of Baghor demonstrated (Kenoyer et al 1983). On the jungle goddess, see also Crooke (1978:I, 114–15).

Graves of powerful spirits, like founders of settlements, ancestors and warrior heroes are visited mainly during the celebration of Muhammad's birth in the region of Bandung, in West Java. Even though people consider that important persons are buried in these graves, their identification is not strictly relevant; in fact it is possible that in some cases no-one is buried in the graves. What is important is that these tombs (or cenotaphs) are physical markers for sites where cosmic power is believed to be accessible (Wessing 1988:44, 51–2). The Bugis of Sulawesi disguise sacred spots—places where the ancestors descended from or ascended to Heaven—as graves, making them more acceptable for orthodox Muslims (Pelras 2002:119, 127–8, 130, fig 8.1). These landmarks devise a magico-religious topography, like around Singapore where ancient animistic beliefs merged into a number of *keramat* (sacred place, sacred person or miracle in Malay).[15] In Singapore, sacred hills, trees and graves are often associated with apocryphal, if not manufactured saints; in fact, even here some *keramat* do not contain any graves (Rivers 2003:94, 115). Other *keramat* can possess healing properties; graves of medicine men and women (*dukuns*) can also become powerful places where people go and ask for particular healings or protection. The grinding stones used by the *dukuns* are usually buried with them. In India, grinding stones are connected to rituals related to marriage, nutrition as well as to healing; they can also be placed in front of images of the rural gods and used as a table for offerings (van der Kroef 1955:29; Crooke 1978:II, 166, 180, 191; Archer 1947:figs 18, 25).

Rags

Near Taiping in West Malaysia there was a famous *keramat*, a tomb of a *dukun*, a healer/midwife, where supplicants used to ask for healing and protection hanging rags, or stones, on the huge tree under which her grave was located (Winstedt 1924:271). Hanging rags, threads, or entire garments to trees connected to holy places, is still a popular practice in India. For example, pilgrims visiting Rāmdev's grave in western Rajasthan offer rags (or clothes) to a large tree in front of Rāmdev's temple, asking for a child or as a vow. Other trees possess curative virtues, thanks to the association with the saint (Binford 1976:131, 141).[16]

---

[15] I would like to thank Dr Leon Comber for stimulating conversations on *keramat* in Malaysia and Singapore.

[16] On Rāmdev's cult, see also Khan (1997) and Bharucha (2003:181–97). On trees and rag offerings in India, see Crooke (1978:I,161–3) and Thurston (1912:155–7).

Figure 14.2 Tree in front of Rāmdev's grave, Rajasthan
(Photograph: W. Parker)

The practice of offerings rags on trees is rather common in Central Asia; in Merv, people ask for protection and for children by hanging textile strips on the trees flanking the tomb of Mukhammed ibn-Zaid.[17] Another sacred tree that still receives offerings in the form of clothes or rags is in the mausoleum of Shah-i-Zinda in Samarkand, where, according to popular tradition, the body of a relative of the Prophet (Kusam Ibn Abbas) is buried (Rozwadowski 2004:108).

At the beginning of the last century, Stein observed votive rags on trees next to the supposed *mazar* (a mausoleum/cenotaph) of the sixth Imam Jafar Sadiq in the environs of Niya, in Xinjiang (Stein 1907:313). The tomb of Mahmud Kashgari, the medieval scholar and lexicographer, attracts flocks of Uygur pilgrims to its location near Wuper (Opal), about 30 kilometres

---

[17] Annaogly (1997:249) defines this practice as a survival of shamanism.

southwest of Kashgar. Whoever desires a child ties a thread, a ribbon or a rag to the branches of a tree at the foot of his mausoleum (see plates 14.1 and 14.2). The tradition has it that Kashgari himself planted it there next to a source. Even though he was not a mystic, a saint, nor an author of religious texts, he is still worshipped as a holy man, a sort of cultural hero for the Chinese Uygur, a symbol of cultural identity and ethnicity.

On the road to the tomb of Mahmud Kashgari, a couple of kilometres before the main entrance to the park of the memorial of Kashgari, there is another, lesser-known *mazar*. 'Seven heroes' appeared in a dream to a farmer who, following their indications, built the cenotaph. In the visionary dream, the man also received detailed instructions about the worship that needed to be offered to each of the seven heroes' tombs (cenotaphs) in order to remove particular illness or disturbance. The place is considered sacred and it is in fact a *mazar*, with a small cemetery formed around it. People worship here, asking for healing; they burn incense to the heroes' tombs and leave rags as a testimony of their visit and prayers.[18]

Figure 14.3 Cemetery outside the mazar of the 'seven heroes'
(Photograph: AA Di Castro)

---

[18] The informants are two Uyghur sisters who are granddaughters of the man who built the *mazar*. These women were interviewed in April 2005 during the survey carried out by the Kashgar Project of Monash Asia Institute (see also Michell, Vicziany and Tsui 2008:14, 131). It is possible that the symbolism of the 'seven heroes' or 'seven Khans' is connected to an archaic astral symbolism of the Turkic peoples already recorded in the 11th century by Mahmud Kashgari (Roux 1990:148).

Figure 14.4 Interior of the *mazar* of the 'seven heroes'
(Photograph: AA Di Castro)

Figure 14.5 *Mazar* of the 'seven heroes'
(Photograph: AA Di Castro)

Muslims of Kazakhstan leave strips of textile as offerings in two important prehistoric rock art sites (Tamgaly and Terekty Aulie), which are integrated into their local pilgrimage. At Tamgaly, the archaeological evidence shows that the area was already used as a funerary ground during the Bronze Age, a much earlier period of the Islamic grave, which lies not far from the rock art figurations. Nevertheless, the sacrality of both sites lies in the Kazakhs' connection to the landscape and the recognition of their cultural and ancestral significance (Lymer 2004; Rozwadowski 2004:108–9).

Footprints

During his survey in the area of Bandung in West Java, Wessing (1988:53–4) recorded the presence of a *batu tapak*, a stone footprint at a place called Gunung Paseban, without any related story, observing that generally the *batu tapak*, or Buddhapāda is connected to a place where the Buddha walked. In a spiritual landscape footprints are important symbolic features; they are signs left in the stone by saints, heroes or mythical personages by which—thanks to these marks—places became sacred. Footprints in Southeast Asia are mainly Buddhist symbols. However, silhouettes of footprints were previously painted on the walls of the cave at Cape Abba, near Darembang on the MacCluer gulf, on the West Coast of New Guinea.[19] Footprints are also objects of devotion of ancestral beliefs, considered traces of supernatural beings left in a mythical time, such as the footprints near Gunung Jati left by Semar (Chambert-Loir 2002:136),[20] or the marks imprinted on a rock on the Nanga Mountain in Flores by a cultural hero (Erb 1988:111–12, fig 115), or the Malay *keramat* associated to footprints of mythical beings (Winstedt 1924:267, 269–70).

In the Buddhist context, the footprint is one of the earliest symbols to allude to the physical presence of the Buddha as well as to the symbolical significance of following the *dharma*, because following the footprints of the Buddha is following his teaching.[21] As an early Buddhist symbol, the footprint indicates the presence of the Buddha and is adopted as a narrative expedient in various relief panels to describe the motion of the Blessed, such as the crossing of the river Neranjara or the famous seven steps at his birth

---

[19] This is the oldest rock painting of this area (see Holt 1967:11, plate 17).
[20] Semar was an old Javanese god transformed into a jester in the Hindu–Javanese drama.
[21] It is possible that the metaphorical significance of the Buddhapāda originated in India by the adoption of pre-Buddhist symbols (Coomaraswamy 1979:16–17). On the conception of the Buddhapāda as a relic, see Kinnard (2000:37–45).

in Lumbinī (Dehejia 1997:figs 132, 154).²² Aśoka visited Lumbinī during his 20th regnal year, as evident by the inscription on the sandstone pillar.²³ The *Aśokāvadāna* narrates that the Maurya king knelt to worship the marks of the seven miraculous steps (Przyluski 1923:251–2).²⁴ According to Seng Cai, a Chinese pilgrim who visited Lumbinī, Aśoka had monumentalised and encased the seven footprints in lapis lazuli (Petech 1950:35–6).²⁵ The Chinese pilgrims, Fa Xien and Sun Yun, inform us about a prodigious Bhuddapāda in Udyāna (Pakistan) that, according to local tradition, Buddha had left on a rock during his visit to north India (Legge 1998:29; Beal 1983:xcvi).²⁶ Fa Xien also mentions the mark left by Buddha on the top of a mountain in Sri Lanka (Legge 1998:103), referring to the famous footprint on Adam's Peak.²⁷ In Tibetan and Nepalese Buddhist beliefs there are numerous sacred places characterised by supernatural marks left by the foot of saints and powerful ascetics (Ferrari 1958:40, 45, 53; Wylie 1962:59, 60, 84–6, 91; 1970:31).

Indian footprint worship is not Buddhist exclusively; there are striking similarities with the footprint of Viṣṇu; even though the origin of the Viṣṇupāda is usually related to the story of the three strides of Viṣṇu narrated in the *Ṛg Veda* (I. 154), the earliest material evidence of footprint appears to be of Buddhist origin.²⁸ In different contexts, footprints in India are associated to memorials, commemorating the death of particular individuals. In Jainism, for example, voluntary death (not considered as suicide) is an old venerated custom that is remembered with the erection of small monuments called *niśidhi*. These monuments, occasionally showing a pair of footprints, mark the *samādhi*, the spot where the ascetic finally attained the ultimate renunciation terminating the last bonds with his/her physical life (Upadhye 1982:45–6; Settar and Korisettar 1982:283–97;

---

[22] For the 'walking' Buddha and footprint's cult in Southeast Asia, see also Brown 1990.
[23] For a translation of the Lumbinī edict, see Thapar (1963:261).
[24] The symbolism of Buddha's first seven steps relates to the power over the cosmos, symbolised by the four directions of the space plus the centre, the zenith and nadir (Snodgrass 1992:275–9).
[25] Author of the *wai-kuo-shih*, Seng Cai was of Yuezhi origin and lived during the Chin dynasty (265–420 CE). No evidence of this lapis lazuli work has been discovered so far.
[26] Stein (1930:60–1, fig 40) had identified the site of this sacred place as well as the actual Buddhapāda and the surrounding monastic ruins (see Tucci 1958:302–3, fig 9).
[27] The Hindus relate this sacred mark to Śiva, while the Muslims ascribe it to Adam (Paranavitana 1958:11). Paranavitana (1958:61–7) believes that the cult of the Adam's Peak footprint has a pre-Buddhist origin.
[28] For the conceptual similarities and the controversial theories about the origin of Viṣṇupāda and Bhuddapāda, see Kinnard (2000:36, 46–52). For the Vedic myth, see the translation and commentary of O'Flaherty (1975:175–6).

Settar 1989:189–90, plates xvii a, b, xviii a, b). Memorials for religious self-immolation in tribal India can also display similar representations (Sontheimer 1982:271–3, figs 21–3). Also in the cult of the Rājpūt hero Rāmdev, where local folk, Hindu and Islamic elements are merged, the footprints play a primary role. In terms of importance, these are second only to the grave of the hero, and as an object of worship they are representing a spiritual manifestation of the saint.[29] In Islam the worship of the footprints of the Prophet is a custom mainly popular in South Asia, the most famous relic probably being the Qadam Sharif in Delhi (Hasan 1993; Welch 1997).[30]

Perhaps the oldest reference of a sacred footprint is in Herodotus (*The histories* IV. 82), who, among the *mirabilia* of the land of the Scythians, mentions a stone footprint of Heracles near the river Tyras (Dniester). This river defined a particularly significant region for the Cymmerians, especially for the presence of the tumuli of their royal ancestors (*The histories* IV. 11, 12). Herodotus' informants indicated the footprint of Heracles as an important piece of memorabilia, a marker left in the landscape by the hero who, according to some local versions, was the ancestor of the Scythian royal lineages. The Scythians would have originated by the union of Heracles and a snake-virgin, representing the chthonic, aboriginal sacredness (*The histories* IV. 8–10). Here again we have the association of the hero as mythical ancestor, footprints and sacred areas marked by graves. A resemblance with the Southeast Asian pattern of an external hero in union with a local snake/ogress princess is also remarkable, perhaps indicating concerns of the legitimation of non-autochthonous descent in a partly matrilineal aristocracy.[31]

Concluding remarks

It is critical in the archaeology of religion to read the landscape with the aim of detecting sacred places. The complexity of this process is increased because of the overlapping and shifting of beliefs generating syncretism and multi-cultic phenomena. In addition to a practical knowledge of the

---

[29] In Rāmdev's cult, interpretations of the footprints change from Islamic to Hindu context according to the 'background' of the devotees, see Khan (1997:106, ff).
[30] Crooke (1978:II, 200) refers to another Prophet's footprint that was in Lucknow before the so-called Indian Mutiny.
[31] For a historical interpretation of the Scythian myths of origins, see Gallotta (1980: 20–30).

material culture and topography of the area, the investigator should be familiar with the myths, iconography, practices and social meanings of the cults performed by ancient as well as contemporary populations. This would facilitate an understanding of the ancient's perception of a sacred place and the distinction between an auspicious place and a dangerous one—the social and spiritual boundaries implying containment and exclusion, such as the dichotomy between a tamed, ordered space of a village and the uncontrolled, potentially dangerous forces of a natural environment like a forest or a desert. Thus, this would assist in recognising how tombs and memorials of the first settler, a founding hero, a king, a chief or that of a holy man mark a sacred place and how these features can create and characterise a spiritual landscape. On the other hand, this characterisation of the spiritual landscape involves notions of legitimacy[32] and territoriality, conferring, moreover, meanings for ethnic, national and cultural identities.

In order to study the characteristic features of sacred places and relevant practices, the adoption of polythetic classification can generate inspiring results. Starting with two basic categories (trees and graves), two supplementary were added (rags and footprints), and the process of adding and highlighting sub-categories by similarities could have been continued. For instance, in considering the cult of Rāmdev, the association of the hero's grave, footprints and miraculous trees has been highlighted. It would be significant to investigate to what extent the cult of the Panch Pirs (Khan 1997:89–92) and the pattern of the five brothers, recurring in many Indian folk narrations and genealogy (Thapar 1979:206), are related, and subsequently to investigate the nature of the associated votive offerings of rag horse figurines in connection with the terracotta figurines of horses with or without riders in India. Another consequential corollary to this would be the comparison of the iconography of the 'spirit rider' from the shores of the Black Sea to the Indonesian islands in order to observe possible structural resemblances in the different socio-economic, religious and anthropologic contexts (Blawatsky and Kochelenko 1966:1–13, figs 1–7; Barbier and Newton 1988:figs 50, 62, 65–7, 122, 127, plates 8, 11, 17, 42; Forth 1998:plates 5, 8). It must be clear that similarity, or even correspondence of features or 'structures', doesn't necessarily imply descent or evolution from a common original source.

---

[32] In some circumstances, Indian memorials might prove also the right of land possession (Thapar 1981:296).

Comparing cults and beliefs related to sacred trees, *keramat*, *mazar* and memorials can help in understanding the nature of ancestors' worship of ancient people. It can also provide important data regarding the process of assimilation of practices generally labelled as local or folk tradition to world religions. There is plenty of scope here for future research projects.

Chapter 15

Imagery of the temple in Old Javanese poetry

Stuart Robson

Adjunct Associate Professor, School of Languages, Cultures and Linguistics, Monash University

Anyone who visits Central Java soon becomes aware of the ancient monuments located in this region, which are a significant tourist attraction. They are rightly famous and worth seeing. The names Borobudur and Prambanan spring to mind, but there are, in fact, many more, some rarely visited. Bearing in mind the damage of 1,000 years, including the removal of stones to build sugar mills during the colonial period, we can use our imagination to perhaps form a mental picture of what the region may have looked like in the year 860 CE, for instance, when the buildings were intact and functioning. It must have been an impressive sight. Of course, the same would apply to East Java, which flourished in the succeeding period when similar buildings were erected.

These remarks clearly call for the better definition of context. The context is the history of early Java, that is, Java of the pre-Islamic period, when the civilisation generally termed 'Hindu–Javanese' (although it had Buddhist elements) was the force that underlay and inspired Javanese culture and society. This does not ignore the complexity of the situation, in which the Indian ('Hindu') component was not shared equally by all the diverse elements of society, but we are here alluding to the more visible reminders of the past. The period taken as a context here can be said to be from the mid eighth century until the end of the 15th century. This gives an idea of the time-span involved—about seven and a half centuries.

It might also be useful to specify the sort of buildings that is being referred to. The ones that have survived are built of stone and brick, but there were also wooden ones that can be seen only in depictions in the reliefs placed on the walls of the stone buildings. The structures of stone or brick are apparently religious buildings, and these are the ones now given the name *caṇḍi*. There were other settlements, however, in the form of hermitages and the residences of teachers and religious communities, and we find a corresponding range of terms to refer to these. The differences were probably ones of function. At least the *caṇḍi* stands apart from the rest and it will be our subject in most of what follows.

Religious institutions of all varieties were to be found in locations spread far and wide across the countryside, sometimes in the lowlands and sometimes on the slopes of mountains, rather than always in the capital at the heart of the kingdom. In short, even at that time, anyone who was travelling about in the countryside of Java would be quite familiar with the sight of a temple, or group of temples, their pinnacles rising above the surrounding greenery and visible across the fields or on the slopes of the mountains.

Who would these travellers, the tourists of early Java, have been? Sometimes the royal court would go out to enjoy themselves in the mountains and along the seashore when the season was right. Others must have been soldiers and traders. Another category of traveller was the professional poet. It is the poets we have to pay attention to here, as they are the ones who have bequeathed us their works, to the extent that they have managed to survive the ravages of time. These works are a product of the same Hindu–Buddhist civilisation that produced the temples and are, therefore, inspired by a comparable set of ideas. Religion had a prominent place in both the temples and the poets' works. It goes without saying that religion, in a general sense, was probably much more in the forefront of people's thinking then than it is now in the West.

The poets wandering through the countryside were, however, not free-range; they were employed within the royal bureaucracy. They had a job to do for the king and often had to put in an appearance at court. Their work too betrays the close links between the institution of kingship and the art of poetry, and this includes function and themes.

The poetry I am speaking of is written in the Old Javanese language, an earlier stage of Javanese. This was a language laden with fine Sanskritic forms and well adapted to the creation of literary works, both poetical and prose. A number of such works have been handed down. With the gradual adoption of Islam in Java from the 16th century onwards, it was the Hindu island of Bali that would preserve and continue the literary tradition of early Java, so that, as is often said, it is Bali we have to thank for the preservation of Old Javanese literature in its purest form and it is Bali that has kept the palm-leaf manuscripts that form our source of knowledge for Old Javanese.

The Balinese refer to the language and its literature as Kawi and both have an important place in their contemporary culture. Here, however, I am referring only to the works written in Java during the Hindu–Buddhist period, so my remarks do not pretend to apply to Bali.

The poetical works in Old Javanese, as distinct from prose, are generally referred to as *kakawin*, a term that means 'verse', which is a kind of verse that is based on the same metrical principles and literary conventions as the Sanskrit *kāvya*. It has recently been pointed out that *kakawin* also owe much to Sanskrit love poetry and the science of erotics (Creese 2004:284). At a somewhat later stage, another type of poetry, an indigenous Javanese one, arose and this is called *kidung*; its language is called Middle Javanese by Western writers.

The various literary works have not received as much scholarly attention as they deserve. Some have been edited, translated and printed, but not many. We know enough already, though, to see that the poetry in Old Javanese can be regarded as an important contribution to world culture, in view of its remarkable aesthetic sophistication. Much more work needs to be done before we have anything approaching a clear idea of the depth of the literature and, as a result, much remains obscure or little understood—even the lexicon and grammatical forms. But we have enough to make a start.

A 'literary tourist' of the 14th century is the poet by the name of Mpu Prapañca. In 1359, this scholar made a journey through East Java, a round trip from the capital, Majapahit, to the south coast, through the mountains to the north coast and back again via many localities and settlements. His trip was not merely for pleasure, but was an official duty. He was accompanying his king, Rājasanagara (also known as Hayam Wuruk), who was attended by a huge train of family members, officers and hangers-on. He had made similar journeys to other regions in earlier years. Prapañca was probably a high court official in charge of Buddhist affairs and, as such, he was expected to be in attendance on the king (and hoped to be seen and gain favour). He also used the opportunity to visit as many Buddhist foundations along the way as he could, giving them support and checking their documents. He lists the villages and establishments they passed through in a detailed account that he compiled in the form of a poem (*kakawin*), to which he gave the title Deśawarṇana ('Description of the Districts', formerly known by the name Nāgarakṛtāgama) and which he completed on 30 September 1365. As well as the description of this journey, the poem also provides details on many other topics that were important to him, such as members of the royal family, the layout of the capital, relations with other islands and regions, history of the king's ancestors (history was apparently a pastime of his), court celebrations and, in particular, complete lists of the various categories of religious establishments and foundations in the kingdom. With all this, he was aiming to show just what a splendid job his young king was doing in promoting the welfare of the land—that he was, in truth, the incarnation of the highest deity. In this way, Prapañca left an account that is absolutely unique—in other words, a work that deviates from the norm for Old Javanese poetry.

Because Prapañca really did join in the expedition of 1359, his descriptions have the quality of an eye-witness account, as when he mentions the oxcarts coming unhitched and slipping on a steep mountain road after unexpected rain. If we turn to his picture of a temple, we can quote what he says about the temple at Kagĕnĕngan (near Singhasāri):

> 37.1 Let us describe the condition of the temple: its layout is matchless,
> On the outside is a very splendid gateway with a surrounding wall, its height measureless;
> Inside its courtyard is terraced, the fine rest-houses arranged around its edge,
> And thick with all kinds of flowering trees—fine *bakula*, *nāgakusuma* and so on—like a vision.
>
> 37.2 The tower-temple in the centre seems amazingly fitting, other-worldly and as tall
> As Mount Meru, a Śaiwa sanctuary with an image of Śiwa within…

Some temples that still exist are also mentioned, Kidal and Jago:

> 37.7 Let us return to the description of the King's journey: the next morning he went to the foundation at Kidal,
> And having paid reverence to the Lord in the afternoon he then went straight on to Jajaghu.
> After he had come again before the holy image of the Buddha, in the evening he lodged there,
> And in the morning he went back to Singhasāri, and without tiring made a stop at Burĕng.
>
> 38.1 The charm of Burĕng is the lake that wells up clear and blue:
> A *caṇḍi* of stone with surrounding wall has been arranged in the midst of it.

> And numerous are the rest-houses that stand on
> the edge and the festoons of flowers;
> It is always the destination of wanderers and
> never fails to give pleasure to those who visit it.
> (Robson 1995)

This is a lovely example of the combined attractions of religious sites and beauty spots in this part of East Java.

An interesting specimen of a description of a temple is to be found in the Old Javanese version of the Rāmāyaṇa. This is a work from a much earlier time, as it was probably written in the mid ninth century and is in fact the first of its kind. A part of the text is based on the Sanskrit Bhaṭṭikāvya. The visitor this time is not a historical figure, but Hanuman on his mission to Lĕngka (Sarga 8, 43–59). Looking down from a mountain, he saw a

> high and great tower-temple (*prāsāda*). It looked like a mountain, because it was carved with reliefs of wild animals and forests. Its courtyard (*natar*) was covered with fine sand—this inspires a comparison of the tower-temple to Mount Mandara and the courtyard to the sea of milk. There was a wall (*tambak*) in ten layers which resembled the waves, and the drum (*paḍahi*) beating within was like the sound of the sea. Outside this there was a wall or screen (*āwaraṇa*) and a number of temples (*prāsāda*) guarding the complex, like a reef lining the shore. The temples outside all contained images, like the gods and demons jostling each other to get the *amṛta*; the images all bore weapons. Among them were door-keepers (*suwuk lawang*) carved with bulging, round eyes. The Lord Śaṅkara was within the temple. Outside the wall the scene was gay with trees, and alongside the wall was a hall (*maṇḍapa*) on a base (*patigan*) and containing various treasures. There were also some temples (*dewagṛha*) arranged as the vehicles (*wimāna*) of those doing the churning and left outside. Beyond these there was a high wall (*tambak*) going around the borders, comparable to the serpent Bāsuki: his crest was then the main gate (*gopura*), and his tusks were the *rākṣasas* standing guard there. Such was the appearance of the sanctuary (*parhyangan*) there in Lĕngka, looking even more beautiful by the light of the moon (Robson 1980:10).

It is worth noting that the author uses imagery in his description of this temple complex that is borrowed from Hindu mythology, for example the

Churning of the Ocean of Milk to produce nectar, or the serpent Bāsuki. This passage does not correspond to one in the Bhaṭṭikāvya, so it has been assumed (Poerbatjaraka 1932:161ff) that the author had in mind an actual Śiwa temple from Java, namely the Lara Jonggrang (Prambanan) complex, which may have been built at the same time as the poem was composed in the mid ninth century.

Another example of a description of temples is to be found in the poem Arjunawijaya (a tale based on the Uttarakāṇḍa), dating from the late 14th century. In the context of this tale, again the king is engaged on a journey through the countryside with his queen. They come upon a temple complex and this is cause for a priest to provide the king with a rather detailed account of the Buddhist deities enshrined there and to mention their Śaiwa equivalents. This makes the passage an interesting statement of 14th-century theology.

25.4 they continued their journey through the rice-fields and settlements,
interspersed with hermitages, ring-communities and cloister-halls;
to the south were lovely *janggan* and *tasyan*.

25.5 Then they came to a wonderful, flawless temple-complex,
situated beneath the ridges they had just passed;
its earthen walls and main gate were high,
and so were the halls before the *alun-alun* yard.

25.6 There the king called a halt to rest for a while;
all the chariots lined up in rows,
and the horses and the elephants crowded together
in the shade of the trees, filling the market square to capacity.

26.1 The king, who was both delighted and amazed
that this hall should rival a palace-court,
stepped down from his jewelled chariot with the queen;
the palace attendants were ready at their service,
and cheerfully they accompanied the king and the queen into the temple-complex, where they soon were lost in admiration…

26.3 The king and the queen then withdrew into the
lofty temple-tower,
from which both the sea and the mountains were
visible, but the royal couple paid no heed to them,
for their thoughts concerned only the statues
which were all equally sublime.
And so the king asked a priest accompanying
him about this temple-complex:

26.4 'Oh honourable priest,' said the king, 'what is
this outstanding temple?'
And the latter replied: *Om, om, om,* this is a
Buddhist temple.
The god Wairocana, the lord of the Jinas, is
represented in the great statue in the centre;
Serene in his peerless hand position of *bodhyagri,*
he is in truth like Śiwasadā.

27.1 To the east is Akṣobhya, he is the god Rudra;
to the south is Ratnasambhawa, the god Dhātṛ;
to the west is Amitābha, the god Māhā;
to the north is Amoghasiddhi, the god Hari.

27.2 Clearly, then, Your Majesty, there is no
distinction between the Deities:
hyang Buddha and Śiwa, the lord of gods,
both are the same [*sic*], they are the goals of the
religions… (Supomo 1977:221–2).

On the other hand, it is striking that many of the descriptions of temples that are found in Old Javanese poetry are actually not of functioning establishments at all, but ones from former times that have been neglected and have fallen into decay. There are examples from different periods. We can look first at one from the 15th century, a time when one might expect a degree of dilapidation after centuries of building. This passage comes from the poem Śiwarātrikalpa, where the hunter Lubdhaka is travelling through the countryside on his way to the woods to hunt and looks down from the ridges on the various sights to be seen below:

3.1 A great temple-complex from ancient times
rose near a mountain stream, and the path there

was lonely.
The carved trunks of the water-elephants
[*makara*] had fallen and crumbled, and for lack
of care its wall had almost tumbled down.
The monster-heads [*cawintĕn*] seemed to be
weeping as their covered faces were overgrown
by a profusion of creepers,
And as though sad and weary the temple-
guardians [*wiwarapāla*] were lying rolled over
flat on the ground.

2. The pavilions in its courtyard were in ruins; some
of the buildings were now only wreckage, while
others were rotting away;
Their roofs were broken and had fallen in, and
beyond repair their pillars stood askew, swaying
back and forth.
Heart-rending was the spectacle of the reliefs;
young maidens were standing gazing skywards,
As if proclaiming their grief at being abandoned
and no more visited by wandering poets.

3. The tower-temple [*prāsāda*] soared on high,
and its pinnacles served as a gathering-place for
weeds;
The sides were cracked, overgrown by a shady
fig-tree which spread luxuriantly.
All the subordinate figures [*pariwarta*] were
cracked by a fearsome tangle of vines,
And only the main deity within was still
immovably in place, standing firm in the centre
of its pedestal [*praṇālaka*].

4. Many of the buildings had fallen in ruins, and all
the spouts were choked and flowed no more;
Likewise the pool and its original appointments
were none of them in their former condition.
The scene was still, without a trace of anyone
coming to visit the deserted courtyards;

> The blossoms of the *kamuning* trees, dropping
> and spreading themselves about, were scolded by
> the buzzing bees. (Teeuw et al. 1969:73–5)

The above is a particularly effective scene, elaborately developed, but there are earlier ones. A brief example can be found in the Arjunawiwāha ('The Marriage of Arjuna'), the earliest *kakawin* from east Java, datable to about 1030. In this story, while Arjuna and his female companion Suprabhā are flying through the air on their way to find the demon Niwatakawaca, they look down and observe the features of the land below. Amongst other things, they see:

> 15.13   A building as if in a dream—how did it become
> overgrown with forest in bygone times?
> A temple of stone had collapsed, and its Kāla-
> head ornament seemed as if about to weep, its
> eyes filled with tears.
> A clump of spreading aśoka trees leaned to one
> side, their terrace undermined by the river,
> And ivory coconuts, lost in reverie and equally
> heavy, let themselves down gently as they fell.
> (Robson 2008)

We will return to the Arjunawiwāha and consider the image of the temple collapsing because of being overwhelmed by trees again shortly. But first I would like to include the description of a neglected hermitage (not strictly speaking a temple) from the poem Bhomāntaka (12th century; formerly known as the Bhomakāwya). In this story, Kṛṣṇa's son, Samba, is enquiring of a sage's son, Guṇadewa, regarding the communities that he can see below among the wooded mountains. In a long account, he says:

> 15.5   "My lord, look around at this enchanting
> hermitage, long abandoned…
>
> 15.6   There was no end to its beauty at that time—
> after all, it was like a heaven of natural beauty…
>
> 15.7   Its great beauties have not been lost, but have
> been shared out over the scenic charms:

> The stones of its galleries have split and been
> broken, undermined by the big trees;
> The cracks in the gate have been forced open by the
> overwhelming roots of the *prih* entwining them,
> And the circle has been broken and destroyed,
> the garden-beds have been broken up and cease
> to be sweet.
>
> 15.8 A block in the wall, carved in the form of a lady,
> has been allowed to elope,
> Neglected and parted, separated from her lover,
> as they had completely collapsed and fallen;
> Does she not know where she should fit, and for
> this reason is pale and dully dazed,
> And so is preparing to cast herself down on the
> rocks, sadly going the way her husband went?
> (Teeuw and Robson 2005).

And so on, for another four stanzas. Each of these descriptions of deserted temples or hermitages serves the poetical purpose of the author. The parts of the buildings function to express emotion, namely that of loneliness and sadness, in the same way that other aspects of the setting—the trees, flowers and creepers—do, using the technique of personification or animation that is typical of accounts of nature in Old Javanese poetry. In particular, we note that it is the carved images, lintels or reliefs that have emotions attributed to them; they have eyes that can weep and thereby express their disappointment at being never visited. Thus, these descriptions of temples do not tell us about human society or the ceremonies once performed there, but they now perform a duty for the poet. They have been 'naturalised' and have become just one more feature of the beautiful world, alongside the trees and flowers to be observed in the Javanese landscape, and they can even serve to provide romantic allusions to separated lovers.

Before going on, I would like to quote another stanza from the Arjunawiwāha, which elaborates on the theme of the collapsed temple, but in a philosophical sense. At this point in the story, Arjuna has achieved the aim of his penance, has been granted powerful weapons, has rescued Heaven from being invaded by a great demon, has enjoyed his reward in the form of marriage to seven nymphs, and is now about to leave Heaven to rejoin his brothers and mother on earth. His father, the god Indra, is exhorting him and says:

35.7   Just like your mind when you were performing austerities, you must not neglect concentration. The lord of yogis, even one who has gained the Eight Qualities, is still devoted to happiness; If you abandon yourself to the senses, you will end up sunk in stupidity and ignorance, and certainly will have to begin again.

35.8   Many a *caṇḍi* has fallen, it will be plain, because of a *waringin*, *bodhi* or *hambulu* tree [kinds of fig], But if their roots are pulled out one by one when still small, how can they do it? The conclusion is: weed out the intoxication and confusion that grow in your heart and sweep them away! If you yield to them, the danger is that their power might then destroy completely the strength you have acquired. (Robson 2008).

This raises the imagery of the temple, collapsing because of the entwining roots of trees, to a new level, beyond the merely romantic, to providing useful teaching on the subtle, destructive power of the objects of the senses for one who has set his heart on a higher ideal.

The preceding remarks are merely an introduction to the use of the temple (*caṇḍi*) as an image on a deeper level within some literary works. There are several examples of this, found in poems dating from various periods. I would like to mention four, taken from the poems Bhomāntaka, Sumanasāntaka, Arjunawijaya and Hariwijaya.

The first, from the opening stanza of the Bhomāntaka, runs as follows: '*mangke caṇḍyā nirêng bhāṣa saphalakĕna yan dewa ning kūng winimba*'. This can be paraphrased as: 'Now let his temple be built of poetic language, and be made a worthy place for the deity of amorous longing to be given a visible form.'

This metaphor should be explained further. The poet is invoking the blessing of the person (perhaps his king, but he is not named) who sponsors and commissions his work. The poem is depicted as having the same function as a *caṇḍi*, because it is the place where the deity descends, takes up his abode and is manifest. The building material for this literary temple is comparable to the carefully carved stones of a *caṇḍi*, as the words of the poem also have to be precisely chosen and arranged in accordance with strict rules. Consequently, the poet who is skilled enough and has been initiated into the secrets of the art is, in fact, a priest; he also uses prayers, mantras, ascetic observances and meditation to bring his work to a successful conclusion. Then the poem will be a worthy place for the god to be present, and communication will be established between the divine and human world, for the benefit of not only the author but also probably all those who read or hear the poem.

The same image can also be found in the opening stanza of the Sumanasāntaka (also 12th century): '*māyākāra winimba nitya sinamādhi manuruna caṇḍi pustaka*'. This means: 'In his illusory form he is pictured in the mind and constantly made the object of mental concentration so that he may descend into the literary temple'. This gives a particularly clear idea of how the god is made to come and occupy his temple in the form of a literary work.

At both the opening and conclusion of the Arjunawijaya (late 12th century), we find the image again:

> 1.2 *Donkw ângastuti jöng bhaṭāra huningan*
> *sĕmbah ning anggöng langö,*
> *Siddhā ning makasang-wulung ya palakungkw*
> *âcaṇḍya bhāṣêng karas,*
>
> The purpose of my praise to the Lord is to
> implore Him to pay heed to the reverential
> homage of the one who devotes himself to poetry,
> So that the carrier of the dark coloured case may
> achieve the perfect goal he has set himself in
> writing—this is what I implore, as I build my
> temple of language on my writing leaf (Supomo
> 1977:181).

The image in Canto 74.4c is less clear. There, the author is disclaiming any ability to compose a good poem and says that it is most unlikely that people will want to lay claim to his work, or to take refuge in it later on as their temple of poetry (my interpretation differs from Supomo's (1977:282)).

Another example is found in the opening stanza of the Hariwijaya (a late poem, perhaps from Bali): '*līlā caṇḍya nirêng palambang inuwus-huwus inapi winarṇa ring karas*'. This can be translated as: 'At his ease let him take as his temple the poem, perfected, adorned and composed upon the writing-tablet.' This, of course, also tells us about the function of the poem in the mind of the author. In many cases, it is the God of Love (Kāma, Smara, Manmatha) who is invoked, as he is the patron of all things beautiful—nature, women and poetry. Poetry embodies ideals of the beautiful, and this is a kind of beauty that inspires rapture, a state of being enchanted, carried away or absorbed in it, and is thus a yogic means of achieving union with the divine. This kind of beauty is called *langö* or *kalangwan* in Old Javanese (Zoetmulder 1974). The poem then can serve as a vehicle to carry the devotee home to the abode of Smara (*'silunglunga ning umulihĕng Smarālaya'*).

This is perhaps the right place to include two rather difficult passages from the Bhomāntaka, where we find the image of a person or persons serving as a 'temple'. In the first, King Kṛṣṇa is addressing Nārada, who has asked for his help in defending the monks in the hermitages, who have been suffering from attacks by demons. He says:

2.15   Oh, your son's heart is as if cut to the quick to
hear this!
Hence let me stake my life to protect every one
of the hermitages.
Though only the fame of having restored the
world to order would serve as a means of
carrying me to the other world,
It will be thanks to you if I should have a shrine
[*caṇḍi*] for the establishment of the welfare of the
world."

In the second example both the figures Kṛṣṇa and Rāmawijaya (apparently Balarāma) seem to be depicted as *caṇḍis*, into which the god Wiṣṇu can descend and be worshipped. Samba is addressing Yajñawati; his life has been saved thanks to the god Wiṣṇu.

49.5   'This is a sign that I and you later on
Should hold a great feast in Dwārawatī,
And should perform special worship of Lord
Keśawa in particular—
Kṛṣṇa and Rāmawijaya will be his *caṇḍi* in the
hall for me' (Teeuw and Robson 2005).

Finally, returning to a more mundane level, the *caṇḍi* serves as a term of comparison, or a metaphor, because of its typical shape in various places in both Old and Middle Javanese poetry. An example is Malat 4.19b: '*karang akeh agung-agung asawang caṇḍi ajajar*' ('a number of large rocks with the appearance of temples in a row').

Further, the imagery of the temple has penetrated to a linguistic level in Old Javanese, as can be seen in certain word forms. There is a substantival form of the word (with reduplication, partial or otherwise: *cacaṇḍi, cacaṇḍyan, caṇḍya-caṇḍyan*) which refers to something that resembles a *caṇḍi*, namely an ornament or perhaps also coiffure (*gĕlung*) (see Zoetmulder 1982: sv *caṇḍi*). The verbal form (*añaṇḍi, cumaṇḍi, cinaṇḍi*) can also mean 'to be *caṇḍi*-shaped, to be formed like a temple', for example, Smaradahana 1.22 '*lor wetanya gunung-gunung marakatângde kung cinaṇḍy aruhur*' ('To the northeast mountains of emeralds aroused feelings of longing—high and temple-shaped').

These verbal forms often apply to flowers or trees, in particular, the *wungu* (Lagerstroemia speciosa), which is a large tree with bunches of purple flowers. However, it is unclear whether the image applies to the shape of the tree or to the bunches of flowers. There also seems to be an association with glowing brightly like a fire.[1]

Given that temples were a familiar feature of the landscape in early Java, it is scarcely surprising that they should be prominent in the literary works of the period. They have been absorbed into the scenery, and in this way can serve as a source of inspiration for poets as they roam the hills and shores in search of suitable images to use in order to arouse the range of emotions which they needed for creating an acceptable piece of poetry. Further, seeing that this activity is closely related to religion, it is also not surprising that poem and temple should have been identified and made one, so that the literary temple is one site where the deity can descend and be apprehended in the form of 'the beautiful'. We also have more factual accounts of temple complexes and monastic foundations, but these do not provide much that can tell us about the ceremonies conducted there or who attended them. In fact, sometimes they are an image of desolation.

---

[1] We are also reminded of the term *caṇḍi bĕntar*, which is apparently not found in Old or Modern Javanese, but is Balinese and also Indonesian, and means literally 'split *caṇḍi*'. It refers to a gateway of a particular shape, namely one that resembles a *caṇḍi* that has been split symmetrically into two halves. In *kidung* texts the word *caṇḍi* can also be found as the name of a melody and a pattern for clothes, called *caṇḍi raras* ('charming temple').

We can speculate that, being associated with the cult of deceased kings, the *caṇḍi* was visited only rarely, perhaps annually, for rituals held by court priests and that, because of their exclusive link with royalty, the rest of society did not participate, except in a supporting role as carriers and cooks. Old Javanese poetry, too, has strong connections with the court, and mentions the lives of ordinary people only by way of exception. Bearing in mind the wide range of religious institutions and centres that existed in early Java, it is probable that the common people—the farming communities in the villages—had their own places of worship associated with founding ancestors and guardian spirits, and that any buildings linked with these were not of stone or brick and were not termed *caṇḍi*. The hermitages occupied by sages and their disciples in the hills may well have had links with the court and have been visited by figures from the capital when they went on journeys through the countryside.

The authors of Old Javanese poetry regularly use the image of the poet (that is, of themselves) wandering through scenes of mountain and seashore, sometimes seated on a convenient rock jotting down the results of their inspiration, in order to make use of these images to arouse the emotions appropriate to the work. Hence, the theme of the journey is well known, and it is only natural that the places of worship that could be seen in such regions should have become intimately embedded in the imagery of Old Javanese poetry.

Chapter 16

Mỹ Sơn and Pô Nagar Nha Trang sanctuaries and the cosmological dualist cult of the Champa kingdom

Trần Kỳ Phương

Co-director of the project 'Crossing Boundaries—Learning from the Past to Build the Future: Archaeological Collaboration between Cambodia, Lao, and Vietnam'

Rie Nakamura

Visiting Lecturer, College of Law, Government and International Studies, Universiti Utara Malaysia

Mỹ Sơn Sanctuary: the royal cult of the North Champa[1] state

The earliest inscription at Mỹ Sơn sanctuary was from King Bhadravarman, who reigned circa 380–413 CE and was called Phạm Hồ Đạt in Vietnamese and Fan Hu-ta in Chinese historical records. The inscription mentions that the king erected a temple dedicated to God Bhadreśvara (Śiva) and confirmed that the land chosen as the site of the royal sanctuary be located in the south of the valley, on the holy mountain named Mahāparvata/Great God of Mountain [C72][2] (Majumdar 1985:4–8; Jacques 1995:5, 204; Trần Kỳ Phương 2004:3–5, 33–5). Nowadays, the local people call it Răng Mèo

---

[1] In this chapter, the terms Champa and Cham refer to elements of the kingdom of Champa, such as Cham art, Cham royal sanctuaries and so on; the term Chăm refers to Chăm ethnic elements, such as Chăm language and Chamic, Chăm people and so on.
[2] Identifying codes in square brackets refer to the location and an inscription number; thus, '[C72]' refers to inscription number 72 at Champa.

Mountain (Cat Mountain) or Hòn Quắp. Mỹ Sơn is a narrow and secret valley, about two kilometres in diameter, surrounded by high mountains; a stream flows through the site from the Holy Mountain of Mahāparvata in the south into the Holy River of Mahānadi, or Thu Bồn, in the north [C147] (Majumdar 1985:7; Jacques 1995:204).

King Bhadravarman's first temple was constructed of wood and enshrined with a *liṅga* that was given the title of Bhadreśvara. This title was possibly composed by coupling the proper name of King Bhadravarman with Īśvara, the other name of Śiva: Bhadravarman + Īśvara = Bhadreśvara (Śiva). The temple-towers of Mỹ Sơn were built continually from the end of the fourth or early fifth until the 13th centuries CE. Groups of structures on the Mỹ Sơn site are labelled A through to H (see Map 16.1). The construction of the Mỹ Sơn B group began early in the tenth century and consisted of:

- the ceremonial long hall (*maṇḍapa*) (D1),[3] the gate tower (*gopura*) (B2), and the main temple (*kalan*) (B1);
- the secondary temples (B3 and B4);
- the tower of the repository for offerings (*kośagṛha*), called the 'fire tower' by Chăm people (B5);
- the tower of the ritual holy water reservoir (B6); and
- the seven small temples (B7–B13) dedicated to the seven gods of the planets (*navagrahas* or *saptagrahas*).

Most of the structures of the Mỹ Sơn B group were built and restored continually from the ninth until the 13th centuries (see Map 16.1).

The biggest temple of Mỹ Sơn B1, which is a reconstruction from the 12th or 13th century, was the largest temple of the site, and is outstanding mainly because of its huge sandstone foundation. It is considered the main temple of the sanctuary because of its decorative fragments dating from the seventh to the 13th century, its relatively large ground plan and its central placement on the site. The temple of Mỹ Sơn B1 enshrines a *yonī-liṅga* called Bhadreśvara (Śiva) *liṅga*. The large pedestal of the *yonī-liṅga* was set in a square hole at the centre of the temple's sanctum to drain the sacred water of the ritual.

Parallel to the Mỹ Sơn B group is the Mỹ Sơn C group; both of them were erected on the east–west axis. The layout of the Mỹ Sơn C group is similar to Mỹ Sơn B group, albeit simpler. It includes:

---

3   Identifying codes in *parentheses* refer to the groups of structures within the Mỹ Sơn site, identified in Map 16.1.

- the main temple (*kalan*) (C1), the *gopura* (C2), and the *maṇḍapa* (D2);
- the fire-tower (*kośagṛha*) (C3);
- the secondary edifice (C4); and
- the secondary temples (C5, C6, C7).

The *kalan* of the Mỹ Sơn C group (C1) is a reconstruction using some earlier architectural fragments such as a lintel and a tympanum. The temple of Mỹ Sơn (C1) enshrines a sandstone icon of Śiva in anthropomorphic form, installed on a large square *yoni* pedestal. This is one of the masterpieces of Cham sculpture measuring 194 centimetres high. Some archaeological findings suggest that the icon was ornamented with a set of golden jewellery during rituals (Boisselier 1963:138–9).

Śiva's costume is a long *sampot* reaching to his knees with long front and rear parts and a belt holding the cloth on the right; this sort of *sampot* was popular in Cham art for only a short period during the late eighth century. The face of Śiva has thick joined eyebrows, two big eyes with round pupils, a straight nose, thick lips with a moustache, and hair woven in a *jata-mukuta*. These are the typical features of Cham sculpture in the early period, from the last quarter of the eighth to the first quarter of the ninth century, before the Đồng Dương style (Trần Kỳ Phương 1988:32–3).

Comparing the two temples Mỹ Sơn B1 and Mỹ Sơn C1, we argue that the installation of these temples reflects the phenomenon of the double cult of Śiva as his *liṅga* and his anthropomorphic statue (Trần Kỳ Phương 2004:34–5). This could indicate that the Cham kings emphasised their absolute belief in the Supreme Śiva in representations of the cosmological symbolic sign, the Śiva *liṅga*, as well as an anthropomorphic Śiva, who became the tutelary deity of their dynasties. Further, we may suppose that the icon of Śiva *liṅga* represented the god Śiva himself, while the icon of the anthropomorphic Śiva represented the deified Cham king.

In addition to the B and C groups, one can find a similar arrangement in the A' and the E groups. The Mỹ Sơn A' group includes several temple-towers built during the early periods. The double cult of Śiva can be seen at the Mỹ Sơn A'1 and A'4 temples: A'1 dedicated to the Śiva *liṅga*, and A'4 to the anthropomorphic Śiva. The *liṅga* of Mỹ Sơn A'1 was looted from the temple, but the anthropomorphic statue of Śiva was found inside A'4. The sandstone statue, set on a high square *yoni* pedestal, has similar features to the Śiva of Mỹ Sơn C1. Technically, the sculptural work on the Śiva statue at Mỹ Sơn A'4 is more sophisticated than on the one at Mỹ Sơn C1, although the two seem to date from the same period (Boisselier 1963:54).

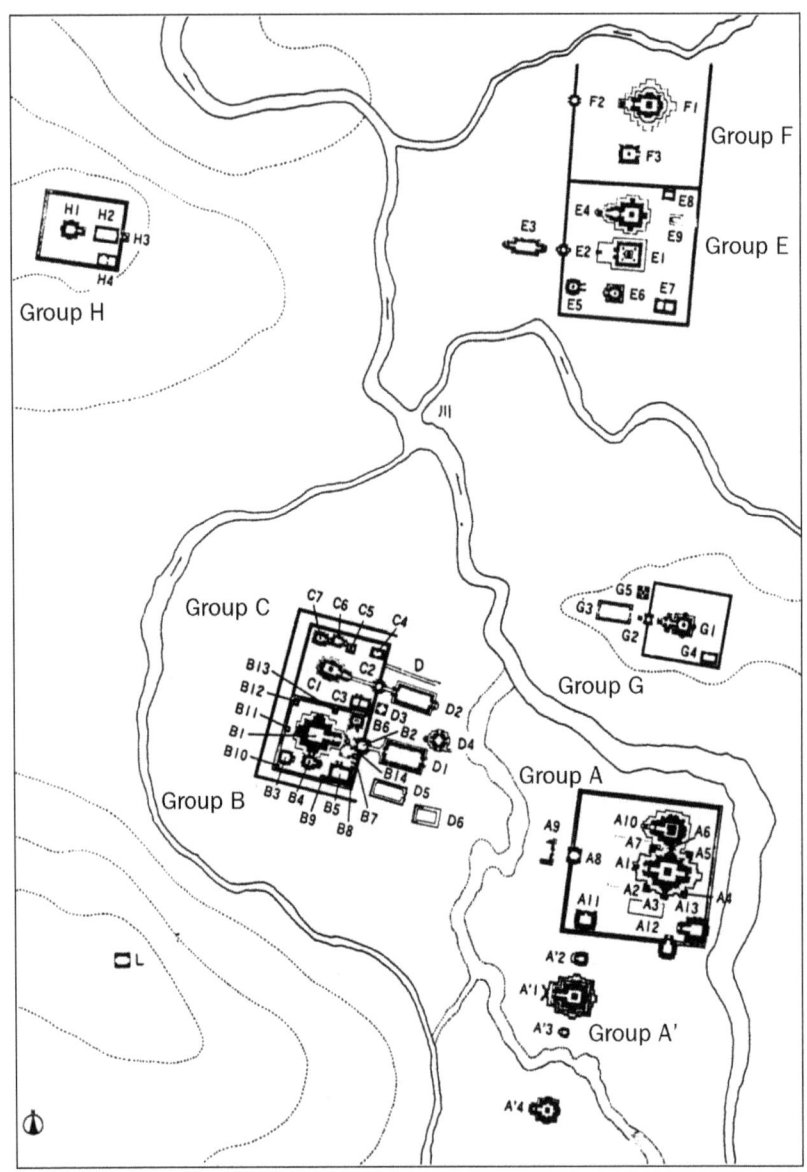

Map 16.1 Plan of Mỹ Sơn site
(According to Parmentier and Boisselier, in Boisselier 1963:Plan C)

Regarding on the Mỹ Sơn E group, Mỹ Sơn E1 housed a Śiva *liṅga* while Mỹ Sơn E4 contained an anthropomorphic Śiva. E1 is one of the earliest structures at Mỹ Sơn and its pedestal is considered a masterpiece of Cham art; both date from the first half of eighth century. The Mỹ Sơn E1 pedestal consists of a *yonī-liṅga* set and was reconstructed by Parmentier at the beginning of the last century (Parmentier 1918:plate CXX).

Mỹ Sơn E4 is located north of Mỹ Sơn E1. The architectural fragments of the temple, such as the large lintel and pediment in sandstone depicting the royal court and the image of Goddess Devī, date the temple to the second half of the 11th century (Boisselier 1963:212–13). It was built, perhaps, under the reign of King Harivarman, circa 1081, when, according to his inscription C90 at Mỹ Sơn, 'he has re-established the edifices and the city of Champa during the troublesome days of the war…and seeing Śrīsanabhadreśvara despoiled of all his possessions at the end of the war, he came to worship the god with a pious heart…' (Majumdar 1985:161–7; Jacques 1995:115–22).

The temple of Mỹ Sơn E4 enshrined the anthropomorphic Śiva standing atop a high square *yonī* pedestal, which is decorated with a row of female breasts that symbolise the goddess Uroja, the founder of the state. Śiva wears a long *sampot* with the long front part decorated with gaps in Z-shape, typical for Cham sculpture dating from the late 11th and early 12th century (Boisselier 1963:212).

Therefore, the icons of Śiva *liṅga* and anthropomorphic Śiva worshipped in the temples of Mỹ Sơn B1 and C1, A'1 and A'4, and E1 and E4 appear to represent the phenomenon of the double cult of Śiva, practised in Mỹ Sơn from the eighth to the 12th–13th centuries. This double cut of Śiva makes Mỹ Sơn unique among Cham religious sites. Except for some images representing Hindu goddesses on pediments at Mỹ Sơn, there are no examples of goddess statues in the round found in the main sanctuaries, which suggests that Hindu goddesses did not play an important role at this royal site.

Pô Nagar Nha Trang Sanctuary: the royal cult of the South Champa state

Pô Nagar Nha Trang[4] lies approximately 450 kilometres south of Mỹ Sơn in Nha Trang city, Khánh Hòa province. The site is located on a small hill next to the estuaries of the Cái and the Hà Ra rivers, the two largest rivers of this region. According to inscriptions, the first wooden temple of the sanctuary was destroyed by a fire in 774 CE; then, in 784, the temple was reconstructed in brick and stone. Archaeological excavations undertaken in the beginning of the 20th century by l'École française d'Êxtrème-Orient revealed ten structures built on this 500 square kilometre hill (Parmentier

---

4   Pô Nagar is the name used by the French for the temple.

1909:111–32). Nowadays, after the damage of war and decay through time only five structures remain. They include:

- a main temple in the north, A;
- two smaller temples in the south, B and C;
- a secondary temple in the northwest, F; and
- brick pillars from a large *maṇḍapa*, M, in the front of the main temple at the foot of the hill.

Inscription C38 mentions that the first icon of Goddess Bhagavatī[5] was erected here during the reconstruction of the sanctuary by King Satyavarman in 784, following his victory over the 'Javanese' pirates in 774 (Majumdar 1985:41–4). Afterwards, statues of the goddess were erected during the years 817 [C31] and 918 [C33]. In 950, the golden icon of the goddess was despoiled by the Khmer [C38]; however, in 965 [C38], King Jaya Indravarman re-erected her sculpture in sandstone. In 1050, the title of Yapu-Nagara/Yang Pu Nagar was given to the goddess by King Śrī Parameśvaravarman [C30], repeated in 1084 by King Paramabodhisatva [C30], and in 1160 by King Jaya Harivarman [C30] (Majumdar 1985:61–4; 138–9; 143–4; 151–3; 194–5); then in 1256, 1267 [C31], and 1275 by Princess Ratnavali [C37] (Schweyer 2004:125).Thus, continuous worship of Goddess Bhagavatī is evidenced in inscriptions for the years 784, 817, 918, 965, and thereafter, under the title of Pô Yang Inu Nagar/Yapu-Nagara, in 1050, 1160, 1256 and 1275, indicating the important role of the goddess as 'the mother of the state' at this royal sanctuary.[6]

The sandstone statue Goddess Bhagavatī at Pô Nagar Nha Trang, enshrined in the main temple (Le Bonheur 1994:225), can be dated to the tenth or 11th century (Boisselier 1963:207–9; Trần Kỳ Phương 1986: 380–2). Its precious material and its excellent craftsmanship emphasise the important role of the statue in the Cham royal cult. The head was restored and its style reflects the artistic style of the Việt or Kinh people. The statue, sitting on the lotus petals of a square *yonī* pedestal, is a ten-arm goddess leaning on a prop decorated with the motif of *kāla-makara*. Of her two forward hands the left one, turning upward on her knee, shows

---

[5] Bhagavatī is a reverential title offered to Goddess Parvatī, consort of Śiva (Liebert 1986:36).
[6] Some researchers believe that the cult of Pô Yang Inu Nagar had existed locally for a long time and was taken over by the Cham even before their exposure to Hinduism (Nguyễn Thế Anh 1995:55).

the *varada-mudra*, the right one, turning frontward on her knee, shows the *abhaya-mudra*. Her other hands hold attributes. On the right, from bottom to top, they hold a dagger, an arrow, a disk (*cakra*) and a lance; on the left, from bottom to top, they hold a small bell, an axe (*ankusa*), a conch (?) and a bow.

Related to the Pô Nagar Nha Trang Sanctuary is a legend of the goddess that has been popularised in the Chăm, as well as in the Việt or Kinh communities living in the region of Khánh Hòa, Ninh Thuận, Bình Thuận provinces. According to the legend, she was born from the cloud and the waves, appeared in the Đai An Mountain, and was fed by a couple of woodcutters. She was a pretty girl. On a flood day, she was embodied into a tree of aloe-wood flowing to the Northern Sea. The tree of aloe-wood was picked up by local people and offered to the Crown Prince of the Northern Sea State. In a moonlit night, she appeared from the tree of aloe-wood and the Crown Prince fell in love with her. They had two children. One day, missing her homeland, she and her children entered into a tree of aloe-wood flowing back to the south. In her homeland, she taught her people to grow rice and weaving. Coming back from the battles, the Crown Prince knew that his wife and his children had returned to her homeland; he tried to look for them with his fleet. Because of the cruel behaviour of the Prince's soldiers towards her people, she used her supernatural power to destroy the fleet of the Prince. The remainder of the fleet became the rocks visible in the estuary. She was the creator of the earth, of aloe-wood and of rice. To show their respect and ensure her to her benediction towards the local people, they built the temple to worship her and her children (Inrasara 1994:36–9; Nguyễn Thế Anh 1995:55; Lý Việt Dũng 2000:115–26).[7]

The annual festival for the goddess takes place at the Pô Nagar Nha Trang on the 23rd day of the third lunar month, usually in April. During the festival, there are many ceremonies dedicated to the goddess, such as

---

[7] From the legend, it seems that two independent states existed in the south and north of the kingdom of Champa. These states, perhaps, had been unified by intermarriage, despite occasional discordance. The main motifs of the legend reflect its cosmological dualist concept: femaleness—heavenly girl—the south, contrasted with maleness—the Prince—the north; aloe-wood and the Northern Sea; the intermarriage; the fact that the south had an advantage over the north (the fleet of the Prince was damaged), and so on. Most of the previous research explained the Northern Sea in the legend as China; however, if considered in the context of the two states or *maṇḍala* that existed in the kingdom, we would interpret the Northern Sea to refer to the Amaravatī State in the north of Champa, in present-day Quảng Nam province.

bathing her statue, changing her dress, and traditional singing and dancing. It is mainly the Việt or Kinh people who participate in the three-day festival. The Cham name of Goddess Pô Yang Inu Nagar was Vietnamised into Thiên Y A Na and the sanctuary was called by the Việt or Kinh people as Tháp Bà (The Lady's temple).

In Central Vietnam, from Thừa Thiên-Huế to Khánh Hòa provinces, the cult of Goddess Thiên Y A Na is popular among the Việt or Kinh people. Most of the temples dedicated to the goddess are built near riverbanks or estuaries. Many scholars argue that the cult of Goddess Thiên Y A Na practised in Central Vietnam has its origin in the worship of Pô Yang Inu Nagar of the Cham inhabitants (Nguyễn Thế Anh 1995:55–67; Nguyễn Hữu Thông et al. 2001:138–66). Nowadays, the Chăm people in Ninh Thuận and Bình Thuận provinces still worship the Goddess Pô Yang Inu Nagar as one of the three main indigenous divinities, together with Pô Kloong Garai and Pô Rame.

The characteristics of the cosmological dualist cult of the two royal sanctuaries of the Champa kingdom

Together with the above-mentioned evidence from artworks and geography, one can see that the respective locations of the two sanctuaries reflect their own characteristics of cosmological dualism. Mỹ Sơn is located in a deep valley surrounded by mountain ranges, while, Pô Nagar Nha Trang is located on a riverside hill near an estuary. Mỹ Sơn belonged to the Amaravati state in North Champa, while Pô Nagar Nha Trang belonged to the Kauthara state in South Champa (Schweyer 2004:116). Thus, from the eighth century until the 13th century, the two royal sanctuaries of Champa seem to reveal their own characteristics: Mỹ Sơn = Bhadreśvara (Śiva)—Mountain—Father; Pô Nagar Nha Trang = Bhagavatī-Pô Yang Inu Nagar—Sea—Mother.

According to Chăm legends, the Champa kingdom was ruled by two clans (Jacques 1995:207–12). The first clan, the Areca, or male, Clan, called Pinang in the Chăm language (Kramuk Vansh in Sanskrit) descended from a mountain clan (Stau Chok, Mountain King). The second clan was the Coconut, or female, Clan, called Li-u in the Chăm language (Narikel Vansh in Sanskrit) and descended from a sea clan (Stau Thik, Sea King) (Trần Kỳ Phương 2004:4–5). Based on the prominent characteristics of the two royal sanctuaries, we argue that the Areca Clan belonged to Mỹ Sơn, or North Champa, and the Coconut Clan belonged to Pô Nagar Nha Trang, or South

Champa.⁸ In other words, the specific functions of the two royal sanctuaries reflected the aspects of the cosmological dualist cult of the reigns of Champa throughout her history.

According to the inscriptions found in Mỹ Sơn and Pô Nagar Nha Trang dating from 12th and the 13th centuries, several kings offered temples and icons to both royal sanctuaries. For example, in 1113–49, King Jaya Indravarman restored temples in Mỹ Sơn and Pô Nagar Nha Trang [C28], and in 1201, King Jaya Parameśvaravarman re-erected all the *liṅga* in the south dedicated to Goddess Pô Yang Inu Nagar (Pô Nagar Nha Trang), as well as ones in the north dedicated to God Śrīsanabhadreśvara (Mỹ Sơn) [C86] (Le Bonheur 1994:272; Schweyer 2004:123–5). The dedications of the kings of Champa to the two royal sanctuaries in the north as well as to those in the south of the kingdom reflect their worship of god and goddess. This cosmological dualist cult should protect the whole kingdom and combine opposite states and/or clans.

Mỹ Sơn / Male	Pô Nagar Nha Trang / Female
Bhadreśvara/ Śiva	Bhagavatī/ Parvatī/ Pô Yang Inu Nagar
Mountain	Sea
Father	Mother
Areca	Coconut
North	South
Valley	Riverside hill near estuary

Table 16.1 Overview of characteristics of Mỹ Sơnand Pô Nagar Nha Trang

The characteristics of the cosmological dualism adapted in the Chăm community

Similar to the dualism observed in the two main sanctuaries of historical Champa, another dualism can be seen in contemporary Chăm communities in the provinces of Ninh Thuận and Bình Thuận along the south central coast of Vietnam, which was the last territory of Champa. Based on their

---

8   Based on the principles of yin–yang, we learn that coconut with its empty heart should belong to the yin/female; and areca with a solid heart should belong to the yang/male. Therefore, the Coconut Clan should belong to female, and the Areca Clan should belong to male.

religions, the Chăm people of this region are grouped into two groups: the Chăm and Bani. The Chăm or Bà-la-môn (Brahmanist) are adherents of an indigenised form of Hinduism, worshipping the god Pô Yang and the deified kings in the old temples, which were constructed between the 13th–14th and the 16th–17th centuries in that region. They are supposed to observe a taboo on beef and are usually cremated when they die. The second group, the Bani are adherents of an indigenised form of Islam. They worship Pô Alwah (Allah) at their mosque called *thang muki* in their villages. They are supposed to not eat pork and are buried after death.

A legend explaining the origin of the division of the Chăm and Bani indicates that it was to bring peace to their society, in which people had been fighting constantly. In the legend, Chăm and Bani are indicated as Ahier and Awal, both words originating in Arabic. Ahier means 'back', 'behind', or 'after' and Awal means 'front' or 'before'. In the legends, Ahier means Chăm and is associated with male, while Awal means Bani and is associated with female. Many Chăm people express a similar idea of Ahier being men and Awal being women. The elderly people in Chăm villages equate Ahier and Awal with plus and minus terminals of a battery; just as we need both to make machinery work, so society needs Ahier and Awal to function.

Doris Blood, who lived among the Chăm people for several years before 1975, pointed out the similar dualistic tendency in the Chăm cosmology based on two realms: father's realm and mother's realm (Blood 1981:43, 48). The male-female or Ahier–Awal dichotomy is essential to the way the Chăm people understand their world. For instance, the Chăm people believe that a person's upper body, from the head to the navel, belongs to Ahier, while the lower body, from the navel to the feet, belongs to Awal. The Chăm regard the sky as the body of a human hunched over with two hands and two feet on the ground; thus they consider from dawn until noon (meaning the upper body, from hands to navel) as Ahier, and from noon until sunset (meaning the lower body, from navel to feet) as Awal. In a week, the first three days—Sunday, Monday and Tuesday—are considered to be Ahier. The last three days—Thursday, Friday and Saturday—are considered to be Awal. Wednesday, the day between Ahier and Awal, is considered the day of equilibrium; it is also the day of the soil, meaning that growth is attributed to this day. The Chăm believe that Wednesday is the best day to organise wedding ceremonies. In the Chăm lunar calendar, one month is divided up to two sections: the first 15 days belong to Ahier, and the last 15 days belong to Awal (Nakamura 1999:130–3).

The maleness of Ahier and femaleness of Awal are also represented by two groups of priests. The gender roles of Chăm priests and Bani priests are expressed by their clothing and behaviour. A Chăm priest, a key person for performing a ritual, wraps their head in a white turban in a special way, the shape of the turban symbolising a *linga*, whereas Bani priests wear an extra cloth on their turban called *khan djram*, which is the cloth for the Bani women. The Bani priests wear the *khan djram* in the same way that Bani women wear them. Chăm priests always sit with crossed legs, as the men sit during rituals, whereas Bani priests sit with their feet under them and to the side as the women sit during rituals.

It is quite interesting that, although Chăm priests symbolise Ahier (male) and Bani priests symbolise Awal (female), they also have things to indicate the opposite gender. Each Chăm priest has a yellow rectangle bag as part of their attire, whereas each Bani priest has three bags as part of their attire. One of the three bags is slightly larger that the other two, which are tied by the same cord. The Chăm priests' single bag symbolises the uterus and the Bani priests' three bags symbolise the penis and testicles (Nakamura 1999:134–8). The priests' bags of Ahier and Awal symbolise their acceptance of their counterparts. This is similar to the notion of 'complementary dualism' articulated by Janet Hoskins, who studied indigenous notions of gender and agency among the Austronesian language-speaking Kodi people at the Western tip of Sumba in the Lesser Sunda islands. She explained the notion of recursive complementary dualism by quoting James Fox:

> A great deal of the symbolic elaboration of dualistic structures in eastern Indonesia involves playing with this principle of recursive complimentarily: Male contains Female, Female contains Male; Inside contains the Outside, the Outside the Inside; Black, White, White, Black (Hoskins 1987:197).

There is a magical sign called *hon-kan*[9] used by priests and the shaman during various rituals. The *hon-kan* is composed of two numbers and two figures. The centre of the symbol is a circle, which indicates the sun, with a crescent underneath. Above the sun is the number 6 and below the crescent is the number 3. The sun and the number 3 belong to Ahier, and the crescent and the number 6 belong to Awal (see Fig. 16.1). The number 3 plus the

---

[9] *Hon-kan* means 'magical sign' in the Chăm language.

number 6 becomes number 9, which is considered to be the most complete number. Thus, the symbol of *hon-kan*, which is composed of the symbols of Ahier and Awal, indicates the most complete form of existence: unity, balance, stability, and peace. In other words, when Ahier and Awal coexist, the world of the Chăm finds unity (Nakamura 1999:87–92).

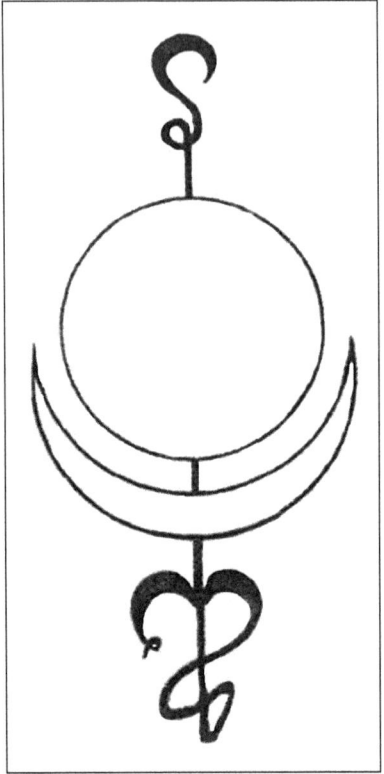

Figure 16.1 The *hon-kan*

The dualism found in the Chăm cosmology and world view, and their notion of unity and peace through acceptance of opposing realms as found in Chăm rituals and as symbolised by the sign of *hon-kan*, seem to provide a possible explanation for the dualism found in the Champa sanctuaries. King Jaya Indravarman, who made dedications to the Mỹ Sơn and Pô Nagar Nha Trang sanctuaries, succeeded the throne without any turmoil: he had all of Champa's agreement to become the King (Maspero 2002:75); perhaps he showed his gratitude for this peaceful succession by constructing two sanctuaries, one each for the male and the female realms. King Jaya

Parameśvaravarman, who also made dedications to both Mỹ Sơn and Pô Nagar, became the King after prolonged Khmer occupation of Champa, which tore Champa apart. King Jaya Parameśvaravarman needed peace and unity among Champa for rebuilding Champa after the Khmer occupation. Both kings sought peace and unity of Champa by showing respect to the two realms: Male and Female, Ahier and Awal.

Ahier (after/behind) /Chăm	Awal (before/front) / Bani
Male (father's realm)	Female (mother's realm)
The Sky	The Earth
The Sun	The Moon
Fire, Hot	Water, Cold
From the dawn until the noon	From the noon until the sunset
Upper body	Lower body
Sunday, Monday, Tuesday	Thursday, Friday, Saturday
First 15 days of a month (bingun)	Latter 15 days of a month (klam)
Number 3	Number 6
Death (?)	Life, birth

Table 16.2 Ahier and Awal
(Nakamura 1999:96)

Conclusion

Champa's economic base was its involvement in maritime trade, and unification of the northern and the southern state of Champa was crucial for their active involvement in this trade. The southern state, Kauthara, was known as the rich land of aloe-wood (Nguyễn Hiền & Võ Văn Chi 1991:6, 34), the most outstanding product of Champa on the international market. The northern state, Amaravatī, known for its prosperous port cities, such as the Great Port of Champa in Hội An area, played an important role in the interaction with China, the largest market for the forest products of Champa (Southworth 2004:226–8; Momoki 2004).

The two royal sanctuaries of Mỹ Sơn and Pô Nagar Nha Trang seem to reflect the Champa royal court's endeavour to unify the northern and the southern states of Champa by applying its cosmological complementary dualism. Mỹ Sơn in the north, which enshrined Śiva and deified kings, represented the realm of Ahier, while Pô Nagar Nha Trang in the south, which enshrined the goddess of the state, represented the realm of Awal. The kings of Champa made tributes to both Mỹ Sơn and Pô Nagar Nha Trang to unify these two states symbolically and to bring harmony to the regions.

The cosmological dualistic tendency of the Chăm people can be seen as deeply rooted in their history, and is commonly observed among the Austronesian language peoples of Southeast Asia (Hoskins 1987:174–94). Cosmological dualism is the key concept to understanding Champa. It guides us our learning about both the structure of the kingdom in the past and the structure of contemporary society of descendants of Champa.

Bibliography

Acharya, PK 1994 [1934], *Architecture of Mānasāra: translated from original Sanskrit*, Manasara series 4, Munshiram Manoharlal, New Delhi.
Acker, R 1998. 'New geographical tests of the hydraulic thesis at Angkor', *Southeast Asia Research* 6(1).
Albrecht, Gerd, Miriam Noël Haidle, Chhor Sivleng, Heang Leang Hong, Heng Sophady, Heng Than, Mao Someaphyvath, Sirik Kada, Som Sophal, Thuy Chanthourn and Vin Laychour 2001, 'Circular earthwork Krek 52/62: recent research on the prehistory of Cambodia', *Asian Perspectives* 39(1/2).
Andrews, Malcolm 1999, *Landscape and Western art*, Oxford University Press, Oxford.
Annaogly, A [n. d. 1997], 'La tradizione sciamanica delle oasi' in Rossi-Osmida, G (ed), *Turkmenistan, Esplorazioni e Rcerche* vol XVI, Centro Studi e Ricerche Ligabue, Venezia.
Aoyama, T 1994, 'A study of the Sutasoma kakawin: a Buddhist narrative in fourteenth century Java', PhD thesis, University of Sydney.
Ar Seinna, U [n.d.], *Tanggyi Taung Pagoda History*, published in Burmese by the author, Khe Taung Sayadaw, Ye Nan Chauk Post office, Sakka Wa Village, Pakkoku district.
Archer, William George 1947, *The vertical man: a study in primitive Indian sculpture*, Allen & Unwin, London.
Arnheim, R 1977, *The dynamics of architectural form*, University of California Press, Berkeley.
ASB (Archaeological Survey of Burma) 1906–65, *Report of the Superintendent, Archaeological Survey of Burma*, Office of the Superintendent, Government Printing, Rangoon.
ASI (Archaeological Survey of India) 1902–36, *Annual report of the Archaeological Survey of India*, Manager of Publications, Delhi.
Atharva Veda—see Bloomfield 1897.
Aung Myint 1998, 'Site characteristics of Pyu and Pagan ruins', paper presented at the seminar 'A Comparative Study of the Dry Areas in Southeast Asia', Kyoto, October 14–16.
Aung Thaw 1968, *Report on the excavations at Beikthano*, Ministry of Union Culture, Rangoon.
—— 1972, *Historical sites in Burma*, Ministry of Union Culture, Rangoon.
Aung-Thwin, Michael 1985, *Pagan: the origins of modern Burma*, University of Hawaii Press, Honolulu.
—— 1998, *Myth and history in the historiography of early Burma*, Ohio University Press for the Center of International Studies, Athens.
—— 2005, *The mists of Ramanna: the legend that was Lower Burma*, University of Hawai'i Press, Manoa.
Aymonier, Étienne 1891, 'Première étude sur les inscriptions tchames', *Journal Asiatique* 17.
—— 1900–01, *Le Cambodge*, 2 vols, Ernest Leroux, Paris.
Barbier, Jean Paul and Douglas Newton (eds) 1988, *Islands and ancestors*, Prestel, München.
Barker, RG 1968, *Ecological psychology: concepts and methods for studying the environment of human behavior*, Stanford University Press, Stanford.

Baskoro D Tjahjono 1993, 'Gejala perubahan orientasi kosmis ke ktonis pada arsitektur bangunan sakral Majapahit akhir', conference paper delivered at *Pertemuan Ilmiah Arkeologi VI*, Batu, Malang Jawa Timur 26–30 July 1992.

Baty, Pierre, Annie Bolle, Socheat Chea et al 2005, 'Extension de l'aéroport de Siem Reap 2004. Rapport de fouille archéologique', APSARA—INRAP, Siem Reap.

Bausani, Alessandro 1966, '"Sopravvivenze pagane nell'Islam" o integrazione islamica?', *Studi e Materiali di Storia delle Religioni* 37 (2).

—— 1984, 'L'Islam: integrazione o sincretismo religioso?' in Lanciotti, Lionello (ed), *Incontro di religioni in Asia tra il III e il X secolo d.C*, Olschki, Firenze.

Beal, Samuel (trans) 1983 [1884], *Si-Yu-Ki: Buddhist records of the Western world*, Oriental Reprint, New Delhi.

Bellwood, Peter 2005, *First farmers: the origins of agricultural societies*, Blackwell, Oxford.

Bénisti, Mirielle 1970, *Rapports entre le premier art khmer et l'art indien*, 2 vols, Mémoires archéologiques 5, École Française d'Extrême-Orient, Paris.

Bergaigne, Abel 1893, 'Inscriptions sanscrites de Campā', *Notices et extraits des manuscrits de la Bibliothèque nationale et autres bibliothèques* 27 (1), 2e fascicule.

Bernet Kempers, AJ 1959, *Ancient Indonesian art*, Harvard University Press, Cambridge.

Bharucha, Rustom 2003, *Rajasthan: an oral history*, Penguin Books, New Delhi.

Bhattacharya, K 1999, unpublished translation of the Lolei inscription, Lehrstuhl für Orientalische Kunstgeschichte, Universität Bonn.

Binford, Mira Reym 1976, 'Mixing in the color of Rām of Rānujā: a folk pilgrimage to the grave of a Rajput hero-saint' in Smith, Bardwell L (ed), *Hinduism*, Brill, Leiden.

Bischoff, Roger 1995, *Buddhism in Myanmar: a short history*, The Wheel publication 399–401, Buddhist Publication Society, Kandy.

Blagden, CO 1917, 'The "Pyu" inscriptions', *Journal of the Burma Research Society* 7(1).

Blawatsky, W and G Kochelenko 1966, *Le culte de Mithra sur la côte septentrionale de la Mer Noir*, Brill, Leiden.

Blood, Doris 1980, 'Aspects of Cham culture' in Gregerson, Marilyn and Dorothy Thomas (eds), *Notes from Indochina on ethnic minority cultures*, SIL Museum of Anthropology, Dallas.

Bloomfield, Maurice (trans) 1897 *Hymns of the Atharva-veda*, Sacred Books of the East, 42, Oxford University Press, Oxford.

Boisselier, Jean 1963, *La statuaire du Champà: recherches sur les cultes et l'iconograpghie*, Publications de l'École Française d'Extrême-Orient 54, École Francaise d'Extrême-Orient, Paris.

—— 1966, *Asie du sud-est: I. Le Cambodge*, Manuel d'archéologie d'Extrême Orient 1, Picard, Paris.

Bosch, FDK 1915, *Inventaris der Hindoe-oudheden op den grondslag van Dr RDM Verbeek's Oudheden van Java*, Dl 2, Rapporten van den Oudheidkundigen Dienst in Nederlandsch-Indië, Bataviaasch Genootschap van Kunsten en Wetenschappen, Batavia.

—— 1931, 'Le motif de l'arc-à-biche à Java et au Champa', *Bulletin de l'École Française d'Extrême Orient* 31.

—— 1960, *The golden germ: an introduction to Indian symbolism*, Mouton, 'sGravenhage.

Braudel, Fernand 1981, *On history*, Weidenfeld and Nicholson, London.

—— 1990, *The identity of France, vol 2: People and production*, Fontana Press, London.

Briggs, Lawrence Palmer 1951, *The ancient Khmer empire*, Transactions of the American Philosophical Society, new series 41, American Philosophical Society, Philadelphia.

Brohm, John 1963, 'Buddhism and animism in a Burmese village', *Journal of Asian Studies* 22(2).
Brown, R Grant 1921, 'The pre-Buddhist religion of the Burmese', *Folklore* 32(2).
Brown, Robert L 1997, 'Narrative as icon: the Jātaka stories in ancient Indian and Southeast Asian architecture' in Schober, Juliane (ed), *Sacred biography in the Buddhist traditions of South and Southeast Asia*, University of Hawai'i Press, Honolulu.
—— 1990, 'God on Earth: the walking Buddha in the art of South and Southeast Asia', *Artibus Asiae* 50(1/2).
—— 2001, 'Pyu art: looking East and West', *Orientations* 32(4).Buckley, Brendan M, Kevin J Anchukaitis, Daniel Penny, Roland Fletcher, Edward R Cook, Masaki Sano, Le Canh Nam, Aroonrut Wichienkeeo, Ton That Minh, and Truong Mai Hong 2010, 'Climate as a contributing factor in the demise of Angkor, Cambodia' in *Proceedings of the National Academy of Sciences of the USA* 107(15).
Burma, 1960 [1921], *Amended list of ancient monuments in Burma*, Superintendent of Government Printing and Stationery, Rangoon.
Casparis, J.G. de (1950), *Inscripties uit de Çailendra-tijd*. Bandung: Pjawatan Purbakala Republik Indonesia (*Prasasti Indonesia* I).
Cerezales, F 1997, *Angkor: 10 siècles de fascination: Voyage au coeur de la civilisation khmère* [CD-ROM], Comme un voyage, Paris.
Chakrabarti, V 1998, *Indian architectural theory: contemporary uses of Vastu Vidya*, Curzon Press, Richmond.
Chambert-Loir, Henri 2002, 'Saints and ancestors: the cult of Muslim saints in Java' in Chambert-Loir, Henri and Anthony Reid (eds), *The potent dead*, Allen & Unwin, Crows Nest and University of Hawai'i Press, Honolulu.
Chan Htwan Oung 1920, 'The thrice named city kingdom of the Shans, the Kantus and the Sakkyas', *Journal of the Burma Research Society* 10(3).
Chandler, Tom (dir) 2009, *Animations of Angkor*, National Geographic Society and Monash University, http://ngm.nationalgeographic.com/2009/07/angkor/angkor-animation.
Charney, Michael Walter 2002, 'Centralizing historical tradition in precolonial Burma: the Abhiraja/Dhajaraja myth in early Kon-baung historical texts', *South East Asia Research* 10(2).
Chit San Win 2003, *A picture of the old Myanmar capital, Tagaung*, (in Burmese), Ministry of Culture, Yangon.
Chou, Ta-kuan (Zhou Daguan) 1992, *The customs of Cambodia*, translated from the French version by Paul Pelliot by J Gilman d'Arcy Paul, Siam Society, Bangkok.
Coe, Michael D 2003, *Angkor and the Khmer civilisation*, Thames and Hudson, London.
Cœdès, George 1906, 'La stèle de Ta Prohm' in *Bulletin de l'École Française d'Extrême-Orient* 6.
—— 1941, 'La stèle du Prah Khan d'Angkor', *Bulletin de l'École Française d'Extrême-Orient* 41.
—— 1952, *Inscriptions du Cambodge*, vol 4, École Française d'Extrême-Orient, Paris.
—— 1968, *The Indianized states of Southeast Asia*, East–West Center, Honolulu.
Colani, Madeleine 1940, *Emploi de la pierre en des temps reculés: Annam–Indonésie–Assam*, Bulletin des amis du Vieux Hué 27, IDEO, Hanoi.
Coningham, R 2000, 'Contestatory urban texts or were cities in South Asia built as images?', *Cambridge Archaeological Journal* 10(2).
Cooley, CH 1974, 'The theory of transportation' in Eliot Hurst, ME (ed), *Transportation geography: Comments and readings*, McGraw-Hill, New York.

Coomaraswamy, Ananda Kentish 1971 [1928, 1931], *Yakṣas*, Munshiram Manoharlal, New Delhi.
—— 1979 [1935], *Elements of Buddhist iconography*, Munshiram Manoharlal, New Delhi.
Coral Rémusat, Gilberte de 1940, *L'art Khmer. Les grandes étapes de son évolution*, Études d'art et d'ethnologie asiatiques 1, Éditions d'art et d'histoire, Paris.
Creese, Helen 2004, *Women of the Kakawin world: marriage and sexuality in the Indic courts of Java and Bali*, ME Sharpe, Armonk and London.
Crooke, William 1978 [1896], *The popular religion and folklore of northern India*, 2 vols, Munshiram Manoharlal, New Delhi.
Cunin, O 2007, 'The Bayon: an archaeological and architectural study' in Clark, J (ed), *Bayon: new perspectives*, River Books, Bangkok.
CyArk 2006, *Angkor*, CyArk, Oakland, http://archive.cyark.org/angkor-info.
Dagens, Bruno 1970–76, *Mayamata, traité sanskrit d'architecture: édition critique, traduction et notes*, 2 vols, Publications de l'Institut Français d'Indologie 40(1-2), Institut Français d'Indologie, Pondichéry.
—— 1989, *Angkor, la forêt de pierre*, Gallimard, Paris.
—— 1995, *Angkor, heart of an Asian empire*, Thames and Hudson, London.
Darmosoetopo, Riboet 1976[?], *Laporan penelitian: peninggalan-peninggalan kebudayaan di lereng barat gunung Lawu*, Proyek PPPT, Universitas Gajah Mada, Yogyakarta.
Datta, Sambit and David Benon 2005, 'A computational approach to the reconstruction of surface geometry from early temple superstructures', *International Journal of Architectural Computing* 3.
Day, Tony 1994, '"Landscape" in Early Java' in Gerstle, CA and AC Milner (eds), *Recovering the Orient*, Harwood Academic, Chur.
Dega, Michael F 2002, *Prehistoric circular earthworks of Cambodia*, BAR international series 1041, Archaeopress, Oxford.
Dega, Michael and Latinis, Kyle 1996 'An introduction to Funan and the archaeology of Angkor Borei, Southern Cambodia', unpublished manuscript.
Degroot. Véronique 2009, *Candi Space and Landscape. A study on the distribution, orientation and spatial organization of Central Javanese temple remains*, Leiden: Sidestone Press (*Mededelingen van het Rijksmuseum voor Volkenkunde*, Leiden 38).
Dehejia, Vidya 1997, *Discourse in early Buddhist art*, Munshiram Manoharlal, New Delhi.
Delaporte, L and F Garnier 1998 [1873], *A pictorial journey on the old Mekong: Cambodia, Laos and Yunnan*, translated and composed by Walter EJ Tips, White Lotus, Bangkok.
Dhammacariya, Ashin 2002, *Kyaung-taw-yar (the sacred place where buddha once resided)* Ministry of Religious Affairs, Yangon.
Dhida Saraya 1999, *(Sri) Dvaravati: the initial phase of Siam's history*, Muang Boran, Bangkok.
Di Castro, Angelo Andrea 2008, 'Archaeology of the goddess: an Indian paradox' in Bapat, Jayant B and Ian Mabbett (eds), *The iconic female: goddesses of India, Nepal and Tibet*, Monash Asia Institute, Melbourne.
Diamond, Jared 2005, *Collapse: how societies choose to fail or succeed*, Viking, New York.
Dieulefils, P 2001 [1909], *Ruins of Angkor, Cambodia*, River Books, Bangkok.
Duijker, Marije 2001, 'The significance of Bhima's weapons in his stone representations: an art historical approach' in Klokke, MJ and van Kooij KR (eds), *Fruits of inspiration: studies in honour of Prof JG de Casparis*, Forsten, Groningen.
Dumarçay, J 1971a, *Phnom Bakheng: étude architecturale du temple*, Mémoires archéologiques 7, École Française d'Extrême-Orient, Paris.
—— 1971b, *Tà Kèv. Étude architecturale du temple*, Mémoires archéologiques 6, École

Française d'Extrême-Orient, Paris.
—— 1993, *Histoire de l'architecture de Java*, Mémoires archéologiques 19, École Française d'Extrême-Orient, Paris.
Dumarçay, J and P Courbin 1988, *Documents graphiques de la conservation d'Angkor: 1963–1973*, Mémoires archéologiques 18, École Française d'Extrême-Orient, Paris.
Dumarçay, J and P Royère 2001, *Cambodian architecture, eighth to thirteenth centuries*, Handbuch der Orientalistik, 3 Abt, Sudostasien, 12, Brill, Leiden.
Dumarçay, J and M Smithies 1991, *The palaces of South-East Asia: architecture and customs*, Oxford University Press, Singapore.
—— 2003, *Architecture and its models in South-East Asia*, Orchid Press, Bangkok.
Durand, EM 1903, 'Le temple de Po Romé a Phanrang', *Bulletin de l'École Française d'Extrême-Orient* 3.
Edwards, P 2005, 'Taj Angkor: enshrining l'Inde in le Cambodge' in *France and 'Indochina': cultural representations*, edited by Robson, Kathryn and Jennifer Lee, Lexington Books, Lanham.
—— 2007, *Cambodge: the cultivation of a nation, 1860–1945*, University of Hawai'i Press, Honolulu.
Einda Swe 2003, 'Images of ancient Tagaung', *New Light of Myanmar*, 24–25 August.
Eldredge, Niles 2000, *The pattern of evolution*, WH Freeman and Co, New York.
Eliade, Mircea 1958, *Patterns in comparative religion*, Sheed and Ward, New York.
—— 2004 [1964], *Shamanism: archaic techniques of ecstasy*, Princeton University Press, Princeton.
Erb, Maribeth 1988, 'Flores: cosmology, art and ritual' in Barbier, Jean Paul and Douglas Newton (eds), *Islands and ancestors*, Prestel, München.
Evans, Damian 2002, 'Pixels, ponds and people: urban form at Angkor from radar imaging', BA Honours thesis, Department of Archaeology, University of Sydney.
—— 2007, 'Putting Angkor on the map: a new survey of a Khmer 'hydraulic city' in historical and theoretical context', PhD thesis, Department of Archaeology, University of Sydney.
Evans, Damian, Christophe Pottier, Roland Fletcher, Scott Hensley, Ian Tapley, Anthony Milne and Michael Barbetti 2007, 'A new archaeological map of the world's largest pre-industrial settlement complex at Angkor, Cambodia', *Proceedings of the National Academy of Sciences (PNAS)* 104(36).
Evers, Hans-Dieter 1984, 'Cities as a "field of anthropological studies" in South East Asia' in de Jong, PE de Josselin (ed), *Unity in diversity: Indonesia as a field of anthropological study*, Foris, Dordrecht.
Fallon, K 1998, 'Early computer graphics developments in the architecture, engineering, and construction industry', *IEEE Annals of the History of Computing* 20(2).
Falser, MS 2007, 'Der prä-angkorianische Ziegeltempel von Preah Ko in Roluos bei Angkor, Kambodscha –: zur Geschichte, Komposition und Konstruktion', *Architectura: Zeitschrift für Geschichte der Baukunst* 37(2).
Ferdinandus, Pieter (no date), 'Kuto Girang research report', unpublished manuscript, Pusat Penelitian Arkeologi Nasional, Jakarta.
Ferrari, Alfonsa 1958, *mK'yen brtse's Guide to the holy places of central Tibet*, Istituto Italiano per il Medio ed Estremo Oriente, Roma.
Finot, Louis 1903, 'Notes d'épigraphie V. Pāṇḍuraṅga', *Bulletin de l'École Française d'Extrême-Orient* 3.
—— 1909, 'Notes d'épigraphie XII. Nouvelles inscriptions de Pō Klaun Garai', *Bulletin de l'École Française d'Extrême-Orient* 9.

—— 1915, 'Notes d'épigraphie XV. Les inscriptions de Jaya Parameçvaravarman I, roi du Champa', *Bulletin de l'École Française d'Extrême-Orient* 15.

—— 1928, 'Nouvelles inscriptions du Cambodge', *Bulletin de l'École Française d'Extrême-Orient* 28.

Fisher, CA 1963, *South-East Asia: a social, economic and political geography*, Methuen, London.

Fletcher, Margaret V 1990, 'Wargasari: a Middle Javanese *kidung*', BA thesis, University of Sydney.

Fletcher, Roland 1992, 'Time perspectivism, *Annales*, and the potential of archaeology' in Knapp, AB (ed), *Archaeology, Annales and ethnohistory*, Cambridge University Press, Cambridge.

—— 1995, *The limits of settlement growth: A theoretical outline*, Cambridge University Press, Cambridge.

—— 1996, 'Organized dissonance: multiple code structures in the replication of human culture' in Maschner, Herbert Donald Graham (ed), *Darwinian archaeologies*, Plenum Press, New York.

—— 2000, personal communication, meeting in Berkeley, California.

—— 2004, 'Materiality, space, time and outcome' in Bintliff, John L (ed), *The Blackwell companion to archaeology*, Blackwell, Oxford.

Fletcher, Roland and Christophe Pottier 2002, 'The gossamer city: a new inquiry', *Museum International* 54(1/2).

Fletcher, Roland, Mike Barbetti, Damian Evans, Heng Than, Im Sokrithy, Khieu Chan, Tous Somaneath, Christophe Pottier and Dan Penny 2003, 'Redefining Angkor: structure and environment in the largest, low density urban complex of the pre-industrial world', UDAYA 4.

Fletcher, Roland, D Penny, D Evans, C Pottier, M Barbetti, M Kummu and T Lustig 2008, 'The water management network of Angkor, Cambodia', *Antiquity* 82.

FOKCI 2007, *Projects: SEACHART*, Friends of Khmer Culture Inc, www.khmerculture.net/seachart.htm.

Forth, Gregory 1998, *Beneath the volcano: religion, cosmology and spirit classification among the Nage of Eastern Indonesia*, KITLV Press, Leiden.

Galaty, Michael L and Charles Watkinson (eds) 2004, *The practice of archaeology under dictatorship*, Kluwer Academic/Plenum, New York.

Galestin, TP 1936, 'Houtbouw op Oost-Javaansche tempelreliefs', Doctor Letteren Rijksuniversiteit te Leiden.

Gallotta, Bruno 1980, *Dario e l'occidente prima delle guerre persiane*, Cisalpino-Goliardica, Modena.

Garami, F and I Kertai 1993, *Water management in the Angkor area*, Angkor Foundation, Budapest.

Gaucher, Jacques 2002a, Archaeology and town planning: an Indian model in Southeast Asia', *Urban Morphology* 6(1).

—— 2002b, 'The "city" of Angkor: what is it?', *Museum International* 54(1/2).

—— 2004, 'Angkor Thom, une utopie réalisée?', *Arts Asiatiques* 59, Paris.

—— 2007, *De la maison à la ville en pays tamoul ou La diagonale interdite: étude sur formes urbaines de la ville-temple sud-indienne*, Mémoires archéologiques 23, École Française d'Extrême-Orient, Paris.

Geertz, Clifford 1960, *The religion of Java*, Free Press, New York.

Giteau, Madeleine 1976, *The civilisation of Angkor*, Rizzoli, New York.

Glaize, Maurice 1936, 1937, 1942, 1943, 1944, *Rapport sur les travaux exécutés dans le groupe d'Angkor*. École Française d'Extrême Orient, Conservation du groupe d'Angkor, Siem Reap.

—— 2009 [1944], *A guide to the Angkor monuments*, Nils Tremmel (trans), theangkorguide.com.

Goens, R van 1856, 'Reijsbeschrijving van den weg uijt Samarangh, nae de konincklijke hoofplaets Mataram, mitsgaders de zeeden, gewoonten ende regeringe van den sousouhounan, groot machtichste koningk van 't eijlant Java', *Bijdragen tot de Taal-, Land- en Volkenkunde van Nederlandsch Indië* 4.

Gould, Stephen Jay 2002, *The structure of evolutionary theory*, Belknap Press, Cambridge.

Griffith, Ralph T H (trans) 1920–1926, *The Hymns of the Rigveda*, 3rd edition complete in two volumes, Lazarus and Co., Benares.

Griffiths, Arlo and William A Southworth 2007, 'La stèle d'installation de Śrī Satyadeveśvara: une nouvelle inscription sanskrite du Campā trouvée à Phước Thiện', *Journal Asiatique* 295(2).

Griffiths, Arlo and William A Southworth 2011, 'Études du Corpus des Inscriptions du Campā II. La stèle d'installation de Śrī Ādideveśvara: Une nouvelle inscription de Satyavarman trouvée dans le temple de Hoà Lai et son importance pour l'histoire du Pān.d.ura.nga', Journal Asiatique 299(1).

Grist, D 1955, *Rice*, Longmans, Green, London.

Groeneveldt, WP 1960, *Historical notes on Indonesia and Malaya compiled from Chinese sources*, Bhratara, Jakarta.

Groslier, Bernard-Philippe 1958, *Angkor et le Cambodge au XVIe siècle d'après les sources portugaises et espagnoles*, Annales du Musée Guimet, Bibliothèque d'étude 63, Presses Universitaires de France, Paris.

—— 1959a, 'Travaux dans la zone sud-oriental d'Angkor. Rapport adressé au Directeur de l'École Française d'Extrême-Orient' in *Mélanges sur l'archéologie du Cambodge (1949–1986)*, 1998, Ecole Française d'Extrême-Orient, Paris.

—— 1959b, 'Nouvelles recherches archéologiques à Angkor', *Comptes-rendus des séances de l'Académie des Inscriptions et Belles-Lettres* 103(2).

—— 1962, 'Recherches archéologiques urgentes: Sambor Prei Kuk', unpublished manuscript.

—— 1966, *Indochina*, Muller, London.

—— 1973, 'Les inscriptions du Bayon' in Dumarçay, J and B-P Groslier (eds), *Le Bayon: histoire architecturale du temple*, Mémoires archéologiques 3(2), École Française d'Extrême-Orient, Paris.

—— 1979, 'La cité hydraulique angkorienne: exploitation ou surexploitation du sol?', *Bulletin de l'École Française d'Extrême-Orient* 66.

—— 1986[1973], 'For a historic geography of Cambodia', *SEKSA Khmer* 8–9, translated from the 1973 original 'Pour une géographie historique du Cambodge', *Les Cahiers d'Outre-mer*, 26, annee, No. 104(Octobre-decembre).

—— 1998, *Mélanges sur l'Archéologie du Cambodge (1949-1986)*, Réimpressions de l'Ecole Française d'Extrême-Orient 10, Paris.

—— 2006 [1959], *Angkor and Cambodia in the sixteenth century: according to Portuguese and Spanish sources*, M Smithies (trans), Orchid Press, Bangkok.

Groslier, Bernard-Philippe and Jacques Arthaud 1966, *Angkor: art and civilization*, Thames & Hudson, London. Guy, John 1999, 'The art of the Pyu and Mon' in Stadtner, Donald M (ed), *The art of Burma: new studies*, Marg Publications, Mumbai.

Hà Văn Tấn (ed) 1999, *Khảo cổ học Việt Nam. Tập II. Thời đại kim khí Việt Nam* [*Vietnamese archaeology. Volume II. The Vietnamese Metal Age*] Nhà Xuất Bản Khoa Học Xã Hội, Hà Nội [Social Sciences Publishing House, Hanoi].

Haendel, A 2005, 'The divine in the human world: sculpture at two tenth-century temples at Angkor', *Artibus Asiae* 65(2).
Hagesteijn, Renée 1989, *Circles of kings: political dynamics in early continental Southeast Asia*, Foris Publications, Dordrecht.
Hall, Kenneth R 1985, *Maritime trade and state development in early Southeast Asia*, Allen & Unwin, St Leonards and University of Hawaii Press, Honolulu.
Hasan, Perween 1993, 'The footprint of the Prophet', *Muqarnas* 10.
Hasson, Haskia 1993, *Ancient Buddhist art from Burma*, Taisei Gallery, Singapore.
Hefner, Robert W 1985, *Hindu Javanese: Tengger tradition and Islam*, Princeton University Press, Princeton.
Heine-Geldern, Robert von 1945, 'Prehistoric research in the Netherlands Indies' in Honig, Pieter and Frans Verdoorn (eds), *Science and scientists in the Netherlands Indies*, Board for the Netherlands Indies, Surinam and Curaçao, New York.
Hendrickson, M 2004, 'New routes for rooting out roads: distant and electronic approaches to studying the medieval Khmer road network', presentation at 'Ancient sites, modern maps: remote sensing and GIS applications in archaeology' symposium, University of California, Berkeley.
Heng, Piphal 2005, 'Preliminary chronology of Sambor Prei Kuk', conference paper, Center for Khmer Studies, Siem Reap.
Heng, Sophady 2002, 'The Memot Centre for Archaeology', *Bulletin of the students of the Department of Archaeology, Phnom Penh* 2.
Heringa, Rens 1997, 'Dewi Sri in village garb: fertility, myth, and ritual in northeast Java', *Asian Folklore Studies* 56.
Herodotus *The histories*, trans. de Sélincourt, Aubrey, new ed, Penguin, London, 1996.
Higham, Charles 1989, *The archaeology of mainland Southeast Asia from 10,000 BC to the fall of Angkor*, Cambridge University Press, Cambridge.
—— 2002, *Early cultures of mainland Southeast Asia*, River Books, Bangkok.
Hoepermans, H 1913, 'Hindoe-oudheden van Java 1864–1867', *Rapporten van den Oudheidkundig Dienst in Nederlandsch-Indië*.
Holt, Claire 1967, *Art in Indonesia: continuities and change*, Cornell University Press, Ithaca.
Hooykaas, C 1958, *The Old-Javanese Rāmāyana: an exemplary* kakawin *as to form and content*, Verhandeling van het Koninklijke Nederlandse Akademie van Wetenschappen 65(1), Noord-Hollandsche Uitgevers Maatschappij, Amsterdam.
Hoskins, Janet 1987, 'Complementarity in this world and the next: gender and agency in Kodi mortuary ceremonies' in Strathern, M (ed), *Dealing with inequality*, Cambridge University Press, Cambridge.
Hpayahtaung Pyu urn inscription 2003, *Myanmar Historical Research Journal* 11.
Hudson, Bob 2003a, 'The founding villages and early palaces of Bagan—an exploration of some chronicle and parabaik sources via computer mapping, field survey and archaeological excavation', *Texts and Contexts in Southeast Asia: proceedings of the Texts and Contexts in Southeast Asia conference, 12-14 December 2001*, Universities Historical Research Centre, Yangon.
—— 2003b, 'Revising the chronology of Bagan (Pagan), Myanmar (Burma)', AINSE 3rd Quaternary dating workshop, 1–2 October, Australian Institute of Nuclear Science and Engineering, Lucas Heights.
—— 2004, 'The origins of Bagan', PhD thesis, University of Sydney.
—— 2005a, 'A Pyu homeland in the Samon Valley: a new theory of the origins of Myanmar's early urban system', *Proceedings of the Myanmar Historical Commission Golden Jubilee International Conference*, 12–14 January, Yangon.
—— 2005b, 'Thoughts on some chronological markers of Myanmar archaeology in

the pre-urban period.' *Yangon University Archaeology Journal* 10th Anniversary Commemorative Volume.
Hudson, Bob, Nyein Lwin and 'Tanpawady' Win Maung 2001, 'The origins of Bagan; new dates and old inhabitants', *Asian Perspectives* 40(1).
Im, S., 1998, 'Réseaux routiers et moyen de transport a l'époque Angkorienne du IX au XIV siècles', unpublished MA thesis, École des hautes études en sciences sociales, Paris.
Inrasara 1994, *Văn học Chăm [Chăm Literature]*, Nhà Xuất Bản Văn hoá Dân tộc, Hà Nội.
Insoll, Timothy 1999, *The archaeology of Islam*, Blackwell, Oxford.
—— 2001, 'Introduction' in *Archaeology and World Religion*, Routledge, London.
—— 2004, *Archaeology, Ritual, Religion*, Routledge, London.
Interdisciplinary Center for Scientific Computing 2007, *Computer modeling, analysis and visualization of Angkor Wat style temples in Cambodia*, University of Heidelberg, www.iwr.uni-heidelberg.de/groups/ngg/AngkorWat/.
Irwin, John 1973, '"Aśokan" pillars: a reassessment of the evidence', *The Burlington Magazine* 115(848).
—— 1976, '"Aśokan" pillars: a reassessment of the evidence: iv symbolism', *The Burlington Magazine* 118 (884).
—— 1979, 'The stupa and the cosmic axis: the archaeological evidence' in Taddei, Maurizio (ed), *South Asian Archaeology 1977*, Istituto Universitario Orientale, Napoli.
Ittaratana, S 1998, 'Méthodologies de recherche et d'analyse des voies anciennes par la télédetection dan la partie méridionale du nord-est de la Thaïlande', PhD thesis, École pratique des hautes études, Paris.
Jacob, J 1978, 'The ecology of Angkor: evidence from the Khmer inscriptions', in Stott, EPA (ed), *Nature and man in South East Asia*, School of Oriental and African Studies, London.
Jacques, Claude 1995, *Études épigraphiques sur le pays Cham*, Réimpressions de l'Ecole Française d'Extrême-Orient 7, Paris.
—— 2005, *Angkor: cities and temples*, River Books, Bangkok.
Jacques, Claude and Michael Freeman 1997, *Angkor: cities and temples*, Thames and Hudson, London.
—— 1999, *Ancient Angkor*, River Books, Bangkok.
Jacques, Claude and P Lafond, 2004, *L'empire Khmer: cités et sanctuaires Ve–XIIIe siècles*, Fayard, Paris.
Janse, Olov RT 1941, 'An archaeological expedition to Indo-China and the Philippines: preliminary report', *Harvard Journal of Asiatic Studies* 6.
Jonge, JKJ de 1878, *De opkomst van het Nederlandsche gezag over Java. Verzameling van onuitgegeven stukken uit het oud-koloniaal archief*, X, Martinus Nijhoff, 'sGravenhage.
Karina Arifin 1983, 'Waduk dan Kanal di Pusat Kerajaan Majapahit Trowulan—Jawa Timur', Skripsi Sarjana, Fakultas Sastra Universitas Indonesia, Jakarta.
Karow, Otto 1991, *Burmese Buddhist sculpture: Johan Mogër collection*, White Lotus, Bangkok.
Kasetsiri, C 2003, 'Thailand–Cambodia: a love–hate relationship', *Kyoto Review of Southeast Asia* 3.
Keith, AB 1920, *A history of Sanskrit literature*, Oxford University Press, London
Kelleher, Matthew 2009, 'Religious spatial behaviour: why space is important to religion' in Nash, George and Dragos Gheorghiu (eds), *The Archaeology of People and Territoriality*, Archaeolingua, Budapest.

Kenderdine, S 2004, 'Avatars at the flying palace: stereographic panoramas of Angkor, Cambodia', *ICHIM04 Digital Culture and Heritage*, Berlin, www.archimuse.com/publishing/ichim04/2507_Kenderdine.pdf.

Kenoyer, Jonathan Mark, Clark, JD, Pal, JN and Sharma, GR 1983, 'An Upper Palaeolithic Shrine in India?', *Antiquity* 57.

Kern, H 1917, *Verspreide geschriften* VII, Martinus Nijhoff, The Hague.

Khan, Dominique-Sila 1997, *Conversions and shifting identities: Ramdev Pir and the Ismailis in Rajasthan*, Manohar, New Delhi.

Kinnard, Jacob N 2000, 'The polyvalent *pādas* of Viṣṇu and the Buddha', *History of Religions* 40 (1).

Kinser, S 1981, 'Annaliste paradigm?: the geohistorical structuralism of Fernand Braudel', *The American Historical Review* 86.

Kirfel, W 1967 [1920], *Die Kosmographie der Inder: nach den Quellen dargestellt*. Georg Olms, Hildesheim.

Klokke, Marijke J 1993, *The Tantri reliefs on ancient Javanese candi*, KITLV, Leiden.

—— 1994, 'On the orientation of ancient Javanese temples: the example of Candi Surowono' in van der Velde, Paul (ed), *IIAS Yearbook*, IIAS, Leiden.

Knebel, J. 1910, 'Distrikt Karang-pandan, onder-distrikt Tawang-mangoe, desa Soekoeh, Lawoe gebergte', *Rapporten van de Oudheidkundige Commissie (Dienst) in Nederlandsch- Indië*.

Kramrisch, Stella 1976, *The Hindu temple*, 2 vols, Motilal Banarsidass, Delhi.

Kroef, Justus Van der 1955, 'Folklore and tradition in Javanese society', *The Journal of American Folklore* 68 (267).

Krom, NJ 1923, *Inleiding tot de Hindoe-Javaansche kunst*, 3 vols, Martinus Nijhoff, 'sGravenhage.

Kummu, M 2004, personal communication, meeting in Siem Reap, Cambodia.

Kusen 1988, *Prasasti Wanua Tengah III. 830 saka: studi tentang latar belakang perubahan status sawah di wanua tengah sejak rake Panangkaran sampai rake watukura dyah Balitung*. Yogyakarta: Ikatan Ahli Arkeologi Indonesia.

—— 1988–89, *Faktor-faktor penyebab terjadinya perubahan status sawah di Wanua Tengah dalam masa pemerintahan raja-raja Mataram Kuna, abad 8-10*, Universitas Gadjah Mada, Yogyakarta.

Lawson, B 2001, *The language of space*. Architectural Press, Oxford.

Le Bonheur, Albert 1994, 'L'art du Champa', in *L'art de l'Asie du Sud-Est*, Citadelles & Mazenod, Paris.

Legge, James 1998 [1886], trans., *A record of Buddhistic kingdoms*, Munshiram Manoharlal, New Delhi.

Levin, Cecelia 1999, 'The Rāmāyana of Loro Jonggrang: Indian antecedents and Javanese impetus', PhD, Institute of Fine Arts, New York University.

Lévy, Paul 1943, *Recherches préhistoriques dans la région de Mlu Prei*, École Française d'Extrême-Orient, Hanoi.

Levy, RM 2001a, *Phimai computer model*, University of Calgary, www.phimai.ca/, accessed 20 March 2010.

—— 2001b, 'Temple site at Phimai: modeling for the scholar and the tourist', *Proceedings of the Seventh International Conference on Virtual Systems and Multimedia*, IEEE Computer Society.

Lieberman, Victor 2003, *Strange parallels: Southeast Asia in global context, c. 800-1830. Volume 1: Integration on the mainland*, Cambridge University Press, Cambridge.

Liebert, Gosta 1986, *Iconographic dictionary of the Indian religions: Hindu-Buddhism-Jainism*, Sri Satguru Publications, Delhi.

van Liere, WJ 1980, 'Traditional water management in the lower Mekong basin', *World Archaeology* 11.
—— 1982, 'Was Angkor a hydraulic society?', *Ruam Botkhwam Prawat Sat* 4.
—— 1989, 'Mon–Khmer approaches to the environment' in *Culture and environment in Thailand: a symposium of the Siam Society*, Siam Society, Bangkok.
Lombard, Denys 1970, 'Pour une histoire des villes du Sud-Est asiatique', *Annales: Économie, Sociétés, Civilisations* 25.
Loti, P 1989 [1912], *Un pèlerin d'Angkor*, La Nompareille, Paris.
Luce, GH 1969, *Old Burma–early Pagan*, 3 vols, Artibus Asiae and the Institute of Fine Arts, New York University.
—— 1985, *Phases of pre-Pagan Burma*, 2 vols, Oxford University Press, Oxford.
Lunet de Lajonquière, É, 1902, *Inventaire descriptif des monuments du Cambodge* I, Publications de l'École Française d'Extrême-Orient 4, Ernest Leroux, Paris.
—— 1911, *Inventaire descriptif des monuments du Cambodge* III, Publications de l'École Française d'Extrême-Orient 9, Ernest Leroux, Paris.
Lunsingh Scheurleer, Pauline 2000, 'Skulls, fangs and serpents: a new development in East Javanese iconography' in Lobo, Wibke and Stefanie Reimann (eds), *Southeast Asian archaeology 1998: proceedings of the 7th International Conference of The European Southeast Asian Archaeologists, Berlin, Aug 31–4 Sept 1998*, University of Hull, Hull.
Ly Vanna 1999, 'Samrong Sen: early workshop of material culture in the flooded area of the Tonle Sap River, Kampong Chhnang, Cambodia', MA thesis, Sophia University, Tokyo.
Lý Việt Dũng 2000, 'Truyện bà Tiên Thiên Y A Na [The story of Thiên Y A Na]', *Tạp chí Thông tin Khoa học và Công nghệ, Số* 2(28).
Lymer, Kenneth 2004, 'Rags and rock art: the landscape of holy site pilgrimage in the Republic of Kazakhstan', *World Archaeology* 36(1).
Lyons, Elizabeth 1979, 'Dvaravati, a consideration of its formative period' in Smith, RB and W Watson (eds), *Early South East Asia*, Oxford University Press, New York.
Mabbett, Ian W 1977, 'The "indianization" of Southeast Asia: reflections on the historical sources', *Journal of Southeast Asian Studies* 8(2).
—— 1983, 'The symbolism of Mount Meru', *History of Religions* 23(1).
Maclaine Pont, Ir H 1925 'Madjapahit, poging tot reconstructie van het stadsplan, nagezocht op het terrein aan de hand van den middeleeuwschen dichter: Prapanca', *Oudheidkundig Verslag 1924* Bijlage D and Q.
—— 1926, 'De historische rol van Majapahit', *Djåwå* 6.
—— 1927, 'Eenige oudheidkundige gegevens omtrent den middeleeuwschen bevloeiingstoestand van de zoogenaamde "woeste gronden van de lieden van Trik" voor zoover zij wellicht van belang zullen kunnen zijn voor eene herziening van den tegenwoordigen toestand', *Oudheidkundige Verslag 1926*, Bijlage G.
MAFKATA (Mission archéologique Franco-khmère sur l'aménagement du territoire angkorien) 2002, *Campagne 2002: Rapport* (première partie). École Française d'Extrême Orient, Centre de Siem Reap, Siem Reap.
Mahlo, Dietrich 1998, 'Frühe Münzen aus Birma:Thesen [Early coins from Burma: some propositions]', *Indo-Asiatische Zeitschrift* 2.
Mair, Victor H 1988, *Painting and performance: Chinese picture veneration and its Indian genesis*, University of Hawaii Press, Honolulu.
Majumdar, RC 1985, *Champa: history and culture of an Indian colonial kingdom in the Far East, 2nd-16th centuries AD*, Gian Publishing House, Delhi.
Malleret, Louis 1959a, *L'Archéologie du delta du Mékong. 1, L'exploration archéologique et les fouilles d'Oc-èo*, Publications de l'École Française d'Extrême-Orient 43, Paris.

—— 1959b, 'Ouvrages circulaires en terre dans l'Indochine méridionale', *Bulletin de l'École Française d'Extrême-Orient* 49.
Mansuy, Henri 1923, 'Résultats de nouvelles recherches effectuées sur le gisement préhistorique de Samrong-Sen (Cambodge)', Mémoires du service Géologique de l'Indochine 10(1).
Marchal, Henri 1924–26, 'Notes sur le Palais Royal d'Angkor Thom', *AAK* 2.
—— 1940, 'Notes d'architecture birmane', *Bulletin de l'École Française d'Extrême Orient* 40.
Maung Cetana 1997, *A history of the Kusinara pagoda, containing a hair relic*, Minister for Immigration and Population, Yangon.
Maung Htin Aung 1970, *Burmese history before 1287: a defence of the chronicles*, Asoka Society, Oxford.
Michell, George 1988, *The Hindu temple: an introduction to its meaning and forms*, University of Chicago Press, Chicago/London.
Michell, George, Marika Vicziany and Tsui Yen Hu 2008, 'Introduction' in *Kashgar: oasis city on China's old silk road*, Frances Lincoln, London.
Miksic, JN 1989, 'Urbanization and social change: the case of Sumatra', *Archipel* 37.
—— 2000, 'Heterogenetic cities in premodern Southeast Asia', *World Archaeology* 32.
Min Han 2003a, *Recent finds: burial urns from Tagaung* (in Burmese), Mandalay University, Mandalay.
—— 2003b, *Recent finds: Pyu silver coins from Tagaung* (in Burmese), Mandalay University, Mandalay.
Momoki, Shiro 1999, 'A short introduction to Champa studies', in Fukui Hayao (ed), *The dry areas in Southeast Asia: harsh or benign environment?* Center for Southeast Asian Studies, Kyoto University.
—— 2004, '"Mandala" Champa seen from Chinese documents', paper given at Workshop on New Scholarship on Champa, Asia Research Institute, National University of Singapore, 5–6 August, 2004.
Mongyway Sayadaw 1823, *Saydi-ya-ka-hta Yazewin Kyoke* undated mimeographcopy from the palm-leaf manuscript by U Htoon Yi under the pen-name Shay haung thu tay thi ta oo ('Archaeological Researcher').
Moore, Elizabeth 1989, 'Water management in early Cambodia: evidence from aerial photography', *The Geographical Journal* 155.
—— 2003, 'Bronze and Iron Age sites in Upper Myanmar: Chindwin, Samon and Pyu', *SOAS Bulletin of Burma Research* 1(1).
Moore, W Robert 1960, 'Angkor, jewel of the jungle', *National Geographic* 117(4).
Mouhot, H 1868, *Voyage dans les royaumes de Siam, de Cambodge, de Laos et autres parties centrales de l'Indo-Chine: relation extraite du journal et de la correspondance de l'auteur par Ferdinand de Lanoye*, Hachette, Paris.
Müller, P, T Vereenooghe, A Ulmer, and L Van Gool 2005, 'Automatic reconstruction of Roman housing architecture' in *Proceedings of the International Workshop on Recording, Modeling and Visualization of Cultural Heritage*, Balkema Publishers.
Müller, P, T Vereenooghe, P Wonka, I Paap and L Van Gool 2006, 'Procedural 3D reconstruction of Puuc buildings in Xkipche' in *Proceedings of the 7th International Symposium on Virtual Reality, Archaeology and Cultural Heritage*, Nicosia.
Mundarjito 1993, 'Pertimbangan ekologi dalam penempatan situs masa hindu-buda di daerah Yogyakarta: kajian arkeologi-ruang skala makro', PhD thesis, Universitas Indonesia, Jakarta.
Mundardjito et al 1986, *Rencana induk arkeologi bekas kota Kerajaan Majapahit, Trowulan*, Proyek Pemugaran dan Pemiliharaan Peninggalan Sejarah dan Purbakala, Jakarta.

Munier, Christophe 1998, *Sacred rocks and Buddhist caves in Thailand*, White Lotus, Bangkok.

Muusses, Martha A 1924, 'De oudheden te Soekoeh', *Djåwå* 4.

Myat Min Hlaing 2002, *Ancient pagodas in Myanmar, vol1*, New Light of Myanmar, Yangon.

Myers, BA 1998, 'A brief history of human–computer interaction technology', *interactions* 5(2).

Myint Aung 1970, 'The excavations at Halin', *Journal of the Burma Research Society* 53(2).

Nafilyan, G 1969, *Angkor Vat, description graphique du temple*, Mémoires archéologiques 4, École Française d'Extrême-Orient, Paris.

Nai Pan Hla 1972, 'Pyu culture ii: epigraphical evidences and archaeological finds', *Working People's Daily*, 2 November.

Nakagawa, TE 2003, *Annual report on the technical survey of Angkor monument*, JSA, Tokyo.

Nakamura, Rie 1999, 'Cham in Vietnam: Dynamics of ethnicity', PhD dissertation, Department of Anthropology, University of Washington.

Needham, Rodney 1975, 'Polythetic classification: convergence and consequences', *Man*, new series 10 (3).

New Light of Myanmar 2004, 'Minister views artefacts excavated in Tagaung and nearby areas', 30 March.

Ngô Văn Doanh 1998, *Tháp cổ Chămpa—sự thật và huyền thoạ I*, Viện Đông Nam Á / Nhà xuất bản văn hóa—thông tin, Hà Nội.

—— 2002, *Chămpa ancient towers: reality and legend*, Institute for Southeast Asian Studies, Giới Publishers, Hanoi.

Nguonphan, P 2009, 'Computer modeling, analysis and visualization of Angkor Wat style temples in Cambodia', Universität Heidelberg.

Nguyễn Hiền, Võ Văn Chi 1991, *Trầm hương (Aloe-wood)*, Nhà Xuất Bản Khoa học và Kỹ Thuật, Hà Nội.

Nguyễn Hữu Thông, Nguyễn Thị Tuyết Nga, Nguyễn Phước Bảo Đàn, Tôn Nữ Khánh Trang, Lê Chí Xuân Minh 2001, *Tín ngưỡng thờ Mẫu ở miền Trung Việt Nam* [*The cults of the worship for the Holy Mothers in Central Vietnam*], Nhà Xuất Bản Thuận Hoá, Huế.

Nguyễn Thế Anh 1995, 'The Vietnamization of the Cham Deity Pô Nagar', *Asia Journal* 2(1).

NIMA (National Imagery and Mapping Agency) 2001, 'Burma names file', *Geographic names*, National Geospatial-Intelligence Agency, www1.nga.mil/ProductsServices/GeographicNames/Pages/default.aspx/ html/entry_files.html.

Noorduyn, J 1982, 'Bujangga Manik's journeys through Java: topographical data from an old Sundanese source', *Bijdragen tot de Taal-, Land-, en Volkenkunde* 138.

Noorduyn, J and A Teeuw 1999, 'A panorama of the world from a Sundanese perspective', *Archipel* 57.

—— 2006, 'Three Old Sundanese Poems'. *Bibliotheca Indonesica* 29, KITLV Press: Leiden.

Nou, Jean-Louis and Louis Frédéric 1994, *Borobudur*, Jaca Book, Milano.

O'Flaherty, Wendy Doniger 1975, *Hindu Myths: a sourcebook translated from the Sanskrit*, Penguin Books, London.

Paranavitana, Senarat 1958, *The God of Adam's Peak*, *Artibus Asiae: Supplementum* 18, Ascona.

Paris, Pierre 1941a, 'Notes et mélanges: Anciens canaux reconnus sur photographies aériennes et les provinces de Takeo, Châu-dôc, Long-xuyèn et Rạch-giá, *Bulletin de l'École Française d'Extrême Orient* 41.

—— 1941b, 'Les bateaux des bas-reliefs khmèrs', *Bulletin de l'École Française d'Extrême Orient* 41.
Parmentier, Henri 1909, *Inventaire descriptif des monuments čams de l'Annam. Tome premier. Description des monuments*, Publications de l'École Française d'Extrême-Orient 11, Ernest Leroux, Paris.
—— 1914, 'L'architecture interprétée dans les bas-reliefs du Cambodge', *Bulletin de l'École Française d'Extrême-Orient* 14(6).
—— 1916, 'Cartes de l'Empire khmer', *Bulletin de l'École Française d'Extrême-Orient* 16(3).
—— 1918, *Inventaire descriptif des monuments čams de l'Annam. Tome II. Étude de l'art čam*, Publications de l'École Française d'Extrême-Orient 12, Ernest Leroux, Paris.
—— 1927, *L'art khmer primitif*, 2 vols, Publications de l'École Française d'Extrême-Orient 21-22, G Vanoest, Paris.—— 1939, *L'art khmer classique: monuments du quadrant nord-est*, 2 vols, Publications de l'École Française d'Extrême-Orient 29, Éditions d'art et d'histoire, Paris.
Patt, Judith 1982, 'Integration with the landscape: the development of an Indonesian aesthetic in the temple plans of the Classical Indonesian period', *Proceedings of the 4th International Symposium on Asian Studies, Hong Kong 1982*, Asian Research Service, Hong Kong.
Pe Maung Tin and GH Luce 1921, 'Chronicle of the City of Tagaung', *Journal of the Burma Research Society* 11(1).
—— 1923, *The Glass Palace chronicle of the kings of Burma*, Rangoon University Press, Rangoon.
Pelliot, P 1903, 'Le Fou-nan', *Bulletin de l'École Française d'Extrême-Orient* 3.
—— 1904, 'Deux itinéraires de Chine en Inde à la fin du VIIIe siècle', *Bulletin de l'École Française d'Extrême-Orient* 4.
Pelras, Christian 2002, 'Ancestors' blood: genealogical memory, genealogical amnesia and hierarchy among the Bugis' in Chambert-Loir, Henri and Anthony Reid (eds), *The potent dead*, Allen & Unwin, Crows Nest and University of Hawai'i Press, Honolulu.
Penny, Dan, Christophe Pottier, Roland Fletcher, Mike Barbetti, David Fink and Quan Hua 2006, 'Vegetation and land-use at Angkor, Cambodia: a dated pollen sequence from the Bakong temple moat', *Antiquity* 80.
Penny, D, C Pottier, M Kummu, R Fletcher, U Zoppi, M Barbetti and S Tous 2007, 'Hydrological history of the West Baray, Angkor, revealed through palynological analysis of sediments from the West Mebon', *Bulletin de l'École Française d'Extrême-Orient* 92.
Péri, N 1923, 'Essai sur les relations du Japon et de l'Indochine aux XVIe et XVIIe siècles', *Bulletin de l'École Française d'Extrême-Orient* 23.
Petech, Luciano 1950, *Northern India according to the Shui-Ching-Chu*, Istituto Italiano per il Medio ed Estremo Oriente, Roma.
Peterson, Larry and Gerald Haug 2005, 'Climate and the collapse of Maya civilization', *American Scientist* 93(4).
Phalgunadi, I Gusti Putu 1990, *The Indonesian Mahābhārata, I, Ādiparva*, International Academy of Indian Culture and Aditya Prakashan, New Delhi.
Phalgunadi, I Gusti Putu 1996, *The Pararaton: a study of the Southeast Asian chronicle*, Sundeep Prakashan, New Delhi.
Phasook Indrawooth 1999, *Dvaravati: a critical study based on archaeological evidence*, Aksonsmai, Bangkok.
—— 2003, 'Dvaravati: political life and thought', *Dialogue* 5(1).

—— 2004, 'The early Buddhist kingdoms of Thailand' in Glover, Ian and Peter Bellwood (eds), *Southeast Asia, from prehistory to history*, Routledge, London.
Pigeaud, TGT 1924, *De Tantu Panggelaran: een oud-Javaansche prozageschrift*, Smits, 's-Gravenhage.
—— 1960–63, *Java in the 14th century: a study in cultural history*, 5 vols, Martinus Nijhoff, The Hague.
—— 1967–70, *Literature of Java: catalogue raisonné of Javanese manuscripts in the library of the University of Leiden and other public collections in the Netherlands*, 3 vols, Martinus Nijhoff, The Hague.
Po Dharma 1987, *Le Pāṇḍuraṅga (Campā) 1802-1835; ses rapports avec le Vietnam*, 2 vols, Monographies 149, École Française d'Extrême-Orient, Paris.
Polkinghorne, M 2007, 'Makers and models: decorative lintels of Khmer temples, 7th to 11th centuries', PhD thesis, University of Sydney.
—— 2008, 'Khmer decorative lintels and the allocation of artistic labour', *Arts Asiatiques* 63.
Pottier, Christophe 1993a, 'Documents topographiques de la conservation d'Angkor', Mémoires archéologiques 21, École Française d'Extrême-Orient, Paris.
—— 1993b, *Préparation d'une carte archéologique de la région d'Angkor*, Mémoire de DEA, Sorbonne Nouvelle, Paris.
—— 1996, 'Notes sur le Bakong et son implantation', *Bulletin de l'École Française d'Extrême-Orient* 83.
—— 1997, 'La restauration du perron nord de la Terrasse des Éléphants à Angkor Thom: rapport sur la première année de travaux (avril 1996 – avril 1997)', *Bulletin de l'École Française d'Extrême-Orient* 84.
—— 1999, *Carte archéologique de la Région d'Angkor: Zone Sud*, 3 vols, PhD thesis, UFR Orient et Monde Arabe, Université Paris III—Sorbonne Nouvelle, Paris.
—— 2000, 'À la recherche de Goloupura', *Bulletin de l'École Française d'Extrême-Orient* 87(1).
—— 2001a, 'Some evidence of an inter-relationship between hydraulic features and rice field patterns at Angkor during ancient times', *Journal of Sophia Asian Studies* 18.
—— 2001b, 'The Contribution of the École Française d'Extrême-Orient with respect to the cultural heritage at Angkor during the past 100 years', *Journal of Sophia Asian Studies* 18.
—— 2003, 'Travaux de recherche récents dans la région d'Angkor', *Comptes-rendus des séances de l'Académie des Inscriptions et Belles-Lettres*, 14 mars.
—— 2004, 'A propos du temple de Banteay Chmar', *Aséanie* 13.
—— 2006, 'Angkor et ses cartes' in Chambert-Loir, H and B Dagens (eds), *Anamorphoses: hommage à Jacques Dumarçay*, Les Indes Savantes, Paris.
—— 2010, 'Nouvelles données sur les débuts d'Angkor', *Archéologues à Angkor*, Ed. Paris Musées, Paris.
Pottier, Christophe and Annie Bolle 2009, 'Le Prasat Trapeang Phong à Hariharālaya: histoire d'un temple et archéologie d'un site', *Aséanie* 24(Décembre).
Pottier, Christophe, Annie Bolle, Eric Llopis, Dominique Soutif, Chea Socheat, Sum Sang, Heng Komsan and Phoeung Dara 2006, 'Bakong, soixante ans après', *From Homo Erectus to the living traditions, Choice of papers from the 11th International Conference of the EurASEAA*, Bougon, 25–30 September 2006, Ed. Pautreau, Coupey, Zeitoun & Rambault.
Pottier, Christophe and Rodolfo Lujàn-Lunsford 2006, 'De brique et de grès: précisions sur les tours en brique de Preah Kô', *Bulletin de l'École Française d'Extrême-Orient* 92.
Przyluski, Jean 1923, *La legende de l'empereur Açoka*, Geuthner, Paris.

Pusat Penelitian Arkeologi Nasional/National Research Centre for Archaeology of Indonesia 1995, 'Research on the Majapahit city at the site of Trowulan, East Java' in JN Miksic and Endang Sri Hardiati (eds), *The Legacy of Majapahit*, National Heritage Board, Singapore.

Raffles, Thomas Stamford 1965 [1817], *The history of Java*, Oxford University Press, London.

Rasmussen, J and G Bradford 1977, *Ground-water resources of Cambodia*, US Government Printing Office, Washington.

Raven, Ellen M 1988, 'The secret servants of Kubera: the *naras* or *guhyakas*' in Hinzler HIR (ed), *Studies in South and Southeast Asian archaeology 2: essays offered to Dr R Soekmono...*, Koentji Press, Leiden.

Ray, Niharranjan 1936, *Sanskrit Buddhism in Burma*, HJ Paris, Amsterdam.

Reid, Anthony 1993, *Southeast Asia in the age of commerce 1450-1680, vol 2, Expansion and crisis*. Yale University Press, New Haven.

Renfrew, Colin 1994, 'The archaeology of religion' in Renfrew, C and EBW Zubrow (eds), *The Ancient Mind*, Cambridge University Press, Cambridge.

Resink, T 1968, 'Bĕlahan or a myth dispelled', *Indonesia* 6.

ṛg *Veda*—see Griffith 1920–1926.

Rivers, PJ 2003, '*Keramat* in Singapore in the mid-twentieth century', *Journal of the Malaysian Branch of the Royal Asiatic Society* 76(2).

Robson, SO 1979, 'Notes on the early *kidung* literature', *Bijdragen tot de Taal-,Land-,en Volkenkunde* 135.

—— 1980, 'The Ramayana in Early Java', *South East Asian Review* 5(2).

—— 1995, *Desawarnāna (Nāgarakṛtāgama)* by Mpu Prapañca, Verhandelingen van het Koninklijk Instituut voor Taal-, Land- en Volkenkunde 169. KITLV Press, Leiden.

Rodrigue, JP, Claude Comtois and Brian Slack 2009, *The geography of transport systems*, 2nd ed, Routledge, New York.

Roux, Jean-Paul 1990 [1984], *La religione dei Turchi e dei Mongoli*, ECIG, Genoa.

Rozwadowski, Andrzej 2004, *Symbols through time: interpreting the rock art of Central Asia*, Institute of Eastern Studies Adam Mickiewicz University, Poznan.

Sakai, Minako 2002, 'Modernising sacred sites in South Sumatra: Islamisation of Gumai ancestral places' in Chambert-Loir, Henri and Anthony Reid (eds), *The potent dead*, Allen & Unwin, Crows Nest and University of Hawai'i Press, Honolulu.

San Win 1993, 'Dating the Payahtaung Pyu stone inscription', unpublished seminar paper.

—— 2003, 'Dating the Hpayahtaung Pyu stone urn inscription', *Myanmar Historical Research Journal* 11.

Santiko, Hariani 1989, 'Bangunan berundak-teras masa Majapahit: benarkah pengaruh punden berundak prasejarah?' *Pertemuan Ilmiah Arkeologi 5, Yogyakarta, 4-7 Juli, 1989*, vol. 2a, Ikat Ahli Arkeologi Indonesia, Jakarta.

Santoso, S 1975, *Sutasoma:a study in Javanese Wajrayana*, International Academy of Indian Culture, New Delhi.

Sarkar, HB 1971, *Corpus of the inscriptions of Java (up to 928 CE)*, 2 vols, Mukhopadhyay, Calcutta.

Sastri, KV and NB Gadre 1990, *Viśwakarma Vāstuśāstram: a text on town-planning etc. Text and commentary*, Thanjavur Sarasvati Mahal series 85, Sarasvati Mahal Library, Thanjavur.

Satari, Sri Soejatmi 1981, *Mountains and caves in art: new finds of terracotta miniatures in Kudus, Central Java*, Bulletin of the Research Centre of Archaeology of Indonesia 15, Proyek Penelitian Purbakala, Jakarta.

—— 2008, 'Ancient gardens and Hindu–Buddhist architecture in Java' in EA Bacus, I

Glover and VC Pigott (eds), *Selected papers from the 10th International Conference of the European Association of Southeast Asian Archaeologists*, NUS Press, Singapore.

Sauvaget, Jean (ed) 1948, *Ahbār as-Sīn wa l-Hind: relation de la Chine et de l'Inde, rédigée en 851*, Belles Lettres, Paris.

Sbeghen (Grimmond), Jo 2005, 'An analysis of the sculpture of Candi Sukuh in Central Java: its meanings and religious functions 1437–1443 CE', PhD, University of Queensland.

Schweyer, Anne-Valérie 2004, 'Po Nagar de Nha Trang', *Aséanie* 14.

—— 2009, 'Les royaumes du pays cam dans la seconde moitié du XIe siècle', *Péninsule* 59.

Scott, G and Hardiman, JP 1900–01, *Gazetteer of Upper Burma and the Shan States*, 2 vols in 5, Government Press, Rangoon.

SCP (Sambor Prei Kuk Conservation Project) 2004, *Conserving and developing Sambor Prei Kuk: final report 3rd Inter-ministerial Conference for the Conservation and Development of Sambor Prei Kuk Monuments and Statute on the Sambor Prei Kuk Conservation and Development Community*, JSRC Printing House, Phnom Penh.

Sedyawati, Edi 1994, *Gaṇeśa statuary of the Kaḍiri and Siṇhasāri periods*, KITLV, Leiden.

Sein Myint 2000, 'Tagaung', *Myanmar Historical Research Journal* 6.

Settar, Shadakshari 1989, *Inviting death: Indian attitude towards the ritual death*, Brill, Leiden.

Settar, Shadakshari and Ravi Korisettar 1982, 'Niśidhis in Karnataka: a survey' in Settar, S and Günther-Dietz Sontheimer (eds), *Memorial stones*, Institute of Indian Art History, Karnatak University, Dharwad.

Settar, Shadakshari and Günther-Dietz Sontheimer 1982, *Memorial stones*, Institute of Indian Art History, Karnatak University, Dharwad.

Shorto, HL 1963, 'The 32 *myo*s in the medieval Mon kingdom', *Bulletin of the School of Oriental and African Studies* 26(3).

—— 1967, 'The *dewatau sotapan*: a Mon prototype of the 37 *nats*', *Bulletin of the School of Oriental and African Studies* 30.

Singh, Purushottam 1970, *Burial practices in ancient India*, Prithivi Prakashan, Varanasi.

Snellgrove, D, 2004, *Angkor: before and after*, Orchid Press, Bangkok.

Snodgrass, Adrian 1992 [1985], *The symbolism of the Stupa*, Motilal Banarsidass, New Delhi.

Soekmono, R 1995, *The Javanese candi: function and meaning*, Brill, Leiden.

Sontheimer, Günther Dietz 1982, 'Hero and Sati-stones of Maharashtra' in Settar, S and Günther-Dietz Sontheimer (eds), *Memorial stones*, Institute of Indian Art History, Karnatak University, Dharwad.

Southwold, Martin 1978, 'Buddhism and the definition of religion', *Man*, new series 13(3).

Southworth, William 2000, 'Notes on the political geography of Campa in central Vietnam during the late 8th and early 9th centuries AD' in Lobo, Wibke and Stefanie Reimann (eds), *Southeast Asian archaeology 1998: proceedings of the 7th International Conference of The European Southeast Asian Archaeologists, Berlin, Aug 31–4 Sept 1998*, University of Hull, Hull.

—— 2004, 'The coastal states of Champa' in Glover, Ian and Peter Bellwood (eds), *Southeast Asia, from prehistory to history*, Routledge, London.

Sox, David Griffiths 1972, 'Resource-use systems of ancient Champa', MA thesis, Department of Geography, University of Hawaii.

Stargardt, Janice 1983, *Satingpra I: the environmental and economic archaeology of South Thailand*, BAR International series 158, Archaeopress, Oxford.

—— 1990, *The Ancient Pyu of Burma: early Pyu cities in a man-made landscape* PACSEA, Cambridge.

—— 1994, 'Urbanization before Indianization at Beikthano, Central Burma, C. 1st Century BC–3rd Century AD?' in *Proceedings of the 5th International Conference of the European Association of Southeast Asian Archaeologists, Paris*, University of Hull, Hull.

—— 2001a, 'The great silver reliquary from Sri Ksetra: the oldest Buddhist art in Burma and one of the world's oldest Pali inscriptions' in Klokke, MJ and van Kooij KR (eds), *Fruits of inspiration: studies in honour of Prof JG de Casparis*, Forsten, Groningen.

—— 2001b, 'Historical geography of Burma: creation of enduring patterns in the Pyu period', *International Institute for Asian Studies Newsletter Online* 25, www.iias.nl/iiasn/25/theme/25T6.html.

Stein, Aurel 1907, *Ancient Khotan*, Clarendon Press, Oxford.

—— 1930, *An archaeological tour in Upper Swat and adjacent hill tracks*, Memoirs of the Archaeological Survey of India 42, Government of India, Calcutta.

Stein Callenfels, PV van 1925, *De Sudamala in de Hindu-Javaansche kunst*, Verhandelingen van het Koninklijk Bataviaasch Genootschap van Kunsten en Wetenschappen 66.

Stern, Philippe 1927, *Le Bayon d'Angkor Thom et l'évolution de l'art khmer*, Annales du musée Guimet 47, Bibliothèque de vulgarisation, Paris.

—— 1934, 'Le temple-montagne khmèr, le culte du linga et le Devarāja', *Bulletin de l'École Française d'Extrême-Orient* 34.

—— 1942, *L'art du Champa (ancien Annam) et son evolution*, Les frères Douladoure, Toulouse.

—— 1951, 'Diversité et rythme des fondations royales khmères', *Bulletin de l'École Française d'Extrême-Orient* 44.

Stone, R 2009, 'Divining Angkor' and 'The Khmer Empire supplement', *National Geographic* 216(1).

Stott, P 1992, 'Angkor: shifting the hydraulic paradigm' in Rigg, J (ed), *The gift of water: water management, cosmology and the state in Southeast Asia*, School of Oriental and African Studies, London.

Stutley, Margaret and James Stutley 1980, *Dizionario dell'Induismo*, Ubaldini, Rome.

Stutterheim, WF 1930, *Gids voor de oudheden van Soekoeh en Tjeta*, De Bliksem, Surakarta.

—— 1956, *Studies in Indonesian archaeology*, Nijhoff, The Hague.

Subhadradis Diskul, MC 1979, 'The development of Dvaravati sculpture and a recent find from northeast Thailand' in Smith, RB and W Watson (eds), *Early South East Asia*, Oxford University Press, New York.

Sukunda-Tessier, Viviane 1997, 'Le sacré à Java d'après les vestiges archéo-philologiques' in Ciarla, Roberto and Fiorella Rispoli (eds), *South-East Asia archaeology 1992*, Istituto Italiano per l'Africa e l'Oriente, Rome.

Sundberg, J (2009), 'The State of Matarām: a review of recent efforts to clarify its history', in M. Long, *Caṇḍi Mendut, womb of the Tathāgata*: 329-362. Newe Delhi: Aditya Prakashan (Śata-Piṭaka series 632).

Supomo S 1977, 'Arjunawijaya: a *kakawin* of mpu Tantular', *Bibliotheca Indonesica* 14, Martinus Nijhoff, The Hague.

Sutherland, Gail H 1992, *Yakṣa in Hinduism and Buddhism*, Manohar, New Delhi.

Taylor, Nora 1998, 'Sculptures of Cham deities: gods or kings?' in Klokke, Marijke J and Thomas de Bruijn (eds), *Southeast Asian Archaeology 1996*, Centre for Southeast Asian Studies, University of Hull.

Teeuw A and SO Robson 2005, *Bhomāntaka, the death of Bhoma*, KITLV Press, Leiden.
Teeuw, A et al 1969, 'Siwaratrikalpa of Mpu Tanakung; an Old Javanese poem, its Indian source and Balinese illustrations', *Bibliotheca Indonesica* 3, Martinus Nijhoff, The Hague.
Tha Myat, U 1963, *Pyu reader*, National Printing Works, Rangoon.
Thapar, Romila 1963, *Aśoka and the decline of the Maurya*, Oxford University Press, Oxford.
—— 1979, 'The historian and the epic', *Annals of the Bhandarkar Oriental Research Institute* 60.
—— 1981, 'Death and the hero' in Humphreys, Sarah C and Helen King (eds), *Mortality and immortality: the anthropology and archaeology of death*, Academic Press, London.
3Dreamteam/Vizerra 2008–10, *Angkor Wat (Angkor Vat)*, Prague, http://vizerra.com/en/locations/angkor.
Thurston, Edgar 1912, *Omens and superstitions of Southern India*, TF Unwin, London.
Tilley, Christopher 1994, *A phenomenology of landscape: places, paths and monuments*, Berg, Oxford.
Trần Kỳ Phương 1986, 'Về ngôi đền chính của nhóm tháp Pô Nagar (Nha Trang – Phú Khánh)' [On the main temple of the Pô Nagar (Nha Trang – Phú Khánh province)], *Những phát hiện mới về khảo cổ học năm 1986*, Viện Khảo Cổ Học, Hà Nội.
—— 1988, *Mỹ Sơn trong lịch sử nghệ thuật Chăm* [*Mỹ Sơn in the history of Cham arts*], Nhà Xuất Bản Đà Nẵng, Đà Nẵng.
—— 2004, *Vestiges of Champa civilization*, Thế Giới Publishers, Hanoi.
Trivedi, K 1989, 'Hindu temples: models of a fractal universe', *The Visual Computer* 5(4).
Tucci, Giuseppe 1958, 'Preliminary reports and studies on the Italian excavations in Swat (Pakistan)', *East and West* 9.
Tulley, JA 2006, *A short history of Cambodia*, Allen & Unwin, St Leonards.
Tun Aung Chain 2003, 'The Kings of the Hpayahtaung Urn Inscription', *Myanmar Historical Research Journal* 11.
Tun Shwe Khine 1992, *A guide to Mrauk-U, an ancient city of Rakhine, Myanmar*, U Tun Shwe, Sittway.
Uchida, E, C Suda, A Ueno, I Shimoda and T Nakagawa 2005, 'Estimation of the construction period of Prasat Suor Prat in the Angkor monuments, Cambodia, based on the characteristics of its stone materials and the radioactive carbon age of charcoal fragments', *Journal of Archaeological Science* 32.
Ünaldi, Serhat 2008, *Reconstructing Angkor: images of the past and their impact on Thai-Cambodian relations*, Humboldt-Universität, Berlin.
UNESCO (United Nations Educational, Scientific and Cultural Organisation), *Convention concerning the Protection of the World Cultural and Natural Heritage: World Heritage Committee, 28th Session, Suzhou, China, 28 June–7 July 2004. Annex 3: World Heritage Tentative Lists by Region*, Document No. WHC-04/28.com/14a Paris, 24 May 2004, http://whc.unesco.org/archive/2004/whc04-28com-14ae.pdf.
Upadhye, AN 1982, '*Nisidhi*—it's meaning', in Settar, S and Günther-Dietz Sontheimer (eds), *Memorial stones*, Institute of Indian Art History, Karnatak University, Dharwad.
Vale, LJ 1999, 'Mediated monuments and national identity', *Journal of Architecture* 4.
Venturi, R 1977, *Complexity and contradiction in architecture*, 2nd ed, Museum of Modern Art, New York.
Verbeek, RDM 1891, 'Oudheden van Java: (383) Soekoeh', *Verhandelingen van het (Koninklijk) Bataviaasch Genootschap van Kunsten en Wetenschappen* 46.

Verhoeven, Marc 2002, 'Ritual and ideology in the Pre-Pottery Neolithic B of the Levant and Southeast Anatolia', *Cambridge Archaeological Journal* 12.
Veth, PJ 1896-1907, Java: geografisch, ethnologisch, historisch, 2nd ed, 4 vols, F Bohn, Haarlem.
Vickery, Michael T 1977, 'Cambodia after Angkor: the chronicular evidence for the fourteenth to sixteenth centuries', PhD thesis, Yale University, University Microfilms, Ann Arbor.
—— 1986, 'Some remarks on early state formation in Cambodia' in Marr, David G and AC Milner (eds), *Southeast Asia in the 9th to 14th centuries*, Institute of Southeast Asian Studies, Singapore.
—— 1998, *Society, economics, and politics in pre-Angkor Cambodia: the 7th–8th centuries*, Centre for East Asian Cultural Studies for Unesco, The Tokyo Bunko, Tokyo.
Visnovcova, J, L Zhang and A Gruen 2001, 'Generating a 3D model of a Bayon tower using non-metric imagery', *International Archives of Photogrammetry and Remote Sensing* 34(5/W1).
Vlis, CJ van der 1843, 'Beschrijving en verklaring der oudheden en opschriften op Soekoeh en Tjetto', *Verhandelingen van het (Koninklijk) Bataviaasch Genootschap van Kunsten en Wetenschappen* 19.
Vogel, JP 1925, *The relation between the art of India and Java*, India Society, London.
Vogler, EB 1953, 'Ontwikkeling van de gewijde bouwkunst in het hindoeïstische Midden-Java', *Bijdragen tot de taal-, land- en volkenkunde van Nedelandsch Indië*, 109(3).
Von Meiss, P 1998, *Elements of architecture: from form to place*. E & FN Spon, London.
Von Plehwe-Leisen, E and H Leisen 2005, 'Wall decoration systems in the temples of Angkor' in Jett, Paul, John Winter and Blythe McCarthy (eds), *Scientific research on the pictorial arts of Asia*, Archetype Publications, Washington.
—— 2008, 'Paint, plaster, and stucco: decorative features of Khmer temples in Cambodia' in Bacus, EA, IC Glover and PD Sharrock (eds), *Interpreting Southeast Asia's past*, vol 2, *Monument, image and text*, NUS Press, Singapore.
Wallace, AR 1869 *The Malay Archipelago*, 2nd ed, 2 vols, Macmillan, London.
Welch, Anthony 1997, 'The shrine of the Holy Footprint in Delhi', *Muqarnas* 14.
Wessing, Robert 1988, 'Spirits of the earth and spirits of the water: chthonic forces in the mountains of West Java', *Asian Folklore Studies* 47.
Westermarck, Edward 1933, *Pagan survivals in Mohammadan civilization*, Macmillan, London.
Wheatley, P 1971, *The pivot of the four quarters; a preliminary enquiry into the origins and character of the ancient Chinese city*, Aldine, Chicago.
—— 1983 *Nagara and Commandery: origins of the Southeast Asian urban tradition*, University of Chicago, Department of Geography, Chicago.
Williams, J 1981, 'The date of Barabuḍur in relation to other Central Javanese monuments' in Gómez, LG and HW Woodward (eds), *Barabuḍur, history and significance of a Buddhist monument*, Berkeley Buddhist studies 2, University of California, Berkeley.
Win Maung, 'Tanpawady' 1997, 'Exploration of the Tagaung area', privately circulated manuscript (in Burmese), Mandalay.
—— 2000, 'Myittha eleven villages exploration record', privately circulated manuscript (in Burmese), Mandalay
—— 2002, 'Some symbolical designs on early silver coins', privately circulated manuscript (in Burmese), Mandalay.
Winstedt, Richard 1924, '*Karamat*: sacred places and persons in Malaya', *Journal of the*

Malayan Branch of the Royal Asiatic Society 2.
—— 1961, *The Malay magician*, Routledge and Kegan Paul, London.
Winter, T 2002, 'Angkor meets *Tomb Raider*: setting the scene', *International Journal of Heritage Studies* 8.
—— 2007, *Post-conflict heritage, postcolonial tourism: culture, politics and development at Angkor*, Routledge, London.
Wisseman Christie, Jan 1992a, 'Water from the ancestors: irrigation in early Java and Bali' in Rigg, Jonathan (ed), *The gift of water: water management, cosmology and state in Southeast Asia*, School of Oriental and Asian Studies, University of London.
—— 1992b, 'Trade and settlement in early Java: integrating the epigraphic and archaeological data' in Glover, I, P Suchitta, and J Villers (eds), *Early metallurgy, trade and urban centres in Thailand and Southeast Asia*, White Lotus, Bangkok.
—— 2001, 'Revisiting Mataram' in Klokke, MJ and KR van Kooij (eds), *Fruits of inspiration: studies in honour of Prof JG de Casparis*, Forsten, Groningen.
—— 2002–04, Register of the inscriptions of Java (from 732 to 1060 CE), consultation draft.
Wittgenstein, Ludwig 1965, *The blue and brown books: preliminary studies for the philosophical investigations*, Harper Torchbooks, New York.
Woodward, Mark R 1988, 'The *Slametan*: textual knowledge and ritual performance in Central Javanese Islam', *History of Religion*, 28.
Working People's Daily 1993, 'Massive stone funerary urn of Pyu King excavated at ancient Srikshetra City', 2 April.
Worsley, Peter 1986, 'Narrative bas-reliefs at Candi Surawana' in Marr, David G and AC Milner (eds), *Southeast Asia in the 9th to 14th centuries*, Institute of Southeast Asian Studies, Singapore.
—— 1988, 'Three Balinese Paintings of the Narrative Arjunawiwaha', *Archipel*, 45.
—— 1991, 'Mpu Tantular's *kakawin* Arjunawijaya and conceptions of kingship in fourteenth century Java' in Ras JJ and SO Robson (eds), *Variation and transformation. perspectives in the study of Indonesian literatures*, Royal Institute for Linguistics and Anthropology, Leiden.
—— 2009, 'Budaya Bahasa Kosmopolit dan Relief-Relief Kisah Rama di Candi Loro Jonggrang, Prambanan (Cosmopolitan vernacular culture and illustrations of the Rama story at Candi Loro Jonggrang, Prambana)' in Henri Chambert-Loir (ed), *Sadur: sejarah terjemahan di Indonesia dan Malaysia*, Kepustakaan Populer Gramedia, Jakarta.
Wylie, Turrell V 1962, *The geography of Tibet according to the 'Dzam-gling-rgyas-bshad*, Serie Orientale Roma, XXV, Istituto Italiano per il Medio ed Estremo Oriente, Roma.
—— 1970, *A Tibetan religious geography of Nepal*, Serie Orientale Roma, XLII, Istituto Italiano per il Medio ed Estremo Oriente, Roma.
Zimmer, Heinrich 1946, *Myths and symbols in Indian art and civilization*, Princeton University Press, Princeton.
Zoetmulder, PJ 1974, *Kalangwan: a survey of old Javanese literature*, Nijhoff, The Hague.
—— 1982, *Old Javanese–English dictionary*, Nijhoff, The Hague.

Lightning Source UK Ltd.
Milton Keynes UK
UKHW022025030321
379739UK00002B/3